LESSONS TO SHARE ON TEACHING GRAMMAR IN CONTEXT

Lessons to Share on Teaching Grammar in Context

edited by
Constance Weaver

Boynton/Cook Publishers
HEINEMANN
Portsmouth, NH

Boynton/Cook Publishers, Inc.
A subsidiary of Reed Elsevier Inc.
361 Hanover Street
Portsmouth, NH 03801-3912

Offices and agents throughout the world

Library of Congress Cataloging-in-Publication Data
Lessons to share on Teaching grammar in context / edited by Constance Weaver.
     p.   cm.
    Sequel to: Teaching grammar in context. c1996.
    Includes bibliographical references and index.
    ISBN 0-86709-394-3
    1. English language--Grammar--Study and teaching. 2. English language--Composition and exercises--Study and teaching.
    I. Weaver, Constance. II. Weaver, Constance. Teaching grammar in context.
    LB1576.L488   1998
    428'.007--dc21

                                            97-51626
                                            CIP

Editor: Scott Mahler
Production: Melissa L. Inglis
Cover design: Jenny Jensen Greenleaf
Manufacturing: Louise Richardson

Printed in the United States of America on acid-free paper
02 01 00 99 98   RRD   2 3 4 5 6 7 8 9

CONTENTS

PREFACE

This book is the promised sequel to my *Teaching Grammar in Context*, published by Boynton/Cook in 1996. It includes articles by both experienced teachers and those just beginning their careers; articles that range from working with young children all the way to working with inservice teachers; and articles covering topics from language acquisition to using grammar checkers on computer software.

The first section, on the learning and teaching of grammar, sets the stage for subsequent sections. The purpose behind the article on how language is learned is to help readers of this book understand that babies and preschoolers acquire the grammar of their language without direct instruction in grammar, by interacting with their environments and generating, though quite unconsciously, increasingly sophisticated and more adult-like grammar rules over time. Furthermore, this process continues through the elementary years and beyond, as a result of exposure to written language in particular. The article on teaching grammar in the context of writing articulates other aspects of the rationale that underlies the emphasis of this book: teaching grammar in the context of its use.

The second section deals with teaching grammar through writing, across the grades. It deals with punctuation, parts of speech, effective word choice and syntax, and conferencing with students to teach revision and editing. The third section focuses partly on style, with an emphasis on sentence composing and on "breaking the rules" for stylistic effect. In addition, this section focuses on the power of dialects and dialects of power. The last section deals with teaching the English language and its grammar through meaningful use of the language, to immigrant students in grades K–12 and to international students at the university level. It includes an article on preparing teachers to teach about language. And finally, the section and the book conclude with an article on using grammar-checking computer software.

While most of the authors illustrate their points with reference to a particular grade or range of grades and levels, many of the ideas could be used or adapted for a very wide age and grade range. Therefore, the book is appropriate for teachers from elementary school through college/university.

Constance Weaver
Western Michigan University

1

How Language Is Learned:
From Birth Through the Elementary Years and Beyond

JANE KIEL

Introduction

Jane Kiel describes language acquisition as a process that begins before birth and continues well into the school years and beyond. Humans are born with a cognitive capacity to learn that no other animal possesses. This ability, coupled with an innate desire to communicate and a language-rich environment, enables us to learn to use and understand language. Kiel explains that from the earliest infant babblings to the more sophisticated speech of a five-year-old, language acquisition follows a fairly predictable course: All children seem to pass through the same stages in the same order—from single word utterances to the mastery of complex grammar structures. Kiel notes that this amazing amount of language learning occurs without any direct instruction. Children who are exposed to a great deal of language—first in the form of spoken language and then through reading—and who are treated as valued communicators, learn how to speak, use complicated syntactic structures, and even learn how to spell better, all on their own. Kiel concludes that children possess a vast mental capacity to understand and learn language and its structures without direct instruction.

What Enables Language Acquisition

An infant is born with an amazing capacity to learn by interacting with his or her surroundings. He or she arrives ready to accept an unbelievable amount and range of stimuli. With this capacity to learn and a language-rich environment, every normal child in the world learns to speak his or her native language in the first few years of life. How is this possible? I believe four components account for a child's language learning: an innate cognitive ability, or capacity, to learn, re-create, and create language; the physical development necessary to produce speech;

1

a need to communicate; and a language-rich environment. These four factors work together within every young child, enabling the child to become a viable communicator by the time he or she reaches the age of five.

Cognitive Capacity

Though infants are born with a very limited capacity to communicate, all children, barring any physical or developmental problems, become competent speakers of their native language by the time they begin school. Even though a newborn seems to be a tabula rasa, a child actually begins life with the cognitive capacity for language development (and, some linguists argue, a specific linguistic capacity— e.g., Chomsky, 1972; Pinker, 1994). While there is still some disagreement as to what portion of language acquisition should be attributed to cognitive factors (nature) or a child's surroundings (nurture), it is rather widely held that both environment and innate capacity play powerful roles in language acquisition (for an in-depth discussion of the nature/nurture controversy, see Sameroff & Fiese, 1988).

Humans are the only animals with the predisposition for speech. After reviewing the research on teaching primates, Lindfors concluded "Human language does appear to be special (specific) to our species, especially in the domain of syntax" (1987, p. 101). This is held as clear proof that we are born programmed for speech. It has been shown that infants as young as three months begin communicating with those around them, through eye contact, gesturing, and vocalizations of differing intonations. Infants and young children also possess the mental capacity to begin to attend to speech, to differentiate meaningful sounds from extraneous noise, and to begin to categorize those sounds into meaningful components (words and phrases). Further proof of this is found in the fact that children can understand spoken language long before they can produce it competently. At eighteen months, my daughter, Grace, had only a handful of words in her vocabulary. Yet, she could carry out a fairly complicated two-part command, such as "Get the big ball and give it to Tristan." Such an ability shows an understanding of the language beyond that which is expressed through speech.

Another example of our cognitive capacity to learn is the fact that language is learned by all children without it ever being taught to them. In the words of Lindfors, "One of the most striking characteristics of children's learning of language is that it is learning without 'teaching' in the usual sense. Adults do not give children explicit instruction in language, nor do they plan a sequenced curriculum for the language-learning child" (1987, p. 6). An example of this is the fact that adults very rarely correct a young child's speech. Adults seem more concerned with the truthfulness of a child's statement than the structural correctness of it. Lindfors states that "adults do not give or withhold reinforcement on the basis of the formal correctness of what children say, but rather on the basis of the truth of the message" (1987, p. 7; see also Slobin, 1972). Grace, a soup lover, pointed to her bowl at dinner when she was twenty months old and announced "I no like it." Both my husband and I quickly corrected, "Oh, you do too. You love soup." To which Grace responded, "Oh," and finished that bowl and another. We were not concerned with the fact that Grace's sentence was grammatically incorrect. We understood it completely and responded to it. But we both were immediately drawn to the untruthfulness of the statement and corrected that.

I never consciously taught Tristan or Grace how to speak. Yet, over a period of several years, they both learned to communicate competently. Language is not, nor could it be, overtly taught: Language is far too complex for that. Yet, because of our cognitive ability to attend to language and make sense of it, we all learned to speak. Tristan is now five years old and can carry on long and complex discussions with an adult or a peer. He learned this to a large extent on his own, without a single flash card or standardized test.

Physical Development

About the same time all of these cognitive processes are taking place, the infant is also developing physically. From the age of four months to the appearance of the first spoken words (usually around twelve months), the muscles used to produce speech are developing. An infant's cooing, and later babbling, are evidence of this fine motor development. Anyone who has been around an infant has heard these first attempts at language, the "agoos" and "oohhhs," and the later "lalalalalala" and "babababba" as muscles become more developed. Fine motor development of the speech muscles seems to be achieved at ten to eleven months, when babbling ends and actual word production begins.

Innate Desire/Need to Communicate

Beyond these physical and cognitive contributors to language development, there lies a very strong need to be understood. Children want to have their needs and desires known and met, beyond what crying or laughing can accomplish. They begin with one-word utterances paired with gestures that express a substantial amount of meaning, especially when the audience is a receptive parent or loved one. Still these single word cues, while powerful, soon become insufficient to fulfill the increasingly complex needs of the developing young communicator.

This is clear to anyone who has tried in vain to understand the request of a toddler. With each repetition, the toddler becomes more exasperated and must often resort to a series of gestures or, if all else fails, may just give up in tears out of frustration. At twenty months, Grace came to me and said "bunnot." I asked her to repeat it and she did, each time with more urgency, until eventually she crumpled to the floor, crying. When I finally asked her to show me "bunnot" she pointed to the bottom of her sweater where I noticed a *button* had come loose. I was finally able to understand. This pattern of reversing middle and final consonants became common practice for Grace between twenty months and two years—bottom was bommot, Adam was Amad, cereal was ceelar. Once I realized this, many such confrontations were averted and I was able to respond to the content of her utterances, while using the correct pronunciation of the word in my verbal response. While this is an example of Grace's need to communicate, it is also an example of how parental response affects language development, further illustrating the interconnectedness of these four separate aspects of language development.

As each level is mastered, inefficiencies in communication become evident and new needs arise that drive the child to develop more and more complex communicative skills. This innate need to communicate plays a very powerful role in a child's language development.

Environment

Finally, though by no means least important, environment is crucial for language acquisition and development. While a child has an innate need to communicate and possesses the physical and cognitive abilities to do so, it is the child's environment that shapes his or her developing language and, indeed, makes it possible for language potential to become actual. From birth an infant is exposed to a vast amount of language. Parents and loved ones speak to, about and/or around the child. We read to infants and toddlers and sing with them, producing a language-rich environment from which the child will learn. By attending to this speech, very young children begin to formulate an understanding of spoken language, including its intonation patterns, words, and structures.

Children who are not exposed to a language-rich environment do not develop the ability to speak. Profoundly deaf children, while they follow the first of the developmental steps toward speech, rarely develop into speakers. Deaf infants will begin to babble at about the same time as children who hear. But, without the ability to hear themselves or those around them, deaf children gradually decrease the amount of babbling, until it disappears around the tenth month. This pattern rarely leads to any word development (De Villiers & De Villiers, 1979). Children in institutions where adult contact is greatly limited also lag behind in language development. Chloe, a child in my care, was adopted from an orphanage in China at the age of seven months and brought to the United States. When she was first adopted, her vocalizations were limited to crying and a throaty animal-like noise. While at seven months cooing and babbling would normally be prevalent, they were nonexistent in Chloe's repertoire.

Due to the stimulation she received from her new mother, within four weeks of arriving at her new home Chloe was producing cooing sounds and by ten months of age, after only three months in the United States and two months in a very stimuli-rich day care setting, she was producing very typical babbling sounds. Now, at eighteen months of age, she is speaking with a vocabulary of fifteen to twenty words and can complete a two-part task when asked to do so. By being exposed to a language-rich environment and having a responsive adult in her life modeling language and rewarding her attempts, Chloe has overcome a seven-month deficit in her language development in less than a year.

Adults play another important role in language development by responding to young children as viable communicators. Adults applaud a toddler's first attempts at words and reward close approximations by producing the desired object or action. That is, we respond positively to the content of the utterance, rather than negatively to the immature form (Slobin, 1971). When Tristan was eleven months old, he said "Dah." We clapped and cheered and he lit up. After that, whenever he said "Dah" my husband would respond. We knew he was trying to say "Dad," and rewarded that attempt by understanding it and producing Dad whenever possible. We treated him like a communicator. When Grace, at twenty months, said "duce" I gave her juice. I didn't wait until she could correctly say "juice" before I rewarded her. I understood her and treated her like a speaker.

Predictable Early Language Acquisition Patterns

Language acquisition follows a very predictable pattern for virtually all children. While all children travel through the different stages at a different rate, virtually all children pass through these stages in the same order. This holds true for languages other than English, as well. (For a more in-depth treatment of this topic, see De Villiers & De Villiers, 1979; Lindfors, 1987; and Slobin, 1972.)

Babbling

The first stages, as discussed earlier, are more a result of developing fine motor skills than an attempt or desire to communicate. The cooing and babbling phases of later infancy seem to be required to develop the musculature needed to produce more coherent speech later on. If these sounds are heard by the child and attended to by an adult, they will be produced with more frequency and the child's language development will progress to the next stage (De Villiers & De Villiers, 1979).

Single-Word Utterances

Next, the child begins to produce single-word utterances. These words are usually nouns for common objects and people in the child's life, but can also be other parts of speech. These words serve the very important purpose of helping children communicate. In this stage—as in all stages to some extent—overgeneralization can occur. Overgeneralization is when a child formulates a rule and applies it too broadly to the language task at hand. In the single-words phase, Grace learned "cow" and "woof" very early on. As she was exposed to more animals, she overgeneralized her label "woof" and all four-legged animals became "woof," with the word "cow" disappearing for a short time from her vocabulary. She then began to distinguish differences between these four-legged animals, and after about six weeks, "cow" reappeared, along with "pig," "kitty," "horse," and "goat." At the age of twenty-two months, however, she still referred to dogs as "woof."

Near the end of the single-word stage, children begin to apply words to other people's behavior, not just their own. Their language becomes less egocentric.

Word Combining: The Beginning of Syntax

This phase of language development continues for years, as the child moves from single-word utterances, to combining first two or three, then many words together to convey richer and richer meanings, using more complex grammar as well. Lindfors writes (1987), "As a child's combinatory speech develops, it moves from a system which at most combines two or three uninflected, heavy content items . . . to a system that incorporates expression of inflections like past tense and plural, grammatical morphemes like articles and prepositions, and embedded and conjoined constructions, all of which contribute to both length and complexity of expression" (p. 126).

As a child's utterances grow in length and complexity, an amazing accomplishment becomes more and more evident: The child has grasped the rules and complexities, or syntax, of the language without ever being directly taught. The fact that the child is creating sentences using many different combinations of the words in his or her vocabulary also proves that the child is not just regurgitating phrases he or she has memorized. Instead, the child is slowly mastering the rules governing the speech around him or her and employing those rules—clumsily at first, but with increasing accuracy—in his or her own utterances.

As the child first moves from the single-word phase to the combinatory phase, he or she begins to combine words in his or her vocabulary into short phrases. These two words, when used together, pack much more meaning than either word used singly. Many of these phrases are noun/verb combinations and seldom contain grammatical morphemes such as articles or auxiliaries (Lindfors, 1987). (For an in-depth discussion on different learning styles in early language acquisition, see Nelson, 1981.) Speech at this stage is often called "telegraphic" because it resembles the speech found in telegrams. Since the sender of a telegram is charged for each word, only high meaning words are used. Some of Grace's early two-word utterances were "Dah work," "Woof out," (when the dog escaped from the house, a common occurrence) and "mine cup."

In the beginning of this phase a child's utterances are more descriptive, telling others about what is occurring around him or her. But as the child's speech develops, he or she begins to use it to act on his or her surroundings. Early in this stage, Grace liked to label things, and phrases like "Mama cup" were common. As her speech developed, she started saying "cup Mama" which served as a request for a drink. She had learned enough about language to understand what a powerful role word order played in determining meaning. And a few weeks later, around twenty-one months of age, she was able to add a third word, again in the right place in the request, to make "mine cup Mama" which relayed more meaning yet. These sorts of phrases are clear, outward examples of the emergence of syntax.

As the child begins to add more words to his or her phrases, several new facets are added to the child's language repertoire (Lindfors, 1987). First of all, grammatical morphemes begin to appear. Brown (1973) identified fourteen grammatical morphemes that emerge in early combinatory speech. Among them are the present progressive *-ing* (I driving), the prepositions *on* and *in* (I on table), the plural, the regular and irregular past tense, possessives, and articles. And, again, use of these syntactic elements develops over time. Once one of these appears for the first time it could be weeks or months before the child can consistently use it correctly.

The second facet to be added is the stringing together of two-term relations, such as combining a subject + verb and a verb + object into one utterance, resulting in a subject + verb + object. Where the child would have previously only been able to string two components together into a single phrase, he or she can now connect three. When Tristan was about sixteen months old, he would ask my husband the same question every night: "Dah do? Do today?" This was his version of "What did you do today, Daddy?" One night, when he was seventeen months old he said, "Do today, Dah?" He had made the leap to stringing two ideas together.

The final component to be added in this second phase of combinatory speech is the child's ability to expand a term in a relation. This is where the child is able to add descriptors to terms already in his or her vocabulary, but that hadn't been paired earlier. Grace often said, "I like juice" and "apple juice" as two distinct, yet related statements. I understood that she wanted apple juice. When she was about twenty-two months old she was suddenly able to combine phrases like these into a single sentence, such as "I like apple juice."

Word Combining: Later Combinatory Skills

As children grow, their speech continues to develop and their combinatory skills increase. More and more elaborate grammatical and syntactic rules are operating to guide their speech development. Again, these rules are never taught. Children infer them from their experiences and feedback when communicating with those around them. From the ages of two to five, children use this feedback to fine-tune the rules they are unconsciously formulating. By the time they reach school age, children will have relatively sophisticated arsenals of grammar and syntax rules under which they are operating.

Some of the rules learned in the second half of the combinatory phase include those used when developing negatives and interrogatives (other than intonation, a common tool in early speech). Children also begin combining sentences and fine-tuning their sound system so their speech more closely matches that of accomplished speakers. As anyone who has ever taught a second language will tell you, these four components are very complicated and difficult to master, as there are so many possible applications and irregular uses of these grammatical structures. Yet, young children learn them, with many mistakes in the beginning, through a cycle of trial and error, more language input as feedback, and the generation of more sophisticated hypotheses. They may start their development of the negative as Tristan did, with statements such as "I no like it" and "He no come home." While these got the point across, he eventually changed his structure to match our own. "I don't like it" was correct, but he overgeneralized that structure, in such phrases as "He don't come home." While this shows developmental progress, it took several months for him to fine-tune his system for negatives to include the large number of possibilities found in the English language. But by the age of four, while his language skills were not as sophisticated as those of adults, he had mastered many rules and rarely made a mistake in grammar or syntax.

A point to be stressed here is that all children develop language through these same basic stages, at different rates but in the same order. They tend to develop the least complex language skills first, which are not necessarily the ones they hear most frequently. As they near mastery of one level, they push on to the next. While all learning is developmental and very rarely takes place in neat, complete increments, these basic stages are easily identified in most children.

When children reach school age they are storehouses full of knowledge about language. By the age of four most children are speaking in clear, grammatically correct sentences. They are able to express complex ideas and desires quite easily. It is important to note that this learning occurs *without direct instruction*. Language evolves because the child has a need and a desire to communicate and the innate ability to do so. The crying of infancy slowly gives way to single-word commands and labels. As the child becomes more of an actor on and within his or her environment, the child's needs and desires change and become more complex. The child's language becomes more complex as well. By the age of three, while their language is by no means flawless, most children are able to form fairly sophisticated sentences and communicate quite easily with those around them.

From the ages of three to five, language grows to include more and more complex vocabulary and grammatical structures. All this learning occurs through listening, modeling, abstracting patterns and hypothesizing rules, and trial and error. Because children are treated like speakers by their audience—both listened to and responded to—they become speakers. (For a more in-depth discussion of this topic, see Wells, 1986.)

How Language Is Learned in the Elementary Years and Beyond

We know that students entering elementary school have large vocabularies and a vast knowledge of spoken language and its grammar. We also know that language skills continue to grow, vocabularies increase, syntactic structures become more complex and refined, and children begin to learn the conventions of written language that are not obvious through speech, such as spelling, punctuation, and formatting the printed page. How do the language and vocabulary skills of these young students continue to grow?

Vocabulary

Elementary school–aged children have a large number of words in their repertoires. By the time they reach the third grade, it is estimated that students have vocabularies ranging in size from 4,000 to 24,000 words, with the median vocabulary containing around 10,000 words (Nagy & Herman, 1987). Further, it is estimated that school-aged children's vocabularies continue to grow at an astounding rate. While it is impossible to measure this gain, it is estimated that children learn between 600 and 5,000 new words annually (Nagy, Herman, & Anderson, 1985). These researchers point out that "this massive vocabulary growth seems to occur without much help from teachers" (p. 234). Where does all this learning come from?

While exposure to spoken language plays a major role in vocabulary acquisition in the toddler and preschool years, its impact decreases greatly during the school years. Spoken language "typically contains a lower proportion of difficult or low-frequency words than written language" (Nagy & Anderson, 1984, p. 327). So the increasingly complex and varied words children pick up after the preschool years probably do not come from listening to conversational language. Once a child reaches the early school grades, Nagy and Anderson point to written language as the main source of subsequent vocabulary acquisition. A child's first exposure to written language typically occurs when he or she is read to. Because young children will encounter words in stories to which they have never been exposed orally, their vocabularies will greatly benefit from listening to adults read. In a study where seven-year-old students were read the same story on three different occasions in a one-week period, Elley (1989) found these students showed significant gains in vocabulary acquisition. Elley states that "The findings . . . support the assumption that young children can learn new vocabulary incidentally from having illustrated storybooks read to them" (p. 184). This learning was found to be relatively permanent. Factors that tended to increase the likelihood that a word would be added to a child's vocabulary include the frequency of occurrence of a word, the amount of additional explanation provided by the teacher, and the helpfulness of the context. Elley concluded that "reading stories aloud to children is a significant source of vocabulary acquisition" (p. 185).

In a similar study, Cohen (1968) had teachers read a story a day to inner-city students over the course of a school year. Those children in the experimental classrooms showed significant gains in vocabulary growth over those students in the control classes. Cohen concluded that "Vocabulary thus appears to be learned best by young children in a context of emotional and intellectual meaning" (p. 213). Because these children were from lower socioeconomic backgrounds, Cohen extrapolated that they "come to school with a paucity of the kinds of words more likely to be found in books than in daily speech at home" (p. 217). Because of this, reading aloud is believed to have an even greater impact on the vocabularies of these students.

Exposure to written language occurs when a child is read to, but beginning in the elementary years it takes place most often when a child reads to him- or herself. Studies have shown that words are also learned most readily from context—from reading new words within the natural text of a story. (See Beck, McKeown, & McCaslin, 1983, for a discussion of the effectiveness of different types of contexts.) Eeds and Cockrum (1985) found that looking new words up in a dictionary—a practice seldom followed by accomplished adult readers but one we encourage in students with earnest—was no more effective than reading words in context: "Students who merely read the novel and responded through discussion, writing, art, or drama appeared to remember almost as many target words as those who laboriously looked them up—and they certainly had more fun. Such simple activities would seem, over the long term, to be much more likely to promote interest in reading and word meanings than a tedious assignment to look up and copy pages of definitions" (pp. 496–497).

Nagy, Herman, and Anderson (1985) found that words were best learned in context. While the likelihood of a new word being learned on the first exposure is only between five percent and twenty percent, just because the word isn't fully understood does not mean that no learning took place. They refer to the "incremental nature of word learning" (p. 236) which follows the developmental model of learning that early language development is thought to follow. Words, it is believed, are learned in small increments, with complete learning of a word's meaning occurring gradually over a long period of time. Therefore, the likelihood of a word being added to a vocabulary increases greatly with each exposure. Given the number of words the average elementary student reads (Nagy, Herman, & Anderson, 1985, estimate it to be over a million), if the child is adding between five percent and twenty percent to his or her vocabulary, the total number is astounding: "A most effective way to produce large-scale vocabulary growth is through an activity that is all too often interrupted in the process of reading instruction: Reading" (p. 252).

White, Graves, and Slater (1990) found reading to be a very effective way to promote vocabulary growth, especially among disadvantaged students. Like Cohen (1968), White et al. felt "the dialect-speaking students . . . were likely to have heard and used different words than the standard-English-speaking students. . . . The result is a mismatch between their oral language experience and school vocabulary" (p. 288). They concluded that minority students need to be encouraged to read and, as Eeds and Cockrum (1985) have stated, need a little direct instruction from teachers on specific vocabulary items in order to close the gap between middle-class and disadvantaged students. However, such direct instruction does not mean an assignment to look up words in a dictionary. It means discussing new words and their meanings with students as they are encountered, in context. By discussing new vocabulary as it occurs in the child's or class's reading, the teacher can greatly increase the likelihood that a word will be remembered.

For vocabulary acquisition to continue at the phenomenal rate it does into the elementary school years, students need exposure to new and more complex words and language structures. This doesn't happen by listening to conversational language and it doesn't come from memorizing vocabulary lessons, as the huge number of words gained each year could never be taught directly. This type of learning comes from being exposed to meaningful written language, either by being read to or by reading it themselves. The teacher isn't completely unnecessary in this process. It was shown that direct teacher input is helpful when students encounter a word in print that needs clarification. But the most important component to continued vocabulary acquisition appears to be reading. It is also important to remember that, like most language learning, vocabulary acquisition is developmental and students will probably need to encounter a new word on several occasions in context before its meaning is fully understood. But with each encounter with a new word, a child is potentially increasing his or her already burgeoning vocabulary. (For further treatment of this topic see Krashen, 1989.)

Spelling

Given our culture's obsession with perfect spelling, it has been taught for decades and still can be found today in modern classrooms. What makes this a rather startling statement is that study after study has shown spelling instruction to have little or no effect on spelling performance. In an 1897 study, Rice concluded that there was little or no correlation between the amount of spelling instruction a student receives and that student's spelling competence. Cornman (1902) produced similar results and also pointed out that a student's ability to spell improved over time whether or not the child received direct spelling instruction. (See Krashen & White, 1991, for an in-depth comparison of Rice, 1897, and Cornman, 1902.) This same conclusion has been drawn again and again by researchers. Hammill, Larsen, and McNutt (1977), in their study of the effectiveness of three basal spelling series, concluded that by the completion of the fourth grade, students who had received no special spelling instruction spelled as well as, and sometimes better than, those who had had direct spelling instruction.

It has also been pointed out that when students finish elementary school, the time when formal spelling instruction often ends, they know how to correctly spell far more words than could have been memorized for weekly spelling tests. Also, because the English spelling system is so complex, with almost as many exceptions as there are rules, memorization of rules is not a viable explanation for spelling competence. It has been shown (Cook, 1912, as cited in Krashen, 1993) that even when directly taught spelling rules, students rarely remembered them correctly, rarely applied them, or applied them incorrectly.

The fact still remains that people learn to spell, some with amazing accuracy. If spelling is not learned through direct instruction, how then do young writers learn to spell the thousands of words in their vocabularies? The strongest evidence points to reading as the major source of children's spelling instruction. Ormrod (1986) showed that some spelling knowledge is gained after encountering a new word just a few times in meaningful text, even when readers were reading for pleasure, not focusing on individual word meanings. Given enough reading, young readers could be exposed to tens of thousands of words every year. Callaway, McDaniel, and Mason (1972), in a study of five different language arts classrooms, found that the students who did a great deal of meaningful reading and writing but had no formal spelling instruction spelled better than those who received formal instruction. The worst spellers were those who did the least amount of meaningful reading and writing yet received formal spelling instruction. Krashen points out that it "is possible that spelling is acquired in a combination of ways, e.g. through reading and writing. Results of read and test studies suggest, however, that reading can do nearly the entire job alone" (1993a, p. 18).

Syntax

As a child's language moves from single-word utterances to multi-word phrases, the child begins to implement rules to govern the formation of these phrases. As the child's language develops, these rules become more sophisticated and the phrases become longer and more complicated. These rules become the child's grammar or syntax. It is this system of rules which enables humans to be language creators, not language imitators.

As with all language acquisition, syntactic development happens over a long period of time. (For an in-depth analysis of the sequence of emergence of different syntactical structures, see Wells, 1985, pp. 188–225, and Miller & Ervin, 1964.) As a child's language is developing, so is his or her understanding of syntax. Beginning with an understanding of word order, a child tries new word combinations and unconsciously formulates syntax to make meaning of the complicated language system the child hears daily. Over time, these rules are abandoned and then reformulated to account for irregularities he or she hears until the child's speech begins to approach that of an adult's. In 1992, Chaney studied the emerging metalinguistic skills of three-year-olds and found "nearly all of the preschoolers were . . . learning to think about the forms of language as well as meanings" (p. 507). Chaney used this discovery to conclude that "metalinguistic skills do not emerge suddenly after age six or eight, but rather develop early in the preschool years" (p. 507). (See also Brown & Fraser, 1964.)

So, by the time the child enters school, he or she possesses a fairly sophisticated system of syntactic rules developed just by listening, trying, and adjusting. Even kindergartners and first-graders use most of the sentence structures used by adults (at least in their simpler forms); for instance, they typically use all three kinds of subordinate clauses (O'Donnell, Griffin, & Norris, 1967). Nevertheless, children's syntactic development continues well into the school years. What is influencing this development as the child gets older?

As with spelling and vocabulary, it has been long thought that good, solid grammar instruction is what our children need to make them good writers and speakers. Just the opposite seems to be true. It has been shown that formal grammar instruction has little or no effect on improving students' writing. As Elley, Barnham, Lamb, and Wylie (1976) stated, "sixty years of empirical studies on the practical value of teaching grammar have failed to demonstrate any consistent measurable effects on students' writing skills" (p. 5). In fact, it has been implied that formal grammar instruction may indeed be detrimental to students in that it wastes valuable time that could be spent on reading and writing (see Smith, 1994, and Elley, et al., 1976).

True, many older people will point out that they had grammar instruction all through school and they have a much firmer grasp of English grammar than young people today. But, these people also spent much more time reading than children do today. They didn't have television to fill their free time—a medium which is largely visual and uses very low-level language—but instead read, listened to radio, and listened to conversations and stories of those around them. Since we have seen that language development is due largely to exposure to meaningful language, it would make sense then that the more complex language a child hears and reads, the more sophisticated his or her language system would become. This same argument seems to carry through to grammar development. Carol Chomsky (1972) writes "The written language is potentially of a more complex nature than speech, both in vocabulary and syntax. The child who reads (or listens to) a variety of rich and complex materials benefits from a range of linguistic inputs that is unavailable to the non-literary child" (p. 23). Reading, then, results in increased syntax development.

In a 1972 study, Chomsky studied children between the ages of six and ten and their learning of complex English syntax. It was found that certain syntactic structures were learned in a set sequence, though at varying rates for different children. This mirrors the pattern of earlier language growth. Also, Chomsky found a strong correlation between reading and syntactic language development: "The child enters the classroom equipped to learn language and able to do so by methods of his own. . . . the best thing that we might do for him . . . would be to make more of it possible, by exposing him to a rich variety of language inputs in interesting, stimulating situations. . . . exposure to the more complex language available from reading does seem to go hand in hand with increased knowledge of the language" (p. 33). Chomsky concluded that children who grew up in rich print environments displayed more grammatical competence than those who did not. Again, children seem to learn language sequentially, at their own pace, and seem well-equipped to do most of it on their own. When exposed to complex, meaningful printed language, children will unconsciously formulate rules to incorporate this new language into their repertoires. Reading, again, was named as an excellent source of that meaningful language.

Elley and Mangubhai (1983) conducted a study with second-language learners to find an effective way to teach (or facilitate the learning of) a new language. Over a period of eight months, 380 Fijian students were given access to 250 high-interest story books in English (known as a "book flood"). At the end of eight months, those exposed to many stories had scores double those of control students in reading and listening comprehension. At the end of twenty months, the gains had increased further and had spread to other facets of language development, including the students' understanding of English structures. Again, a greater amount of grammar was learned by students exposed to books. (See Elley, 1991, for a review of nine such second-language acquisition studies using book flood techniques.)

Krashen (1989), in his studies of second-language acquisition and varying methods of instruction, concluded that students learn very complex rules of grammar which they have never been overtly taught. He cited the example of adult immigrants who were able to learn their new language to a fairly high degree without any direct instruction. Also, he reported numerous examples of students who had participated in free reading programs doing better than control groups on tests of writing, reading, and grammar. Finally, he discussed findings that students who report more pleasure reading outside of school write better than nonreaders. Reading, again, seems to be the key to higher levels of language learning, including grammar.

Syntax, then, is learned developmentally. Children begin to unconsciously construct grammar rules very early in their language development. A child's language becomes more complex as his or her rules to govern its production evolve. In the beginning, this evolution is influenced by the child's listening to and interacting with speakers. As the child matures, he or she begins to draw input from more linguistically advanced and diverse sources, most likely printed language. First, while the child is read to and, later, when reading on his or her own, the child continues to hone syntactic rules, and the resulting language becomes more and more sophisticated.

While it is very difficult to study and determine exactly how each complex syntactic structure is learned, it has been shown that it is not through direct instruction. All children seem to learn the same rules in about the same order, though at differing rates—depending, in part, on their exposure to rich and complex language. Children, therefore, learn syntactic patterns and rules when they are developmentally able and ready, not when the teacher decides to teach it. It is through exposure to meaningful language that a child learns these structures. One of the best sources of meaningful language is written material. And in using reading to learn, each child can assimilate what he or she needs when he or she is developmentally ready. Therefore, ten different children could hear the same story and use it to learn ten different things. Reading is an invaluable source of grammar instruction.

Conclusion

When humans are born, they possess the innate ability to learn language. Because they are exposed to language from the moment they are born—and before—they begin to develop the ability to create language. Human children are spoken to from birth as if they are valued communicators, capable of understanding and communicating. First their cries, and later their first attempts at speech, are greeted with prompt action and responded to and understood. As children begin to speak, this pattern continues. Parents respond to children as if they are competent communicators. They don't correct their errors in speech or refuse to respond until a request is stated correctly. Instead, parents attempt to understand what is being said and act accordingly. By hearing language, having their language responded to, and being treated like true communicators, children develop in language use until their command of language, especially grammar, very closely resembles that of adults. Again, this is accomplished without any direct instruction, but through the children's desire to communicate, access to a language-rich environment, and adults treating the young speakers as communicators.

As a child's language becomes more sophisticated, the child begins to develop rules to govern the production of speech. The child continually adds words to his or her ever-growing vocabulary, and blatant errors gradually disappear. Printed material becomes the basis for much of his or her later learning. It has been proven that school-aged children learn much, if not most, of their vocabulary, spelling, and grammar from exposure to printed material (either by being read to or by reading it themselves). Very little is learned through direct instruction. Given the vast amount of language they have already learned on their own before starting school, this fact really should not surprise us. Language is learned when we are exposed to, and engaged with, meaningful language, not because we are taught. So, as Frank Smith (1994) and many others have said, maybe we should spend more instructional time not on instruction, but on giving the students a chance to interact with language in a meaningful way: through reading and writing for an audience. It is through such contact that true language learning takes place.

References

BECK, I., MCKEOWN, M., & MCCASLIN, E. (1983). Vocabulary development: All contexts are not created equal. *Elementary School Journal, 83,* 177–181.

BROEN, P. (1972). The verbal environment of the language learning child. *Monograph of the American Speech and Hearing Association*, No. 17.

BROWN, R. (1973). *A First Language.* Cambridge, MA: Harvard University Press.

BROWN, R., & FRASER, C. (1964). The acquisition of syntax. In U. Bellugi & R. Brown (Eds.), The acquisition of language. *Monographs of the society for research in child development*, No. 29, 43–79.

CALKINS, L. (1983). *Lessons from a child: On the teaching and learning of writing.* Portsmouth, NH: Heinemann.

CALLAWAY, B., MCDANIEL, H., & MASON, G. (1972). Five methods of teaching language arts: A comparison. *Elementary English, 49,* 1240–1245.

CHANEY, C. (1992). Language development, metalinguistic skills, and print awareness in three-year-old children. *Applied Psycholinguistics, 13,* 485–514.

CHOMSKY, C. (1972). Stages in language development and reading exposure. *Harvard Educational Review, 42,* 1–33.

CHOMSKY, N. (1972). *Language and mind.* New York: Harcourt Brace Jovanovich.

COHEN, D. (1968). The effect of literature on vocabulary and reading achievement. *Elementary English, 45,* 209–217.

CORNMAN, O. (1902). *Spelling in the elementary school.* Boston: Ginn.

DE VILLIERS, P., & DE VILLIERS, J. (1979). *Early language.* Cambridge, MA: Harvard University Press.

EEDS, M., & COCKRUM, W. (1985). Teaching word meanings by expanding schemata vs. dictionary work vs. reading in context. *Journal of Reading, 28,* 492–497.

ELLEY, W. (1989). Vocabulary acquisition from listening to stories. *Reading Research Quarterly, 24,* 176–187.

ELLEY, W. (1991). Acquiring literacy in a second language: The effect of book-based programs. *Language Learning, 41,* 375–411.

ELLEY, W., BARNHAM, I., LAMB, H., & WYLIE, M. (1976). The role of grammar in the secondary school English curriculum. *Research in the Teaching of English, 10,* 5–21.

ELLEY, W., & MANGUBHAI, F. (1983). The impact of reading on second language learning. *Reading Research Quarterly, 19,* 53–67.

GENISHI, C., & DYSON, A. (1984). *Language assessment in the early years.* Norwood, NJ: Ablex Publishing.

GLEASON, J., & WEINTRAUB, S. (1978). Input language and the acquisition of communicative competence. In K. Nelson (Ed.), *Children's language, vol. 1.* (pp. 171–222). New York: Gardner Press.

HAMMILL, D., LARSEN, S., & MCNUTT, G. (1977). The effects of spelling instruction: A preliminary study. *Elementary School Journal, 78,* 67–72.

KRASHEN, S. (1989). We acquire vocabulary and spelling by reading: Additional evidence for the input hypothesis. *Modern Language Journal, 73,* 440–464.

KRASHEN, S. (1993a). How well do people spell? *Reading Improvement, 30,* 9–20.

KRASHEN, S. (1993b). *The power of reading: Insights from the research.* Englewood, CO: Libraries Unlimited.

KRASHEN, S., & WHITE, H. (1991). Is spelling acquired or learned? A reanalysis of Rice (1897) and Cornman (1902). *ITL: Review of Applied Linguistics,* 1–48; 91–92.

LINDFORS, J. (1987). *Children's language and learning* (2nd Ed.). Englewood Cliffs, NJ: Prentice Hall.

MILLER, G. (1977). *Spontaneous apprentices: Children and language.* New York: Seabury.

MILLER, W., & ERVIN, S. (1964). The development of grammar in child language. In U. Bellugi & R. Brown (Eds.), The acquisition of language. *Monographs of the society for research in child development, 29,* 9–34.

NAGY, W., & ANDERSON, R. (1984). The number of words in printed school English. *Reading Research Quarterly, 19,* 304–330.

NAGY, W., & HERMAN, P. (1987). Breadth and depth of vocabulary knowledge: Implications for acquisition and instruction. In M. McKeown & M. Curtis (Eds.), *The nature of vocabulary acquisition* (pp. 19–35). Hillsdale, NJ: Erlbaum.

NAGY, W., HERMAN, P., & ANDERSON, R. (1985). Learning words from context. *Reading Research Quarterly, 20,* 233–253.

NELSON, K. (1981). Individual differences in language development: Implications for development and language. *Developmental Psychology, 17,* 170–187.

O'DONNELL, R., GRIFFIN, W., & NORRIS, R. (1967). *Syntax of kindergarten and elementary school children: A transformational analysis.* (Research Report No. 8). Urbana, IL: National Council of Teachers of English.

ORMROD, J. (1986). Learning to spell while reading: A follow-up study. *Perceptual and Motor Skills, 63,* 652–54.

PINKER, S. (1994). *The language instinct: How the mind creates language.* New York: William Morrow.

RICE, J. (1897). The futility of the spelling grind. *Forum, 23,* 163–172; 409–419.

SAMEROFF, A., & FEISE, B. (1988). The context of language development. In R. Scheifelbusch & L. Lloyd (Eds.), *Language perspectives: Acquisition, retardation and intervention* (p. 3). Austin, TX: Pro-Ed.

SLOBIN, D. (1972). They learn the same way all around the world. *Psychology Today, 6* (July), 71–74; 82.

SMITH, F. (1994). *Writing and the writer.* Hillsdale, NJ: Lawrence Erlbaum Associates.

WATSON, R. (1987). Learning words from linguistic expression: Definition and narrative. *Research in the Teaching of English, 21,* 298–317.

WEAVER, C. (1996). *Teaching grammar in context.* Portsmouth, NH: Heinemann.

WELLS, C. (1985). *Language development in the pre-school years.* Cambridge: Cambridge University Press.

WELLS, C. (1986). *The meaning makers: Children learning language and using language to learn.* Portsmouth, NH: Heinemann.

WHITE, T., GRAVES, M., & SLATER, W. (1990). Growth of reading vocabulary in diverse elementary schools: Decoding and word meaning. *Journal of Educational Psychology, 82,* 281–290.

WILDE, S. (1990). A proposal for a new spelling curriculum. *Elementary School Journal, 90,* 275–289.

2

Teaching Grammar in the Context of Writing[1]

CONSTANCE WEAVER

Introduction[2]

Articulating some of the key points in Weaver's *Teaching Grammar in Context* (Boynton/Cook, 1996), this article serves as a bridge between that book and this.

After discussing the general conclusions of decades of research on the effects of teaching grammar as an isolated subject, Weaver follows the lead of Rei Noguchi (1991) in arguing that "less is more," with respect to teaching grammar in order to improve writing. That is, teaching selected aspects of grammar in the context of their use promises to be more effective than teaching grammar more thoroughly, but in isolation. Weaver then offers a scope-not-sequence chart outlining key aspects of grammar that might be taught over the years, from kindergarten through graduate school. Critical to the argument for teaching grammar in the context of writing is her discussion of the underlying learning theory, a constructivist theory rather than the behavioral theory that has guided the traditional teaching of grammar in isolation. Her article concludes with sample lessons from teachers at the fifth and the seventh grade, and from the secondary and university levels.

While I was doing research for my book *Teaching Grammar in Context* (1996b), I was surprised to discover that during the Middle Ages, grammar was considered the foundation of all knowledge, the necessary prerequisite for understanding theology and philosophy as well as literature. As Huntsman (1983) puts it, "Grammar was thought to discipline the mind and the soul at the same time" (p. 59). I was even more surprised to discover that a major publisher of textbooks used in home schooling and in fundamentalist schools describes a certain middle-grade grammar and writing program (*God's Gift of Language Series*) by saying that "Grammar is taught with the purpose of making clear to the students the orderly structure of their language, a picture of God's orderly plan for the world and for their lives" (A Beka Book, 1996, p. 36). Clearly some people think that grammar should be taught as a formal system because it represents order, authority, and something that—to them—seems absolute, without question (Chapman, 1986; Holderer, 1995; Gaddy, Hall, & Marzano, 1996).

With such deep-seated beliefs, some parents and community members argue vociferously for teaching grammar as a system—formally, and not necessarily in conjunction with writing. They argue for grammar on what, for them, are moral and religious grounds. And when other stakeholders in education realize that grammar is not being taught as a formal system and that students are not necessarily mastering some of the conventions of edited written English, it is easy for them to simply assume a causal relationship and believe that English teachers are not doing their duty when they don't teach grammar as a complete subject.

As professionals teaching the English language arts, we too are sometimes convinced that *we* learned practical things about sentence structure, style, and editing from doing exercises in our grammar books; for instance, I can tell you very specifically some of what I learned that has helped me as a writer (though I'll admit I only needed one or two semesters of intensive grammar study to reap its potential benefits, not the six semesters to which I and my classmates were subjected). Because some of us are convinced we benefited at least somewhat from the formal study of grammar, it can be difficult for community members and English teachers alike to believe what decades of grammar studies tell us: that in general, the teaching of grammar does not serve any practical purpose for most students (Hillocks & Smith, 1991). It does not improve reading, speaking, writing, or even editing, for the majority of students—nor does the teaching of English grammar necessarily make it easier for students to learn the structure of a foreign language (indeed, many students who have studied English grammar *learn* the structure of English consciously for the first time when studying a foreign language).

The Research

Typically the research studies have not been fine-tuned enough to reveal that the study of grammar does have at least limited benefits for a few of us as writers. But even this more optimistic conclusion is called into question somewhat by a landmark study done by Finlay McQuade. He taught an elective, junior-senior level Editorial Skills class that enrolled students who, it appears, were typically college-bound. The students reviewed parts of speech and basic sentence structure, then dealt with application of such principles as "agreement, reference, parallel construction, tense, case, subordination" to the task of finding errors in sentences written expressly for that purpose. Students, parents, and the teacher were happy with the course, until some students who had succeeded in the Editorial Skills class were assessed in reading, writing, mechanics, and vocabulary, then assigned to a course in writing mechanics on the basis of that assessment. This unhappy result led McQuade to investigate the effects of his course.

What he found was startling. Overall, students showed as much gain on their Cooperative English Tests in years that they hadn't taken the Editorial Skills class as in the year that they had (McQuade, 1980, p. 28); the ES class seemed to make no difference in students' preparation for the College Entrance Examination Board's Achievement Test in Composition (p. 29); the class average on the pre-test was actually higher than the average on the post-test (p. 28); most of the reduction in errors was a reduction in relatively simple errors (mainly capitalization) by just a few of the students (pp. 29–30); and though the students' pre-course essays were not spectacular, their post-course essays were "miserable" and apparently "self-consciously constructed to honor correctness above all other virtues, including sense" (p. 29). No wonder that this and other studies have led research summarizers like George Hillocks (1986) to conclude that

> None of the studies reviewed for the present report provides any support for teaching grammar as a means of improving composition skills. If schools insist upon teaching the identification of parts of speech, the parsing or diagramming of sentences, or other concepts of traditional grammar (as many still do), they cannot defend it as a means of improving the quality of instruction. (p. 138)

Or to put it even more bluntly, "School boards, administrators, and teachers who impose the systematic study of traditional school grammar on their students over lengthy periods of time in the name of teaching writing do them a gross disservice" (Hillocks, 1986, p. 248; cited also in another important summary, Hillocks & Smith, 1991, p. 596). For other choice quotes from research summaries, see my fact sheet on the teaching of grammar that NCTE published as a SLATE Starter Sheet in the spring of 1996 (also in Weaver, Gillmeister-Krause, & Vento-Zogby, 1996).

What, then, are teachers to do? Should we teach formal grammar to all our students, knowing full well that only a few are likely to make practical use of what we've taught? Or should we abandon the teaching of grammar entirely, unless we teach it as a subject for inquiry (Postman & Weingartner, 1966) or as a subject simply of intellectual interest, if not religious/moral value?

Probably neither extreme is the best option. In an article critiquing the earlier research summaries, Martha Kolln (1981) pointed out that teaching grammar in the context of writing might be much more effective than teaching grammar as a separate subject (as evidence, she cites, for instance, a study by Harris, 1962, which is reported at length in Braddock, Lloyd-Jones, & Schoer, 1963). Later studies by Elley et al. (1976) and by McQuade (1980) do not invalidate this point. On the other hand, it is by no means clear that "application" of selected aspects of grammar cannot be done just as effectively, and a lot more efficiently, without detailed, explicit grammar study, as illustrated by O'Hare's experiments in sentence combining (1973). This is the argument advanced by Rei Noguchi (1991) and it's the argument advanced in my own book as well (Weaver, 1996b). Though the research investigating this issue has been meager, it is definitely promising. For example, Lucy Calkins found that third graders learned punctuation much better in the context of writing and "publishing" than by studying punctuation rules in isolation. Furthermore, an experimental study at grades four through six showed that students who were taught the conventions of language in the context of their writing generally made better use of writing mechanics than did students who had studied these skills in isolation (DiStefano & Killion, 1984).

What Aspects of Grammar Should We Teach

Of course, some educators may still want to teach at least an elective course or unit in the structure of the English language, simply on the grounds that studying the language is interesting and/or intellectually challenging—or can be made so (Postman and Weingartner, 1966). What all students need, however, is guidance in understanding and applying those aspects of grammar that are most relevant to writing.

FIG. 2–1 *A minimum of grammar for maximum benefits (Weaver, 1996). Teaching the application of these grammatical concepts does not require teaching or conscious mastery of English as a complete grammatical system; indeed, it probably requires no more than a dozen terms.*

1. TEACHING CONCEPTS OF SUBJECT, VERB, SENTENCE, CLAUSE, PHRASE, AND RELATED CONCEPTS FOR EDITING
Objectives
- *To help students develop sentence sense through wide reading.*

- *To help students learn to punctuate sentences correctly (according to accepted conventions) and effectively (judiciously violating the rules on occasion, for rhetorical effect).*
  By identifying subjects and verbs (predicates).
  By identifying fragments, run-ons, and comma splices, which includes understanding the concept of a grammatical sentence (T-unit); distinguishing between independent and dependent clauses, and between clauses and phrases (including near-clauses); recognizing when a verb is not a properly formed main verb.

- *To help students learn to make verbs agree with their subjects.*
  According to the conventions of Edited American English, as differentiated from the conventions of other dialects.
  In special cases, such as when the subject is modified by a prepositional phrase; when the subject is inverted; when the subject is compound.

- *To help students learn conventions for punctuating subordinate clauses.*
  Introductory adverbial clauses (and long phrases).
  Restrictive and nonrestrictive adjectival clauses.

2. TEACHING STYLE THROUGH SENTENCE COMBINING AND SENTENCE GENERATING

Objectives

- *To help students combine sentences.*
  Coordinating clauses and phrases.
  Subordinating some elements to others.
  Reducing clauses to phrases.

- *To help students expand their syntactic repertoire in order to write more syntactically sophisticated and rhetorically effective sentences.*
  Using free modifiers (especially appositives, participial phrases, and absolutes).
  Using structures particularly associated with exposition and argumentation, such as qualifying clauses and phrases.

3. TEACHING SENTENCE SENSE AND STYLE THROUGH THE MANIPULATION OF SYNTACTIC ELEMENTS

Objectives

- *To help students learn techniques to arrange and rearrange sentence elements for readability and effectiveness.*
  Moving adverbial free modifiers.
  Using parallel grammatical elements when appropriate.
  Putting free modifiers after a clause or before it, rather than between the subject and verb.
  Eliminating dangling modifiers by removing or reconstructing them.
  Experimenting with *wh* words, *it* and *there* transforms of basic sentence structures.
  Understanding the relative advantages of the active and passive voices and being able to use both.

4. TEACHING THE POWER OF DIALECTS AND DIALECTS OF POWER

Objectives

- *To help students gain an appreciation for various community and ethnic dialects, through literature, film, and oral discourse.*

- *To help students understand grammatical differences between these dialect forms and the Language of Wider Communication used in business, government, and many everyday situations.*

- *To help students determine which dialects are most appropriate in what kinds of situations (perhaps through inquiry and investigation of their own).*

- *To help students use, as desired, the forms of various dialects (e.g., for literary effect and rhetorical purposes).*

- *To help students edit their writing for the grammatical forms and word usages* that characterize Edited American English (e.g., EAE subject-verb agreement, negation, pronoun use, and verb forms and use).

- To help students edit for basic usage distinctions (e.g., it's versus its, their versus they're and there, your versus you're).

- To help students edit for the grammatical forms and usages that differentiate the language of privilege and prestige (cultivated English) from the general English used in daily speech and writing by most people comfortable with the Language of Wider Communication.

- Editing for the finer points of subject-verb agreement, pronoun-antecedent agreement, and other issues of pronoun use.

- Editing for at least the more basic forms and usages that differentiate the prestige English from general English (e.g., some of the distinctions listed in glossaries of usage).

5. TEACHING PUNCTUATION AND MECHANICS FOR CONVENTION, CLARITY, AND STYLE
Objectives
- To help students edit for appropriateness the relevant aspects of punctuation that are not associated with the grammatical elements in the other categories.
Period, question mark, and exclamation mark.
Quotation marks.
Comma.
Semicolon.
Colon.
Apostrophe in possessives.

Other aspects of punctuation and mechanics, such as parentheses and dashes.

- To help students learn to use various aspects of punctuation not only for conventional correctness but for clarity and stylistic effectiveness.

- To help students to capitalize proper nouns used in their writings and to avoid capitalizing other nouns.

Figure 2–1 presents my suggestions of a minimum of grammar for maximum benefits (Weaver, 1996b, pp. 142–144). This is what I call a "scope-not-sequence" chart, covering relevant concepts that might be taught sometime between kindergarten and graduate school. While this chart includes most of the grammatical concepts needed for sentence revision, style, and editing, and while some concepts are listed in the developmental sequence found in research studies, the lists should not be interpreted as presenting a sequence for instruction. What's appropriate at any given time will vary considerably from school to school, class to class, and especially from individual to individual. Therefore, I would suggest that teachers consider the chart, examine their own students' writing, and offer the kinds of guidance their students need—mostly at the point of need (though some basic grammatical concepts may need to be taught aside from the writing process itself). At the very least, I would recommend that teachers in a school or school system decide what their own students should be taught at each level, with considerable overlap. Better yet, teachers could collectively decide what the teachers at each grade level should be responsible for teaching, but only to the students who demonstrate the need or readiness for these predetermined concepts and skills in their writing.

Underlying Learning Theory

There are no miracles here. That is, teaching grammar in the context of writing will not automatically mean that once taught, the concepts will be learned and applied forever after. On the contrary, grammatical concepts must often be taught and retaught, to individuals as well as to groups or classes, and students may long afterward continue to need guidance in actually applying what they have, in some sense or to some degree, already learned. There is no quick fix.

In part, this is because the learning of grammatical concepts is so complex. For example, Harris and Rowan (1989) point out that practice, practice, and more practice usually does not promote adequate understanding (see also Kagan, 1980). In part, this is because the practice exercises in grammar books are carefully crafted to be relatively easy; they do not give students the opportunity to grasp the critical features of a concept like *sentence*. In their study of college students' concept of sentence, Harris and Rowan (1989) found that many students were confused by the meaning-based definitions of sentence that they had been taught ("A sentence is a group of words that expresses a complete thought"). Many of the students could not reliably differentiate between grammatical sentences and fragments or a run-on or comma splice. In order to understand the concept of *sentence*, they also needed to understand what was *not* a sentence, and vice versa—but they had a firm grasp of neither.

I am convinced that one reason our traditional teaching of grammar has little transfer to writing situations is the underlying behaviorist learning theory. We have simply taken for granted the behaviorist ideas that practice makes perfect and that skills practiced in isolation will be learned that way and then applied as relevant. We have assumed that this is the way teaching and learning should work, despite the overwhelming evidence that it doesn't. With respect to grammar, Harris and Rowan (1989) show quite convincingly that a conscious grasp of grammatical concepts requires a depth of understanding that is not often gained through practice exercises alone. Figure 2–2 reflects one of my attempts to contrast a behaviorist, transmission theory of learning and teaching with the constructivist, transactional theory that better reflects how people learn in general and how teachers may better promote the learning of concepts and complex processes (Weaver,

1994, p. 365; Weaver, 1996, p. 149). The learning of grammatical concepts is itself a complex process.

FIG. 2–2 *Ends of a Behavioral-Constructivist Continuum (Weaver, 1994)*

BEHAVIORAL PSYCHOLOGY	COGNITIVE PSYCHOLOGY
Transmission	Transactional
Reductionist	Constructivist
Habit formation	Hypothesis formation
Avoiding mistakes prevents formation of bad habits	Errors necessary for encouraging more sophisticated hypotheses
Students passively practice skills, memorize facts	Students actively pursue learning and construct knowledge
Teacher dispenses prepackaged, predetermined curriculum	Teacher develops and negotiates curriculum with students
Direct teaching of curriculum	Responsive teaching to meet students' needs and interests
Taskmaster, with emphasis on cycle of teach, practice/apply/memorize, test	Master craftsperson, mentor: emphasis on demonstrating, inviting, discussing, affirming, facilitating, collaborating, observing, supporting
Lessons taught, practiced or applied, then tested	Minilessons taught as demonstration, invitation; adding an idea to the class pot
Performance on decontextualized tests is taken as measure of learning of limited information	Assessment from a variety of contextualized learning experiences captures diverse aspects of learning
Learning is expected to be uniform, same for everyone; uniform means of assessment guarantee that many will fail, in significant ways	Learning is expected to be individual, different for everyone; flexible and multiple means of assessment guarantee all will succeed, in differing ways
Adds up to a failure-oriented model, ferreting out students' weaknesses and preparing them to take their place in a stratified society	Adds up to a success-oriented model, emphasizing students' strengths and preparing them to be the best they can be in a stratified society

---

Certain aspects of the constructivist theory of learning seem especially relevant for the teaching of grammar. One is that the learner must form hypotheses about concepts, in the process of coming to understand them. This means that we teachers must give a wide range of examples to illustrate a concept (such as *grammatical sentence*) and also that we must contrast these with common non-examples that are frequently mistaken for instances of the concept, such as a dependent clause (which has a subject and predicate—a characterization that often occurs in handbook definitions of a sentence—but which is grammatically not complete as a sentence). Another significant implication is that errors are common and probably even necessary in the process of formulating more sophisticated hypotheses—or to put it more simply, errors are a necessary concomitant of growth (Shaughnessy, 1977; Kroll & Schafer, 1978).

Thus we should not be surprised if students make new kinds of errors after we have taught a "new" syntactic structure or editing concept, nor should we penalize students for taking the risks that have resulted in these errors. Instead, we should praise students for what they've attempted, then gently show them how to eliminate what we perceive as error (Weaver, 1982). We also need to adopt a stance of humility before we undertake to *correct* students' writing, or to help them correct it themselves. As Connors and Lunsford (1988) put it,

> Teachers' ideas about error definition and classification have always been absolute products of their times and cultures. . . . Teachers have always marked different phenomena as errors, called them different things, given them different weights. Error-pattern study is essentially the examination of an ever-shifting pattern of skills judged by an ever-shifting pattern of prejudices. (p. 399)

And this doesn't even begin to address the issue of dialect differences.

Kinds of Lessons: Some Examples

The kinds of grammar lessons I suggest in *Teaching Grammar in Context* are incidental lessons, wherein (for example) grammatical terms are used casually, in the course of discussing literature and students' writing; inductive lessons, wherein students may be guided to notice grammatical patterns and derive generalizations themselves; teaching grammatical points in the process of conferring with students about their writing; minilessons, which present new and useful information (to a class, group, or individual) in a brief format (Atwell, 1987; Calkins, 1986); and extended minilessons, which typically involve students in trying out or applying the concept, briefly and collaboratively, in order to promote greater understanding (Weaver, 1996b). Here, I would like to offer three examples of extended minilessons, which are common and often productive. Individual conferencing is perhaps even more valuable, as illustrated with one example. These lessons were taught by teachers from fifth grade to upper-level undergraduate, but all are appropriate for secondary students. Each example reflects one or more of the principles of constructivist learning theory. Each also illustrates the teaching of a grammatical concept, an editing concept, and/or a stylistically effective use of language.

Ann

Ann, a fifth-grade teacher, had noticed that when her students answered comprehension questions in reading, science, and social studies classes, they frequently responded with dependent clause fragments, especially those starting with *because*. She admits that when students wrote subordinate clauses for answers, she used to add independent clauses in red ink "to help them see the error of their ways. But to no avail: the subordinate clauses keep coming with all the tenacity of the Energizer Bunny."

Before taking a course in grammar and teaching grammar, Ann had been inclined to think that she should teach grammar as a formal system in order to help students eliminate such fragments from their writing. As a result of research read and ideas discussed in the class, Ann decided to teach just extended minilessons on areas of particular concern: in this case, writing grammatically complete sentences instead of dependent clause fragments. She taught two such lessons, one focusing exclusively on the subordinating conjunction *because*, since it is so often used in answers and in other writing. She had students work in pairs and added a peer editing component, asking pairs to trade and check one another's work.

Ann learned several lessons as a result of this experiment. First, the students understood the examples very well and asked a lot of questions about applying the "rules" to their writing. However, Ann also discovered that her transparencies involved, perhaps, too much information for her fifth graders. Furthermore, though the worksheets seemed simple and obvious to Ann, some kids had trouble, especially with the terms and concepts of *subordinate clause* and *independent clause*. And in spite of the minilesson examples and the examples at the top of the activity sheets, some students forgot capitals, commas, or periods; others misplaced commas; and others capitalized the subordinating conjunctions even though they occurred in the middle of sentences. Furthermore, many of these errors were overlooked during peer editing. Ann also discovered that the practice took longer than she had anticipated—almost half an hour. In other words, neither Ann's lesson nor the students' responses achieved perfection.

"Lastly," Ann reports, "in subsequent student writing the Bunny was back. Students were still using subordinate clauses as sentences." However, Ann did not become discouraged, for she knew better than to expect one minilesson to produce mastery, even when extended with some practice. Ann writes, "As Lois Matz Rosen (1987) puts it, 'Learning to use the correct mechanical and grammatical forms of written language is a developmental process and as such is slow, unique to each child, and does not progress in an even uphill pattern'" (p. 63).

Sarah

Taking the same course in grammar and teaching grammar as Ann, Sarah had likewise been inclined to teach traditional grammar; in fact, she admits that "Last year, I have realized, I did too much traditional grammar, and sadly enough I am afraid I did not teach my students how to become better writers." (For a fuller discussion, see Sarah Woltjer's article in this book.)

So it became Sarah's goal to improve her teaching of writing and not concentrate on the traditional grammar lessons. She writes, "Already this year, it has been exciting to watch the difference in my classroom as I implement new teaching ideas. This year I see much more enthusiasm for writing and grammar because the students are not fully aware they are being taught grammar. Disguising my grammar lessons behind the minilesson format in the writer's workshop has prevented me from having to endure a repetition of last year's groans regarding how boring grammar is."

Sarah had previously encouraged her seventh-graders to use adjectives and adverbs in their writing, but found that often her students' "descriptive" poems or paragraphs included little description and no details to make the pieces come alive. When it was suggested that she guide her students in writing a "five senses" poem about fall, Sarah decided to experiment with two different ways of encouraging students to use adjectives and adverbs. First, she asked the students to write about fall but gave them little direction, except for mentioning "Be sure to use those adjectives and adverbs for detail!" The students turned in their writings at the end of class.

About two weeks later, Sarah guided the students in writing their second fall poems, the "sense" poems. She explains:

> The Monday before, I had each student bring in one or two leaves, so by Wednesday we had a large basket of them. Before writing on Wednesday we did prewriting exercises together as a class. My students loved it! We threw the basket of leaves in the air and watched them fall in different directions. Then the students took turns placing their leaves on the hot air register and watched as their leaf got blown up toward the ceiling. After this they went around the classroom sharing a favorite fall memory or Thanksgiving tradition. Finally, with that introduction, I explained the writing assignment as using the five senses and they began writing. Those that had trouble with the first fall writing assignment now had previous knowledge and ideas from the prewriting activities on the five senses to provide organization. The difference in their writings was amazing!

Figure 2–3 shows the "before and after" poems from two students. One important thing to notice is that many of the descriptive words in the "after" poems aren't necessarily adjectives or adverbs; they are nouns ("razor blades") or verbs ("mulched"), as in the sense poem from Tom, a student in Sarah's lower language arts class, who disliked writing and reading. Another important point is that while the "before" poems used some adjectives and/or adverbs, the "after" poems

FIG. 2–3   *"Before" and "after" poems from Sarah's seventh-graders*

Tom's poems
Before
It is fall you rake the leaves crustily over a pile "o" mud. It is nearly ear shattering when you rake the flames on the ground. How chilling it be, no one knows. It (fall) is so unpredictable.

After
Smells like destruction when burned.
Clogging your lungs.
Tastes like the dirt of the earth, *destroying your taste buds.*
See the leaves on the trees fall effortlessly to the ground,
Where they will be raked, mulched, and burned.
Touch them—they feel like razor blades, when you jump on them.
Hear them? You can't!
But if you can't hear them, do they really fall?

Amy's poems
Before
Fall is the leaves changing colors; they can be green, yellow or red.
Fall is the cold and the freezing at night.
Fall is when your backyard is covered with leaves.

After
I can smell the apple pie *baking in the oven.*
I can smell the burning leaves in the neighbor's yards.
I hear the leaves *crackling under my feet* as I trudge through the yard.
I hear children *yelling* as they jump in a pile of leaves.
I see blended colors on the leaves like someone painted them.
I touch the leaves and I feel the veins.
I touch the leaves and sometimes they break in my hands.
I taste the turkey as the grease runs down my throat.
I taste the pumpkin pie and now I know it is fall!

used a much greater variety of constructions that function adjectivally, to modify nouns, or adverbially, to modify verbs or whole clauses. One example is the participial phrases in the "after" poem by Amy, a student in Sarah's advanced language arts class. (The italicized words and phrases in both "after" poems are present participle phrases functioning like adjectives, to modify the preceding nouns.)

What is to be learned from Sarah's experience? Several things, I think:

1. Various kinds of prewriting experiences can greatly enhance the quality of students' writing. This is something Sarah already knew and typically practiced.

2. A variety of adjectival and adverbial constructions will probably emerge when students are guided in focusing on the details of experience, rather than on grammar.

3. Asking students to focus on "adjectives" and "adverbs" might actually limit students' use of the more sophisticated structures they would use naturally.

The last two lessons were important ones Sarah learned—and important, I think, for many of us to learn, as teachers. (For a fuller version of Sarah's story, see Chapter 5 in this book).

Renee

Secondary teacher Renee uses a conference approach to teach writing, including sentence revision and editing. Figure 2–4a shows a sophomore's first draft of his

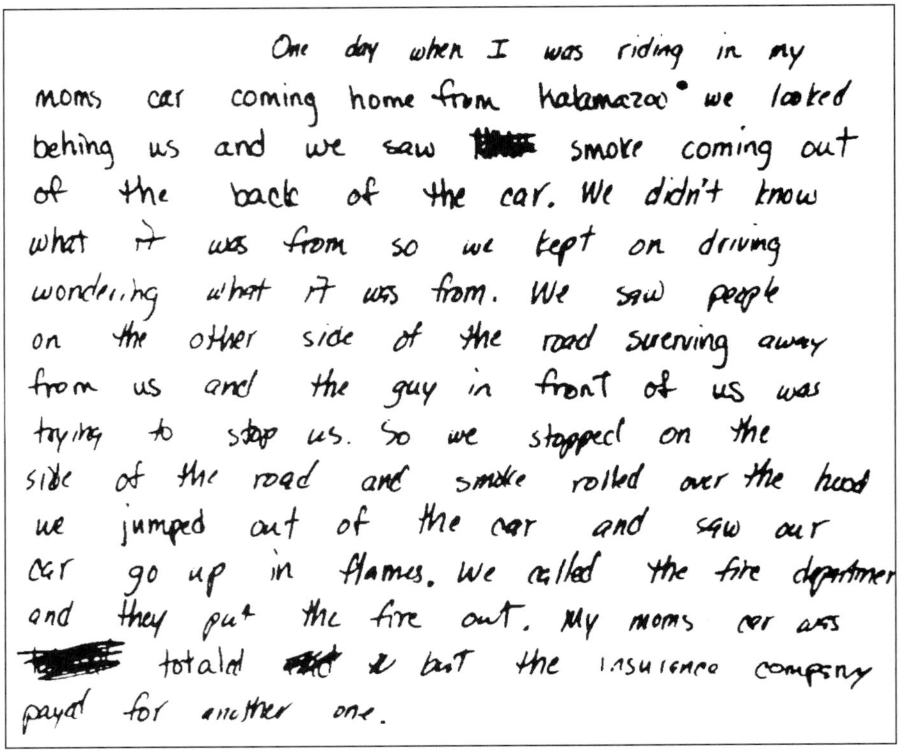

FIG. 2–4a *Sophomore's first draft (Weaver, 1996b).*

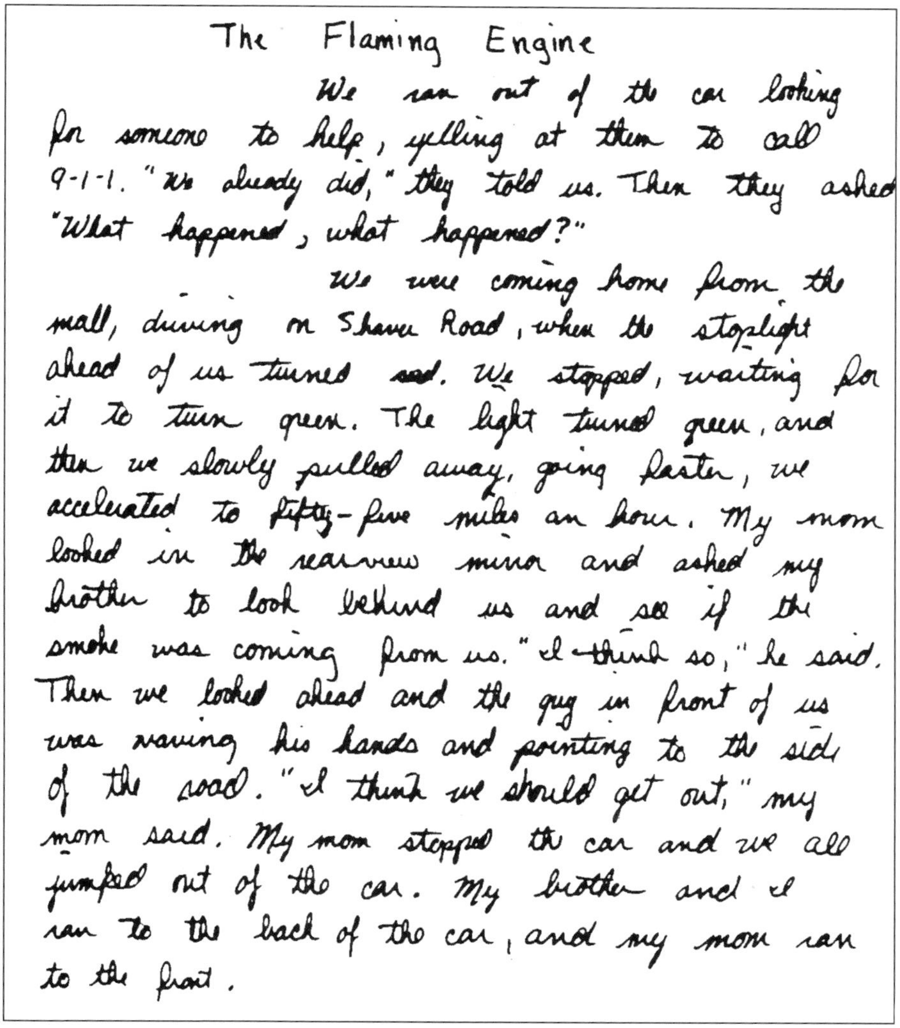

> ### The Flaming Engine
>
> We ran out of the car looking for someone to help, yelling at them to call 9-1-1. "We already did," they told us. Then they asked "What happened, what happened?"
>
> We were coming home from the mall, driving on Shane Road, when the stoplight ahead of us turned red. We stopped, waiting for it to turn green. The light turned green, and then we slowly pulled away, going faster, we accelerated to fifty-five miles an hour. My mom looked in the rearview mirror and asked my brother to look behind us and see if the smoke was coming from us. "I think so," he said. Then we looked ahead and the guy in front of us was waving his hands and pointing to the side of the road. "I think we should get out," my mom said. My mom stopped the car and we all jumped out of the car. My brother and I ran to the back of the car, and my mom ran to the front.

FIG. 2–4b *First paragraph of sophomore's sixth draft (Weaver, 1996b).*

paper, while 2–4b shows the first paragraph of a much longer sixth draft. First, Renee suggested to the writer that he consider an opening that "grabs the reader's attention." She further suggested that conversation can do that. In working with a later draft, Renee guided the writer in seeing how to put the reader "there," in using participial phrases to convey narrative detail, and in using punctuation conventionally. In a subsequent conference, she and the writer might still consider whether one or both of the comma splices should be left as is or eliminated (Weaver, 1996b, pp. 84–85).

FIG. 2–5 *Comma Splices*

A "comma splice" occurs when two grammatically complete sentences (independent clauses) are joined with just a comma.

On rare occasion, comma splice sentences are found in published writing. This usually occurs only when the two grammatically complete sentences are short and, for the most part, grammatically parallel.

Examples:
1. The students that need to touch the book can, the children that need to verbalize their thoughts are responded to.
2. And they learn on their own, they in a sense teach themselves.
3. These children are not stupid, they just learn and understand in different ways.

Usually, however, comma splices are considered a "no no." Below are examples of comma splice sentences that don't meet the conditions for acceptability: ones that should be "corrected." With a neighbor, please consider effective ways of eliminating these comma splices by using different punctuation, restructuring the sentence, or adding a connecting word like *and* or *but* (a coordinating conjunction).

1. I was very impressed, the teacher pointed to the words as the students said them.
2. Then the students were blindfolded and given a button, they had to name the characteristics they felt the button contained.
3. This little exercise really worked, as soon as she started singing the children started singing right with her.
4. My first expectation was the shared book experience, this seems to be one of the most fundamental aspects of whole language.
5. The first is a poetry notebook, it is the first item on the agenda that day.

In teaching upper-level undergraduates who are preparing to be teachers, I have often found that even these students do not evidence much concern for the mechanics of writing before they have "turned in" their papers. (This is in so-called content area classes, wherein I do not routinely lead students through stages of the writing process unless they request or obviously need such help.) The motivation is somewhat higher when students have gotten their papers back with "corrections," accompanied usually by an explanation and occasionally by the general reminder that "You need to get a grasp on this, because it's something you'll be expected to teach even elementary-level students!" Sometimes I just put a checkmark in the margin where something needs to be attended to.

At this point, I have found some success with, in effect, treating the returned paper as a not-quite-final draft (for many related ideas, see Rosen, in this volume). So far, I have developed information sheets on two of the most common "errors" in mechanics: use of just a comma between two independent clauses (the "comma splice") and absence of the apostrophe in possessive nouns. First, I distribute the handout(s) to students and explain the concept(s), using the examples on the sheet(s), which have been taken from actual student papers. Then I organize the students into groups and invite them to play around with correcting the other sentences, which again have been taken from students' papers, as in the handout in Figure 2–5. I also give each group a grammar handbook, asking them to check the phenomenon in question, and/or other kinds of "errors" that have been marked (see Figure 2–6 for some quality handbooks for different levels, as well as good resource books for teachers). The students are also asked to discuss with each other what needs correction in their own papers (not necessarily just comma splices or possessives), to determine what they still don't understand, and to ask me for clarification and help as I circulate around the room. I encourage students to help each other edit future papers, to use a grammar handbook to help with grammatical problems they *know* they have, to seek my help in an individual conference if needed, and to take risks with grammatical constructions.

This procedure has typically reduced the incidence of these kinds of errors in subsequent papers—not only the one or two kinds of errors on my handouts, but other kinds as well. In addition, though, I usually find "new" kinds of errors, such as students punctuating ordinary plurals and verb endings with apostrophes, not just using the apostrophe in possessive nouns. My favorite overgeneralization is from the earnest young man who wrote "mathematic's" after learning about the apostrophe in possessives (e.g. "the mathematician's knowledge"). I greet such new kinds of errors with a smile and a chuckle, reminding the preservice teacher that new errors will occur, almost inevitably, as writers try to apply concepts that are new to them and only partially understood. I remind them that as teachers, they too should encourage risk-taking and growth in the use of language by responding to children's new errors in a similar manner.

Conclusion

As I indicated before, there are no miracles here. No matter how students are taught grammatical concepts, syntactic constructions, and stylistic devices, or language conventions and editing concepts, they will not automatically make use of these in their writing. However, the relevant research confirms what everyday experience reveals: that teaching *grammar* in the context of writing works better than teaching grammar as a formal system, if our aim is for students to *use* grammar more effectively and conventionally in their writing.

FIG. 2–6 *References for recommended grammar texts and reference books (Weaver, 1996b).*

High School and College

BELANOFF, P., RORSCHACH, B., & OBERLINK, M. (1993). *The Right Handbook: Grammar and Usage in Context* (2nd ed.). Portsmouth, NH: Boynton/Cook. This book is refreshingly honest about how language is actually used by educated people, as opposed (sometimes) to what the usual handbooks prescribe. Designed as an aid for writers, the book can also spark appreciation for the richness and diversity of language and an understanding of how language and language standards change. Valuable and interesting for teachers and students, especially at the college level.

EBBITT, W. R., & EBBITT, D. R. (1990). *Index to English* (8th ed.). New York: Oxford University Press. This alphabetically organized index comes close to providing everything you ever wanted to know about grammar—provided you can figure out which headings to use. The book is particularly valuable for its honesty regarding the degree to which certain words and constructions are and are not accepted—in what kinds of writing, and by whom. The guide is not as unrealistically conservative as some of the grammar handbooks on the market, nor so liberal that it provides an inadequate guide to usage in the broadest sense. A valuable classroom or library reference to have available for teachers and serious students of language.

GLAZIER, T. F. (1994). *The Least You Should Know About English Writing Skills* (Form B., 5th ed.). Fort Worth, TX: Harcourt. Deals with just a few of the most persistent editing problems. It has exercises and answers so students can check their own understanding. Therefore, it is useful for those motivated to teach themselves certain conventions of Edited American English. Suitable for junior high through college.

GORDON, K. E. (1993). *The Deluxe Transitive Vampire: The Ultimate Handbook of Grammar for the Innocent, the Eager, and the Doomed* (2nd ed.). New York: Pantheon. The example sentences make the book highly entertaining to many students, even though this book is not necessarily the best teaching tool. See also Gordon, *The New Well-Tempered Sentence: A Punctuation Handbook for the Innocent, the Eager, and the Doomed* (expanded and revised edition), 1993, New York: Ticknor & Fields.

HACKER, D. (1991). *The Bedford Handbook for Writers* (3rd ed.). Boston: Bedford Books of St. Martin's Press. This book runs a close second to Troyka et al. in completeness and clarity of its explanations. The instructor's annotated edition provides valuable references for further exploration. This high quality text is especially popular at the college level, perhaps in part because there are so many ancillary materials available. These include a bibliography of professional resources for teachers of writing, a collection of background readings for teachers, a guide for writing tutors, and various materials more directly linked to teaching with and from the handbook itself.

HACKER, D. (1995). *A Writer's Reference* (3rd ed.). New York: St. Martin's Press. For simplicity, clarity, and ease of use, this handbook ranks number one. Its spiral binding is a particular blessing for those who want a book to lie flat while they are consulting it. However, the book is relatively conservative in its prescriptions. Suitable for junior high through college.

HARRIS, M. (1994). *Prentice Hall Reference Guide to Grammar and Usage* (2nd ed.). Englewood Cliffs, NJ: Prentice Hall. Harris's explanations are unusually clear, thanks to years of one-on-one tutoring in a university writing center.

KOLLN, M. (1991). *Rhetorical Grammar: Grammatical Choices, Rhetorical Effects.* New York: Macmillan. Straightforward presentation of grammatical concepts and their stylistic effects. Especially suitable for college level, or for precollege high school students.

LUNSFORD, A., & CONNORS, R. (1995). *The St. Martin's Handbook* (3rd ed.). New York: St. Martin's Press. About four-fifths of this handbook focuses on grammar, mechanics, and punctuation, but it does so in the context of writing.

LUNSFORD, A., & CONNORS, R. (1997). *The Everyday Writer: A Brief Reference.* Similar in format to Hacker's *A Writer's Reference* (above), but somewhat more detailed—more for the college level. Especially helpful with information on how to reference electronic sources.

RICE, S. (1993). *Right Words, Right Places.* Belmont, CA: Wadsworth. Includes wonderfully rich examples from literature and emphasizes the rhetorical effects of language choices, not grammar for the sake of grammar. Particularly interesting to students of literature and creative writers, this book seems most appropriate for college students who are not easily intimidated by Rice's thorough explanations.

SEBRANEK, P., MEYER, V., & KEMPER, D. (1990). *Writers Inc.* (2nd ed.). Wilmington, MA: Write Source. This compendium of information has an encyclopedic quality; it includes information on various topics, grammar being only one of them. Suitable for students from junior high through college, if they can make use of a text that defines grammatical terms more than it explains them.

TROYKA, L. Q., WITH DOBIE, A. B., & GORDON, E. R. (1992). *Simon & Schuster Handbook for Writers* (3rd ed.). Englewood Cliffs, NJ: Prentice Hall. Of the various books listed here, this one is by far the most complete in its treatment of grammar, with lots of insights rarely found in other books. The format is inviting and easy to read; the annotated instructor's edition is a wonderful resource of ideas for explaining grammatical concepts clearly. Most suitable for teachers and others seriously interested in understanding the structure of English and ways of explaining that structure effectively.

Elementary and Middle School/Junior High

KEMPER D., NATHAN, R., AND SEBRANEK, P. (1996). *Write Away.* Wilmington, MA: Write Source. For young writers, approximately grades 2–3. Emphasizes writing, with attention to basic mechanics.

KEMPER, D., NATHAN, R., & SEBRANEK, P. (1995). *Writers Express: A Handbook for Young Writers, Thinkers, and Learners.* Wilmington, MA: Write Source.

Suggested for grades 4 and 5, this book—like *Writers Inc.*—has a useful reference section (maps, historical time line). However, the major focus is writing and the writing process. A chapter titled "The Proofreader's Guide" deals with punctuation, spelling, and mechanics.

SEBRANEK, P., MEYER, V., & KEMPER, D. (1995). *Write Source 2000: A Guide to Writing, Thinking, and Learning* (3rd. ed.). Wilmington, MA: Great Source. Suggested for grades 6 through 8 but also for "students of all ages," this book is similar to the one just listed, but it has more—more of everything, including a rather complete "Yellow Pages Guide to Marking Punctuation."

Of course I make no claim to having examined *all* the grammar handbooks, but, on the other hand, I have selected these from among quite a few that were examined. Some readers may note that *Warriner's English Grammar and Composition* series (1986) is not included in this list, nor is the single handbook *Warriner's High School Handbook* (1992). A far better reference tool for high school and even junior high students is Diana Hacker's *A Writer's Reference*.

Endnotes

1. This article has been reprinted almost verbatim from the author's article by the same title, which appeared in the November 1996 issue of the *English Journal*.

2. The author wishes to thank Renee Callies, Ann Miner, and Sarah Woltjer for permission to describe some of the ways they teach grammar in the context of writing.

References

A BEKA BOOK. (1996). *Home school catalog.* Pensacola, FL: A Beka Book.

ATWELL, N. (1987). *In the middle: Writing, reading, and learning with adolescents.* Portsmouth, NH: Heinemann.

BRADDOCK, R., LLOYD-JONES, R., & SCHOER, L. (1963). *Research in written composition.* Urbana, IL: National Council of Teachers of English.

CALKINS, L. (1980). When children want to punctuate: Basic skills belong in context. *Language Arts, 57,* 567–573.

CALKINS, L. (1986/1994). *The art of teaching writing.* Portsmouth, NH: Heinemann.

CHAPMAN, J. (1986). *Why* not *teach intensive phonics?* Pensacola, FL: A Beka Book.

CONNORS, R., & LUNSFORD, A. (1988). Frequency of formal errors in current college writing, or Ma and Pa Kettle do research. *College Composition and Communication, 39,* 395–409.

DISTEFANO, P., & KILLION, J. (1984). Assessing writing skills through a process approach. *English Education, 11,* 98–101.

ELLEY, W., BARHAM, I., LAMB, H., & WYLLIE, M. (1976). The role of grammar in a secondary English curriculum. *Research in the Teaching of English, 10,* 5–21. (Reprinted from *New Zealand Journal of Educational Studies, 10* (May 1975) 26–42).

GADDY, B., HALL, T., & MARZANO, R. (1996). *School wars: Resolving our conflicts over religion and values.* San Francisco: Jossey-Bass.

HARRIS, M., & ROWAN, K. (1989). Explaining grammatical concepts. *Journal of Basic Writing, 8* (2), 21–41.

HARRIS, R. (1962). *An experimental inquiry into the functions and value of formal grammar in the teaching of written English to children aged twelve to fourteen.* Unpublished doctoral dissertation, University of London.

HILLOCKS, G., JR. (1986). *Research on written composition: New directions for teaching.* Urbana, IL: ERIC Clearinghouse on Reading and Communication Skills and the National Conference on Research in English. Distributed by the National Council of Teachers of English.

HILLOCKS, G., JR., & SMITH, M. (1991). Grammar and usage. In J. Flood, J. Jensen, D. Lapp, & J. Squire (Eds.), *Handbook of research on teaching the English language arts* (pp. 591–603). New York: Macmillan.

HOLDERER, R. (1995). The religious right: Who are they and why are we the enemy? *English Journal, 84,* 74–83.

HUNTSMAN, J. (1983). Grammar. In D. Wagner (Ed.), *The seven liberal arts in the Middle Ages* (pp. 58–95). Bloomington: Indiana University Press.

KAGAN, D. (1980). Run-on and fragment sentences: An error analysis. *Research in the Teaching of English, 14,* 127–138.

KOLLN, M. (1981). Closing the books on alchemy. *College Composition and Communication, 31,* 139–151.

KROLL, B., & SCHAFER, J. (1978). Error analysis and the teaching of composition. *College Composition and Communication, 29,* 242–248.

MCQUADE, F. (1980). Examining a grammar course: The rationale and the result. *English Journal, 69,* 26–30.

NOGUCHI, R. (1991). *Grammar and the teaching of writing: Limits and possibilities.* Urbana, IL: National Council of Teachers of English.

O'HARE, F. (1973). *Sentence combining: Improving student writing without formal grammar instruction.* (Research Report No. 15.) Urbana, IL: National Council of Teachers of English.

POSTMAN, N., & WEINGARTNER, C. (1966). *Linguistics: A revolution in teaching.* New York: Dell.

ROSEN, L. (1987). Developing correctness in student writing: Alternatives to the error-hunt. *English Journal, 76,* 62–69.

SHAUGHNESSY, M. (1977). *Errors and expectations: A guide for the teacher of basic writing.* New York: Oxford University Press.

WEAVER, C. (1982). Welcoming errors as signs of growth. *Language Arts, 59,* 438–444.

WEAVER, C. (1994). *Reading process and practice: From socio-psycholinguistics to whole language* (2nd Ed.). Portsmouth, NH: Heinemann.

WEAVER, C. (1996a). *On the teaching of grammar.* SLATE Starter Sheet—Fact Sheet Series (pp. 7–8). Urbana, IL: National Council of Teachers of English.

WEAVER, C. (1996b). *Teaching grammar in context.* Portsmouth, NH: Boynton/Cook.

WEAVER, C., GILLMEISTER-KRAUSE, L., & VENTO-ZOGBY, G. (1996). *Creating support for effective literacy education.* Portsmouth, NH: Heinemann.

3 Dora Learns to Write and in the Process Encounters Punctuation

PAT CORDEIRO

Introduction

Drawing on many years' experience in the classroom writing with children and a three-part study of children's use of periods in their writing, Pat Cordeiro describes a pathway of progress made by many young writers as they learn how to conventionalize written language. She discusses how children grow in developing conventional endmarking and in defining "sentenceness." In the classroom, learning punctuation is often relegated to a worksheet or a boardwork exercise; in the writer's process, punctuation is often seen as a set of details to be added "at the end" so that the writing will conform to a standardized form. Rarely is the punctuation system seen or taught for what it is: an essential code for organizing units of thought and language, the key to making meaning in writing. Just as breath, pause, body language, eye contact, and intonation help the speaker structure meaning in oral discourse, punctuation—ranging from the small, subtle comma to the large, overt paragraph—helps re-create the writer's meaning for the reader. And in the process of being applied to a written text, punctuation helps the *writer* understand the writer's own meaning. In this chapter Cordeiro discusses children's development of punctuation usage in their own writing and how we might help them—and ourselves—learn this shared convention from the perspective of punctuation as a system that organizes and governs the sharing of meaning, helping both the reader and the writer know what the writer wants to say.

This is the story of an imaginary first-grader named Dora and how she learns about writing and its conventions. The story of Dora is typical and the portrayal of her is a composite of the process and products of many children I have observed, as both a teacher and a researcher, over twenty-five years of thinking about how we learn to write. As a teacher I worked and wrote with children in grades one through six. As a researcher I observed the writing process and product of three classes, grades one, three, and six, analyzing all writing done throughout the year during writing time at each of the grade levels. As I looked, I focused on how children learn to put periods in their written text. I found this one aspect of learning to write, learning punctuation, to be pivotal, both for children as they strive to master the written code, and for teachers as they seek to understand children and their language-learning processes. I found that learning where to place periods in text is key: understanding how children learn this significant convention provides a window on how children learn about the structure of the language and how they set about mastering the code, conventions, and meaning potential of written communication.

So we call on Dora to tell us her story, to help us to understand more about what might be going on with early language learners as they do what language learners do—create hypotheses, test and modify them, and evolve rules to live by in their writing.

Dora's Early Learning

When Dora first began to write, she was sure that what writers did was put letters on paper. When she and her friends wrote together at the writing table, they showed each other the letters and marks they were making, saying, as the teacher did, "Let's read your writing." Somehow those letters had to match the way the words sounded when you said them out loud. So when it was writing time Dora did just that. She said the words very slowly and carefully and she wrote down all the letters that she thought matched the sounds she heard in the words she said. What she wrote was this:

YERCOMAYERAMOSDARA
(We are coming home. We are almost there.)

Her teacher seemed very pleased, and Dora wrote like this for several days. Each day Dora's teacher asked her to talk about her writing and then asked her to read what she had written. Dora would read and the teacher would write down in the corner of the page what Dora said. One day Dora's teacher asked, "Dora, did you ever notice in your reading book that all the letters don't run together one after the other? Did you ever notice that each word gets its own place?" Dora's teacher got a book and showed Dora that, sure enough, the letters didn't all run together. Sometimes they were separated. Dora and her teacher used their hands to frame the words in Dora's story so that she could see that each one could have its own place.

The next time Dora wrote, she thought she would try to separate the letters into words. She asked her friends at the writing table what they did, and some of them said they had thought about how words were separate, too. One of the children showed Dora how she put little dots in between the words. Dora tried that. When she got to the end of what she thought was the first word, she made a little dot. For the rest of the story Dora put a dot wherever she thought the word ended. Sometimes she wasn't sure where words ended, but she worked very carefully. Her story looked like this:

```
THE CAT
IS.SHASING.A.
BTR.FI.
THE.BAK.AV.THE. HOWS.
(The cat
is chasing a
butterfly.
The back of the house.)
```

Dora wrote several stories with dots in between each word. Her mother said Dora "really seemed to be getting the words." Her father read the whole story without Dora's help. Dora was very pleased. Then one day in the class when Danny was reading, the teacher said that he needed to read in "sentences." She said that he needed to "stop at the periods at the end of the sentences" and she showed Danny, Dora, and the others the dots she called "periods." The teacher showed them that there were many periods in the story, and she read a little to demonstrate to them how to stop reading when they came to one of these "periods."

Later on, when it was writing time, Dora thought about how to put periods in her story. She and her friends talked about what had happened while they had been reading, and everyone seemed confused when they tried to figure out what to do with those little dots. Dora decided to keep on putting dots in between each word because then she knew where each word in her story ended and it made it easier for her to read.

When she was finished with her story she got out the picture storybook they had been using. She saw that her story looked different from the one in the book. Her story looked like she had too many dots in it, and she wasn't sure how she was going to be able to put in what the teacher called "periods" if she had so many dots already. Dora stopped thinking of her marks as *dots* and began thinking of them as *periods*. She thought she'd try to decide where they might go if she only used a few. It seemed to her that it was going to be very hard to figure out this rule. It was hard to think about this and not forget her story at the same time. And there was all that spelling. Dora got tired.

The next day at writing time, Dora talked with her friends about where to put the periods. Everyone agreed that the teacher and the book must be right: periods didn't go after every word you wrote. Everyone was pretty clear about what a word was, although sometimes the teacher helped them when they thought two words were one word, like with "Thank you," which everybody at the writing table thought was only one word until the teacher said it was two words.

Dora decided that she'd put periods at the end of each line. She wasn't quite sure what to do after each word, so she looked back at her reading book. Since there wasn't any mark in between the words, Dora did the same—she left a space, although it seemed funny to be doing such a special thing as writing a word without making a mark where it ended. Once in a while Dora put a dot in between words the way she had before, maybe because it seemed wrong to just leave a space, or maybe because she forgot. Her story looked like this:

WE ARE.GOING BIKRTING WE ARE AT.THE BIKRTING PAK WE.ARE BIKRDING NOW.
(We are going bikeriding. We are at the bikeriding park. We are bikeriding now.)

One day Dora read a story she had written to the teacher. It was about Dora's visit to her friend's house, and she had been working on it for a long time. It was now finished, and the teacher was helping her use *the rules* to put in *punctuation*. Dora was happy that she had figured out where to put the periods at the end of each line, so she was quite surprised when the teacher said that Dora "needed some help in learning where to put the periods." The teacher asked Dora to read her story again, and so Dora did. After she had read a little bit, the teacher asked Dora to talk about the writing and how she had decided to place the periods. Then the teacher asked, "Remember how you read this part? We talked about this mark called the period, and how when we're reading we let our voice drop down, like this . . ." The teacher read Dora's story back to her, but she stopped at the end of the line where the period was and sounded like she was finished. It didn't sound right to Dora and she said so. The teacher said, "That's right, this isn't a sentence. That's why we don't put a period there."

The teacher asked Dora to read her story again. This time, when Dora stopped at the end of the first part, the teacher said "That's a sentence; put a period here." And so Dora did. Then the teacher showed Dora the picture storybook Dora had been reading that morning. She showed Dora that there weren't periods at the end of each line, but that the periods happened at different places on the page. She asked Dora to go back over her story by herself and see if she could find other places where periods would go at the end of sentences.

Dora and her friends at the writing table worked on this problem for a long time. Dora couldn't figure out why she had been wrong. Everything seemed to fit so well. And she couldn't figure out what a *sentence* was. Finally Dora erased all the periods at the end of the lines and put a period at the end of the writing on each page. This seemed to look more like what she remembered from the reading book. Dora read the story over to her friends and she stopped reading when she came to the period at the end of each page. The story sounded good and her friends liked it a lot. When she stopped at the periods, it seemed that things were finished and not kind of odd, like when the teacher had read and stopped at the period at the end of the line. One page of Dora's story looked like this:

MY FAD HD A CAT I PLAD WT THE CAT.
(My friend had a cat. I played with the cat.)

The next story Dora wrote was very long and it was the first time Dora thought about putting periods right in the middle of things instead of at the end of a word, line, page, or story. She was working on a long story called "How ToSwm" (How to Swim). It looked like this:

Frs Get In The Wter
Then Put Yur Hol Bdy Undrwatr.
Then Mv Yur Ams Lik Ths:
Then Kik Yr Feet Togtr.
Because If You Dod Do It Togetr.
You Mit Snk And Drown.
Don Forgt To Bret.
(First get in the water. Then put your whole body underwater. Then move your arms like this. Then kick your feet together. Because if you don't do it together you might sink and drown. Don't forget to breathe.)

Dora had been working on this story for quite a long time and was very proud of it. She had gone back to putting periods at the end of each line. Putting one at the end of each page didn't seem to be enough. Her teacher hadn't said anything about it, and at this point Dora hadn't thought much about it either. She had been too busy with the stories she wanted to write. Now that she was getting better with the letters her mother and father said that they were very proud. Dora's friends liked the stories Dora wrote, and when they were at the writing table, kids would often ask her to read her stories and to help them with theirs. They often talked about new things they were learning.

Dora found that she had lots of things to write about. She didn't always think about details like periods. She kept on using the same old idea she had before: Periods go at the end of the page. That seemed to give just about the right number when she compared it to what she saw in her reading book. But this particular day she was working on "How to Swim," going back over the story, trying to fit in things she had learned. When she got toward the end, she came to the part that said "Then kick your feet together." She had just put a period at the end of the last line after "together." It may have seemed to her that "Because" was an important beginning, or she may have thought that "together" was a good place to stop. She put a period in between these two causal thoughts, creating the simple sentence "Then kick your feet together" and the causal adverbial clause "because if you don't do it together you may sink."

When Dora's teacher asked her to read her story, she asked Dora, as she always did, to read it "the way it was meant to be." She reminded Dora to "stop at all the periods" and she said to be sure to read it in sentences. Dora's teacher had given her contradictory instructions. It was impossible for Dora to stop at the periods as she had placed them and to read meaningful sentences. If she stopped at her period placements and dropped her voice at the natural end of her sentences as we do in English, then the text would sound choppy and strange. If she dropped her voice at her period placements and at the ends of the syntactic sentences, then the text would sound meaningless. Dora had to choose between attending to her punctuating marks or reading with meaning.

Dora started to read. She read it the way it was supposed to sound. She forgot about the periods at the ends of the lines. Children commonly read their own text without regard for the punctuation marks which they themselves have placed. They read the text as they know it in their heads, not as they have tried to write it in standard form. Marks like periods, which have not yet gained meaning, are ignored.

When Dora got to "Then kick your feet together," she stopped and let her voice drop down. Then she read "because if you don't do it together you might sink and drown." It sounded right. This was an important time for Dora and her teacher. It was the first time Dora had deliberately placed an endmark to mark off a clause.

When Dora read her story and stopped at the period after "together," Dora's teacher smiled. She knew that Dora was beginning to develop a workable hypothesis for period placement which would eventually lead to correct, standardized endmarking. After trying out all the placement rules based on units of text, such as interword, endline, and endpage, Dora had begun to develop a syntax-based hypothesis. The teacher asked Dora to talk about the writing she had done, and Dora explained all the hard thinking she and the children at the writing table had been doing.

Dora was pleased when she saw her teacher smile. Her teacher said, "I especially liked the way you stopped when you read the period after 'Then kick your feet together.' It made the story sound good." Dora said, "I knew that one was right." Her teacher asked, "What will you write next?"

What's Going on with Dora?

Dora's teacher could have said many things. She could have questioned Dora about why she had placed a period between clauses. However, children may interpret teachers' questions as criticism (Stubbs, 1976). Dora's response might well have been a silent one as she erased the period and tried to *correct* what she had come to see as an *error*. Faced with a challenge, learners may revert to an amalgam of abandoned hypotheses, ones which have been disproved but which once seemed valid. Some of this was apparent in Dora's switch from endline to endpage and back to endline. And, children—like the rest of us—may at times simply forget. Wilde (1992) writes, "My sense is that he knew how to use them [commas] but sometimes forgot, particularly once he got involved in what he was writing" (p. 7).

The teacher could have taken the opportunity to tell Dora that she had not marked a sentence, that even though it sounded *good* to both of them, it was just a clause. But Dora's teacher saw that Dora was just beginning a long process of syntactic awareness, one with important implications for language learning in general. She chose to point this out with praise. As Hall (1996) points out, "one thing is clear to all teachers of young children—young learners treat punctuation in the same generative way that they deal with spelling" (p. 7). Dora's teacher knew that punctuation is negotiable, an agreement between writer and reader (Quirk & Greenbaum, 1973). Sometimes, for literary purposes, authors may choose to isolate a phrase or a clause to lend additional emphasis. Not all authors would punctuate a text in the same way. Young children have been known to argue in favor of a nonstandard form of punctuation because it emphasizes a particular point. (See Martens & Goodman, 1996, for a discussion of invented punctuation.) Often young writers use dark, boldface writing or many exclamation points to create excitement in text. Sometimes deliberate isolation of a phrase is used to create an effect.

Most important, Dora's teacher was concerned with allowing Dora to develop a workable hypothesis based on data that confirms the language user's thinking. She allowed Dora the freedom to overuse and overgeneralize appropriate environments for period use (Ferreiro & Zuccermaglio, 1996). Dora's teacher talked and listened to children's explanations of their own thinking. As Anderson (1996) points out, "By allowing children to reflect on, and discuss the way language is used both by them and around them we give them the possibility to extend and refine their strategies" (p. 63). In the world of period placement, every sentence is a new experience. The writer is constantly faced with rule adjustment, with hypothesis modification. In early writing experiences the child is often faced with abandoning an alternative hypothesis which seems to be valid. Sometimes there is no ready hypothesis to take its place. Rule formation becomes very difficult under these circumstances. "Getting it right" can be very scary.

Dora's confusion is compounded by many factors. What will continue to block her developing understanding of the units of language is her tendency to write complete sentences before she turns the page of her writing booklet. Giacobbe (personal communication) and Armstrong (1996) both hypothesize that when observed children wrote in stapled booklets using picture paper they seemed to use the turning of the page as an endmarker. Thus, the physical act seemed to serve to commemorate the end of the thought. Children using lined paper often accomplish the same thing by chaining clauses together with "and—and" or "then—then" or a combination of the two. This chaining allows the writer to avoid the problem of sentence demarcation altogether, and allows the child to begin to capture the complexity of oral language. It may also represent more closely the child's actual thought units. Kress (1982) points out that speech does not provide a clear and definable model for sentence identification. Speech tends to be chained rather than hierarchical. We do not automatically know from our history as speakers where to endmark in writing; speech and writing are two distinct forms of language use and inform each other only up to a point.

Dora will begin to learn the form of simple sentences through her developing understanding of the syntactic structures of the language as she experiences them through writing. Simone (1996), writing about use of the comma, points out that acquiring standardization in punctuation appears to have a structural basis: "The first commas that children acquire are those indicating a smaller quantity of structure and those requiring less cognitive processing" (p. 175). Once Dora is tuned in to periods she may begin to attend to separate instances and to generalize across the cases to refine a rule. This is what language learners do (Kress, 1982). But as Dora develops a sense of where periods go in simple sentences, she will keep upping the ante on herself through the content and syntactic structure of her writing, thus confounding the *rule* she has begun to form. Because Dora is learning rapidly in so many domains, she will begin to write in more complex sentences, ones which do not fit the sense of rule she has developed. And, since every sentence that is generated is unique, it will be hard for Dora to mentally set up categories of similar sets of sentence patterns. Dora's teacher will need to be especially careful to give Dora leeway to work on this very complex understanding.

Once Dora develops the knowledge that "I went downtown." is a sentence and deserves an endmark, she will search in her writing for similar sentence patterns. But because in her writing she is primarily concerned with story, she may write something like "I went downtown with my mother" and she may well punctuate it like this:

I went downtown. with my mother.

As children grow in writing experience, they must generalize across many kinds of unique sentences.

Understanding Dora

As children begin to write, they are faced with many problems. Elementary teachers are familiar with the sound-letter correspondence problem. Those of us who have worked with very young writers know how hard they work on this. Sounding out a word as simple as *dog* is no small task for a beginning writer. This is a very complex, microphonic problem. And while a child is focusing on the letters that are involved in writing a word, it is no surprise that other, more discreet signs like periods are overlooked. After all, writing is making words. And making words is done with letters, not funny little marks like commas and periods. Young writers/readers seem to experience a kind of sign blindness. That is, they may not see all the marks which are present on a page of text. Not knowing how to respond to signals, young writers and readers may not initially *see* periods, commas, apostrophes, capital letters, paragraphs, and so on. They are very busy with all those letters. We all experience something similar when we drive a car—some signs we respond to, some we may not even be aware of, until we are stopped for speeding, or failing to yield. The more subtle the sign and its response, the more likely it is to be overlooked as we hurry through the *text*.

For Dora, *real* writing begins with the making of letters. Dora seems to have already had plenty of time to play with writing-as-scribbling. She has now accepted the fact that *true* writing is composed of recognizable and agreed-on symbols called *letters*. And this is where she begins. As Dora begins to try to place letters in some orderly fashion, she attends only to this one feature: letters make sounds which make what she wants to say—nothing else matters. We see this in her first example,

YERCOMAYERAMOSDARA (We are coming home. We are almost there.)

Dora may continue working with letters, trying to accomplish more shared sound-letter correspondence, for several stories. Some students work on this for many months, sometimes through more than one grade level. Many crucial factors affect progress: hearing, attention, perception of sound-letter correspondence, exposure to other print media, experience with writing, encouragement, and patience.

One of Dora's early struggles in writing will be *word-ness*. Where one word ends and another begins is not always easy to hear in speech. For instance, we cannot easily tell whether "Good bye" or "Get well" are each one word or two. Certainly, they, and many other similar phrases, are one thought. It may be hard for children to sort out the difference between a word and a thought. What defines a word is hard to say. People talk very fast and we have no oral device or gesture for word demarcation. Young writers are on their own and may not segment words as we adults have learned to perceive them.

Dora, like other young writers, will begin to segment the speech stream into units. Ferreiro and Zucchermaglio (1996) point out that children begin to attend to punctuation marks only when they begin to work with the alphabetic principle and with spelling standardization. They will call these units "words," although that may not always be the case. The most common first use of periods is inter-word, as a word separator.

I.HAD.A.SPRIS.PRD. (I had a surprise party.)

It is important to note that at this stage children like Dora are not just writing simple sentences (i.e., subject-verb-object) like "I saw a ball." The sentence "My mom's friend thought that I was going to walk out the door" is a complex one, comprised of a major clause (My mom's friend thought) and a subordinate clause (that I was going to walk out the door). The writer is not concerned with writing sentences that fit a known pattern. Here, the involved writer is concerned with writing sentences that express the author's meaning. Children who wrote the samples used in this chapter are unafraid: they write what they need to say. They look to their editors—their friends, teachers, and parents—to help them conventionalize their writing. It is also important to comment on Ferreiro and Zucchermaglio's (1996) observation that "children are very sensitive to the textual function of punctuation marks . . . sometimes using punctuation as an alternative means to other lexical and textual solutions" (p. 204). Perera (1996) also found evidence of children's sensitivity to punctuation as they read and responded to early work with text.

Dora and others like her have been nurtured in a trusting environment (Graves, 1984, and others) and so they try out many alternative hypotheses before they begin to *get it right*. What are those alternative hypotheses? Where do they come from? And, how do children eventually come around to standardization?

Dora's Sequence of Learning

The pattern of error that Dora went through is one shared by children I have studied (Cordeiro, 1988; Cazden et al., 1985; Cordeiro et al., 1983). Wilde (1992) uses the term "developmental punctuation" (p. 5) and points to students' use of "gradually more sophisticated hypotheses." Here, while considering children's modification of language hypotheses, we will look at the products of those hypotheses as they reveal evolving knowledge of syntax and units of language. While this evolution is certainly developmental, it seems to reflect children's experience with written language more than their cognitive development. This hypothesis certainly requires more study.

In the samples I studied, beginning writers often first used period placement as an *interword* marker. Dora's subsequent period placements were also predictable, but not always found in all children's writing. The deliberateness of Dora's period placements, the consistency of those placements from story to story, and the specific sequence all point to a changing set of alternative hypotheses on Dora's part. As she begins to deal with larger and larger units of text, Dora's concept of what constitutes a markable segment changes. In the beginning of her writing history, Dora is concerned with the unit *word*. In demarcating this, she begins to learn about the segmentation of the speech/thought stream.

But soon Dora learns that in writing we are concerned with larger units. She begins to use her period placement as a signal to herself and the reader that a particular unit of text is complete. The first larger unit which is commonly demarcated is the line itself. Children making *endline* marks are starting to grasp the concept of sentence, but are looking at a visual sign—the end of the line—rather than a syntactic or semantic one. Endline placements may occasionally coincide with the end of a sentence, but the endline hypothesis is recognizable by its consistency and by the child's failure to endmark sentences that stop during a line of text.

Young writers may next use *endpage* periods placed *only* at the end of a page of text. Such placements are without regard for how many sentences are on the page or whether the ongoing sentence continues to the next page. These writers sense that periods are used to mark larger units of text than a single line. This endpage hypothesis—all periods go at the end of a page—may continue throughout a story and may go on for several pieces of text. A writer may be lucky when using this alternative hypothesis and may actually punctuate sentences correctly, providing that a sentence ends on a page and does not continue from page to page. A teacher encountering the *endpage* hypothesis, however, would recognize it by its consistency and by its disregard for sentences that end *within* a page, and not at the end of the page.

An extension of the endpage hypothesis is the *endstory* hypothesis. Here writers put a period only at the very end of the story. The story itself may be composed of separate sentences or may be chained together with *and* or *then*. Again, this hypothesis is recognizable by its consistency within a text and by the writer's failure to endmark sentences *within* the text itself.

The final hypothesis young children work with as they try to master correct period placement is the *phrase structure* placement, and represents an overt and demarcated grammatical awareness. These phrase structure placements are what would be commonly referred to as "fragments" (Cooper et al., 1984; Gefvert, 1980; Shaughnessy, 1977). They are often treated as being of the same nature, when in fact they are quite various (Harris, 1981), representing a variety of syntactic boundaries. Phrase structure placement is distinguished because it is a period placement which is based on syntax or semantics and marks a final step toward mastery of conventionalized period placement. It is characterized by putting periods at the end of intact phrases or clauses and contains substeps in its application. Dora used phrase structure placement in the sentence "I went downtown. with my mother." when she separated the adverbial phrase "with my mother" from the rest of the sentence.

These then are the six alternative hypotheses that guide young writers' period placements:

1. interword

2. intraword (a rare use)

3. endline

4. endpage

5. endstory

6. phrase structure

The seventh category, of course, is conventional placement at the end of a sentence—as determined by the writer. Most of the writing I looked at from first-graders used each of these categories, generally in a progression from one category to the next. A few third-graders used the beginning categories, but generally, once children began to make phrase structure placements, they rarely returned to the other hypotheses.

This classification scheme for fragments created at the phrasal/clausal level utilizes Halliday's (1976) concept of functional structure and Quirk and

Greenbaum's (1973) five parts of the sentence. Not all beginning writers use all six hypotheses; however, the categories often represent a progression. Sometimes more than one hypothesis can be seen at the same time, as in the following sample which mixes correct usage with interword period placement:

I AM CM.ING TO MY HOS. I HD A LON RD.
(I am coming to my house. I had a long ride.)

The following sample demonstrates shifts from interword placement to endline, as the text shifts from the personal narrative to the section called "About the Author." Note that the text also contains one intraword placement, "treat.ing."

WE.ARE.TREK. (We are trick)
OR.TRIT.ING. (or treating.)

ABAWOT THE ATHT. (About the Author)

I LAK TO PLAY WETH.
MY BAST FRANDES.
THE.
END
(I like to play with
my best friends.
The
End)

In samples such as these we see writers in the process of modifying alternative hypotheses, constantly creating new environments as they write unique and complex sentences, and revising old hypotheses in the light of new data.

Helping writers as they progress through the categories of hypotheses for period placement seems to be a combination of exposure, experience, and explanation. Young writers need to be exposed to samples of text punctuated conventionally during reading and other print activities. Conversations need to be held about these conventional punctuations, particularly after the child has begun to experiment and develop hypotheses. As writers and readers in the classroom, we always honored the story first in a text, and then discussed details such as punctuation later, but often I found I need not have worried. Children devour story naturally and it's hard to interrupt that process for the avid reader. Likewise, I found children were equally curious about the details of text and how it was constructed. Punctuation actually interested them.

Helping children refine hypotheses also requires a great deal of experience. Children need to write, and they need time to explore the printed page that they are creating. We have only to watch children at the work of drawing to appreciate the amount of experience many children give themselves in this medium of expression.

Finally, we do need to talk with writers about the details of writing, like punctuation. It is hard for any of us to focus simultaneously on all there is to do in creating print, in telling the story, and in making meaning. We all need explanation and feedback.

What Older Writers Do

As children mature in age and writing experience they become aware through various sources that periods are used in writing to endmark sentences, and they begin to develop an awareness of the nature of a written sentence (Kress, 1982; Robinson, 1996). As these two learnings come together, children begin to produce a different kind of error. They first begin to isolate whole parts of sentences. These phrase structure separations are classifiable on the basis of syntactic and semantic considerations, and represent overt and demarcated grammatical awareness. Referred to as *fragments* (Cooper et al., 1984; Gefvert, 1980; Shaughnessy, 1977), they are commonly treated as being all of the same nature. In fact they are quite various (Harris, 1981), representing many hypotheses at a variety of stages of perception. Children using these phrase structure placements may also begin to endmark correctly but will probably continue to omit periods at the end of some sentences.

Idiosyncratic misplacements occur, the products of rules individually constructed and ventured. Connectives may end pseudosentences, subjects may be isolated from verbs, and subject-verbal combinations may be isolated from objects. All indicate children's attempts to begin to try to operate systematically and according to rules (Donaldson, 1978; Piaget & Inhelder, 1969). Children's errors indicate their strategies about what's being learned (Milz, 1980; Kroll, 1980; Barritt & Kroll, 1978; Lamb, 1977; Corder, 1976; Brown & Fraser, 1964; Weaver, 1982).

In the writing I studied, all children used some alternative hypotheses. In both the first- and the third-grade data there was no child who, when beginning to demarcate sentences correctly, never made an alternative period placement. Most of the first-graders made certain kinds of placements such as interword, endline, endpage, and endstory before they made others based on sentence parts and structural function. Most of the third-graders made misplacements based on major sentence parts. All sixth-graders in the study conjoined sentences and created phrase structure placements.

In studying third-grade writing, I found that those children generally moved directly to misplacements which could be classified syntactically and semantically as phrase structure. Only four third-graders made period misplacements typical of early first-grade work, such as interword, endline, and endpage. These students quickly and spontaneously abandoned these uses in favor of honoring syntactic and semantic boundaries. Two third-grade students who were receiving remedial reader services made idiosyncratic misplacements that were near but not at the phrasal/clausal boundaries.

In analyzing the writing of sixth-graders, I found that what was most typical in their misplacements was *lack* of endmarking, creating what are commonly called "conjoined sentences" or "run-on" sentences. As these older writers continued to hypothesize about the units of language, they also began to experiment with paragraphs and chapters, creating larger and larger units of thought. The common injunction we repeat to students, "Put the period at the end of the complete thought," is not a good guide to help children learn where syntactic units end.

I believe that by studying the punctuation errors in children's writing and not simply committing them to the realm of mistakes we can grasp a sense of how children perceive their own language and how they express an innate sense of style. By building on those insights we can lead them toward a mastery of the evolving symbolic written code that adults agree works best in American English (Roberts, 1956; and others).

The Writer as Editor

A typical editing conference with a sixth-grader often went like this for me:

> I think I need to put a period after 'school'—that's one thought, that part is all together. I think I'll put a comma between 'home' and 'she'—they're part of the same thing, but they need to be separated a little. I'm going to change this— This part here, this has to be a new paragraph, that's a whole different thing from all of this and there's going to be people talking so I have to let the reader know— The reader's going to need a lot of blank space to understand this part—

Students in my sixth grade usually typed finished, handwritten stories on the word processor, copying from a draft on paper, editing as they typed, with me sitting by. In some cases there might be no punctuation at all in the handwritten copy and the student would insert punctuation as the story developed on-screen. I found that when students worked this way, adding in punctuation, they often changed the story, added new thoughts, scrapped whole sections, clarified and crystallized ideas. The use of this intricate symbol system, punctuation, served to focus thinking about what the writer really did mean, and what the reader would make of it. These writers worried about whether the reader would know what the writer meant, whether the reader would lose track of who was speaking, and where the subplots were going. They worried about how the reader would understand what the writer was trying to say. For writers, the process of editing was a process of making meaning, what Wells (1986) calls "being an active constructor of her own knowledge" (p. 65). Students who write this way understand that words alone do not convey a writer's meaning. They know that a more powerful symbol system, punctuation, is needed to create meaning beyond the words.

On occasion, I worked with students who had come from other schools, with large classrooms and teacher-indicated editing. When these students began composing in our process-oriented writing time, they would often use almost no punctuation spontaneously, although they often wrote extensively. One girl told me that she "loved to write five-page book reports in her other school." She must have written them completely unpunctuated. And the teacher must have edited for her in her absence. The teacher's efforts seem to have had little or no impact on this girl's acquisition of punctuation, for she had no spontaneous punctuating systems when she came to my class. As a writer she was a product of instructional systems that did not promote writing as a process. I was not surprised that she was having trouble with the process of punctuating.

Calkins (1983) once asked punctuating students what they thought they were doing, and what various marks meant. She compared students in classrooms that emphasized the processes of writing to students in classrooms in which writing instruction followed the prescriptions of a language arts textbook. Calkins (1980) found that 47 percent of the explanations *writers* gave for punctuation referred to the way it affects the pace and inflection of language. Only 9 percent of *nonwriters'* definitions referred to this (p. 570). Calkins (1983) writes, "In my punctuation mark study, I asked each child from the two classrooms to tell me what each mark meant and how it was used. I found that Pat's third-graders (who had no formal instruction but learned through writing) could explain an average of more than eight kinds of punctuation. The children from Mrs. West's room, who had studied punctuation through classwork, drills, and tests, but had rarely written, were able to explain fewer than four kinds" (p. 35).

Students whose writing is unpunctuated until the last moment are not exceptions, even in a process-writing classroom. I have worked with a few students who have spent their whole school careers focusing on writers' process and have not developed spontaneous punctuating systems. The problems with educating for punctuation are broader than how writing is taught.

When I talk to students about the need for us to work on making these systems spontaneous, they understand what I mean. They have tried many times to remember what they meant to say when reworking a piece of writing, trying to segment the text. From working with their own texts, these students know what it is like to be a reader of a piece of unpunctuated writing, a reader with only the words as guidelines to the author's intention.

Punctuation is the most intricate symbol system used by literate writers and readers. It is the catalyst for a negotiation between readers and writers, and represents the writer's best means of communicating intention. As students who write know, words are not enough to convey meaning. In order for writers to speak clearly to readers, they need to make use of punctuation symbols, which segment thoughts and specify the various language functions in use.

In order for such students to become the successful writers they should be, they need to begin to integrate editing into the writing process, developing spontaneous systems, at least those which allow a rudimentary segmenting of text even in the first draft. Such students need a helper at their elbow in the beginning, for they must make up for lost time. As sixth-graders, these students are advanced thinkers, literate young writers. The writing they compose is complex and flows from these writers. This makes editing at the end a nearly impossible task.

If punctuation instruction is to become successful, we must abandon our view of content before form and adopt instead a view of integrated symbol systems. As those of us in process writing classrooms have observed, content changes as the writer edits. Teachers must stop punctuating for students in their absence. Editing is part of the writer's process. But in almost all writing instruction, punctuation is usually added on; editing comes last. In the traditional classrooms I learned in, most of the editing of what I wrote was done alone by the teacher and handed back to me without comment. Today, some students still learn writing skills in these hands-off, student-proof ways.

Even for those students learning to write in process writing classrooms, punctuation is often still added on. In the process writing concepts, writers are encouraged to compose thoughts and focus on content first—and for substantial lengths of time. Revision precedes editing, content precedes form. Form is usually taken to mean punctuation—those elements of text that conventionalize the writing. Form is later added on, usually with the teacher at the elbow. Historically in education, at a time when punctuation was taken by many teachers to be worth more than ideas, process writing returned ideas and meaning to the forefront of the writing process, the place where meaning belongs. But somehow, punctuation as an active, meaning-making system was overlooked. Process writing also stressed the need to relieve the cognitive overload suffered by young writers as they strive to activate many, many complex systems in order to perform writing (Flower & Hayes, 1980). Punctuation became one of the lost children of the process, listed somewhere near the end of the writer's concerns. Lost was the concept that punctuation enabled the writer to structure meaning out of strings of words from the very beginning of the writing process.

Even for children, writing is an orchestration of integrated symbol systems. Writers use punctuation to create meaning as they write. As I watch sixth-graders decide whether to use a period or a comma, whether to paragraph or continue, I see them making content decisions: What ideas go together? At what point do the ideas shift? At what point do I want the reader to abandon one train of thought and open up another? As I watch myself right now, deciding whether to endmark with a period or a comma, or whether to start a new paragraph, I am thinking about what these choices do to the meaning I wish to convey. I imagine myself inside my reader's head, storing one sequence of syntax and opening up a new one, relating ideas in meaningful ways. The reader and I are negotiating a shared communication, using punctuation as the guidemap.

What's a Writer to Do?

I began my research with the assumption that children know what they are doing when they create what we have traditionally viewed as *errors* (Cordeiro, 1988;

Weaver, 1982; Corder, 1976). For punctuation, this overturned the teaching lore which held that students "put periods any old place" and don't know what they are doing. I believe writers punctuate from a set of hypotheses that they have formed based on prior experience. For children, identifying and endmarking sentences that they themselves have constructed in a series within a meaningful text is quite different from performing workbook activities on period placement, a common way of teaching punctuation. The first is a productive process in context, the second a receptive process in isolation. In workbooks, sentences are usually presented one at a time without the syntactic and semantic overlap that happens when children must punctuate their own ongoing text (Gentry, 1981; Cronnell, 1980). The child as punctuator is not involved in the author's meaning beyond the necessities of the assignment. From these studies, I have concluded that punctuation is a process, acquired over time, with developmental implications. I now look to children's knowledge of punctuation as an indicator of language awareness and development. I have evolved a way of talking and teaching about punctuation that seems to inform me and my students, a way of viewing punctuation as a cognitive roadmap for writers and readers.

We can look at the process of punctuation from two sides: One side is the nature of punctuating, how these special marks on a page are part of a process that enables meaning-making. The other side is the process a writer goes through when learning to punctuate, a process with developmental implications.

As a teacher of writing, I now generalize about punctuation as a process from conclusions I drew from studying the placement—and misplacement—of the period. This most common endmark provides a common ground for talking about all punctuation. All teachers have worked with children on endmarks and sentence identification. Period placement is a persistent problem from children's first efforts up through mature writing, so it provides a rich source of information as a productive, interactive, and expressive process for creating meaning through text.

I started out looking at punctuation as a matter of learning the rules, the way I thought I had learned it. But as I observed children from kindergarten on, I found myself considering much more than memorizing rules. I found that there was more to learning this abstract set of skills than I had thought. I found that when I looked closely, beyond the rules and at the work of children, I could see their knowledge of their language revealed on paper.

What Punctuation Does

The term "punctuation" refers to all the forms and symbols that make my writing readable by you—the endmarks, commas, capital letters, dialogue markings, and apostrophes. I include paragraphs, chapters, and titles, too. These editing marks, these conventions that make a story readable and shareable, are abstract symbols that have been standardized over time. They are marks and spaces that make the story able to stand alone without the author's intervention. The two ways we use punctuation are the two main functions of punctuation in writing: segmenting and identifying (Quirk & Greenbaum, 1973). They enable the writer to tell the reader how the text is separated and how certain words are being used.

Endmarks like periods, commas, and semicolons are the best example of marks that *segment.* These marks go beyond syntax to tell the reader how the structure of the language is being used. Cognitively, these marks notify the reader of how much text must be retained in short-term memory in order to derive the author's intended meaning.

If I had written the above paragraph without any endmarks or paragraph breaks, an experienced reader would be in despair by now. Having started to read in good faith, the reader would soon realize that the writer did not understand the concept of cognitive overload or the topic. The reader would still be holding the first thought about endmarks in short-term memory, having assumed that knowledge of it was necessary to understanding the whole sentence. But short-term memory isn't big enough for all that text. Endmarks let the reader drop the old and move on to something new.

The same holds true when we paragraph. Here we give the reader many signals that the old is finished and the new is beginning. When we paragraph, we begin by placing a period. We then break the text, go to the next line, indent, and start with a capital letter—even if the word is not a proper noun. This gives the reader time to relax. When a young writer talks about how much white space the reader will need, she demonstrates an awareness of the reader's cognitive process as meaning is being reconstructed.

The second function of punctuation is shown by marks that *identify* word form. These are typified by apostrophes. These marks distinguish between ambiguities that are built into the language. When I write, "I ate the lizards," you may quietly gag at the thought. But if I punctuate my sentence correctly, you may find that I did not eat lizards, but rather find that "I ate the lizards' eggs." This may not please you either, but then it's all a matter of swallowing writers—swallowing writers' tastes, that is. Cognitively and syntactically, marks that identify also help us to reckon with the apparent problem of having two plural nouns in a row: lizards and eggs. Having fit the first noun, lizards, into our cognitive reconstruction of meaning, we have to decide what to do with the second noun, eggs, which seems to be left hanging. The punctuation that identifies, the apostrophe, placed on the first noun (lizards' eggs) clears it all up. Punctuation is how writers and readers communicate with each other beyond letters. As a language process, unique and flexible, it allows writer and reader to create meaning symbolically and interactively. It is the catalyst for a negotiation between readers and writers.

A writer constructs punctuation within a text, according to the needs of the new and original sentences. Old rules of punctuation formulated and used by the writer in previous pieces of text may serve as guidelines up to the point that the new sentences diverge in structure and intent from the old ones. Then the writer must develop new strategies for defining meaning. Having only orthography and punctuation to work with, the writer must use punctuation as a creative tool with each new text.

Punctuation is, in effect, an *ad hoc* language process in which the rules change each time we build a new structure in writing. The rules developed in previous language environments may guide or mislead in the new environment that we create. Producing punctuation in a written piece by referring to a list of rules on hand—as we often ask students to do—results in an unnatural, second-order relationship with the meaning-making devices available in writing.

Punctuation is the agent for standardization in the written language event. This guarantee assures the readers and writer that they are working within the same reference system, that ambiguity will be avoided, that the recording system is a shared one, and that the symbols for defining text are meaningful. The list of rules in hand is legitimate only up to the point that it reassures all participants that the symbol system in use is shared.

Characteristics of Today's Punctuation

Punctuation rules are flexible in today's writing; Hall (1996) calls it a "system in change" (p. 10). Meyer (1983) makes wonderful sense of the semantic and syntactic thicket in which the writer wanders. Meyer uses categories to show how punctuation is used in three different writing styles: informal (journalism), formal (learned writing), and narrative (fiction). He compares the practice of punctuation markings in these three styles to the rules of usage generally given in style manuals and finds many differences.

Meyer argues that American punctuation is not all of a kind, that there are various styles which permit a variety of correct usages. Meyer discovered variations in how the prescriptions of style manuals were realized in mature writing, related to the style of writing. The learned style was punctuated *more* than the others: "The percentage of unpunctuated sentences coordinated by 'and' was much lower in the learned style . . . than in the journalistic and fictional style" (p. 60). Meyer attributes this to the shorter main clauses found in the latter styles. Learned writing tends to be lengthy and complex, thus requiring more punctuation, rather than less. However, the learned style contained fewer instances of interclausal period placement: "The learned style is generally a very formal style, and is perhaps more likely to adhere to the prescriptive rule that orthographic sentences should not begin with 'and' or 'but'" (p. 63).

Meyer argues that American punctuation in *practice* is quite different from those rules which are prescribed in *theory:* "Rarely has there been an attempt to present punctuation as a system rather than as a collection of ad hoc rules and exceptions" (p. 1). Meyer argues that punctuation performs two functions: It helps the reader to understand the text, and it allows the writer to create stylistic variation (p. 36). Effective punctuation, like effective writing, is the result of good judgment, not of one's ability to follow so-called rules of good punctuation or writing (p. 148).

This conclusion from Meyer's study emphasizes the problem that many children face as they begin to write in school: oral language practices, common fictional punctuation usage, and underdeveloped skills all conflict with the full and formal style which is taught as academic writing. Schools are primarily concerned with teaching learned punctuation and writing, a full and formal style far removed from speech and everyday communication (Stubbs, 1976).

Defending the formal, essayist model as "the language refined and biased under the impact of literacy . . . the specialized tool of analytic thinking and explicit argument" (p. 251), Olson and Torrance (1981) argue that the child coming to school must learn to deal with formal text and thus "specialize his language to better serve . . . ideational or logical functions" (p. 253). However, in our schoolish insistence on one exclusive set of rules for punctuation—that of a learned formal form—we are denying the practical facts of common usage and the creative aspects of style in writing.

Many punctuation misplacements seem to reflect children's response to perceptual and stylistic considerations, often the same considerations that guide non-prescriptive adult use. In practice, American punctuation is not always what is spelled out in great detail in style manuals. Meyer (1983) points to many examples of adult practice in common and accepted usage that are outside the rules taught for punctuation in school. The practices exhibited in children's writing often imitate with period placement the more subtle punctuations practiced in the mature form.

To some extent punctuation appears idiosyncratic, Smith (1982) notes. However, "no one has complete freedom; we are not permitted to scatter periods or quotation marks across the page at random. But there is a wide range of variation from one writer to another. . . . To some extent these evident differences among writers reflect stylistic preferences; not so much for the punctuation itself as for the kinds of sentence structures that demand particular marks of punctuation" (p. 159). When children become aware either for reasons of prosody, length, or complexity that a unit is too big for comfortable processing, they may punctuate it as best they know how. They may even punctuate for stylistic reasons, just as adults do, particularly in the fictional style.

Children—and adults, according to Meyer—often use creative punctuation when using adverbials in writing. These adverbials, punctuated as they are, can be read as examples of emphatic intonation, particularly those in sentence-final position. For instance, third-grader Chet writes: "he said son stop son so I can get in the boat. *before he eats me.*" The father in the water who is being chased by the shark certainly might intone the isolated adverbial emphatically. He might even yell it quite separately from the rest of the syntactic sentence. And another example, from third-grader David: "To program in basic you have to Put the computer on and press control Reset. *At the same time.*" Programming in basic with two hands is a hard thing to learn to do, and children sometimes have difficulty in trying to learn the two-handed coordination. Some of us might be able to do it *at the same time.*

Many children write a variety of adverbials that are isolated from the surrounding related text by period placement. Some may reflect a child's stylistic use of the period in the narrative form for emphasis and effect. In the adult writing, in all styles, Meyer (1983) found that "syntactic, semantic, prosodic, stylistic, and pragmatic factors all affected the punctuation of adverbials" (p. 120). It seems that rules need not apply.

In the red-lead philosophy of being educated into learned, formal writing, all adverbials must adhere to certain rules. These fragments created out of sentence-initial and sentence-final adverbials would have been subjected to censure without regard for cause or effect. Furthermore, observations such as those made by Meyer about actual adult use would not be taken into account.

When a third-grader wrote, "So Garfield stayed after school for a week. Still looking for it," the effect of the week-long search was clear, thanks to the extra period. Corrected, his stylistic effect might have been lost.

And Jack's poignant Christmas story might lose some of its Christmas wonder: "But before he went to bed he put cookies on the table and a glass of milk for Santa. and for his reindeers." In fiction, an afterthought should be written as one. Punctuation can be used and taught successfully when viewed cognitively, by writers talking about readers. Punctuation is a shared symbol system which works to tie together the writer's cognitive arrangement of schemas and ideas with the reader's.

Toward a Theory of Punctuation

Using punctuation can be understood by applying Passmore's (1980) categories of skills. He divides skills into two categories, those which are *closed capacities* and those which are *open capacities.*

Closed capacities are those skills which can be learned in a final, routinized form. Mechanical efforts such as typing, walking, and hammering are classified as closed capacities. Closed capacities are those skills that do not require judgment but can be taught in a final form.

Open capacities are those skills that can always be improved and do not allow for total mastery. Skills like driving, cooking, sewing, and carpentry are open capacities. Open capacities are those skills that cannot be converted into routines, and are relative to evolving judgment. Passmore (1980) says that they are characterized when "the student can take steps which he has not been taught to . . . [which do] not necessarily follow as an application of a principle in which the teacher has instructed him" and are subject to "a certain degree of wildness" (pp. 39–42).

By grouping punctuation, spelling, handwriting, and capitalization all together as mechanics of writing and working with them together and last in the writing process, we have misled teachers and authors into believing these aspects of writing are all of a kind. In fact, spelling, handwriting, and capitalization are skills of a closed nature, and can be routinized and made subliminal, subject perhaps to individual whim, but learnable in a single, final form. Punctuation, however, stands alone as an open capacity, "subject to a certain degree of wildness."

Punctuation is a persistent and troublesome aspect of writing because of our misconception of it as a mechanical skill that can be routinized and made subliminal. It is forever open to negotiation, and represents a semiotic transaction between writer and reader. It is not a closed-capacity skill that can be practiced, defined, and mastered in a final form. By reducing the art of punctuating to a list of rules, we have convinced ourselves that this "reference card" method will suffice.

How we perceive and classify punctuation affects what share of the writer's attention we expect it to get. By recognizing punctuation as an open capacity, we enable writers to give this ad hoc language process its share of meaning-making attention. Punctuation hovers on the edge of a writer's awareness, sometimes peripheral and sometimes focal, slipping into either rubric depending on the complexity and singularity of the sentence under construction.

Meyer (1983) writes "Effective punctuation, like effective writing, is the result of good judgment, not of one's ability to follow so-called rules of good punctuation or writing" (p. 148). And Gardner, in a 1984 handbook for writers, reiterates the argument: "It is true that punctuation . . . is a subtle art; but its subtlety lies in suspending the rules . . ." (p.17). Hall (1996) refers to it as "flexible" (p. 8). Punctuation is constantly open to negotiation and improvement. This is true both for punctuation as a means of expression, and in its life as a writer's skill.

Teaching About Punctuation

When I teach students where to put a period, I approach it from a pyscholinguistic perspective, saying something like this: "A period is a signal to a reader that they can let go of the past string of words safely. A period lets readers know that something new is starting, and they can either forget what has gone before or store it in a longer-term memory, and get ready for a new idea." We do writers a great disservice when we teach punctuation by aphorism, a pedagogical tradition that feels like it comes from a behaviorist perspective, such as when we say and have them memorize, "Put the period at the end of the sentence." The notion of sentence-ness is not clearly defined, as I hope I have shown, and locating the end of an undefined unit of thought-as-syntax is a formidable task. As Dawkins (1995) writes, "It is a mistake to assume that the sentence is the basic element in prose; it is also confusing, for it is the wrong basis for analyzing written language" (p. 535).

We complicate matters severely when we enjoin writers to "Put a period at the end and a capital letter at the beginning." For many years I always taught punctuation and capitalization together, since that is how I was taught. Now I believe that these two sets of hypotheses, those surrounding punctuation and those surrounding capitalization, are not kept in the same cognitive *compartment*, nor are they innately related. In fact, they may well conflict, since capitalization is only related to punctuation in one particular place syntactically—at the point of end-marking when intact phrases are sequential in text. Ferreiro and Zucchermaglio (1996) point out that punctuation introduces "graphic elements that are alien to the main principles of an alphabetic writing system. Children must deal with them as an autonomous subsystem that does not affect the letters themselves" (p. 179) except for using upper case at the beginning of a sentence. While I can't explain things in this way to young writers, it is important for me to remember this difference as I try to help young writers sift, sort, and modify their own sets of hypotheses around this very complex process, writing.

Once I interviewed many of the children in our 120-student school, asking the simple question, "How do you know when to put a period in your writing?" The answers were many and varied but fell generally into five categories:

1. Aphoristic/Memorized: "Put a period at the end of the sentence."

2. Syntactic: "When the sentence comes to an end."

3. Rhetoric: "When it's the end of a thought."

4. Speech-based: "When you say something you just know where to put them."

5. Instinct: "I just know when the subject ends."

6. A class by itself: "When, what you're going to say stops."

Furness (1960) pointed out that ". . . in general, punctuation is difficult to acquire, or it has not been and is not being well taught in our schools" (p. 185). Wilde (1992) believes that teachers "develop punctuation minilessons based on children's writing; since punctuation seems like a smaller body of knowledge than spelling, it may seem like an easier one to develop one's own curriculum for" (p. 56). She proposes a three-part curriculum in punctuation (1992) and speculates about the power of minilessons for writers of all ages, particularly around complex conventions like the semicolon (1996).

Dawkins (1995) proposes providing many examples and sufficient writing time for writers to learn to make choices, thus encouraging "students to analyze their semantic and rhetorical intentions" (p. 544). He also suggests that teachers and students spend time studying samples of writing from good literature and "raising and lowering" the punctuation in use to collaboratively study the effect on meaning. An example of "raising" punctuation would be to insert a comma where the author had placed none and an example of lowering would be to change the author's use of period to a semicolon or comma. Dawkins writes, "By teaching raising and lowering, we will be adding to our students' repertoire of skills; we will be encouraging students to clarify the meaning of sentences and to gain intended emphasis" (p. 548).

Furness (1960) suggests that inquiry should more profitably look "into the field of thinking than into the field of grammar. What basic relations exist among ideas, and how are marks used to indicate those relations to readers? . . . If the writer has a modicum of intuition about separation, connection, diversion, and insertion of meaning and can associate those functions with the proper marks, and if he really knows what he wants to say, he can write sentences that a reader can follow" (p. 186). We must also consider the effect of cognitive overload on a writer. Punctuation has been viewed as one consideration too many for a writer and so we have not considered how it might be taught to writers as a cognitive assistant.

During the process of writing, punctuation is one of the many skills, open and closed, that must be considered by the writer as constraints (Bartlett, 1982; Murray, 1978). Short-term memory—the agent of composing—is limited, and the many constraints of the writing process place serious burdens on the young writer (Daiute 1981, 1984). Faigley and White (1984) say that "many things students write are still in progress due to the multitude of textual aspects which must be considered" (p. 106). Children's ability to incorporate new principles and procedures into their composing processes must depend in part on what they are able to hold in mind while writing, and this will surely depend on underlying factors as to how much they can retain in short-term memory for how long, how many things compete for attention while they write, and how efficiently they can distribute attention to these demands (Scardamalia et al., 1982).

Children have received various types of information about skills like punctuation. These standardizations are learned by children from many sources. In an active print environment, children acquire editing from all around them, from each other, from the teacher, from their reading, from worktexts, and from reading each others' writing. Britton (1982) says that "How this is picked up from alphabet books and cornflake packets, picture books, TV advertisements, and street signs remains something of a mystery, though two governing conditions seem likely: a context of manipulative play and picture-making, and the association of this learning with the purpose of producing written stories" (p. 167). Students acquire punctuation usage as a process over time. Editing is an interactional, social, and integrated function of the writing process. As writers write and revise, they edit. As they edit, they make meaning. Emergent writers edit in their heads as they compose with the alphabet. We hear evidence of this mental editing when they reread the text orally to us. Writers know where punctuation marks should go. If you ask young writers who have just reread to tell you "where the period goes," they usually know.

Teaching lore holds that children should know where to put periods in writing because they know all about sentences from their history as speakers. However, Kress (1982) argues persuasively that we speak in clausal complexes rather than sentences, and that the main business of teaching in writing instruction is the nature and substance of the English sentence. Thus children, in attempting to learn how to punctuate the ongoing stream of writing, are in fact learning a new form of language organization: the sentence. In writing, forms of language expression are learned that are not learnable in oral speech. Arthur (1996) comments that "if more were known about children learning punctuation . . . teachers might be allowed to concentrate on instilling an enthusiasm and love for language, which would in itself lead to an understanding of the mysteries of punctuation" (p. 108).

The insistence on rules in language instruction, coupled with the failure of educational reformers to effect change, caused the teaching of punctuation in writing to be directly linked with old traditions of upper-class classical learning. Rule application and acquisition were earmarks of higher learning, and continue even today to be seen as signs of true literacy:

> meritocratic pressures of upward social mobility that stereotyped the audience and purposes of writing in particular ways [were] . . . associated with the polish and trappings of social class . . . Writing was openly presented to students as a kind of "proper talk"—an important outward sign of a presumed inner grace: "educated man." (Nystrand, 1982, p.4)

As writing became included in the academic definition of an educated person, one of standing and social class, standards relating to the product rather than the process became the norm:

> The teaching of English and the development of standards in writing and oral language came increasingly to be associated with normative judgments about standards not intrinsic to the linguistic code, but to the individual creators of language. . . . The strong implication was that those who wrote and criticized well had more intelligence, morality, and industry than did their fellow students. A class consciousness was developing on the basis of the language used and the standards of writing perpetuated in the classroom. (Heath, 1981, p. 35)

Bucholz (1979) advances the unique view that punctuation is "one of the ultimate manifestations of power . . . Strategic application of punctuation may be the key to future wealth, position, and fame. If nothing else, punctuation strategy gives one new self-esteem, catapulting the wise tactician far ahead of those left behind in the punctuation power void" (p. 227). Whitehall (1963) says "Man has been speaking for well over 700,000 years. Man has been practicing alphabetic writing only for about 3450 years. Man has punctuated, in the modern sense, for less than 250 years" (p. 224). The marks that define the relationships between the units continue to be active tools in the writer's hand. Falling back on experience and evolved patterns of usage, the writer manipulates these symbols. The writer creates text silently, visually, with an array of meaningful symbols. Like Lewis Thomas's (1974) semicolons, "You cannot hear them, but they are there, laying out the connections between the images and the ideas"(p. 185).

References

ANDERSON, H. (1996). Vicki's story: A seven-year-old's use and understanding of punctuation. In N. Hall & A. Robinson (Eds.), *Learning about punctuation*. Portsmouth, NH: Heinemann.

ARMSTRONG, M. (1996). *The leap of imagination: An essay in interpretation.* Unpublished manuscript.

ARTHUR, C. (1996). Learning about punctuation: A look at one lesson. In N. Hall & A. Robinson (Eds.), *Learning about punctuation.* Portsmouth, NH: Heinemann.

BARRITT, L., & KROLL, B. (1978). Some implications of cognitive-developmental psychology for research in composing. In C. Cooper & L. Odell (Eds.), *Research on composing: Points of departure.* Urbana, IL: National Council of Teachers of English.

BARTLETT, E. (1982). Learning to revise: Some component processes. In M. Nystrand (Ed.), *What writers know: The language, process and structure of written discourse.* New York: Academic Press.

BRITTON, J. (1982). Spectator role and the beginning of writing. In M. Nystrand (Ed.), *What writers know: The language, process and structure of written discourse.* New York: Academic Press.

BROWN, R., & FRASER, M. (1964). Acquisition of syntax. In U. Bellugi & R. Brown (Eds.), The acquisition of language. *Monographs of the society for research in child development,* No. 29, 43–79.

BUCHOLZ, W. (1979). Punctuation: The dynamics of obscure marks. *Phi Delta Kappan,* 227.

CALKINS, L. (1980). When children want to punctuate. *Language Arts, 57,* 567–573.

CALKINS, L. (1983). *Lessons from a child.* Portsmouth, NH: Heinemann.

CAZDEN, C., CORDEIRO, P., & GIACOBBE, M. (1985). Spontaneous and scientific concepts: Young children's learning of punctuation. In G. Wells & J. Nichols (Eds.), *Perspectives on language and learning.* England: Falmer Press.

COOPER, C., CHERRY, R., COPLEY, B., FLEISCHER, S., POLLARD, R., & SARTISKY, M. (1984). Studying the writing abilities of a university freshman class: Strategies from a case study. In R. Beach & L. Bridwell (Eds.), *New directions in composition research.* New York: Guilford Press.

CORDEIRO, P. (1986). *Punctuation in a third-grade class: An analysis of errors in period placement.* Unpublished doctoral dissertation. Harvard Graduate School of Education.

CORDEIRO, P. (1988). Children's punctuation: An analysis of errors in period placement. *Research in the Teaching of English, 22,* 1, 62–74.

CORDEIRO, P., GIACOBBE, M., & CAZDEN, C. (1983). Apostrophes, quotation marks, and periods: Learning punctuation in the first grade. *Language Arts, 60,* 323–332.

CORDER, S. (1967). The significance of learners' errors. *International Review of Applied Linguistics, 4,* 162–170.

CRONNELL, B. (1980). *Punctuation and capitalization: A review of the literature.* Los Alamitos, CA: Southwest Regional Laboratory, technical note # TN 2-80/27.

DAIUTE, C. (1981.) Psycholinguistic foundations of the writing process. *Research in the Teaching of English, 15,* 5–22.

DAIUTE, C. (1984). Performance limits on writers. In R. Beach & L. Bridwell (Eds.), *New directions in composition research.* New York: Guilford.

DAWKINS, J. (1995, December). Teaching punctuation as a rhetorical tool. *College Composition and Communication, 46,* 4, 533–548.

DONALDSON, M. (1978). *Children's minds*. New York: W. W. Norton.

FAIGLEY, L., & WITTE, S. (1984). Measuring the effects of revision on text structure. In R. Beach & L. Bridwell (Eds.), *New directions in composition research*. New York: Guilford.

FERREIRO, E., & ZUCCHERMAGLIO, C. (1996). Children's use of punctuation marks: A case of quoted speech. In C. Pontecorvo, M. Orsolini, B. Burge, & L. Resnick (Eds.), *Children's early text construction*. Mahwah, NJ: Lawrence Erlbaum.

FLOWER, L., & HAYES, J. (1980). The dynamics of composing: Making plans and juggling constraints. In L. Gregg & E. Steinberg (Eds.), *Cognitive processes in writing*. Hillsdale, NJ: Lawrence Erlbaum.

FURNESS, E. (1960). Pupils, pedagogues and punctuation. *Elementary English, 37*, 184–189.

GARDNER, J. (1984). *The art of fiction*. New York: Knopf.

GEFVERT, C. (1980). Training teachers of basic writing. In L. Kasden & D. Hoeber (Eds.), *Basic writing: Essays for teachers, researchers, administrators*. Urbana IL: National Council of Teachers of English.

GENTRY, L. (1981, March). *Punctuation instruction in elementary school textbooks*. Los Alamitos, CA: Southwest Regional Laboratory, technical note 2–81/02 (ED 199 757).

HALL, N. (1996). Learning about punctuation: An introduction and overview. In N. Hall & A. Robinson (Eds.), *Learning about punctuation*. Portsmouth, NH: Heinemann.

HALLIDAY, M. (1976). A brief sketch of systemic grammar. In G. Kress (Ed.), *Halliday: System and function in language*. London: Oxford University Press.

HARRIS, M. (1981). Mending the fragmented free modifier. *College Composition and Communication, 32*, 175–182.

HEATH, S. (1981). Toward an ethnohistory of writing in American education. In M. Whiteman (Ed.), *Writing: The nature, development and teaching of written communication*. Hillsdale, NJ: Lawrence Erlbaum.

KRESS, G. (Ed.). (1976). *Halliday: System and function in language*. London: Oxford University Press.

KRESS, G. (1982). *Learning to write*. London: Routledge & Kegan Paul.

KROLL, B. (1980). Developmental perspectives and the teaching of composition. *College English, 41*, 741–752.

LAMB, M. (1977). *An application of error analysis to comma splices and fused sentences*. Paper presented at the Annual Meeting of the Conference on College Composition and Communication.

MARTENS, P., & GOODMAN, Y. (1996). Invented punctuation. In N. Hall & A. Robinson (Eds.), *Learning about punctuation*. Portsmouth, NH: Heinemann.

MEYER, C. (1983). *A descriptive study of American punctuation*. Unpublished doctoral dissertation, University of Wisconsin at Milwaukee.

MILZ, V. (1980). First-graders can write: Focus on communication. In C. Galloway (Ed.), *Theory into practice, 19*, 179–185.

MURRAY, D. (1978). Internal revision: A process of discovery. In C. Cooper & L. Odell (Eds.), *Research on composing: Points of departure*. Urbana, IL: National Council of Teachers of English.

NYSTRAND, M. (1982). Rhetoric's "audience" and linguistics' "speech community": Implications of understanding writing, reading, and text. In M. Nystrand (Ed.), *What writers know: The language, process and structure of written discourse.* New York: Academic Press.

NYSTRAND, M. (Ed.). (1982). *What writers know: The language, process and structure of written discourse.* New York: Academic Press.

OLSON, D., & TORRANCE, N. (1981). Learning to meet the requirements of the written text: Language development in the school years. In C. Fredrickson & J. Dominic (Eds.), *Writing: The nature, development and teaching of written communication.* Hillsdale, NJ: Lawrence Erlbaum.

PASSMORE, J. (1980). *The philosophy of teaching.* Cambridge, MA: Harvard University Press.

PERERA, K. (1996). Who says what? Learning to "read" the punctuation of direct speech. In N. Hall & A. Robinson (Eds.), *Learning about punctuation.* Portsmouth, NH: Heinemann.

PIAGET, J., & INHELDER, B. (1969). *The psychology of the child.* New York: Basic Books.

QUIRK, R., & GREENBAUM, S. (1973). *A university grammar of English.* London: Longman.

ROBERTS, P. (1956). *Patterns of English.* New York: Harcourt Brace.

ROBINSON, A. (1996). Conversations with teachers about punctuation. In N. Hall & A. Robinson (Eds.), *Learning about punctuation.* Portsmouth, NH: Heinemann.

SCARDAMALIA, M., BEREITER, C., & GOELMAN, H. (1982). The role of production factors in writing ability. In M. Nystrand (Ed.), *What writers know: The language, process and structure of written discourse.* New York: Academic Press.

SHAUGHNESSY, M. (1977). *Errors and expectations.* New York: Holt, Rinehart, & Winston.

SIMONE, R. (1996). Reflections on the comma. In C. Pontecorvo, M. Orsolini, B. Burge, & L. Resnick (Eds.), *Children's early text construction.* Mahwah, NJ: Lawrence Erlbaum.

SMITH, F. (1982). *Writing and the writer.* New York: Holt, Rinehart & Winston.

STUBBS, M. (1976). *Language, schools and classrooms.* London: Methuen.

THOMAS, L. (1980). Notes on punctuation. In *The medusa and the snail: More notes of a biology watcher.* Boston: G. K. Hall.

WEAVER, C. (1982). Welcoming errors as signs of growth. *Language Arts, 59,* 438–444.

WELLS, G. (1986). *The meaning makers: Children learning about language and using literature to learn.* Portsmouth, NH: Heinemann.

WHITEHALL, H. (1963). The system of punctuation. In L. Dean & K. Wilson (Eds.), *Essays on language and usage.* New York: Oxford University Press.

WILDE, S. (1992). *You kan red this! Spelling and punctuation for whole language classrooms, K–6.* Portsmouth, NH: Heinemann.

WILDE, S. (1996). Just periods and exclamation points: The continued development of children's knowledge about punctuation. In N. Hall & A. Robinson (Eds.), *Learning about punctuation.* Portsmouth, NH: Heinemann.

4 *Teaching Writing and Grammar in Context*

SCOTT PETERSON

Introduction

Much has been said about the role of skills in the whole language classroom. Lately, there has been a drift toward more skills at the expense of writing process activities. The theme of this essay is that the teaching of grammar and the writing process are not mutually exclusive activities. The teaching of grammar and writing skills need not be exiled to a language text. Rather, grammar can be taught and learned within the context of a meaningful writing activity. Grammar is learned best when applied directly to a real writing situation. The author backs up his claim with an abundance of examples and ideas that can be directly applied to any classroom.

Part I: Ryan's Story

No matter what I did or how hard I tried, I couldn't get Ryan to buy into the writing process. It's not that he lacked ideas: He was bright and a warehouse of knowledge filled his brain. He had an absorbent mind that soaked up ideas like a thirsty sponge, and he thrived on the trade books we used in place of a basal reader in our classroom.

He even looked like a scholar. Small and thin as a wire, his round face was topped with thick black hair mowed short. His eyes were enlarged by pop-bottle thick glasses, giving him the owlish look of someone who enjoys dealing with ideas.

No, the problem was not lack of brain power. The problem was fishing them out of Ryan's well-stocked mind. He always started strongly with a well-written sentence or two. Anything beyond a good start challenged him, however. He simply could not make his ideas come alive. He stubbornly refused to add the depth and detail needed to make his writing worth reading. It had no feeling, no heart to it. There was nothing vivid or sharp to make his ideas come off the page. It was an empty, barren style with nothing inside.

Ryan soon became a low-grade behavior problem. His strong start seemed to burn him out, and he would spend his writing time staring into space or doodling a picture to illustrate his original idea. Eventually, he would drift into what he would call "helping others." A more accurate spin on the situation was that he was bothering those around him and keeping them from focusing on their writing. I was losing him. Day by day, he was putting more distance between himself and his writing.

Then, one Monday morning things began to open up. Ryan came skipping down the hall yelling, "Mr. Peterson, Mr. Peterson, look at this!" Barely able to contain his excitement, his story came out in a torrent of words. He had gone bowling over the weekend and had thought it "the coolest thing in the world." He had loved everything about it—the rumble of the bowling ball, the crash of the pins, the greasy fast food—simply everything. When he got home, he grabbed his pencil and out came these words:

Bowling
Bowling is as loud as a thunderstorm
The pins are set up like the head of an arrow
The pins roar like a lion
Rolling a strike is like throwing a star down an aisle

Finally, the life and vividness I had looked for was there. Ryan had given a piece of his life. Finally, he was beginning to connect with his writing.

Part II: Creating an Impact that Sticks

Ryan's story points out an important lesson for teachers: Students write better and learn more when they are directly involved in the writing process. Personal involvement in the writing process, while learning the basics of writing, brings stronger, more meaningful results than teaching skills in isolation. To use writing skills and techniques to communicate a message important to the writer has far more value and is retained longer than teaching skills within the isolation of a textbook. As Lucy Calkins writes in *The Art of Teaching Writing* (1994), students learn best when they are "deeply involved in their self-sponsored work and they bring them together to learn what they need to know in order to do their work. This way they stand a chance of being active meaning makers."

An example of an activity that allows students to apply skills within the context of a meaningful activity is our theme unit centered around the *Titanic*. This doomed ship, with its themes of grand hopes and failed technology, class divisions, bravery, and needless tragedy, sucks kids into its story and grips them tightly as few historical events do.

"Not all were Rich"
Types of Passengers

Name Ryan Schreiber

First Class	Second Class	Third Class
Welthiest people	① To start a new life.	① To start a new life 7id
1,500 to 4,500	② Engineer	third class passengers
John Jacob Astor	③ teacher	② wanted Jobs and new farms
Charles Guggenheim—mining give money	④ lourior	③ chased out
Ida and Isidor Straus—Macys	⑤ doctor	④ poor and wanted best
department store	⑥ Journalist	⑤ opportunity
Smith—Perfect safety record best in	⑦ minister	⑥ don't speer english
the world	⑧ buishessman	⑦ bottom of the ship
Braught servents and maids	marble sinks. rear of the	seasick least safe
J. J. Astor wealthiest man in the	ship fancy wood trim. smaller	couldn't mingle with other
world	than first but still comfy.	class. gates fences to keep
Thayer—R.R. Exutive	Nice resturants	them seprate bunk beds.
Harper—Puplishing Co.		dormetories. smaller less fancy
Molson-Beer Co.		seprate deck
Molly Brown-Entertainer		
There there for fun and		
Vaction Social Event		
rooms-million air sweets		
three rooms-private deck-		
parlor-private bathroom.		
Windows-instead of porthole		
On top of ship-you don't get		
Seasick, safer cielings to cover		
up pipes and wires. Antic		
Furniture Marble sinks fancy wood trim		

FIG. 4–1 *Titanic passenger list*

The first step of the unit is to gather as much information as possible about the *Titanic*. Using a variety of sources, the students harvest as much knowledge and facts as they can about the great ship. They examine such issues as the "unsink-ableness" of the *Titanic*, its grandiose size and scope, and the incredible luxuries and amenities offered to its passengers. They compare the differences between first, second, and third class passengers, look at some of the richest people who boarded the ship, and examine the social forces at play during that era that added to the tremendous tragedy that was the *Titanic*.

Very quickly, a large amount of information is extracted from the students' reading. Left by itself, this information could be dumped into the students' brains in a huge pile of disorganized, disconnected information. To help students put their knowledge into some kind of order, they sort and classify their information into three main categories:

1. The qualities of the ship that led people to believe that it was unsinkable

2. The incredible features, materials, and craftsmanship that gave the ship its air of privileged pleasure

3. The types of passengers on the ship and the very different pathways that led them to board the *Titanic* in April of 1912 (See Figure 4–1)

This process helps the students sort out the mass of knowledge they have acquired into manageable chunks that can later be retrieved and woven into a writing project.

Next, the class studied the genre of historical fiction. Using such books as *Beethoven Lives Upstairs* and *My Great Aunt Arizona,* we studied how the authors tied the fictional aspects of their story around the historical core of the tale. Students charted what they thought was created by the author and what actually happened. When students had a solid understanding of the concept of historical fiction, we were ready to move on to the next step.

To close out the unit, students were to write their own piece of historical fiction based on what they knew about the *Titanic.* They were to take on the persona of a child boarding the great ship on the day before its fateful voyage. They decided what class of passenger they were, what features might particularly interest them, and what activities they might partake in as a child on the *Titanic.* They then wrote a letter to a close friend or relative, weaving as much fact as they could into their made-up tale. They first webbed or clustered the ideas they wanted to include, organized their information by paragraphs, and presented their story in the form of a letter (see Figure 4–2).

What skills were incorporated into this one activity? Note taking and nonfictional reading strategies were modeled in the beginning research portion of the activity. Paragraphing as a way to organize and present information was modeled and applied as students clustered their ideas. The characteristics of historical fiction were covered in some detail, and the conventions of the friendly letter were used by students.

All of these skills could have been covered in an English book or a basal reader. This assignment, however, took the skills out of the isolation of a text and placed them at the heart of a writing assignment. In other words, several skills were put into one package and presented to the students as one activity.

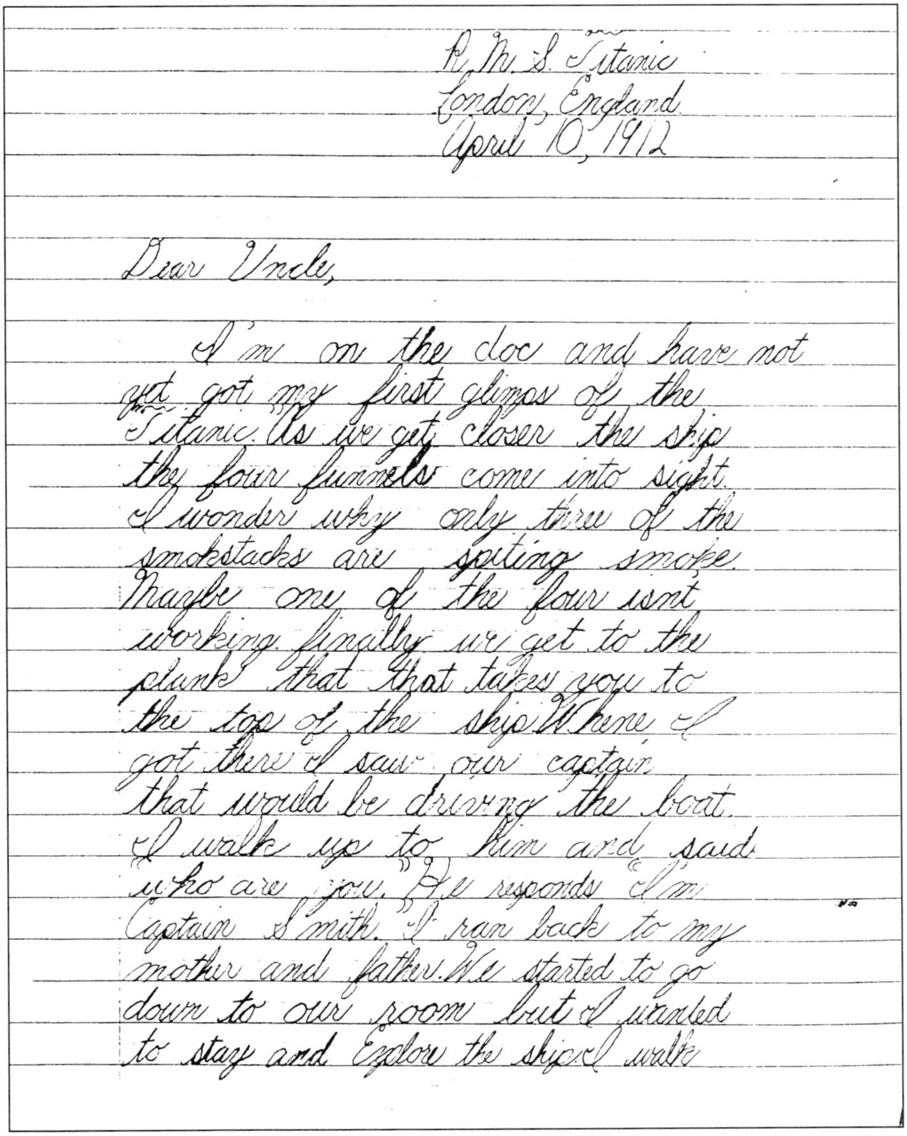

R, M, S, Titanic
London, England
April 10, 1912

Dear Uncle,

I'm on the doc and have not yet got my first glimps of the Titanic. As we get closer the ship they four funnels come into sight. I wonder why only three of the smokestacks are sorting smoke. Maybe one of the four isnt working finally we get to the plank that that takes you to the top of the ship. When I got there I saw our captain that would be driving the boat. I walk up to him and said who are you. He responds I'm Captain Smith. I ran back to my mother and father. We started to go down to our room but I wanted to stay and Explore the ship. I walk

FIG. 4–2a Titanic *letter*

Part III: What Works

Teaching skills in context requires that teachers design their own lessons to meet the writing needs of their class. Instead of depending on a grammar text or English book to fill the room with meaningful activities, teachers will have to come up with lessons that actually tie directly into the writing process. The question is,

around and see a lot of people
that have their suitcases being
dragged around by other people.
Only one of the people I know
wich is John Jacob Astor
the wealthiest man in the world.
I found out the titanic is
880 feet long, 10 stories tall,
and 92 feet wide. The titanic
is 4,000 tons! One anchor
length is 172 lbs! This ship is
unsinkable. It has 2 bottomms
and 16 warter tight compalments.
The captain found me exploring
and asked if I wanted to steer
the boat. So I got to steer
the boat. Then I went to the
side of the boat and saw a
fish at least 5 ft. long. Then
I went to my cabin with my
mom and Dad.
    As I walked down to
my cabin I saw the first heated
swimming pool to be on a boat.
As I walked past the gym there

FIG. 4–2b Titanic *letter*

why bother preparing your own materials when there are so many wonderful textbooks and commercially prepared materials to fall back on? Why bother doing the troublesome and time-consuming dirty work of preparing your own lesson plans when you can simply use a textbook? After all, they are so attractively packaged, well organized, and just sitting on a shelf begging to be used. Why not take advantage of their services?

The answer is that teaching grammar and writing within the isolation of a was somebody on the exersize like with a dress and a nice shirt. Another person was on a electrical camel that made your hart and liver going. There was a barber shop with automatic shampoo and hairdryers. I also met another kid my age and he was in the cabin right next to mine. We became best friends. I found one of the four elevators. My friend and I went up and down the elevators and had a great time. One time we stopped on a floor that we didn't push the button on and it was first class. When the door opend Captain Smith was there. When we got to the floor we wanted we stopped of the elevator. Then we went back to our "cabin. I said see you tomorrow." Then I was in my 2nd class cabin.

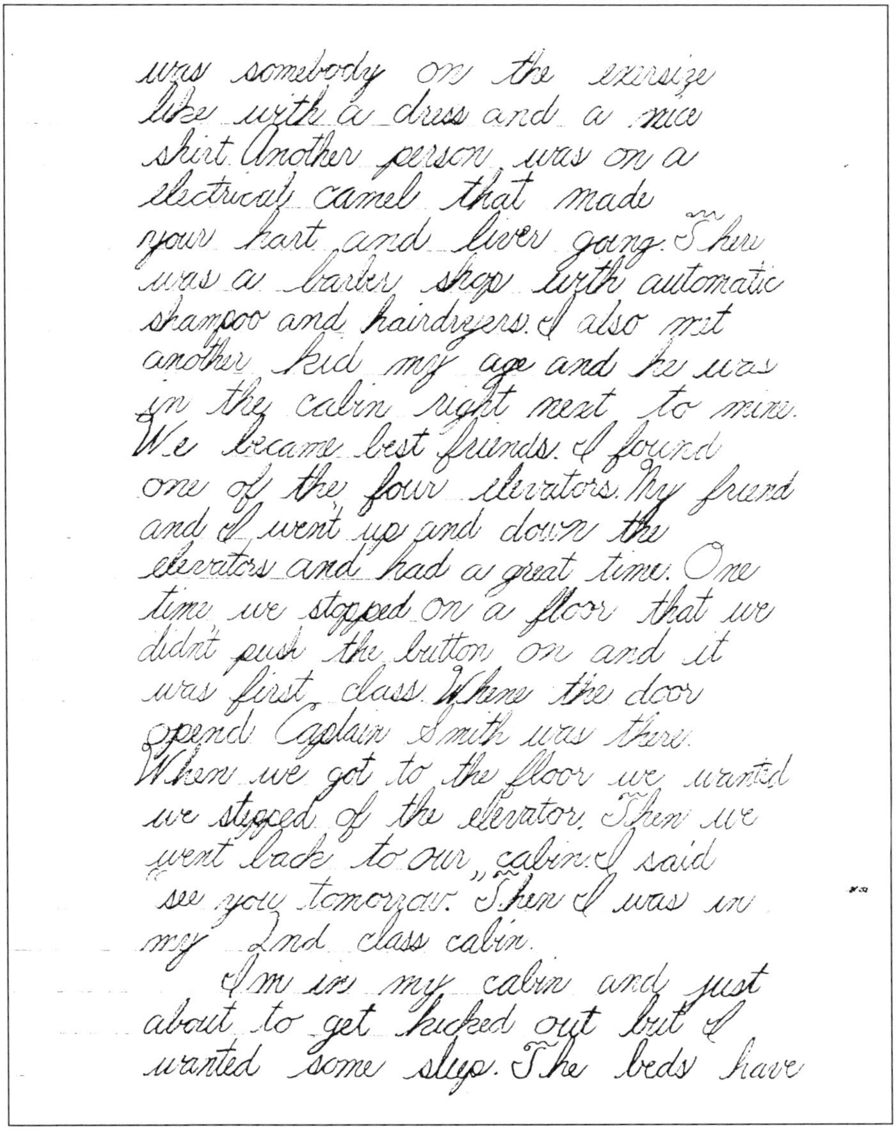

I'm in my cabin and just about to get kicked out but I wanted some sleep. The beds have

FIG. 4–2c Titanic *letter*

textbook simply does not work. It may do a lot of things, but it does not improve a student's ability to write. In fact, there is evidence that teaching grammar out of a book may have just the opposite result. Listen to this conclusion from a 1963 report entitled *Research in Written Composition*:

> In view of the widespread agreement of research studies based upon many types of students and teachers, the conclusion can be stated in strong and unqualified terms:

the teaching of formal grammar has a negligible or, because it usually displaces some instruction and practice in actual composition, even a harmful effect on the improvement of writing. (Braddock, Lloyd-Jones, & Schoer, 1963, pp. 37–38)

The conclusion of George Hillocks's 1986 study, *Research on Written Composition,* is even stronger:

> In short, the findings of research on the composing process give us no reason to expect the study of grammar or mechanics to have any substantial effect on the writing process or on writing ability as reflected in the quality of written products. Experimental studies show that they have little or none. (p. 228)

> School boards, administrators, and teachers who impose the systematic study of traditional grammar on their students over lengthy periods of time in the name of teaching writing do them a gross disservice which should not be tolerated by anyone concerned with the effective teaching of good writing. (p. 248)

Some people may argue that English texts have changed, and that the new research on grammar has penetrated into the offices of the major educational publishing houses. They have seen the light, and the new texts bear little resemblance to the dusty, moldy old ones used in bygone eras. Instead, the new texts place the writing process at the center of their programs. No longer do they isolate grammar from writing. Rather, they mix and blend the two together into a delicate balance much like the ingredients of a favorite recipe so that what comes out is a delicious morsel that meets the needs of all concerned.

Not so, according to some experts. The new process writing texts do not provide much in the way of writing experiences. Mary Ellen Giacobbe reports in "Choosing a Language Arts Text" (1988) only 31 percent of the pages in second-grade English texts are labeled as composition pages. Further, fully one quarter of the 31 percent is actually transcribing and copying the words of others. Only 2 percent of those pages labeled as composition required true authorship of the students.

Not only do the grammar texts fall far short in their attempt to get students involved in the writing process, they serve as a poor role model for emerging writers. Their stilted, dead language is nearly the exact opposite of how nonfiction should be composed. As Neil Postman writes in *The End of Education* (1995), "Of the language of grammar texts, I will not even speak. To borrow from Shakespeare, 'it is unfit for the Christian ear to hear.'"

Part IV: What Works

Teach skills but don't use a language text. Sounds like yet another conundrum for the classroom teacher. Fortunately, however, this riddle has an answer that makes sense and is easily applicable to the writing process: The best way to teach writing skills is within the context of a meaningful writing activity. Teaching the principles of language so that they can be directly applied to a writing project gives relevancy to even the most abstract of language concepts. Conversely, to isolate skills within the confines of a language text is to strip it of any usefulness. It becomes an empty kind of knowledge that has little practical value so that it is quickly washed out of the brain.

Research by Graves (1984) and Giacobbe (1988) shows that the typical language program has a tremendous amount of repetition and redundancy. Texts continuously spiral back so that skills covered in one grade level are repeated over and over again throughout other grade levels. This is not surprising given the valuelessness of the knowledge covered. There is little use for such skills and they must be continuously repeated through all levels of the program to keep such empty knowledge from draining out of the brain. The knowledge acquired from the grammar text has no use and simply will not stick.

Knowledge acquired within the context of a meaningful writing activity, on the other hand, has a much better chance of being used and retained. If teachers can show that a particular skill can help to improve the quality of writing, then the skill becomes a useful thing to know. No longer is the skill taught in isolation for no other purpose than its own sake. It can be utilized to write more clearly and with greater impact. The skill has a purpose and a point. As Regie Routman (1988) writes, "skills and subskills can be effectively taught in the context of good literature as well as through minilessons for reinforcement. Attention to these details occurs within the whole meaningful context, never in isolation" (p. 202).

The above presents a pretty convincing case against using an English text as a pathway to better writing. If grammar does not improve writing, then an even bigger question becomes obvious: What exactly *does* improve student writing? How do we turn students into proficient writers? How do we get students to write as well as they can?

The answer to that question is what many teachers already involved in the writing process intuitively know—the best way to improve student writing is to let students write. Just as the only way to learn to ride a bike is to jump on the seat and start pedaling, the best way to learn to write is to pick up a pencil and start to put words on paper. Students can't develop a knowledge of writing by dictating sentences out of a book to them. Instead, they have to saturate and immerse themselves in words. They need to play and experiment with words so they can grow into a sense of language. As one teacher (Brennan, 1988) writes, "Children learn to write by frequent writing. The value and knowledge of writing is as much caught as taught by teachers who value writing in their own lives" (p. 277).

Anyone involved in sports already knows this. A coach can round and smooth out the rough edges of talent, and can add the fine details that can mean the difference between success and failure. Talent, however, basically emerges and evolves through constant repetition and use. As Donald Graves (1984) puts it, "So much time is devoted to blocking and tackling drills that there is no time to play the game, writing" (p. 65).

In light of this new research and the idea that writing is best learned by writing, do we need to teach skills and grammar at all? Why not just let kids write and write, all the while letting their knowledge and skills unfold and blossom while expressing poetic thoughts and getting in touch with their better sides? Do we need to go to the bother at all, or should we let students come to an understanding of language in a natural way as they compose their way through school?

The answer is a resounding *yes*. The surface appearance and presentation of a composition is crucial to its acceptance by its intended audience. A writer's meaning will be severely tarnished by a poorly presented product no matter how strong the ideas it contains. Donald Graves (1984) puts it quite powerfully when he writes:

> A new orthodoxy holds that grammar, spelling, and handwriting are unimportant as long as the information is good. Not so. These skills, or surface features, are very important in their place. Once the information has been developed, then the final touches that will enhance the meaning need to be added. If a sentence is not punctuated properly, is illegible or convoluted, the reader has to struggle unnecessarily. It appears that the writer cares little for their information or their audience. The full job of teaching is not done until the teacher has helped the children handle the surface features on their own. (p. 192)

Teachers also need to think of their own best interest. Hardly a day goes by without a new attack on public education. This continual state of crisis has spawned a conservative, back-to-basics movement in virtually every part of the country. When teachers allow their students to experiment and put their own thoughts into language, they put themselves out on a limb, an easy target for anyone who would like to take a shot at them. As one writer (Gill, 1992) put it, "To the public, a piece of writing filled with misspelling looks unfinished, uninformed, indicative of poor writing, and/or the product of a writer with a disability" (p. 444). For our own safety and protection, teachers must work hard to help students produce the best surface presentation possible.

Part V: Choosing Skills, or, "If I See One More _____ I'll Die" Test

Throwing out a textbook leaves a huge void in any curriculum. No longer is there the comforting cushion of preplanned, preselected lessons and dittos to fill a large portion of the language arts program. Given this, a very important question leaps to the forefront: How do I fill the crater left by the removal of the language text from the curriculum? How do I fill the void that was occupied by my English text?

The first step in answering this question is to decide what to teach. There are several places to look to help find the solution to this question. The first thing to do is to dust off the curriculum guide that has been stuck in a forlorn corner on your bookcase for so long. This may shed some light on the minimum requirements of your grade level. The next place to look is at any standardized or state assessment tests students are required to take in your school district.

Tests can promote an empty, shallow kind of teaching and learning that flies in the face of current research on reading and writing. Nonetheless, they are playing a bigger and bigger role in public education. Results are highly publicized and often used to punish poorly performing schools or to bash public schools in general. To ignore this reality is to do a real disservice to students. To pretend these tests don't exist is like sending children into an important baseball game without any instruction or practice in the key elements of the game. It is to your advantage to work into your curriculum any skills that will help students perform well on standardized assessments.

The last and most important place to look is also the most obvious—student writing. The first step in any writing program is to get students over the fear of the blank page. Once they become fluent writers and begin to produce a body of work, certain trends and tendencies become apparent. Many of these tendencies and flaws can be handled on an individual basis during the revision conference. Some, however, are shared by a significant number of their classmates. I know these tendencies have reached a critical mass when I am reading through folders and begin to mumble to myself, "If I see one more _____ I'll die!" Then I know that this flaw is shared by enough students to merit becoming a part of my curriculum. For example, my students tend to start out the year writing bland, flat, sentences with little or no punctuation. We begin the year, then, with sentence-expanding activities and work on run-on sentences. My list looks something like this:

1. Sentences
   subjects and predicates
   sentence expanding
   punctuation
   similes and metaphors

2. Parts of Speech
   nouns
   verbs
   adjectives
   adverbs
   pronouns

3. Mechanics
   basic punctuation and capitalization

4. Showing and Not Telling
   incorporating the five senses
   writing with style

Part VI: Ryan's Story Revisited

So Ryan did begin to write. It began with his short but vivid poem about his first trip to the bowling alley, and expanded into other areas. Writing would never come naturally or easily for him. Words and ideas would never flow easily from his cluttered mind. His writing would be a bit on the thin side, and not always contain the depth and detail needed to completely fill out his ideas. But he did begin to get on the bike and pedal. Ryan continued with the playfulness that he showed in his short poem about bowling. All of his work had at least one striking image and his sentences had a richness and density that made his work interesting to read.

While Ryan was pedaling he learned the basics of language. He learned that grammar and language concepts were tools that steadied his ride while going down the writing pathway. They had a purpose and could be used to make his ride a little easier. Ryan did not learn the elements of language within the narrow confines of an English text, as something to be memorized for a test and then quickly lost from the brain. Instead, the rules of language had a purpose and a use. Because the knowledge was useful, it lodged in a safe, secure part of the brain, where Ryan could easily retrieve it as his ride became more complex. Each time he used his knowledge, it became stronger and less likely to be confined to a dusty, forlorn corner of his brain. Ryan had begun his journey. He was on his way down a path that would lead him to regard writing as a meaningful and useful part of his life.

Appendix

The following are ideas and activities that incorporate language skills and concepts into meaningful writing situations. All have been classroom tested and students respond well to these activities. They serve as a springboard from the assignment into everyday writing tasks. Students carry over skills learned in these activities to writing in other areas of the curriculum. Similes, for example, pop up more frequently after doing the comparison poem activity.

A good way to begin the year is by helping students write better sentences. The following three activities help students write richer, more detailed sentences. They also introduce and define the terms *subject, predicates, similes,* and *metaphors.* When taken together, the activities will help students build better, more expressive sentences.

Activity 1: Sentence Expanding

1. Start by putting a simple, two-word sentence on the board or overhead projector and ask if it is a complete sentence.

   Example: Bird flew.

Most, if not all students, will respond no. Tell them that it is indeed a complete sentence. Tell them a sentence consists of a subject (the who or what part of a sentence) and a predicate (the action or what they did part of the sentence). Bring out that while "Bird flew" is a complete sentence, it is not a good one and that they are going to build one that is more representative of an image that they have in their mind.

2. Next, have students close their eyes and picture a specific bird in their mind. Prompt students with such questions as:

What color is your bird?
Is it large or small?
What type of beak does it have?
Does it have long or short legs?

Ask students to describe their bird in terms that will cause others to share their mental image of their bird. They then add their descriptive words to the subject part of their sentence. Their new sentence might look something like this:

The large brown bird with a sharp beak flew.

3. Next, focus attention on the predicate part of the sentence by asking students to think about what the bird is doing. Is it in a hurry or is it floating in a graceful arc over a meadow? Is it in flight from a predator? Where is it going and why? Students then collect their thoughts and add them to the predicate part of their sentence. Their final, expanded version might look like this:

The large brown bird with a sharp beak flew in graceful circles over a meadow, looking for a tasty morsel for dinner.

Students then share their final products with the class and compare them with the simple sentence they started with. Most recognize the final version as a definite improvement over the original (See Figure 4–3).

4. Have students display their favorite example of an expanded sentence. Start with two pieces of blank paper. Label one *subject* and the other *predicate*. They then copy one of their original two-word sentences onto the paper, putting the one-word subject on one sheet and the one-word predicate on the other. Phase two involves putting their expanded subject and one-word predicate on the second line. On the third line they put their final expanded sentence. Students complete the project with a picture to illustrate their expanded sentence. This gives students a graphic, concrete illustration of how their sentence has grown, as well as providing an opportunity to share and display their work (see Figure 4–4).

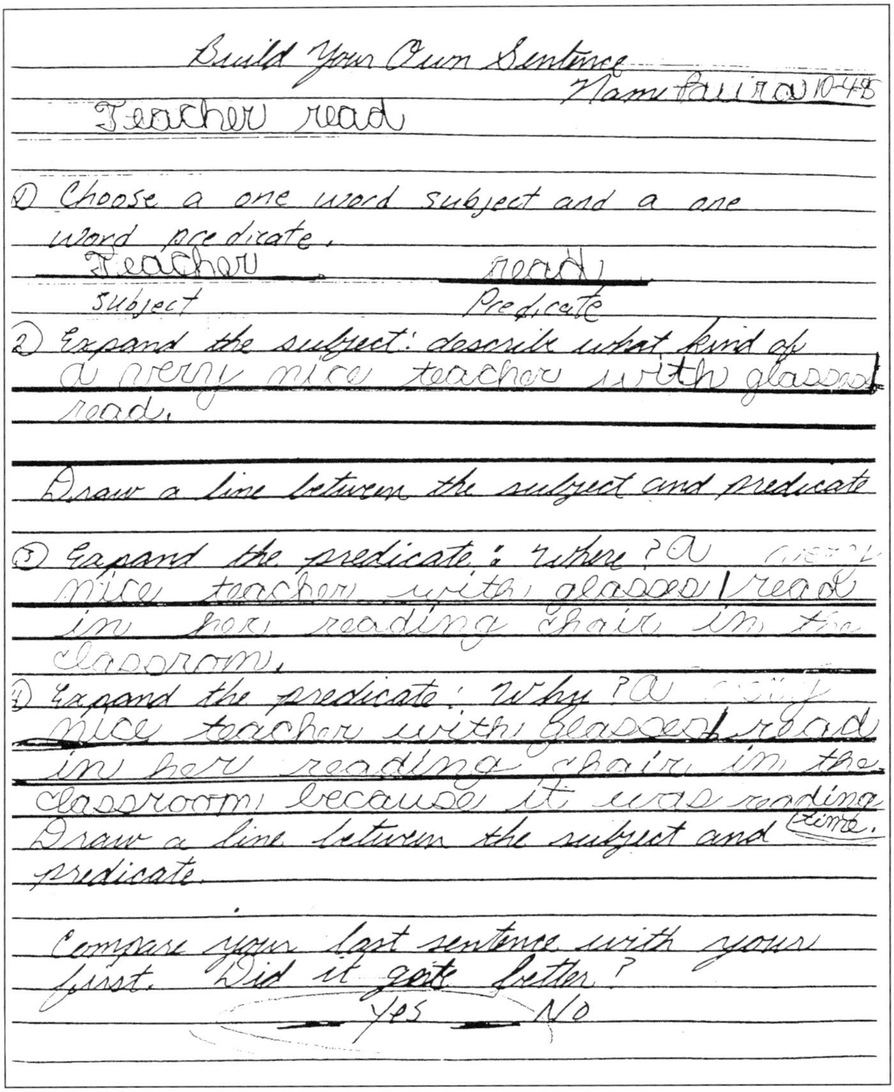
Build Your Own Sentence
Name [illegible]
Teacher read
1) Choose a one word subject and a one word predicate.
Teacher read
subject Predicate
2) Expand the subject: describe what kind of
a very nice teacher with glasses | read.
Draw a line between the subject and predicate
3) Expand the predicate: where? a very nice teacher with glasses | read in her reading chair in the classroom.
4) Expand the predicate: Why? a very nice teacher with glasses | read in her reading chair in the classroom because it was reading time.
Draw a line between the subject and predicate.
Compare your last sentence with your first. Did it gote better?
Yes No

FIG. 4–3 *Build your own sentence*

Activity 2: Comparison Poems

1. The inspiration for this activity comes from Kenneth Koch's *Wishes, Lies, and Dreams.* Start by reading some of the poems from the section entitled "Comparisons." Ask students to guess the age of the authors. After several guesses, inform students that the poems were written by primary-age children. Point out that powerful images reside in all of us regardless of age, and that

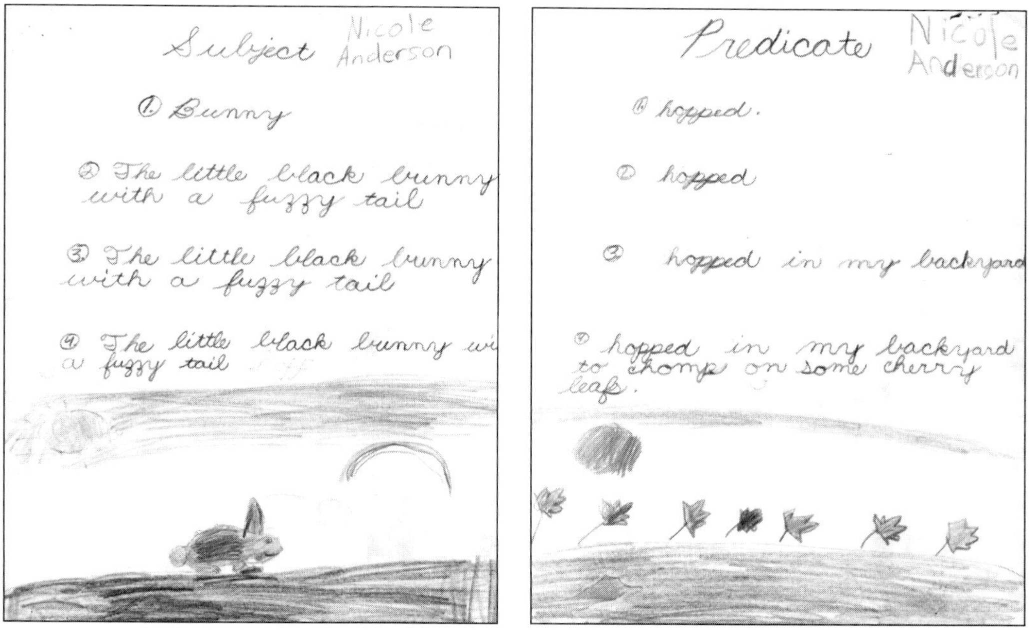

Subject Nicole Anderson

① Bunny

② The little black bunny with a fuzzy tail

③ The little black bunny with a fuzzy tail

④ The little black bunny wi[th] a fuzzy tail

Predicate Nicole Anderson

① hopped.

② hopped

③ hopped in my backyard

④ hopped in my backyard to chomp on some cherry leafs.

FIG. 4–4   *Subject/predicate allies*

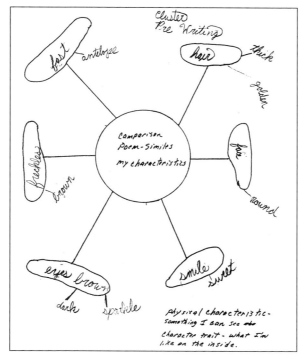

FIG. 4–5   *Self-portrait cluster*

one of the ways of getting these powerful images onto paper is by using strong, vivid comparisons.

2. Discuss comparisons and how they can be alike yet quite different.

   Example: Ice on a pond and the top of a table
   Snow and a piece of paper

Explain that comparing two things using *like, as,* or *than* is called a simile.

3. Have students write a comparison poem about themselves. Start by having kids cluster physical and character traits about themselves. Extend the cluster by finding things they can compare themselves with. Blond hair, for example, can be compared with the down on a baby chick (see Figure 4–5).

4. Have students turn the images from their cluster into sentences and a comparison poem. Collect their poems and read out loud, seeing if the class can identify the author based on their comparisons. Display the poems with a self-portrait (see Figure 4–6).

5. Close the project by having students write comparison poems about subjects of their choice.

Activity 3: Color Poems

Color poems are another way of getting vivid comparisons onto paper, though using metaphors instead of similes. This activity also helps students link abstract concepts with concrete, tangible images such as color.

1. Using the chart in Figure 4–7, have students choose a favorite color and list it in the proper column.

2. Next, students list images, ideas, and emotions associated with the color and the five senses. For example, the color blue might be associated with the taste of blueberry, or the color yellow might feel like the warmth from the summer sun. The same brainstorming or prewriting purpose can be accomplished with a cluster as well.

3. Using their chart or cluster as a springboard, students write color poems with sentences containing metaphors (see Figure 4–7).

The next group of activities centers around parts of speech. They are intended primarily to define and make students aware of the functions of nouns, verbs, and adjectives. Other skills, such as sentence expanding, paragraphing, and prewriting techniques, are indirectly brought into play. (The beauty of any writing project is that it cannot be limited to one function or purpose. A variety of skills and thought processes are called upon and applied.) Because these skills are used within the context of a meaningful writing activity, students see them as something functional and useful in the writing process.

Me Myself and I

My hair is as golden as the sun
when it sets.

My eyes sparkle like a shooting star
falling through the atmosphere.

My smile is as sweet as brownies
that just came out of the oven.

I'm as fast as an antelope from a
hungry cheetah.

My freckles are as brown as wet
sand on a beach.

My face is as round as an apple
in the fall.

FIG. 4–6 *Self-portrait poem*

> Red
>
> Red is the taste of fresh strawberrys
> right off the bush.
>
> Red is the smell of a sweet rose
> on a hot summer day.
>
> Red is the feeling of an embarassed
> kid on their first day of school.
>
> Red is the sound of an apple
> crunching in my mouth
>
> Red is the color of my mouth
> all over inside.
>
> By Ashley Ricblin

FIG. 4–7 *Color poem "red"*

Activity 4: My Favorite Sandwich

1. Start by dipping into the library to find information about John Montague and the invention of the sandwich. Share the information with the class.

2. Have students make a cluster showing the ingredients and condiments that make up their favorite sandwich. Then have students add words that describe each ingredient. The words *bright* and *yellow,* for example, might be used to describe mustard, or *creamy* and *smooth* to describe mayonnaise (see Figure 4–8).

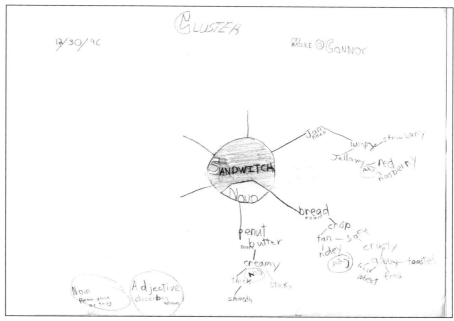

FIG. 4–8 *Sandwich cluster*

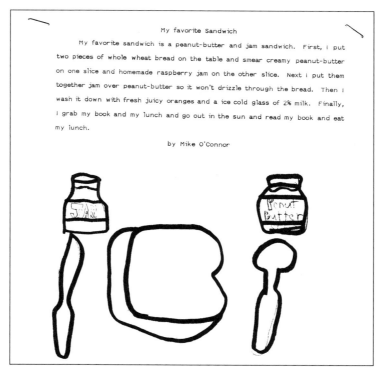

My favorite Sandwich

My favorite sandwich is a peanut-butter and jam sandwich. First, I put two pieces of whole wheat bread on the table and smear creamy peanut-butter on one slice and homemade raspberry jam on the other slice. Next I put them together jam over peanut-butter so it won't drizzle through the bread. Then I wash it down with fresh juicy oranges and a ice cold glass of 2% milk. Finally, I grab my book and my lunch and go out in the sun and read my book and eat my lunch.

by Mike O'Connor

FIG. 4–9 *My favorite sandwich*

3. Finally, have students write a paragraph describing how they make their favorite sandwich using adjectives to help taste their creation (see Figure 4–9).

Activity 5: Adjective/Verb Poems

1. Start by having students choose a topic for their poem. Place the topic in the center of the cluster as shown in Figure 4–10.

2. Students then think of words that describe their topic. *Messy,* for example, might be used to describe a pet. Explain that words that describe a noun are called adjectives. Students place the adjectives in the proper place in their cluster.

3. Next, students think of action words that go along with their adjectives and nouns. A messy pet, for example, might splash. Explain that action words are called verbs and add their action words to their cluster. A completed cluster might look like the one in Figure 4–11.

4. Close out the project by having students write expanded sentences based on their clusters in the form of a poem (see Figure 4–11).

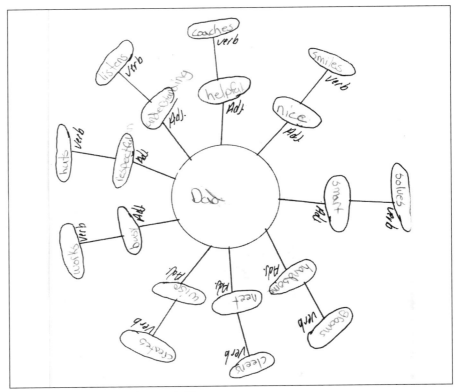

FIG. 4–10 *Poem topic cluster "dad"*

Dads.

By Marisa Espinoza

Nice, helpful   dad's   coaches softball

Smart, wise   dad's   solve problems

Handsome, neat   dad's   clean messes

Busy, understanding   dad's   work very hard

Neat, wise   dad's   creat different
                                              things

Smart, understanding   dad's   listen to
                                              problems

Respectful, wise   dad's   hunt animals

FIG. 4–11   *Poem—expanded sentences "dad"*

Activity 6: Adjective Picture

1. Start by having students think of five objects and make simple outlines of each object on five separate sheets of paper.

2. Next, students write as many adjectives describing the object as will fit around the outline of the object (see Figure 4–12).

3. Staple or bind together the finished outlines to make a book. Another alternative is to color and decorate the outlines and display around the room as pictures.

FIG. 4–12 *Adjective picture*

Activity 7: Menus from *My Side of the Mountain*

Children's literature serves as excellent models and springboards for writing activities. The next activity is based on Jean Craighead George's fine novel, *My Side of the Mountain.*

1. Read the book *My Side of the Mountain.* Take notes or keep track of the many meals and recipes prepared by Sam during his stay on the mountain.

2. Next, have students create their own imaginary restaurant featuring only Sam's recipes and creations. Make good use of adjectives by having students think

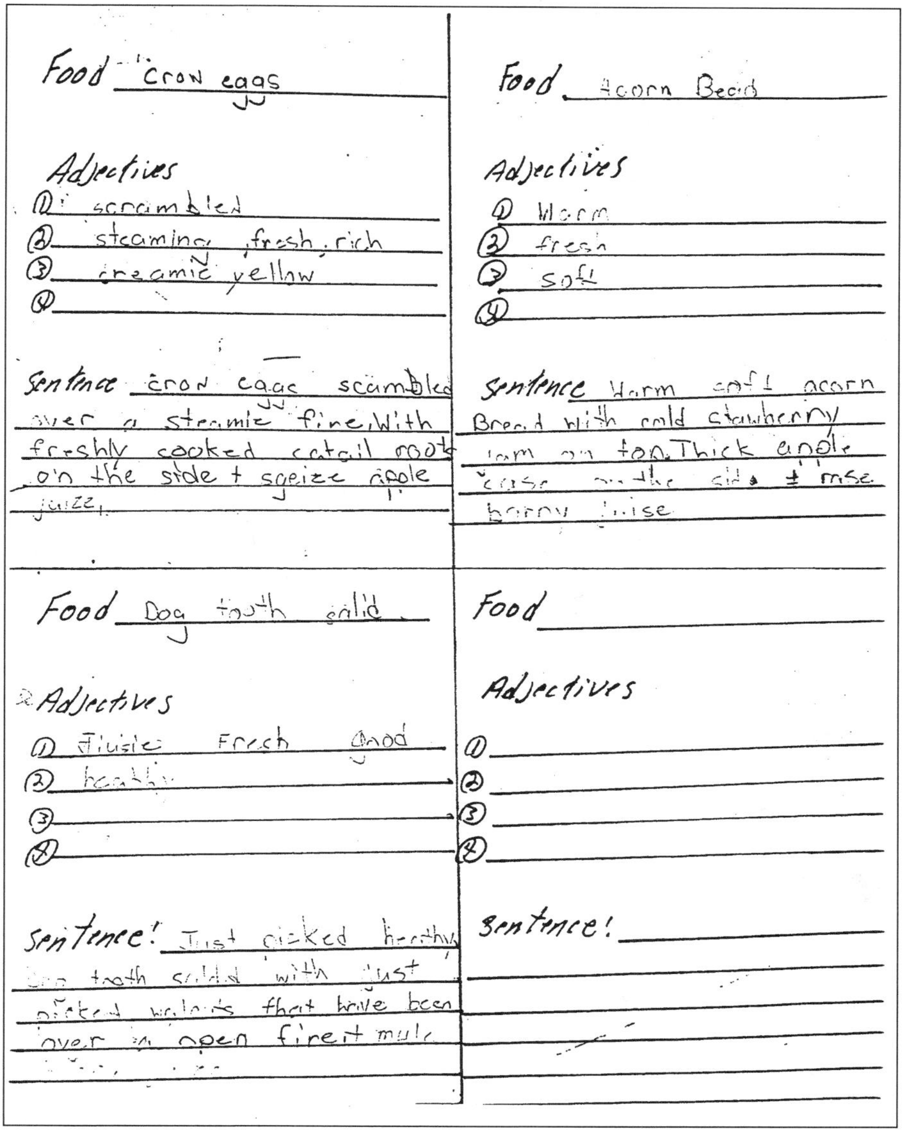

FIG. 4–13 *Restaurant food sentences*

of words that describe their meal and then writing a sentence describing their creation (see Figure 4–13).

3. Close out the project by having students use their sentences to write an annotated menu describing each meal in all its mouth-watering glory. Have them come up with a name for their restaurant and a cover for their menu, bind together, and share with the class (see Figures 4–14a and 4–14b).

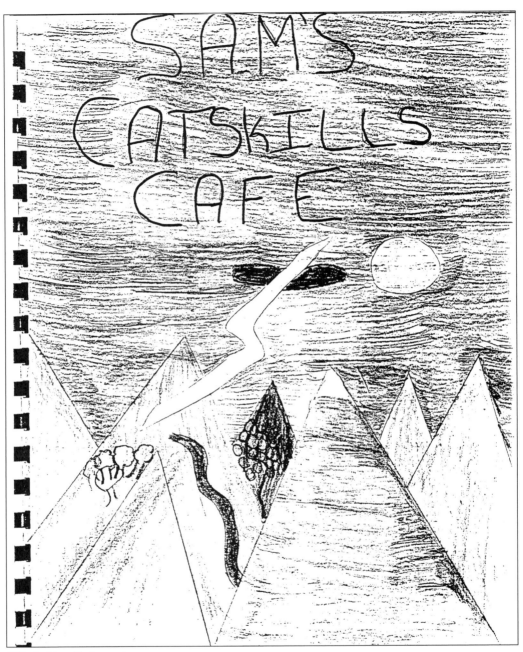

FIG. 4–14a *Restaurant menu*

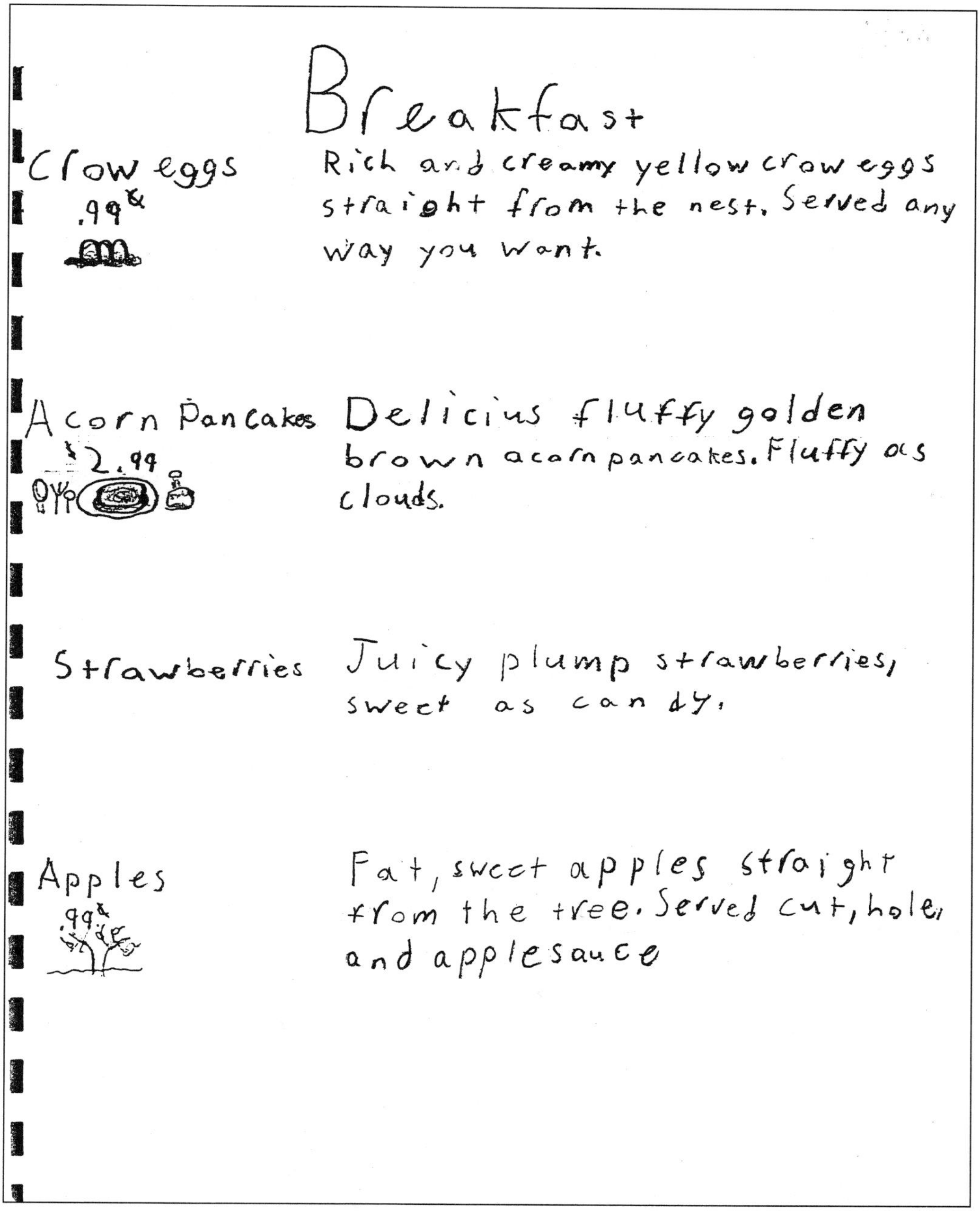

Breakfast

Crow eggs
.99¢

Rich and creamy yellow crow eggs straight from the nest. Served any way you want.

Acorn Pancakes
$2.99

Delicius fluffy golden brown acorn pancakes. Fluffy as clouds.

Strawberries

Juicy plump strawberries, sweet as candy.

Apples
.99¢

Fat, sweet apples straight from the tree. Served cut, hole, and applesauce

FIG. 4–14b *Restaurant menu*

Activity 8: Showing and Not Telling

This activity is not designed to teach a particular grammar skill. Instead, it is designed to, first, get students to show and not tell character traits and feelings and, second, have students incorporate the five senses into their writing. It is an effective way to make their writing more detailed, vivid, and sharp.

1. Start with a simple telling sentence such as:

   The night was scary.

   Ask students if this sentence did, indeed, produce fear in their hearts. Point out that the sentence lacks impact because the author told rather than showed how the reader should feel.

2. Next, have students write "scary night" in the middle of a cluster. Ask the students to add to their cluster things they might hear on a scary night (the cry of a wolf, the hoot of an owl, etc.). Then have students add things they might see on a scary night (a full moon, dark shadows, etc.). Repeat this process with the rest of the five senses (see Figure 4–15).

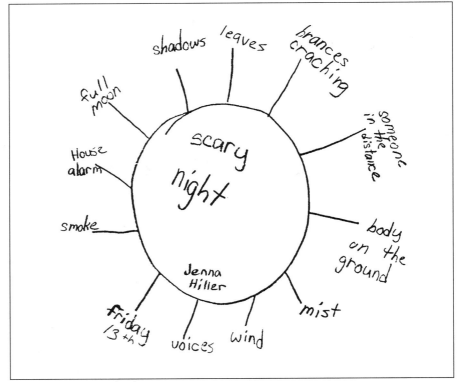

FIG 4–15 *Scary night cluster*

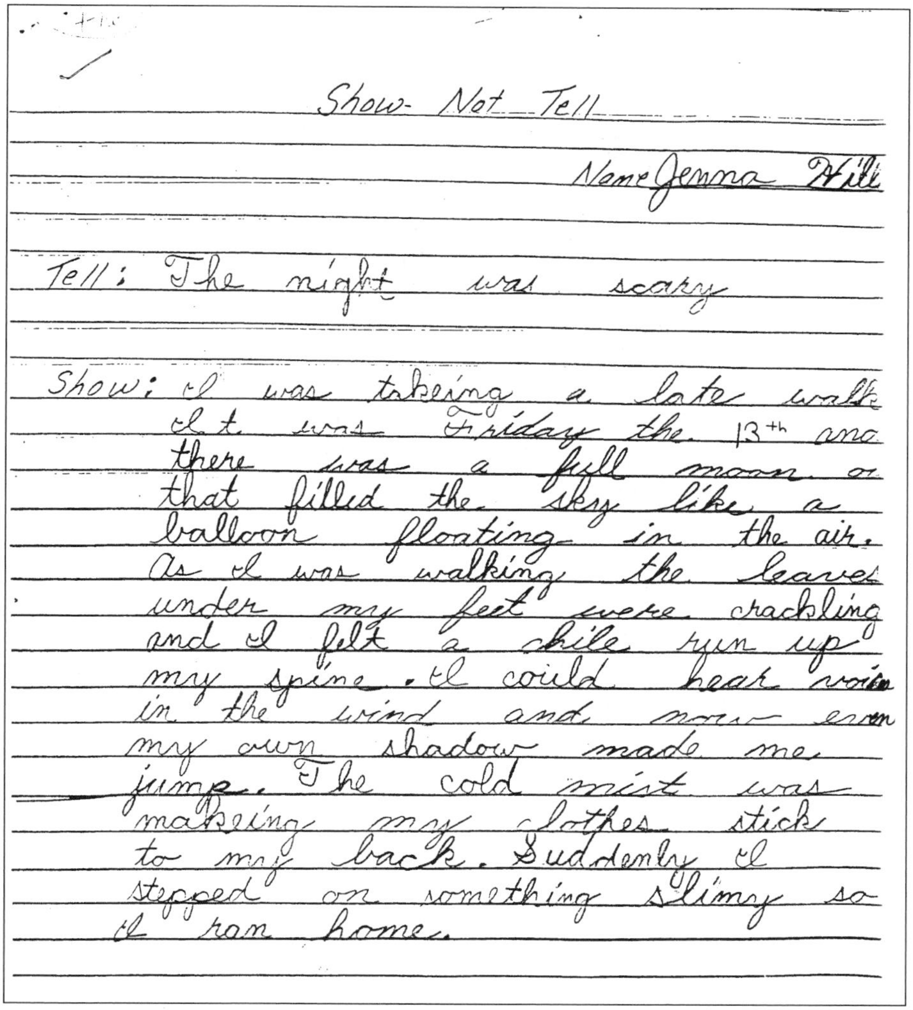

Show-Not-Tell

Name Jenna Hill

Tell: The night was scary

Show: I was takeing a late walk. It was Friday the 13th and there was a full moon that filled the sky like a balloon floating in the air. As I was walking the leaves under my feet were crackling and I felt a chile run up my spine. I could hear voices in the wind and now even my own shadow made me jump. The cold mist was makeing my clothes stick to my back. Suddenly I stepped on something slimy so I ran home.

FIG. 4–16 *Scary night paragraph*

3. When their cluster is filled with scary images incorporating the five senses, tell students they are going to write a paragraph describing a scary night. They must follow two rules, however: First, they must use images from all five senses and, second, they cannot use the words "scary" or "night." This requires that they show and not tell what is going on in their paragraph (see Figure 4–16).

References

Braddock, R., Lloyd-Jones, R., & Schoer, L. (1963). *Research in written composition*. Urbana, IL: National Council of Teachers of English.

Brennan, C. (1988). How to cover a language arts text: Sit on it. In T. Newkirk & N. Atwell (Eds.), *Understanding writing: Ways of observing, learning, and teaching* (2nd. Ed.). Portsmouth, NH: Heinemann.

Calkins, L. (1994). *The art of teaching writing* (2nd Ed.). Portsmouth, NH: Heinemann.

Giacobbe, M. (1988). Choosing a language arts textbook. In T. Newkirk & N. Atwell (Eds.), *Understanding writing: Ways of observing, learning, and teaching* (2nd Ed.). Portsmouth, NH: Heinemann.

Gill, T. (1992). Development of word knowledge as it relates to reading and spelling instruction. *Language Arts*, October, 444–452.

Graves, D. (1984). *A researcher learns to write: Selected articles and monographs*. Portsmouth, NH: Heinemann.

Hillocks, G., Jr. (1986). *Research on written composition: New directions for teaching*. Urbana, IL: National Council of Teachers of English.

Postman, N. (1995). *The end of education: Redefining the value of education*. New York: Alfred A. Knopf.

Routman, R. (1988). *Transitions: From literature to literacy*. Portsmouth, NH: Heinemann.

5   *Facilitating the Use of Description— and Grammar*

SARAH WOLTJER

Introduction

As all teachers do, Sarah Woltjer has struggled with the challenge to reach the variety of learning styles and levels within her classroom. Some students excel at writing and love to devote time to it, while others lack confidence in their writing abilities. However, it is important to motivate all students to write. In order for students to become better writers, it is essential to give them time to write within the language arts classroom. Sarah devotes one seventh-grade class period each week strictly to writing. It is an opportunity for students to put words on the page and experiment with different voices and styles. Frequently, throughout the month each student will choose pieces of his or her writing to publish for the classroom anthology. This article shares how prewriting and brainstorming activities can aid in producing good student writing. The activity is sure to inspire student writers of all learning styles and levels.

My teaching and research has shown me that in order for students to have an effective learning experience, grammar cannot be isolated exercises that are practiced but receive little relevant application. As Jean Sanborn (1986) states, "The study of grammar requires an act of self-consciousness that literally asks young people to step outside themselves and examine a process which they perform unconsciously . . ." (p. 77). This is a difficult task, and in large part an unnecessary one for young writers. Sanborn also expresses concern that our students begin to view language as a mystery that cannot be understood, when actually it is something they have known and developed instinctively since birth. As long as language is actively being used in the classroom it will develop, but I do not want my students to become fearful of language. Traditional grammar exercises tend to make my students shy away from language; therefore, I believe grammar will most effectively be developed if taught in the context of writing.

As a teacher at the middle-school level, it is one of my goals to see my students' writing improve, but I was discouraged by the grammatical errors that seemed to be repeated in my students' work, even though the grammatical concepts were ones that the students have rehearsed in traditional grammar exercises for years. We had studied adjectives and adverbs, too, yet I had little success at encouraging students to write with expression, feeling, and description through the use of adjectives and adverbs. Finally, through the development of a class period for writing, minilessons, peer-editing, and a classroom writing anthology, I began to see some improvement in my students' writing as well as grammar. As you will see through the following lesson, I found that by offering prewriting activities, and not constraining students to just adjectives or adverbs, I enabled them to use much more effective detail in their writing.

The assignment was to write a fall poem, using the students' five senses as a guideline for developing the poem. The Monday before, I had asked each student to bring in one or two leaves, so on Wednesday we had a large basket of them. Before writing on Wednesday we did prewriting activities as a class. My students loved it! We threw the basket of leaves in the air and watched them fall in different directions. Then the students took turns placing their leaf on the hot air register and watched as it was blown upward. After this they went around the classroom sharing a favorite fall memory or Thanksgiving tradition. Finally, with that introduction, I asked them to write their fall-sense poem. Even those students who typically had trouble with descriptive writing assignments now had the knowledge and ideas from the prewriting activities to provide organization to their thoughts.

Two weeks earlier I had also given my students an assignment to write a fall poem. Unlike our preparation for writing the sense poem, I gave no prewriting activities and left the assignment open-ended, except to mention: "Be sure to use those adjectives and adverbs for detail!" These poems were written and turned in by the end of class. I then put them away until after the sense poems were written, when I took them out for comparison. The differences in the students' sense poems compared with their previous writings on fall were amazing!

Fall Poem

Fall is a time when leaves turn color and fall off the tree.
You step on them and make a crunching noise.
You rake the leaves up and put them in a pile, jump
on them and mess them all up again.
Fall is a time to go outside and play and eat lots of candy.
Jill

Sense Poem

It smells like a gush of fresh air blowing
across my face while I'm walking.
It sounds like somebody crumbling up a
piece of paper and throwing it away.

It tastes like fresh donuts and hot cider on a
      cold frosty day.
It looks like a shriveling old crinkling flower
      in the cold air.
It feels like a scratchy hard piece of sand
      paper scraping against the door.
Jill

Fall Poem

Fall is the leaves changing colors; they can be green,
    yellow, or red.
Fall is the cold and freezing at night.
Fall is when your backyard is covered with leaves.
Amy

Sense Poem

I can smell the apple pie baking in the oven.
I can smell the burning leaves in the neighbor's yard.
I hear the leaves crackling under my feet as I trudge
    through the yard.
I hear children yelling as they jump in a pile of leaves.
I see the beautiful trees with yellow, red and brown leaves.
I see blended colors on the leaves like someone painted them.
I touch the leaves and I feel the veins.
I touch the leaves and sometimes they break in my hands.
I taste the turkey as the grease runs down my throat.
I taste the pumpkin pie and now I know it is fall!
Amy

Fall Poem

Fall is a fun time, a jump in the leaves time,
      a cook turkey time, and a have a good time time.
Fall is green, yellow, red, and brown. Fall is warm and cold.
Fall is a tall tree with green leaves, then with yellow and red
      leaves, and finally with leaves
      on the ground next to it.
Fall is a nice time to have.
Sandy

Sense Poem

As I walk outside I look around.
I see the leaves, slowly falling to the ground.

I hear the wind, as it moves the tree branches.
I touch the ground, it is cold and almost frozen for winter.
I smell the distant aroma of smoke from burning leaves.
I taste the rain, as it gently falls from the sky.
I know fall is here.

Then I walk inside, and look around.
I see my mom and sister, getting ready for Thanksgiving.
I hear my dad, playing off-tune hymns on the piano.
I touch the plates, as I set them on the table.
I smell the turkey, almost ready to be carved.
I taste the dinner, with all its good food.
I know that fall is here!
Sandy

The above poems are selected from three students. Their two poems offer a few key points for writing teachers to remember. First, prewriting activities are of tremendous value and can enhance the quality of students' writings. Second, students who may feel intimidated by the need to include certain grammatical constructions in their writing suddenly feel free to express themselves in a variety of syntactic ways when asked to focus on the experience of fall rather than the grammar to be included. Third, in their sense poems, the students clearly express their feelings and thoughts about fall, without using just adjectives or adverbs. Some of the most descriptive words used in their sense poems are nouns ("sand paper" and "aroma") or verbs ("trudge" and "falling"). Participial phrases such as "crackling under my feet" also bring the description to life. Had I instructed my students to include such grammatical constructions, I believe I might have lost some of their creativity that comes naturally through their unconscious command of syntax.

All writing, including descriptive writing, needs to be inspired through students' creative thoughts and ideas, not simply through the use of adjectives and adverbs. If we give our students clear-cut grammatical requirements, will it be at the expense of their experimentation and syntactic growth? As Lois Rosen (1987) says, "Students learn to write by writing, and they learn to write correctly by writing, revising, and proofreading their own work" (p. 64). It is not the repetitive traditional grammar lessons that are going to produce better writers within our classrooms, but a combination of sufficient reading time, purposeful writing experiences, and hands-on applicable minilessons, which will create a positive attitude and promote the development of our students' use of language. It will also take sufficient guidance and support at different phases of the writing. Providing a supportive classroom atmosphere that allows risks to be taken will produce more willing and successful writers and a positive contagious attitude within our classrooms. It will take extra time and effort to build this supportive environment, but I believe the results, such as the poem below, will be well worth the effort.

Fall Senses

I see smoke rising from chimneys into the cool air,
and leaves sailing across the grass escaping an assailing rake.
I hear autumn wind whistling through barren trees,
and leaves crunching and crackling beneath my feet.
I smell hot turkey roasting in grandma's oven,
and, outdoors, the smoke from piles of smoldering leaves.
I taste cool apple cider as it goes slipping down my throat,
and warm, steaming, fragrant pumpkin pie.
I feel warmth seeping through me as I sip hot chocolate,
and cold air biting at my cheeks as I step out into the cold.
I know that fall regrets the lost summer and dreads the winter to come.

Helen

References

ROSEN, L. (1987). Developing correctness in student writing: Alternatives to the error-hunt. *English Journal,* March, 62–69.

SANBORN, J. (1986). Grammar: Good wine before its time. *English Journal, 75* (3), 72–80.

Using Minilessons to Promote Student Revision
Helping Students Realize Their Power over Words

SUE ROWE

Introduction

Frustrated by her students' reluctance and apparent inability to make revisions in their writing, Sue Rowe developed minilessons using examples from their own work and true information about her personal life. Textbook lessons on revising were ineffective; the writing samples bore no resemblance to the students' writing; and the instructions contained no concrete techniques to help the students examine and make changes in their compositions. Drawing from her research into the writing process, she used two separate techniques to give students ideas for improving the style of their writing: sentence-combining and the elimination of verbs of being.

Bill Strong's practical suggestions and ready-to-use examples provided a basis for her sentence-combining lessons, but the substitution of examples from the students' writing made the lessons more effective. Young writers, particularly those who don't view themselves as *good* at writing, respond well when their work is the focus of the class's attention. With the help of their peers, they begin to see how they can manipulate the language and produce more interesting, complex, and varied sentences. Elimination of *be* verbs is a technique borrowed from J. E. Sparks (1982), the creator of the *Power Writing* program. By class brainstorming the use of more vivid verbs, students begin to see how they can turn colorless prose into a piece that flows with interesting vocabulary. They become more willing to make changes in their writing because they have concrete goals.

One of the most frustrating aspects of being an English teacher is getting students to *revise* their writing. Unlike spoken language, which can be reacted to by the listener and clarified by the speaker, the written word most often serves as a non-interactive communication. How can we get students to realize that their writing may be read and analyzed by a reader who will not know or come in contact with them as a writer? State writing assessments indicate to the test-takers that their compositions will be read by "interested adults" who will score them on the basis of style, clarity, and correctness, as well as content. Students need to understand that the good ideas in their heads must be communicated effectively in order to be understood by their readers. If students realize that they have the power to manipulate the written language to produce clear, precise writing, they will be more willing to change their words, and not just correct their mistakes.

When I question my students about unclear passages in their writing, their most common refrain is, "But you know what I mean!" Sometimes I do. Often I do not.

Unclear pronoun referents are one of the most common problems. An opinion statement about a current events issue may read: "They shouldn't require restaurants to ban smoking completely."

"Who is *they*?" I ask the class.

"You know, the people who said they should ban it!" the students respond indignantly, as if I were a fool for asking.

"And who are these *people*?" I ask.

Reluctantly, the better students reread the article to find the answer. Many others dismiss my question; what they have is good enough, and the social studies teacher for whom they are writing the paper won't be as picky as the language arts teacher.

They're wrong.

Since we have teamed up in "pods" in our school, the quality of student writing in the content areas has improved dramatically. As language arts professionals, the English teachers work with math, science, and social studies teachers to make students more aware of the important role language plays in all aspects of their lives. The ability to read competently and communicate effectively is central to their success in all subject areas. In fact, many assignments count as a grade in two or more classes. For example, every other week the social studies teacher asks students to find an article in the newspaper that embodies an issue, and then formulate an opinion and support it in a short persuasive paragraph. The social studies teacher grades the piece on content; I may take a language arts grade in addition, based on development, clarity, and mechanics—issues we have addressed during language arts class. Students are more likely to produce a thoughtfully revised and polished paragraph if they know that their audience includes the English teacher, and that they will be held accountable for the same criteria for which they are responsible in the language arts classroom.

Unclear pronoun referents are one thing; once the pronouns are identified, students can easily replace them with specific nouns. But getting students to play around with their sentences, to say the same thing in a different way, is more of a challenge. As far as revision, I have found two different types of minilessons that produce significant results: sentence-combining and elimination of verbs of being. By replacing *be* verbs with more vivid (preferably action) verbs, students find their writing is less wordy and contains less repetition. Of course, this distresses some students who have been taught that the longer a piece of writing is, the better their grade will be. But they soon discover that they can attach details to short sentences in order to make their writing more interesting. Usually, I use samples from students' own writing to teach these lessons. They are proud to have an example of their work displayed on the overhead and enjoy the attention of their peers. They also see that the sentence(s) they wrote can be worded in a number of different ways, as we rewrite the sample according to the day's lesson. In addition, I use information from my own life as examples for the students to work with, which makes me more of a "real person" to the students and provides fuel for interaction. Since they know my husband and I have two cats, plant a large garden in which we grow several types of hot peppers, and love to attend rock and roll concerts, they share their own cat stories and pictures, bring in produce (usually something hot) from their family garden or ask to play CDs during our lunch hour that they're sure I'll like. The students get my attention, while I become more than just an English teacher.

Eliminating Verbs of Being

Replacing verbs of being with more interesting language is one of the stages of *Power Writing*, a program developed by J. E. Sparks (1982). Language arts teachers throughout our school system use the program because it provides an easy, step-by-step approach to the writing process, particularly at the elementary level. To introduce the concept of eliminating verbs of being, I put the following sentence on the overhead and ask the students to copy it, and then underline the verb.

I am a teacher.

No problem. I've been working with the students on identifying subjects and verbs in warm-up sentences. They all know that "is," "are," "am," "was," "were," "be," "been," or "being" is a verb or part of a verb. I challenge them to rewrite the sentence, replacing "am" with another verb, keeping the meaning of the sentence. Before they become too frustrated, I give them a hint: "What do I *do?*"

"Oh!" A few of the students come up with the following sentence.

I teach.

As I circulate around the room, commenting and encouraging, other students catch on. Soon the students try to outdo each other by adding bits of information to the original clause. After a few minutes I solicit some responses and write them on the overhead.

I teach at Vicksburg Middle School.

I teach seventh grade at Vicksburg Middle School.
I teach seventh-grade language arts at Vicksburg Middle School.

They are on a roll, frantically trying to outdo each other as they realize their ability to add details to the main clause. I write each expanded sentence on the overhead, pointing out how each writer has embellished it with a prepositional phrase, a direct object, and modifiers. I don't take the time to explain each term, but the students are impressed that they are able to add such important-sounding details. They are awed by their own abilities.

David's example gives us an opportunity to discuss how a rewrite can involve a subtle change in meaning. He writes:

I enjoy teaching little children with brainwashed minds.

Most students realize that the original sentence doesn't include the fact that I *like* to teach, merely that I teach. They also point out that they are neither "little children" nor "brainwashed." They do, however, admit that David's example is creative, and in five or ten minutes they have glimpsed their power to manipulate the language, a power that most of them don't know they have. They clamor for another sentence, but I have to get on with the rest of the day's agenda.

The next day I give a similar sentence as a warm-up:

I am a football player.

This sentence appears in several students' "collage" paragraphs, pieces of writing to explain a collage of pictures they have constructed to describe themselves. The collages go into their middle-school portfolios, which they will take with them when they graduate from eighth grade. Each item in the portfolio is accompanied by a reflective piece of writing that explains the item.

This time, the students need no prompting to come up with the basic rewrite:

I play football.

Again, they add bits of information: where, when, how, the positions they play, etc. I display various examples on the overhead and we discuss the pros and cons of each. Again, David's is the most creative and unusual. Here it is, in his own handwriting.

I play football because smashing brains is a way to relieve stress.

Needless to say, David reads avidly. Mostly, he devours fantasy fiction, but he does read a lot, and I am able to make the point to the class that reading enables us as writers. It not only adds to our vocabulary, but also helps us with wording and ideas.

The following day, I use another common sentence from the collage paragraphs, one where the students list their favorite activities. I deliberately choose an unlikely combination so that no one will feel picked on or left out:

The activities I like to do best are volleyball, reading, and wrestling.

By this time the students are "experts." They whip off examples so fast that I am unable to circulate completely and make comments. No matter; they are busy sharing their ideas with each other and discussing the merits of each others' sentences. Before I can even ask for examples to display on the overhead, more than half the class has a hand in the air. I call on Sarah.

I like to play volleyball, wrestling, and to read.

We all agree that Sarah has improved the sentence by rearranging the list ("Sports should be together!"), but that the sentence itself doesn't "sound right." I point out that it lacks parallelism, explaining that items in a list need to be worded similarly. They quickly grasp the idea that "*to* play" and "*to* read" are different from "wrestl*ing*." I mention the words "participle" and "infinitive," but the students don't need labels; they recognize the difference between the two constructions and immediately understand the concept of parallelism.

Ben's group encourages him to contribute the next example:

I read, wrestle and play volleyball in my space time.

Students point out that the sentence is well worded, sounds "right," and contains the same basic ideas as the original. I also point out that Ben has changed nouns to verbs ("read" and "wrestle"). He's a magician! At this point, I collect the warm-ups to give a grade and assess the students' progress.

One problem with having students eliminate verbs of being is that sometimes they do just that: they *eliminate* them completely. Jeff writes the following sentence.

The activities I like to do volley, ball, reading, and wrestling.

To protect Jeff's self-esteem, I present a similar sentence to the group the next day, as usual, asking them to identify the verb:

The things I like to eat pizza, ice cream and candy.

Most underline "to eat" as the verb. I point out that the phrase "to eat" answers the question *What?* after the word "like." It can't be a verb; only nouns and pronouns answer the question *What?* I refer to the phrase "to eat" as an "infinitive," but only to explain in passing that some verbs masquerade as nouns. These are called "verbals." If you "like" something, that is an action, so "like" must be a verb, at least in this sentence.

I ask the students to rewrite the sentence so that it makes sense. Most put an "are" between "eat" and "pizza." When I ask them to eliminate this verb of being from the sentence, they become frustrated.

"That's impossible!"

"No way!"

"But it's not a sentence without the verb!"

Our time is up, so I quickly show the students how they can eliminate the "are" by simply crossing off the first two words. "Besides," one student comments to another, "it makes the sentence shorter and more to the point." In some cases, "The things I like to eat are . . ." is an effective construction because it places emphasis on the fact that these are the writer's favorites, but the point I'm trying to make to the students is that verbs of being can be eliminated easily, sometimes by simply ridding the sentence of "excess baggage." Besides, when students write about themselves, they are often prone to repeat sentence constructions: "The things I like to eat are . . ." "The things I like to do are . . ." "The dreams I have for the future are . . ." This repetition often bores both the reader and writer unless there is a stylistic reason for it.

Sentence-Combining

After using several canned examples from various sentence-combining authorities, I decide to use real information from my own life. My husband and I have been looking forward to an upcoming Rolling Stones concert in Lansing, which will also be an opportunity to visit our daughter, who attends Michigan State University there. I present the students with the following sentences.

> George and I are going to the Rolling Stones' concert Friday.
> We will take Jessica out to eat first.

This minilesson produces so many different responses that it turns into a maxi-lesson. It wreaks havoc with my week's lesson plan, but it is so fruitful that I have to react to the variety of my students' responses. We have a lively discussion about the differences among student-generated rewrites. Tom contributes this sentence.

George and I are going to the Rolling Stones concert, but first we must take Jessica out to eat on Friday.

We discuss the fact that this sentence implies that the concert can take place any time after Friday, and that taking Jessica out to eat is mandatory.

George, Jessica and I will go out to eat before the Rolling Stones concert Friday.

Scott's revision gives the impression that Jess is going to the concert with us. Some students miss the point that the two sentences are related and *spoken* by the same writer. They make an incorrect pronoun substitution in the second sentence, writing something similar to the following.

George and I are going to the Rolling Stones' concert, but first *they* will take Jessica out to eat.

I'm not quite sure how to handle this, but the students help me out. One points out that the reader doesn't know who "they" are; it sounds as though "they" are the Rolling Stones. And that's not who will be taking Jessica out to eat. Another proposes that if "they" is changed to "we" the sentence makes more sense, but omits the fact that the concert takes place on Friday.

Will, a student who has difficulty with written expression, contributes this sentence.

George and I are going to take Jessica out to eat before we go to the Rolling Stones concert on Friday.

The class agrees that it maintains the integrity of the original sentences, but is unclear about exactly *who* will be attending the concert. Will is impressed with his ability to play around with the wording; he doesn't think of himself as a writer and feigns disinterest in all schoolwork. The recognition and approbation of his peers does wonders for his self-esteem. He continues to involve himself in the lesson, offering opinions about other students' examples, and making changes to his own.

In the end, all feel that Kim's sentence is the best combination of the two original sentences, for precise meaning and conciseness:

Friday night, George and I will go to the Rolling Stones concert after we take Jessica out to eat.

But the entire class has been exposed to myriad examples and has discussed the pros and cons of each. And even students for whom written expression is a difficult task have been successful.

Sentence-Combining to Eliminate Verbs of Being

Quite often, attaching a sentence containing a *be* verb to the one that precedes or follows it is an easy way to eliminate the verb of being. I provide the students with the following sentences. Again, they are typical of those found in the collage paragraphs:

> My best friend is John Doe.
> He lives in Anytown.

In no time at all, they come up with two basic constructions.

> My best friend, John Doe, lives in Anytown.
> John Doe, my best friend, lives in Anytown.

I congratulate them for rewriting so quickly and for reducing an entire sentence to a phrase, an appositive, as well as getting rid of a colorless verb of being. We discuss how the placement of the words slightly affects the emphasis of the writer. In the first combined sentence the words "best friend" seem to be the more important idea, because they begin the sentence. In the second, the name seems more important for the same reason.

Often, combining sentences to eliminate a verb of being can lead students into more sophisticated phrasing, like the construction of absolutes. Consider the following sentences:

> The boy went out to play with his friends.
> His homework was finished.

Invariably, one of the students comes up with a construction containing an absolute phrase, similar to this.

> His homework finished, the boy went out to play with his friends.

This provides an opportunity to mention absolutes and praise the students for their ability to compose interesting and sophisticated sentences. They will never remember the labels I give their phrases and clauses, but that's okay. It's not important that they *learn* the grammatical terms I introduce, only that they use varied sentence structures to enliven their writing.

While the minilessons don't completely solve the problem of students' reluctance to revise, I see real growth in their attempts to work with and manipulate their words. Although few of the collage paragraphs undergo drastic changes, many students work hard to reduce their verbs of being and produce longer, more interesting sentences containing more detail. Most important, even students who lack confidence in their writing abilities find they have a power over words that they haven't realized. They are able to reduce sentences to phrases and clauses and attach them to other sentences to produce a more sophisticated piece of writing.

For the most part, this year's collage paragraphs are the best I've seen. I enjoy reading the final products, and the students proudly place them in their portfolios along with their collages.

References

SPARKS, J. (1982). *Power writing*. Los Angeles: Communication Associates.

Suggested Resources

ATWELL, N. (1987). *In the middle: Reading, writing, and learning with adolescents*. Portsmouth, NH: Boynton/Cook. Chapter 6 contains ideas for minilessons on style.

CALKINS, L. (1994). *The art of teaching writing*. Portsmouth, NH: Heinemann. The ultimate guide to teaching and learning about writing. Calkins provides numerous ideas, suggestions, and examples of how to encourage students to grow as writers.

CROWHURST, M. (1983). Sentence combining: Maintaining realistic expectations. *College Composition and Communication, 34* (1). A caveat about sentence combining: Although it may raise students' level of syntactic maturity, it doesn't necessarily contribute to overall writing improvement.

DAIKER, D., KEREK, A., & MORENBERG, M. (1985). *Sentence combining: A rhetorical perspective*. Carbondale: Southern Illinois University Press.

DAIKER, D., KEREK, A., & MORENBERG, M. (1990). *The writer's options* (4th Ed.). New York: Harper & Row. Unit 5 offers suggestions for sentence combining by constructing absolutes.

HILLOCKS, G., JR. (1986). Grammar and the manipulation of syntax. *Research on Written Composition*. Urbana, IL: ERIC/NCRE and the National Council of Teachers of English. The author's main point is that sentence combining facilitates students' writing quality by expanding their repertoire of syntactic structures.

KROGNESS, M. (1995). *Just teach me, Mrs. K.* Portsmouth, NH: Heinemann. Many case studies of the writing process at work. Concentrates on the reluctant learner.

MALMSTROM, J., & WEAVER, C. (1973). *Transgrammar: English structure, style, and dialects*. Glendale, IL: Scott, Foresman. Contains a section on expanding the basic sentence using absolutes and participles.

O'HARE, F. (1973). *Sentence combining: Improving student writing without formal grammar instruction*. Research Report no. 15. Urbana, IL: National Council of Teachers of English.

RIEF, L. (1992). *Seeking diversity*. Portsmouth, NH: Heinemann. A handbook for the middle-school language arts teacher, it picks up where Atwell left off. Includes many practical ideas and suggestions with numerous examples of student work.

SEBRANEK, P., MEYER, V., & KEMPER, D. (1995). *Write source 2000*. Wilmington, MA: Great Source. Some excellent sections on combining and styling sentences. Stresses practice and experimentation. A great handbook for the middle-school student.

SPARKS, J. (1982). *Power writing*. Los Angeles: Communication Associates. Some may argue that power writing techniques produce formulaic student writing. This is true if the writing program is based solely on Sparks's philosophy and strategies. His methods, however, provide students with a system for organizing and prioritizing their ideas, support, and details in a logical manner. It also gives content area teachers a leg up when assigning writing in their classrooms. In addition, Sparks provides lessons and examples for eliminating verbs of being and varying sentence openers.

STRONG, W. (1986). *Creative approaches to sentence combining*. Urbana, IL: ERIC/RCS and the National Council of Teachers of English. Contains sample exercises and ideas for introducing students to the concept of sentence combining.

WEAVER, C. (1993). Postscript: Sentence combining revisited. In *Language issues: Readings for teachers*. New York: Longman. Advises against unrealistic expectations from sentence-combining activities and exercises.

7 *When Grammar Matters*
Guiding Students Through Revision

RENEE CALLIES

Introduction

Formerly a high-school English teacher, Renee Callies describes the reluctance of her students to use the writing process and its stages of drafting, revising, polishing, and publishing. She explains how, during the revision stage, she used compliments and questions, either in written comments on papers or during student-teacher conferences, to address grammatical incongruities. Asking questions that delved into the meaning of their pieces, Renee describes how this successfully convinced students to ponder whether or not their point was clear. By the use of these nonthreatening compliments and questions, she gained their trust as an interested reader, not a technical authority. Finally, she shows, through student writing samples, that when she was in this role of involved reader, the students responded to her suggestions and concerns seriously and, oftentimes, enthusiastically.

Like many teachers, I bring to my teaching of writing a synthesis of the commonsense research and training of several widely respected professionals—Tom Romano, Donald Murray, and Peter Elbow. All of them recognize and espouse the importance of students learning to edit within the context of their own writing. Only then can students begin to see the significance of effective, captivating writing—the type of writing people anticipate reading. And only then, when they revise and edit their own sentences, do students see grammar as relevant.

For my high-school students, the notion of engaging readers with stories, poems, and essays is attractive, but writing more than one draft is initially a struggle, and, for some, can remain a year-long debate. Eventually, however, I hear an affirmation for the process when other teachers tell me about their students' requests to rewrite assignments. Revising teaches even the reluctant students that mistakes occur naturally in the process, and opportunities to correct those mistakes exist. Revising teaches them how to compose and how to edit. Most important, revising teaches students to value good writing, and the process of writing well.

As I guide my students through drafts of their writing, my editing techniques evolve with my successes and failures. While originally I would point out all errors, content and grammatical, I now realize that even though the students peer- and self-edit, they lack the reading experience and writing practice necessary to do this editing completely. These skills are honed over a lifetime of reading and writing. With this in mind, I choose to ask questions about content and meaning first, issues more readily apparent to their young eyes, before going on to aspects of grammar. In practical terms, why bother asking the writer to make spelling and punctuation corrections if the passage is going to change significantly?

When responding to students' writing there are three principles I follow to guide them through the editing process. Note, too, that many of these revisions should be addressed in early drafts, especially when mechanical errors create confusion. I typically comment, either verbally or by hand, as follows:

1. I compliment the writing, telling the students what they do well, always finding something to admire, even if it is simply their choice of title or topic.

2. I question the points I do not understand in their papers. These questions can address pronoun errors, as well as discrepancies in meaning. Anytime I compliment or question, I try to make my remarks specific, explicitly stating strengths or problems. I no longer put a question mark next to a confusing sentence, or "awkward" next to a poorly constructed paragraph. I tell my students what works, and what I don't understand.

3. I make a general observation about the entire piece—perhaps congratulations for taking a risk, or a word of empathy about the subject matter. Through this process, not only are issues of content and organization addressed, but also issues of grammar, and all within the context of the students' writing.

For teachers unaccustomed to guiding students through several drafts of their writing, it may be useful to see how these types of responses work in practice.

In my first reading of an elaborate short story written by Brad, a sophomore, I could not contain my excitement and expressed it at the end of his story with a compliment (see Figure 7–1). He proceeded to write the fifth, sixth, and seventh drafts, finally showing me the eighth. The changes were dramatic. He combined several short, ineffective paragraphs, recognizing that the information that belonged together would make more sense in one paragraph. In addition, he added descriptive detail to passages, elaborating on the images.

Although it was doubtful the compliment was the catalyst to Brad's editing, I believe it made him more receptive to the content questions and grammatical incongruities I noted in the margins of his piece. In his fourth draft, I identified a comma splice, indicated by the italicized sentence in the paragraph below:

> He needed a break, for he was usually pretty tired at this point. He stopped and opened up his canteen of tropical punch Kool-Aid which hung from a steel-beaded chain around his neck. *He looked at the floor below him, he could see the path through the numerous limbs and branches below him.*

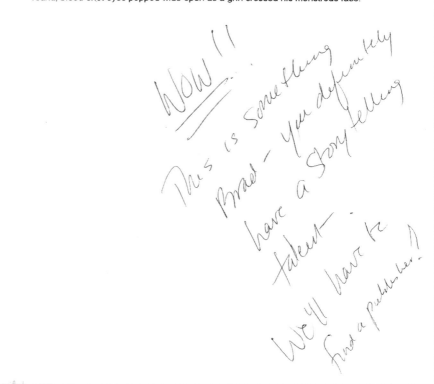

Then the pulse ceased. "Get this kid on a stretcher!" he yelled to his partner. They hauled him in, hooked him up to every machine in the truck, and sped off.

Within the ambulance, the paramedics were working on him frantically. Employing every trick they had learned over their short careers. But still, the whine of the flatline over the heart rate monitor dominated the scenario. "Give up," one finally said, "no hope for this one, just let him go. He'll never make it, even if it were for a miracle."

At that moment, a hard strong beep emitted from the monitor, and Steve's round, blood-shot eyes popped wide open as a grin crossed his monstrous face.

FIG. 7–1 *Brad's writing*

Brad, in his fifth draft, changed the first independent clause of that sentence to a participial phrase—ultimately constructing a more effective sentence:

> He needed a break, for he was usually pretty tired at this point. He stopped and opened up his canteen of tropical punch Kool-Aid which hung from a steel-beaded chain around his neck. *Looking at the floor below him, he could see the path under the cover of the numerous limbs and branches that supported him.*

I learned early, in fact, while taking a college course on the teaching of writing, that compliments like these soften any perceived blow inflicted on the esteem of a high-school writer. Tom Romano (1987) further elaborates on the necessity of *not* curbing whatever talent/instinct/motivation pushes students to write, by overemphasizing what they do wrong.

Dr. Celeste Resh (1995) not only reiterated this necessity for compliments, but also gave me a softer way of nudging my students. By asking questions about their writing—instead of pointing out errors or confusion—I successfully encouraged the students to think about what they wrote, and they, in turn, revised for meaning. Oftentimes, the students answered my questions verbally in conferences. I then suggested they add that information to their papers, because other readers would likely share my confusion.

Again, Brad, in the eighth draft of his story, wrote the paragraph below, describing a type of miraculous healing:

> He looked down and saw his wounds closing. He even felt them mending on the inside of his body. *As the pain in his ribs disappeared, two large, dark-skinned hands appeared from the air and were resting on his chest.* They raised up and wrapped their fingers around the back of Steven's skull. They then placed their thumbs over his eyelids and pressed them shut.

As a reader, I found the lack of parallelism in the italicized sentence distracting. I pointed out that the writing implied that the hands were already on the character's chest, and asked if that was what Brad wanted the reader to think. We had a quick conference in which I explained parallelism to Brad. In the next draft, he changed the line, eliminating the ambiguity:

> He looked down and saw his wounds closing. He even felt them mending on the inside of his body. *As the pain in his ribs disappeared, two large, dark-skinned hands appeared from thin air and rested upon his chest.* They raised up and wrapped their fingers around the back of Steven's skull. They then placed their thumbs over his eyelids and pressed them shut.

Specificity of comments, I soon realized, also improved the students' revisions. Oftentimes, if I wrote "unclear, reword" or "awkward sentence" on their papers, they would either leave the sentence alone, or remove it completely. Drawing attention to the specific problem by asking a question nudged the students to think about the possible responses before deciding their editing solution.

Seth, in his story about a family trip to Tennessee, showed me just how ineffective the use of the remarks "awkward" and "unclear" could be. Rather than saying specifically that I did not understand how the rings of resin related to the crack in the rocks, I just marked the area as "awkward" (see Figure 7–2). In addition, while he tried to explain what he saw in the sentence following, I wrote simply "unclear, reword."

Neither comment told him specifically his problem—the use of convoluted words and phrases he had picked up from his reading. Although he created comma

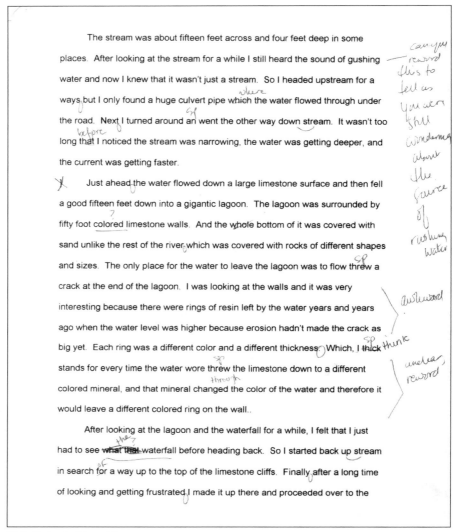

The stream was about fifteen feet across and four feet deep in some places. After looking at the stream for a while I still heard the sound of gushing water and now I knew that it wasn't just a stream. So I headed upstream for a ways but I only found a huge culvert pipe which the water flowed through under the road. Next I turned around an went the other way down stream. It wasn't too long that I noticed the stream was narrowing, the water was getting deeper, and the current was getting faster.

Just ahead the water flowed down a large limestone surface and then fell a good fifteen feet down into a gigantic lagoon. The lagoon was surrounded by fifty foot colored limestone walls. And the whole bottom of it was covered with sand unlike the rest of the river which was covered with rocks of different shapes and sizes. The only place for the water to leave the lagoon was to flow threw a crack at the end of the lagoon. I was looking at the walls and it was very interesting because there were rings of resin left by the water years and years ago when the water level was higher because erosion hadn't made the crack as big yet. Each ring was a different color and a different thickness. Which, I thick stands for every time the water wore threw the limestone down to a different colored mineral, and that mineral changed the color of the water and therefore it would leave a different colored ring on the wall..

After looking at the lagoon and the waterfall for a while, I felt that I just had to see what that waterfall before heading back. So I started back up stream in search for a way up to the top of the limestone cliffs. Finally after a long time of looking and getting frustrated I made it up there and proceeded over to the

FIG. 7–2 *Seth's writing*

splices and run-on sentences, he took risks in his writing. He tried something he knew only remotely how to accomplish, and I rewarded his effort with those few generic criticisms. His response was equally indifferent: he completely dropped the idea from the story.

I had success, however, when I made deliberate comments about the errors I saw in my students' writings. In Figure 7–3, James' first draft of his poem, "The Wind in the Highlands," he referred to the same wind by using the pronouns "they," "his," and "it." I drew his attention to this by underlining all the instances and stating my confusion. In his subsequent draft, James changed all of his pronouns

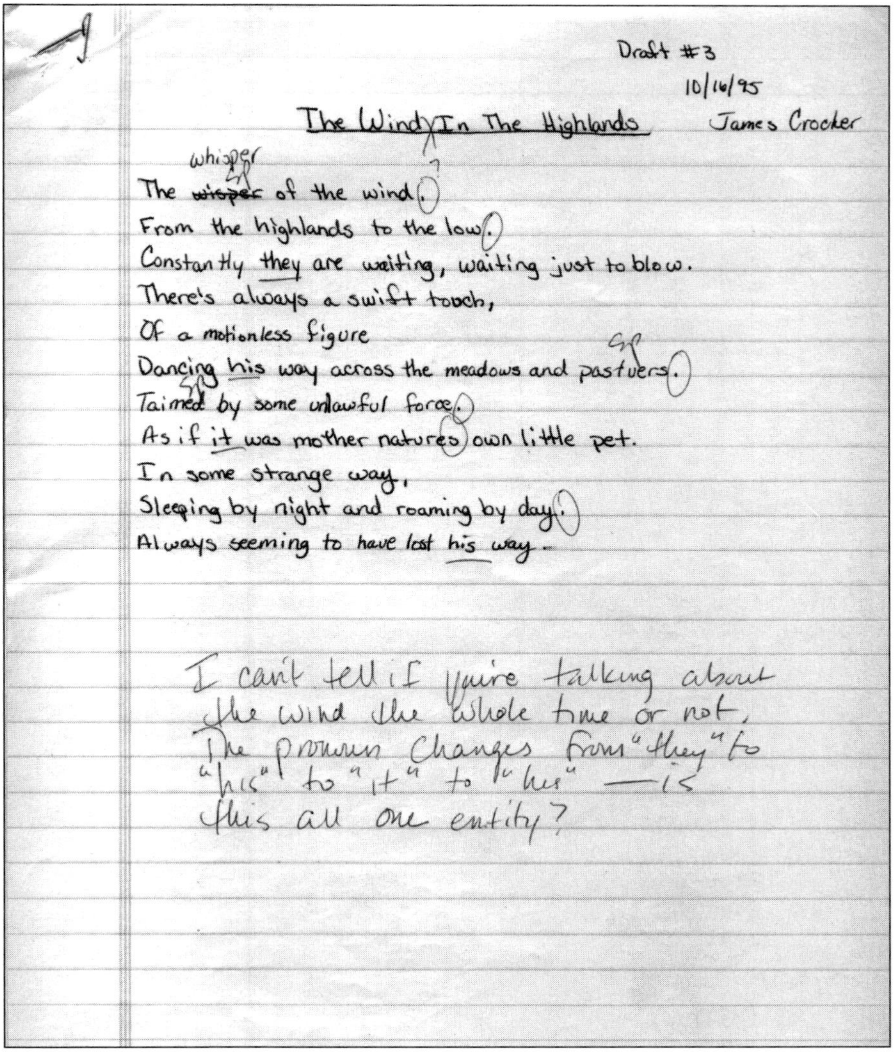

Draft #3
10/16/95

The Wind In The Highlands   James Crocker

whisper
The whisper of the wind.
From the highlands to the low.
Constantly they are waiting, waiting just to blow.
There's always a swift touch,
Of a motionless figure
Dancing his way across the meadows and pastuers.
Taimed by some unlawful force.
As if it was mother natures own little pet.
In some strange way,
Sleeping by night and roaming by day.
Always seeming to have lost his way.

I can't tell if you're talking about
the wind the whole time or not.
The pronoun changes from "they" to
"his" to "it" to "his" — is
this all one entity?

FIG. 7–3 *James' writing*

to "it." In a quick conference, we looked at his corrected draft, and I pointed out that using the pronoun "this" instead of the article "a" in line five made it clear to the reader James was talking about the same wind. He made the change in his final draft.

In addition to complimenting writers and asking questions, at the end of almost every paper I expressed my overall reaction to the piece. For a long report, my response could be extensive and detailed. For a quick piece, thrown together for credit, I still said something about its appropriateness, or about the writer's topic choice. I always started with the positive, then proceeded to the problem

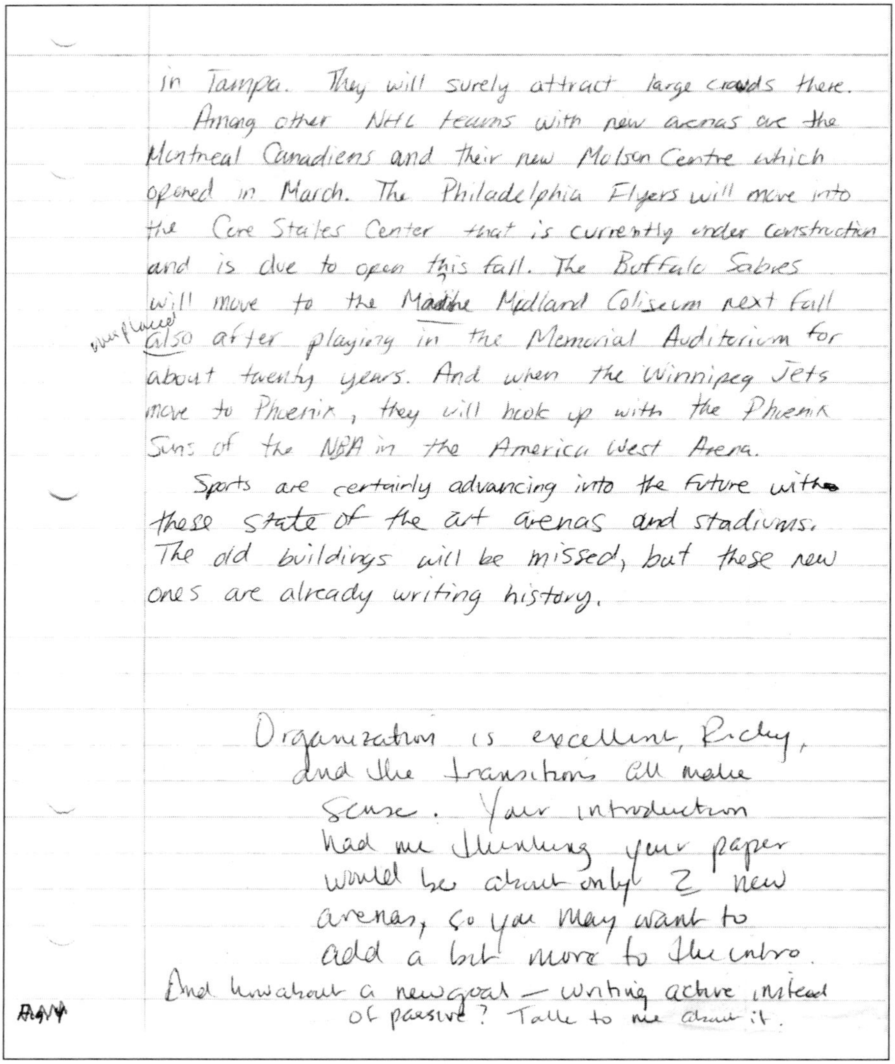

in Tampa. They will surely attract large crowds there.
Among other NHL teams with new arenas are the Montreal Canadiens and their new Molson Centre which opened in March. The Philadelphia Flyers will move into the Core States Center that is currently under construction and is due to open this fall. The Buffalo Sabres will move to the Marine Midland Coliseum next fall also after playing in the Memorial Auditorium for about twenty years. And when the Winnipeg Jets move to Phoenix, they will hook up with the Phoenix Suns of the NBA in the America West Arena.
Sports are certainly advancing into the future with these state of the art arenas and stadiums. The old buildings will be missed, but these new ones are already writing history.

Organization is excellent, Ricky, and the transitions all make sense. Your introduction had me thinking your paper would be about only 2 new arenas, so you may want to add a bit more to the intro. And how about a new goal — writing active instead of passive? Talk to me about it.

FIG. 7–4 *Ricky's writing*

areas. I quickly discovered this was the ideal area to address repetitive mechanical errors or to nudge writer experimentation.

For example, Ricky, a prolific sports writer in my class, obviously had a passion for reporting. It was easy to go beyond the basics and have him work on more advanced issues of writing. At the end of his third draft on an essay about the new arenas being built for sports teams (see Figure 7–4), I complimented him on the organization of the piece, asked a question about some confusion in the introduction, and then suggested he consider a new goal—writing using active voice

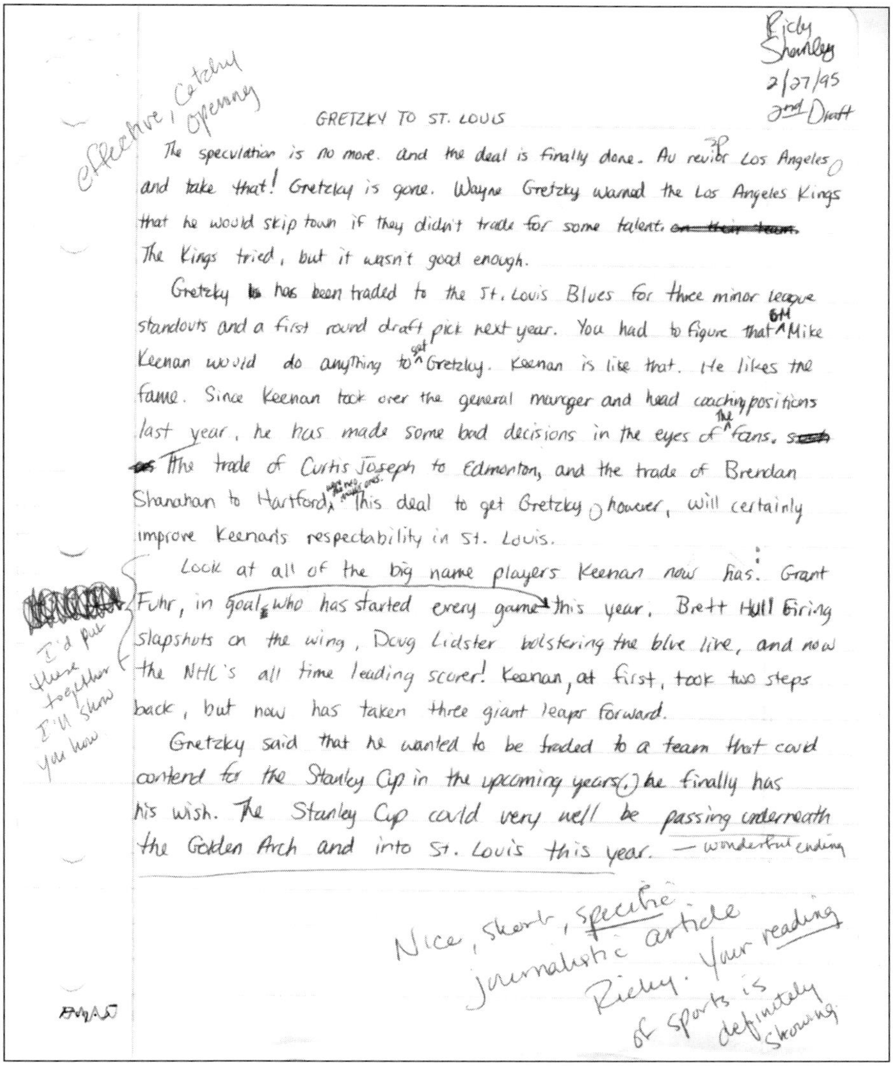

Ricky Shanley
2/27/95
2nd Draft

GRETZKY TO ST. LOUIS

effective, catchy opening

The speculation is no more. and the deal is finally done. Au revoir Los Angeles and take that! Gretzky is gone. Wayne Gretzky warned the Los Angeles Kings that he would skip town if they didn't trade for some talent. ~~on their team.~~ The Kings tried, but it wasn't good enough.

Gretzky has been traded to the St. Louis Blues for three minor league standouts and a first round draft pick next year. You had to figure that GM Mike Keenan would do anything to get Gretzky. Keenan is like that. He likes the fame. Since Keenan took over the general manger and head coaching positions last year, he has made some bad decisions in the eyes of the fans. The trade of Curtis Joseph to Edmonton, and the trade of Brendan Shanahan to Hartford. This deal to get Gretzky, however, will certainly improve Keenan's respectability in St. Louis.

Look at all of the big name players Keenan now has: Grant Fuhr, in goal, who has started every game this year, Brett Hull firing slapshots on the wing, Doug Lidster bolstering the blue line, and now the NHL's all time leading scorer! Keenan, at first, took two steps back, but now has taken three giant leaps forward.

I'd put these together I'll show you how

Gretzky said that he wanted to be traded to a team that could contend for the Stanley Cup in the upcoming years. he finally has his wish. The Stanley Cup could very well be passing underneath the Golden Arch and into St. Louis this year. — wonderful ending

Nice, short, specific journalistic article Ricky. Your reading of sports is definitely showing

FIG. 7–5 *Ricky's writing (St. Louis)*

instead of passive voice. We talked about it in a quick conference, an easy and effective way to get talented writers to stretch their capabilities. Although Ricky did not revise the arena paper for active voice, he began editing for it in subsequent writing. In a short piece on hockey player Wayne Gretzky's trade to St. Louis (see Figure 7–5), Ricky had Brett Hull "firing," and Doug Lidster "bolstering." When writers like Ricky have success with their stories, when the writing effectively grabs the reader, they become more open to trying additional approaches.

Poetry offered unique opportunities for students to take similar risks, to play with the conventions of writing. When writing poems, students viewed themselves as artists, and their fragile egos frequently materialized. Because of this, my responses to poetry had to be calculated. If I had problems fathoming the writer's message, asking questions about the meaning could be misconstrued as either an insult to his or her skill as a poet, or incompetence on my part as a reader. My frequent request to have them give their interpretation as a clarification almost always resolved this dilemma. If the students could not voice their intended message or support their message from the context of the poem, they had to revise. Requiring the students to justify the words, structure, and mechanics of their poems helped them appreciate the idea that all poets write with purpose. This also kept students who did not know how to use punctuation in poetry from simply avoiding it. If they used words, phrases, or punctuation in an unconventional manner, they had to tell me what they changed and why. They had to know the rules before they broke them.

Erin, who began writing several poems at the end of the year, also began experimenting with the structure of her poems. In a poem titled "i am," she used several images to convey a sense of waiting and anticipation (see Figure 7–6). When I asked her about her use of the lowercase "i," she explained she wanted people to read the poem and see themselves, not just the narrator. She also wanted to suggest that the character represented by "i" had not reached his/her potential, which she felt was implied with an uppercase "I." Her explanation of this nontraditional usage made me comfortable with her grammatical choice. Erin deliberately made the error to emphasize, believing it a more effective technique.

Similarly, in the poem written by Deacon, he chose to use no punctuation, and had a nonstandard verb form (see Figure 7–7). First I made a specific compliment: I liked the metaphor implicitly comparing the stars in the sky to holes in a

---

i am

i am a flower, yet to bloom.
i am a fetus, in the womb.
i am a star, yet to shine.
i am a diamond, lost in a mine.
i am a television, yet to be used.
i am a tourist, lost and confused.
i am a dress, yet to be worn.
i am a newspaper, old and torn.
i am a prize, yet to be won.
i am a prune, dried by the sun.
i am a bed, yet to be made.
i am a debt, never repaid.
i am a customer, yet to be billed.
i am wish left unfulfilled.

FIG. 7–6 *Erin's poem*

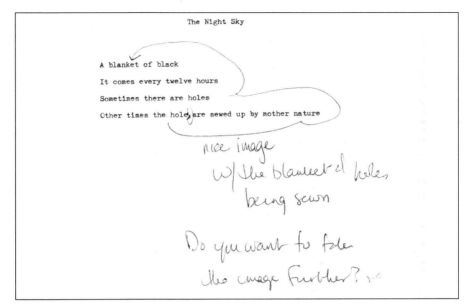

The Night Sky

A blanket of black
It comes every twelve hours
Sometimes there are holes
Other times the holes are sewed up by mother nature

nice image
w/ the blanket & holes
being sewn

Do you want to take
the image further?

FIG. 7–7 *Deacon's poem*

blanket. Later, in a conference, I addressed the use of the word "sewed" and asked him about the absence of punctuation. He admitted a lack of knowledge of the correct past participle for "sew," and changed the verb to "sewn." He wanted to omit any punctuation, however, feeling the line breaks indicated enough pause for the reader. He also explained the conventional punctuation he could have used. This indicated both a sense of artistic privilege and grammatical competence.

While my methods continue to undergo their own revisions, my tenets of specifically complimenting and questioning the writing will remain because I believe the results of those tenets reflect the thoughts of an interested reader, rather than the thoughts of a critical teacher. In trying to get students to write more and to write effectively, I do not want to discourage their efforts, nor do I want to falsely commend their skills. Teaching students to revise and edit their writing for clarification and effectiveness helps them create sentences that will reach me, and others, as readers—ultimately, the goal of any writer.

References

RESH, C. (1995). A composition class that teaches itself: Structuring an effective collaborative conversation. *Language Arts Journal of Michigan, 11* (2), 80–83.

ROMANO, T. (1987). *Clearing the way*. Portsmouth, NH: Heinemann.

8

Learning to Use Grammar with Precision Through Editing Conferences

ELLEN BRINKLEY

Introduction

From her experience with writers at many levels, Ellen Brinkley has learned that the grammar students learn "for keeps" is grammar that is taught within conversations with student writers about crafting and editing their own work. In this chapter she discusses the importance of the individually tailored teaching of editing skills that are supported by grammatical structures, rather than traditional methods of intensively teaching grammatical structures and hoping that student writers will apply what they learn to their own writing. She demonstrates the role that sharply focused editing "microlessons" can play within the writing conference setting, and explains how they can be used in conjunction with other strategies for teaching editing skills and choices.

Student writers have something worth saying that the rest of the world needs to hear. We teach writing so that students can develop their voices to express ideas and views about issues that are important to them. If we as teachers don't equip them with the skills, including editing skills, that they need to become confident writers, we as a society will miss hearing from those whose voices are silent. Editing conferences, and the sharply focused microlessons that can occur within them, help refine skills and increase students' confidence in themselves as writers. It is our responsibility, therefore, to create and use the contexts and structures—including editing conferences and precisely focused grammar instruction—that will enable our students' otherwise "submerged voices" to emerge (Macedo, 1994, p. 4).

As a teacher of writing I have learned the value of sitting with students one-to-one to listen to their writing as they read aloud, and then to confer about the work in progress and its possibilities. At Madeira High School in Cincinnati, I worked with two colleagues—Pam Murphy and D. J. Hammond—to establish an award-winning schoolwide writing center and writing assistance program that gave every English teacher the chance to confer with student writers for two class periods each day. Now as I work with preservice and practicing English language arts teachers, and as I direct the Third Coast Writing Project at Western Michigan University, I can't imagine teaching writing, or teaching teachers of writing, without writing conferences.

The Writing Conference

A writing conference is possible whenever a writer and a listener/consultant meet to have a conversation about a piece of writing or the prospect of developing one. Muriel Harris refers to such conversations as "collaborative talk" that helps students "acquire the practical information they need" (Harris, 1995, p. 34). Even first-grade students and their teachers can experience the kind of conversation and collaboration that lies at the heart of writing conferences. For example, when Vania, a first-grader, read her newly published book in a conference with her teacher, Tim O'Keefe, she read, "Once upon a time there was a cat and a dog and they saw a snake. And then the dog ate the cat and the cat ate the . . ." She paused midsentence and asked, "Mr. O'Keefe, what's that word?" In response, O'Keefe reread Vania's text aloud so that she could hear her own language and focus on the meaning, and he provided a signal that suggested the word she needed: "And then the dog ate the cat and the cat ate the /s/ . . ." (Mills, O'Keefe, & Stephens, 1992, p. 8). Through this brief exchange Vania asked for the practical help she needed to read her own writing. And her teacher provided just enough help in order for her to proceed—a way to use her intended meaning to support her skill as a writer and reader.

Writing conferences consist of natural conversations focused on an individual student writer and the writing she or he is working on. Most of us have learned from Peter Elbow, Donald Graves, Donald Murray, Lucy Calkins, and a host of others to refine our conferring strategies and to confer with students throughout the composing process (Elbow, 1973; Graves, 1994; Murray, 1985; Calkins, 1994). Frequently we introduce writing conferences early in the year, by conducting a conference with a student volunteer while the rest of the class watches. Discussion following the conference gives our students a chance to analyze what happened and to understand how writing conferences work. Students can then pair up and try out the role of writer and of listener/consultant as they discuss their own works in progress. Further debriefing discussion from time to time helps students continue to refine their conferring skills.

When I conduct demonstration conferences, I often provide a guidesheet of suggestions (such as the following) for students' reference. This conference model is designed for occasions when the writer has at least a rough draft. It can be adapted for almost any grade level and should always be offered as a *suggested* guide rather than as an assigned set of steps to be followed:

FIG. 8–1 *Suggested Process for Writing Conference*

- The writer explains or introduces the piece of writing and explains what he or she is especially wondering about or wanting response to.

- The writer reads the piece or excerpt aloud. (Alternatively, the listener can read the piece while the writer listens.)

- The listener responds by "mirroring" . . .
  — saying what she or he heard or noticed
  — telling what he or she especially liked

- The listener and writer engage in conversation, with listener . . .
  — responding to specific requests for response made before the piece was read
  — asking questions about what she or he would like to know more about
  — making suggestions or recommendations as seems appropriate
  — offering a "spark," since the most important result is for the writer to want to keep writing on this piece and/or on others.

- The writer reflects on the listener's comments and decides what action to take.

Seldom would actual conferences follow this protocol exactly. Some conferences, for example, consist of a simple checkup: "How's it going?" The response might be: "Okay, but I need more details so readers will know what happened." If instead the response is "I'm stuck," that's the signal for a more substantial conference. Often writing conferences operate serendipitously, so that a response or suggestion offered by the listener/consultant sparks an idea that takes the writer in a different, but possibly better, direction than either could have predicted.

There are many reasons teachers of writing use writing conferences:

- Conferences allow students to test their writing on a real audience and to discover new ideas as they think aloud about their writing.

- Conferences provide individualized instruction that can be tailored to an individual writer's learning style and that is always based on the writer's own needs and interests.

- Conferences help writers generate ideas, discover a direction, keep going mid-draft, rethink and revise, and edit an almost publishable piece.

- Conferences provide intervention for all students, especially for those who need it and for those who seek it.

- Conferences allow teachers and students to know each other in a personal way often not possible in whole-class activities.

- Conferences build confidence in insecure writers.

- Conferences help student writers become more articulate in describing themselves as writers and their own writing processes.

- Conferences help teachers understand the logic of students' thinking about their writing.

- Conferences help teachers recognize what student writers know already and what they still need to learn.

- Conferences help students understand the source of their difficulties with writing and recognize what they still need to learn.

- Conferences nudge students to become confident, independent writers.

Of course, students don't need to confer about every piece of writing. When a writer starts scratching out ideas on paper, she or he may decide simply to file the piece in a classroom writing folder for possible use at another time. Also, quickly written, writing-to-learn pieces usually don't need to be revised or edited, since their purpose has been served—to think on paper about a topic or idea. But for pieces that students want to revise and eventually publish (even if they're "published" in a letter mailed to a single reader), conference conversations teach students to interact with their own written text in ways that improve their writing and make them better writers.

Teaching Editing

We encourage students to delay focusing primarily on editing tasks until late in the composing process, though writers do focus on grammar and surface features throughout the writing process as they decide on syntactic arrangements of words and ideas. It's during the editing phase of the writing process, however, that grammar and *correctness* issues get more attention. It's at that point that we have a responsibility to teach enough grammar and usage to enable student writers to manipulate the language and the meaning of their own sentences and texts.

Calkins (1994) cautions that we need to teach language as a skill, not a content. For too long many of us have taught the *content* of editing; that is, we have taught rules and assigned workbook or handbook sentences to be corrected, then tested students on their understanding of, and their ability to apply, the *content* of the *rules* involved. We have taught editing as content. Teaching from a handbook, and teaching a heavy dose of grammatical terms, often hinder rather than enrich students' facility with language. We have "awk"ed, "dang"ed, and "frag"ed our students to death. Seldom do students who write a dangling modifier know what one is or how to correct it, and many of our technical explanations are what Patrick Hartwell (1985) refers to as COIK—"clear only if known" (p. 119). As we work with student writers, in most cases we can avoid falling into the COIK trap by discarding most of the technical jargon and focusing primarily on writers' choices in conveying meaning.

Students need to learn strategies that will help them to remember and address the many editing tasks that writers must face as they polish a piece of writing. Whole class editing minilessons can effectively and efficiently "add information to the class pot" to be retrieved as needed (Calkins, 1994, p. 200). A teacher can, for example, use a page from her own writing to show students how she reads through and deletes unnecessary words, demonstrating that writing has greater impact when every word works hard to convey meaning. Students can discuss and help the teacher decide which words could be cut while preserving meaning; they can then be encouraged to examine their own drafts to try tightening their own prose.

I frequently use the following "Editing = Polished Writing" (see Figure 8–2) sheet as a handout reference and reminder for student writers and for myself, as I anticipate which editing minilessons will be especially helpful.

FIG. 8–2 *Editing = Polished Writing*

Editing is

- rereading and anticipating a reader's response

- listening for precision of language

- tightening and linking

- clarifying and sharpening

- smoothing out and reordering

- listening for pace and rhythm

- creating or refining a title

- finding ways to engage and support a reader

- anticipating a critic's attention to detail

- noticing and correcting

Editing means making changes, when needed, to

- words: seeking words with the precision that will express exactly the meaning the writer intends

- length: paring away redundant words and phrases or adding telling details that extend and enrich meaning

- pacing: creating short, quickly read sentences that add emphasis or drama;

adding transitions that show relationships between ideas; slowing the pace so that the reader can make connections; or untangling long convoluted sentences

- emphasis: underlining, italicizing, boldfacing, capitalizing, or bulleting

- spelling: using computer spell-checks and dictionaries for every word the writer isn't sure about

- punctuation: selecting punctuation options to clarify and to convey the desired level of formality

- capitalization: consulting a handbook to check conventional usage

- paragraphing: indicating logical sequences and relationships between ideas

- verb tense: creating consistency for the reader's sake

- person: considering who potential readers are in order to decide how best to address them by using first, second, or third person

- grammatical constructions: noticing and correcting lack of agreement between subjects and verbs, or between pronouns and antecedents; lack of parallel phrasing; lack of complete sentences (some computer grammar checkers will help highlight these problems)

- visual presentation: deciding on font and point size, margins, graphics, spacing, and arrangement

Editing Conferences

By sitting side by side with student writers and conferring with them about their own texts we can teach editing as a skill, not as content, through individually taught minilessons. Within the conference context the writer and teacher can focus with precision on such issues as how to use a specific grammatical concept or how to correct a particular surface feature error—all based entirely on what a particular student needs to know or is ready to learn for a real purpose. We might call these sharply focused interactions "microlessons" (as suggested in Figure 8–3) rather than minilessons, since they often pinpoint a single concept or strategy based on a single student's own language and syntax.

Graves (1994) illustrates a microlesson when he discusses very brief conversations based on what the teacher notices in a particular student's writing. For example, as he talks to young writers about their work, he might say, "I see you've got that capital on the city. How did you know how to do that?" Just raising the question can generate interest in the textual feature being discussed. If the student doesn't seem able to explain the feature, the teacher can demonstrate, invit-

FIGURE 8–3 *Editing mini/microlessons*

Editing Minilesson

- brief, 5–10 minutes

- teacher explains and/or demonstrates, with little interaction

- lesson presented to whole class, group, or individual

- idea or strategy added to the "class pot," to be used as needed

- no assigned follow-up

- topic and time determined by teacher from "kid-watching"

Editing Microlesson

- brief, 1–5 minutes

- constant interaction between teacher and student

- lesson occurs within one-to-one conversation

- idea or strategy may be used in student's current text

- follow-up possible when a pattern of error is evident

- topic and time determined by student or by teacher

ing the student to "look what this can do for you" (p. 192). The conversation Graves describes might, depending on the student's response, take less than a minute. As he listens, he can learn what the writer knows and might be ready for. If he offers to teach a microlesson the writer could then decide whether and when to use the "lesson" information or strategy.

Many teachers make good classroom use of both the minilesson and the microlesson to teach editing skills as they work with whole class groups and with individual writers. Editing conferences, however, should occur only when student writers already have experience conferring about generating and revising content and ideas. Too often teachers short-circuit the writing process by moving students quickly through lockstep assignments, from first draft to editing, missing that important revision time for rethinking and organizing. Unless we teach students how to use conferences to focus primarily on content and ideas, during prewriting all the way through revision, they won't grasp the significance of the larger context in which editing issues can be addressed as they prepare writing for final publication. What we want to avoid, therefore, is emphasizing editing conferences too soon and sending the message that correctness is more important than anything else.

The Editing Conference in Action

When I teach undergraduate courses, especially those for K–12 preservice teachers of writing, I read and respond to the polished writing that's done outside class—sometimes at the end of the term in a portfolio, sometimes during the semester with individual pieces. As I read, I use Post-It notes or penciled marginal notes to comment briefly on the ideas I encounter as a reader. I usually also put a dot in the right-hand margin next to each line that contains a grammatical or writing convention error. I explain that the dots are there for students to use as a means of improving their own skills. I don't require that they do anything with the dots; they're simply there for them to learn from if they decide to. Sometimes in class we'll work in small response groups to help each other decide what the dots mean (a strategy they may want to use eventually in their own classrooms). Always I invite them to ask me about any dots they can't figure out. Typically only a few students take me up on my offer. Beth Mead, preservice elementary teacher, was one who did.

Enthusiastic and articulate in class, Beth spoke with ease and insight during our class discussions about teaching writing in elementary school. But when she received her first paper with marginal dots, she saw dots next to twelve of her first twenty-two lines of text. After class Beth made an appointment to bring in her paper for a writing conference, to see what she might do about all the errors. Although we could have focused a writing conference on content or stylistic issues, she wanted to learn why there were so many dots, what she could do to correct the errors, and how she might avoid the same errors in the future.

When I sat side by side with Beth in my office, I noticed two things about her errors: Almost all of the errors were surface feature errors, i.e., they would not have been noticed by listening to Beth read the paper aloud but would show up only when a reader read the text on the printed page; and just two or three types of errors seemed to account for the majority of dots at the ends of lines.

I asked Beth to read aloud the sentences that had marginal dots next to them to see if she could identify the error(s) that each dot signaled. She read the first sentence:

Beth: "Developing effective writing strategies for upper elementary students can be challenging, and successful."

At this point I could have jumped in to explain why the comma was unnecessary between the two predicate adjectives. Instead I waited for her to continue.

Beth: I think I know what it is [as she pointed to the comma] because I had this discussion with someone at work. I remember from having college English that when you have just two things joined together you don't have to use a comma, you can just say 'and.' That was the rule I remembered, but then at work one of the guys (and he's actually published some things) said no, you do it this way [pointing to the comma in her text]. So I started checking in everyday books and novels, and I saw it with a comma and the "and" and so I started doing it too.

Now I understood what I could only know from listening to Beth's explanation: she was following what she thought was the advice of someone who seemed to know what he was talking about, and we needed to clear up how to punctuate (or not punctuate) coordinate adjectives but also to discuss commas as they appear in items in a series and in compound sentences. Through my conversation with Beth, I could discover the logic and the intelligence in her mistakes (Shaughnessy, 1977). Only then could I use what I learned from her to decide how to focus the micro-lesson that would be most helpful.

Starting with what I thought was easiest, we talked about how many items there were—in this case two, not three. In less than a minute I discovered that Beth already knew how to punctuate three items in a series and that most compound sentences linked with "and" have a comma following the first independent clause. From there, we could address the compound predicate adjective—a grammatical label I did not use or explain:

Ellen: In your sentence you say that "Developing . . . strategies" can be two things— "challenging" and "successful." Both of those words describe "developing . . . strategies." You have two things, not three . . . so the comma isn't needed.

After this brief exchange, Beth continued to read lines from her text and soon discovered on her own another error based on number of items—though in this case she had used two objects of a single preposition:

Beth: "Writing is a journey"—see, there it is again—"filled with discovery, and adventure."
Ellen: Right, good.
Beth: So my old rule I remembered was right.

At this point Beth had corrected her confusion about using a comma between coordinate elements, and she had confirmed that her "old rule" still worked. Eventually she encountered the same problem in a much longer sentence, and she got sidetracked as she read aloud, guessing at other possible errors but missing the misplaced comma. I was there, however, to point to the phrase in question, and she quickly spotted the error and corrected it, thereby reinforcing our earlier conversation. Later, she read and corrected another instance of punctuating two coordinate elements, in this case a compound predicate, without my assistance:

Beth: "This simple technique helps to maintain control in the classroom, and facilitates trust." See, here we go again.

We shifted to a slightly different microlesson when we looked at sentences that had commas and periods inappropriately placed outside quotation marks. That discussion led Beth to ask about the placement of parentheses in conjunction with periods, which led eventually to this response:

Ellen: There is one thing I want to caution you about. I said that commas and periods almost always go inside quotation marks. But the "rules" change if you've got punctuation marks that are taller. For instance, if you've got a semicolon or an exclamation mark, a question mark, or a colon, sometimes they're *outside* the quotes rather than inside. This is something you'll probably want to look up to be sure. For now, just keep in mind that it's those little tiny things that are right on the line that go inside because they look so strange when they're sitting out there by themselves.

This microlesson commentary doesn't sound like grammar handbook language, but the first priority of conversation within an editing conference is to find practical ways to help students increase their skill and their confidence as editors of their own writing. In this case, I was able to turn the official teacher language of the handbooks into student language (Harris, 1995), and Beth could use my "taller" and "tiny" labels as a visual mnemonic strategy to remember the appropriate punctuation sequence for most commas and periods. Rather than bewilder her by discussing the conventional usage of each of the other marks of punctuation, I reminded her to check her handbook, which she could use simply as a reference tool to provide insight into conventions of mechanics and usage, which Hillocks and Smith suggest is the more appropriate use of such texts rather than as a "course of study" (1991, p. 600).

Beth and I focused on one other microlesson about commas:

Beth: "It is important to establish classroom boundaries with consequences, which all students understand."

I asked Beth to talk about her meaning—about what she meant by "consequences" and what she meant when she said that all students would understand. Once I understood her intended meaning, I could explain the effect of her comma:

Ellen: If you put a comma after "consequences," it's almost like saying the rest of the sentence is kind of incidental. It's like saying, what's really important comes first: "It is important to establish boundaries with consequences." Oh, and by the way, "which all students understand." I think instead I hear you saying that the consequences need to be ones that all students understand.
Beth: Yeah. Exactly.

Beth could learn from our highly focused conversation the difference in *meaning* that commas can make. She learned it as we worked together—teacher and student writer—with her own text and meaning. I didn't mention restrictive and nonrestrictive clauses, though I might have if she'd been interested and if our conference had focused only on this one microlesson.

Although we might have talked at length about the content and ideas in Beth's paper, on this occasion we talked about meaning only as it influenced—or was influenced by—the surface features. Mina Shaughnessy (1977) insists that when students want to learn about grammar and conventions, they express a "healthy desire to control language" (p. 11). That's what Beth wanted at that moment. This conference helped her to use meaning as well as conventions to make comma decisions, and it helped her to understand what she still needed to work on.

In retrospect, I think by tackling three separate issues, we may have tried to do too much for one editing conference session. The biggest danger with editing conferences is that if we do too much we end up exacerbating the student's confusion. On the other hand, when I typed up the transcript of the conference session, I worried a bit that the microlessons might not have been thorough enough to make them stick. But I take heart in knowing that Beth will have other occasions to build on our session. She can't learn it all from me. One conference isn't enough, but conference microlessons add grammatical and surface feature skills that help students like Beth to become more confident as writers.

Other Structures for Teaching Editing

Most teachers can't depend entirely on editing conferences, minilessons, or microlessons. Many teachers also use editing checklists as a way to teach students to reflect on their writing and to self-edit. Figure 8–4, a "Checklist for Self-Editing," shows a sample sheet used for elementary intermediate grades.

FIGURE 8–4 *Checklist for Self-Editing*

Author: _____ Date: _____

Title: _____

____ 1. Read your piece.

____ 2. Does it have complete sentences?
   • Add words or rewrite each incomplete sentence so it will be complete.

____ 3. Does your piece make sense?
   • Rewrite any sentences you want to make clearer.

____ 4. Circle all the words that may be misspelled.
   • Try writing out the word different ways to see if one spelling looks correct.

- Check the words in a dictionary.
- Find the word in the room or in a book.
- Ask a friend to help.
- Ask me if you still need help.

___ 5. Underline all words that begin with capital letters.
  - Be sure to use a capital letter for the first letter in each sentence.
  - Are all the other underlined words proper nouns?

___ 6. Put a box around all punctuation.

. Period	, Comma
? Question mark	! Exclamation mark
" " Quotation marks	

  - Revise punctuation when needed.

___ 7. Have a writing conference with a friend.
  Name:_____

Such a sheet should only be used after students have learned strategies for revising their writing, i.e., to reflect on and reconsider the content and organization of the writing. Once students have learned through revision conferences and writing response groups to see the possibilities of their own and others' texts in progress, and once they have a text that's important enough to want to "publish," then students are ready to edit. And that's when such checklists can be useful as a first step in attending to editing tasks.

Another first step to editing is to use or adapt the dot-in-the-margin system described earlier. Teachers, especially secondary teachers who work with great quantities of student writing, can simplify their editing response task by putting marginal dots on selected student texts. I prefer this practice for the following reasons: It takes little time to "dot" lines with errors; it produces relatively little defacement of students' papers; it gives some (albeit minimal) indication where errors exist; and it requires that students look more closely at their own texts at the sentence level to determine what's needed. I ask preservice teachers to find and correct (on their papers, by hand, in color) the errors to drive home the point that they as classroom teachers will need to have flawless editorial skills if they want to have any credibility among parents. (Indeed, elementary teachers who advocate students' use of invented spelling, i.e., temporary phonetic spelling, and secondary teachers who advocate teaching targeted grammar lessons in context, get little respect and support from parents if they send home notes with misspelled words and usage errors.)

Another structure used to teach editing skills is *Daily Oral Language* (Vail & Papenfuss, 1989–1990), a publisher-produced set of lessons that are easy to use and provide a focused minilesson on a particular editing or usage topic. DOL lessons, however, use isolated sentences taken out of context, and they have relevance only when and if they're applied to students' own writing or speaking. On the other hand, writing microlessons taught in an editing conference always occur within the context of a particular student's composed text and allow the writer to use the intended meaning to make choices about sentence structure and conventions. Some teachers whose curriculum includes DOL have found ways to modify the daily lessons, such as basing the lesson on sentences from students' writing or asking students after the lesson to search their own drafts for places where the targeted correction might be needed.

In many classrooms teachers also encourage peer editing, although some teachers unfortunately seem to use the expression "peer editing" to refer to any response to writing, with the result that students don't learn to rethink the bigger questions about meaning that get addressed during revision. Careful use of terms will help students better understand both the revision and editing processes. We must remind ourselves that peer editing is for editing.

As students use what they learn in editing minilessons in their own writing, they can conduct peer editing conferences with each other, noticing errors and discussing possible corrections. Some students will be better editors than others, but many students can intuitively rely on what "sounds right" to sense when something is wrong and can encourage each other to try something else to see if it works. Peer editing conferences work effectively as a part of first-step editing within blocks of time in the classroom devoted to writing workshop. Using peer editing as a first step can take care of many editing questions and allow teachers, whose time to spend with any individual student is limited, to use their knowledge, experience, and skill to become the final arbiter of editing questions and to conduct final editing conferences with students who especially need them.

When such an arrangement becomes an established part of the classroom writing workshop, the teacher's conferencing role might change during the year. For example, in the beginning of the year teacher-student conferences might focus more on prewriting strategies and helping reluctant writers generate ideas. The conference focus will shift to "keep going" strategies for students who struggle to push through to the end of a draft. Eventually conferences will focus more on responding to drafts and teaching revision strategies, and finally conferences will begin to address editing issues. Throughout the year the teacher will teach and value the entire writing process by conferring with students about each part. But as students become more adept at responding to their peers' content and ideas, teachers can often devote more time to editing microlesson conferences.

The Value of Conferring with the Teacher

An ideal program for teaching editing combines whole class minilessons, individual self-edit strategies, peer editing, and teacher-student editing conferences—all within a classroom writing workshop context. Teacher-student writing conferences are the most difficult part of the program to carry out because of the time they take, but they're probably also the most important.

Kathy Edlefson, fifth-grade teacher at Washington Elementary School (Kalamazoo, Michigan), used an end-of-year survey to ask her students about what helped them learn to be better writers. When she asked about teacher-student conferences ("How has teacher conferencing helped you as a writer?"), her students told her that they especially valued the chance to learn from her:

Juanita: It helped because if there was something a peer did not tell me then the teacher will tell me.
Kim Dang: She helped me with errors and plus, they have been living long enough to know about Writer's Workshop.
Ashley: She has helped me by hearing the things I may say wrong. She can hear something I might not have noticed.

Another survey question asked, "If you could only choose one method of response to your writing, which would you prefer: peer response, teacher conferencing, or response groups? Explain your answer." Some of the fifth-graders said response groups "because you get more opinions" and "because it gives me more ideas of my stories, how it goes, and what needs changing." Others chose the teacher conference:

Dawn: She knows more about the writing of stories.
Doniel: I like it when my teacher is proud of me. It makes me feel good, for an example, my basketball story.
Juanita: I chose the teacher because when I conference with peers something that I need to know could be left out.
Andrew: It's more fun . . . she is the teacher and she knows more about stuff.

Kathy worried that some students seemed to think of the peer conferences and the teacher conferences as "fix-it sessions," but clearly these fifth-graders understood that their teacher could provide some help better than anyone else. It's interesting to notice that they don't as a group seem to regard Kathy's *response* as more valuable, perhaps because they know who their audience is—peers usually—and they seek response from them. They seem convinced, however, that the teacher is the more knowledgeable, preferred consultant for editing issues.

A national survey of exemplary elementary and secondary teachers confirms Kathy's survey responses. Teachers reported that writing conferences were the only type of feedback that teachers consistently agreed was helpful, and students reported that talking to their teachers was the best technique for helping them write (Freedman et al., 1985, cited by Harris, 1986, p. 3). Many teachers who have read *The Art of Teaching Writing* (1994) are impressed by Calkins's description of the value of her writing conferences with Pulitzer Prize winner Donald Murray. These conferences were so important to her growth as a writer that she drove two-and-a-half hours each way for a conference that lasted just fifteen minutes (p. 15).

Those who conduct writing conferences need to be persons who have experience with writing, who know how to use time efficiently, who understand what to look for, and who can offer strategies to overcome problems (Reigstad & McAndrew, 1984). My editing conference with Beth was grounded in my own knowledge of grammatical constructions and writing conventions. Years of conferring with student writers have taught me that classroom teachers can't teach editing skills through editing conferences and through teacher-created minilessons *unless* they know what they're talking about, i.e., unless they possess a firm grammatical knowledge base to ground their minilessons and conference conversations. This is not to say that classroom teachers need to *teach* all or most of what they know about grammar and editing but rather that they need to *know* it to be able to teach it skillfully. I'm convinced that the only way I could explain what Beth needed to know— without getting lost in a tangle of jargon that might actually prevent her from learning—was to know it myself so well that I could articulate the concepts involved in language she could understand. She came wanting to understand the "rules" better. What I did was to try to explain the concepts based on her own writing.

Encouraging Skillful Writing and Confident Writers

All of the discussion about conferences is based on the belief that conferring helps students become more independent as writers. As they learn from their own and their classmates' emerging texts, and as they learn to be articulate in describing their own work and the work of others, they internalize the conversations about writing. They learn how to advise themselves about their own texts, as a seven-year-old student did when she explained to her teacher that she was "pretend-sharing" about her writing, that is, she was anticipating the questions her peers would ask her about her writing and thinking through how she might answer their questions (Calkins, 1994, p. 221).

Some student writers may not immediately welcome the responsibility of making their own decisions about their writing. From a teacher's perspective it might "seem easier and faster for both teacher and student if we just tell them what their papers should say, and how they should change them" (Calabrese, 1991, p. 13). But if we want students to control their writing, we must be willing to teach the editing strategies and the grammatical concepts they need to gain that control. Surely the editing conference is a more effective way to teach students editing skills than the old ways of writing all over students' papers or correcting their errors for them. Such schemes may have sharpened teachers' editing skills, but they have crippled student writers by keeping them dependent on an external editor.

Individual editing conferences can be the most efficient use of a teacher's time and a student's time, since they can focus precisely on a particular skill without having to explain more than the student needs to know. Many teachers complain, however, that they don't have enough time to conduct individual conferences with students. If they're expected to teach 150 student writers a day, they're right to complain. Given the limits on in-class time, there's no way to do justice to the needs of individual writers. For this reason, secondary schools are establishing school-wide writing centers to make writing conferences available to more students more of the time. The writing center provides two crucial elements that make more writing conferences possible: a time and a place to confer. Thus they make all the benefits of writing conferences more available to more student writers. All of the reasons for using writing conferences cited earlier in this chapter provide a rationale for a school-wide writing center.

Those of us who've been fortunate enough to work day by day with individual student writers have learned from experience the value of one-to-one attention during the composing process. We've witnessed the difference that writing intervention can make. And we've appreciated the thanks offered by serious writers who welcome honest feedback and critique. If we believe that students need to be able to express their ideas well, and if we believe editing skills are important in presenting those ideas, we'll reject the skills-in-isolation assignments that have silenced too many student writers for too long (Christensen, 1994). Instead, we'll provide the editing conference context and the precision teaching needed to produce skillful writing and confident writers.

References

CALABRESE, M. (1991). Will you proofread my paper? Responding to student writing in the writing center. *Writing Lab Newsletter, 15* (5), 12–15.

CALKINS, L. (1994). *The art of teaching writing.* Portsmouth, NH: Heinemann.

CHRISTENSEN, L. (1994). Whose standard? Teaching standard English. In B. Bigelow, L. Christensen, S. Karp, B. Miner, & B. Peterson. *Rethinking our classrooms: Teaching for equity and justice* (pp. 142–145). Milwaukee: Rethinking Schools.

EDLEFSON, K. (1996). *The writing conference.* Unpublished manuscript, Western Michigan University, Kalamazoo.

ELBOW, P. (1973). *Writing without teachers.* New York: Oxford University Press.

FREEDMAN, S., ET AL. (1985). *The role of response in the acquisition of written language.* Final Report to the National Institute of Education, NIE-G-083-0065.

GRAVES, D. (1994). *A fresh look at writing.* Portsmouth, NH: Heinemann.

HARRIS, M. (1986). *Teaching one-to-one: The writing conference.* Urbana, IL: National Council of Teachers of English.

HARRIS, M. (1995). Talking in the middle: Why writers need writing tutors. *College English, 57* (1), 27–42.

HARTWELL, P. (1985). Grammar, grammars, and the teaching of grammar. *College English, 47* (2), 105–127.

HILLOCKS, G., JR., & SMITH, M. (1991). Grammar and usage. In J. Flood, *Handbook of research on teaching the English language arts* (pp. 591–603). New York: The Free Press.

MACEDO, D. (1994). *Literacies of power: What Americans are not allowed to know.* Boulder, CO: Westview Press.

MILLS, H., O'KEEFE, T., & STEPHENS, D. (1992). *Looking closely: Exploring the role of phonics in one whole language classroom.* Urbana, IL: National Council of Teachers of English.

MURRAY, D. (1985). *A writer teaches writing.* (2nd Ed.). Boston: Houghton Mifflin.

SHAUGHNESSY, M. (1977). *Errors and expectations: A guide for the teacher of basic writing.* New York: Oxford University Press.

REIGSTAD, T., & MCANDREW, D. (1984). *Training tutors for writing conferences.* Urbana, IL: ERIC Clearinghouse on Reading and Communication Skills and the National Council of Teachers of English.

VAIL, N., & PAPENFUSS, J. (1989–1990). *Daily oral language: Levels 1–12.* Evanston, IL: McDougal Littell.

9

Developing Correctness in Student Writing
Alternatives to the Error Hunt

LOIS MATZ ROSEN

Introduction

The following article by Lois Matz Rosen presents a compilation of specific strategies for helping students learn the mechanical/grammatical skills of writing and produce more fully polished final drafts.

Lois first became interested in this aspect of teaching writing when she was engaged in a research study analyzing the comments teachers made on students' papers. The teachers in her study were spending inordinate amounts of time and effort marking mechanical/grammatical errors on students' papers with little evidence that this process led to more correct writing in future papers. These findings led her to seek alternative methods teachers could use to help students become more correct writers. In this chapter, Lois describes the results of her case study of six secondary writing teachers and then explores both theory and practice in avoiding the "error hunt," while at the same time helping students become proficient at the mechanical/grammatical skills of writing. Strongly advocating a process approach to writing instruction at all levels, she outlines numerous methods for teaching correctness as an integral part of a rich classroom reading and writing environment, in which students are continuously engaged in writing, revising, and sharing their pieces.

"Developing Correctness in Student Writing" was first published in *English Journal* (1987, March) as both a research report and a methods summary for recommended practice in dealing with the mechanical and grammatical skills of writing. It has since been reprinted in two edited volumes for teachers and used in numerous English methods courses for prospective teachers. Inasmuch as the article was first published ten years ago, when Connie Weaver asked for permission to reprint it in this volume, I felt a need to update it, adding recent research and methods, making some changes I'd wanted to make since the day of its publication. This presented a unique opportunity not often offered a writer: to revise a published article.

My recent search into the articles and books of the past decade revealed several new developments in the area of teaching "correctness" in writing. For one thing, I did most of my present search in front of a computer screen, using ERIC databases, the Wilson index, the World Wide Web, and numerous other computer databases that hadn't existed just a decade previously, when I'd meticulously hand-searched the bound volumes of ERIC indexes and hunted through the yearly indexes of a dozen or more education journals. This explosion of computers at home and in the classroom adds a new dimension to our work with students' writing skills. Research studies have proliferated, trying to document the relationship between students' writing, revising, and proofreading skills and the use of computers with word processors and spelling and grammar checkers. The mixed impact of computers on students' mechanical/grammatical skills is discussed in the revised article below.

At the time when I researched and wrote the original version—the mid-1980s—the movement toward teaching writing as a process and mechanical/grammatical skills as part of that process was just beginning to spread and appeared to be better accepted in elementary classrooms than in secondary classrooms. As a result, most of the techniques I presented in 1987 came from writing teachers and theorists who worked at the elementary level. One of the first things I realized in updating this article was that attention to teaching mechanics and grammar within the process of writing and revising was now given prominent attention at the secondary level. For example, in *English Journal*, the EJ Focus for October 1987 was "Grammar and Beyond"; the EJ Exchange for December 1988 was "Going by the Rules: Conventions of Written English"; another EJ Focus in February 1993 was entitled "Polishing, Proofreading, Publishing"; an EJ Exchange on "The Great Grammar Debate Once Again—with a Twist" was published in September 1993; and, most recently, the November 1996 issue devoted the entire journal—twenty articles—to "The Great Debate (Again): Teaching Grammar and Usage." Of course, the whole issue of teaching grammar, usage, and mechanical skills in writing has always been a primary concern for secondary teachers—the Great Grammar Controversy is still going strong. And not all of the articles from *English Journal* support teaching mechanical/grammatical skills as part of the writing process. However, articles written within the last ten years are more likely to reflect the principles and approaches described throughout this volume than pieces written earlier. Many of the strategies I outlined in 1987 are now actively used in classrooms K–12, while secondary teachers have added their own approaches to correctness, described in the following revision.

Finally, an unexpected controversy was introduced with publication of Lisa Delpit's articles questioning the efficacy of the process approach for students who speak a nonmainstream dialect (1986, 1988). This, too, merits consideration, given the ever-growing linguistic, racial, and ethnic diversity that now characterizes so many English language arts classrooms throughout the United States.

Although no new research either proving or disproving these approaches to mechanical and grammatical correctness in writing has been done in recent years, as more and more teachers adopt writing process strategies into their classes, teaching correctness in the context of the students' own writing becomes more wide-spread. The updated article below confronts this lack of recent substantive research, making recommendations for the future.

Developing Correctness in Student Writing, 1987–1997

> I don't understand why good students leave out possessives when I've taught it, reinforced it, quizzed it. . . . Yet even after all this, there are those errors in the title, in the very first sentence!

> Do I read a paper and ignore all punctuation? What good is that for them?

> I put 5X on their papers and they have to write it over five times. It's so stupid, obviously. But I can't reinforce this by doing nothing.

> We spend hours at night with papers. It's not fun after a while and it gets to you. . . . I'm not sure the students get as much from it as the time I spend on it.

These comments by high-school English teachers discussing the process of marking student papers reflect the dissatisfaction and frustration of many teachers over the problem of dealing with errors in student writing—the obvious mistakes in spelling, punctuation, capitalization, grammar, and usage that often pepper student papers and refuse to disappear despite the teacher's most diligent attention. Traditionally, teachers have worked to eradicate error in two ways: by teaching mechanical and grammatical correctness through drill exercises in grammar/usage texts, and by pointing out all errors when marking student papers, perhaps also expecting students to make corrections when papers are returned. Although numerous research studies show that there is little or no transfer of learning from isolated drills to actual writing experiences and that the time-intensive practice of the teacher's "error hunt" does not produce more mechanically perfect papers, this 100-year-old tradition still persists. (See Braddock et al., 1963; Haynes, 1978; Rosen, 1983, for discussion of research in this area.) The presence of grammar/usage texts in almost any language arts classroom attests to this approach to correctness, as do the results of several recent studies into teachers' marking procedures.

The Error Hunt

Harris (1977) found that 66 percent of the corrections and annotations the high-school teachers in her study made on student papers were on mechanics and usage. Searle and Dillon's study (1980) of the commenting done by nine teachers in grades four through six revealed that teachers in their study tried to correct all errors in spelling, usage, and punctuation, which led to a heavy emphasis on what the researchers characterized as "Form-Correction Response" (p. 239). Applebee's 1981 study, *Writing in the Secondary School: English and the Content Areas,* reflects the same pattern:

> The major vehicle for writing instruction, in all subject areas, was the teacher's comments and corrections of completed work. Errors in writing mechanics were the most common focus of these responses; comments concerned with the ideas the student was expressing were the least frequently reported. (pp. 90–91)

A study I completed in 1983 of patterns in responses by the high school English teachers quoted at the opening of this article showed similar results. Almost 50 percent of their combined responses (defined as any type of written feedback to the student including underlinings, symbols, phrases, corrections, suggestions, and comments) on their students' papers focused on mechanical and grammatical errors. Each of the six teachers in my study had a specific approach to dealing with errors on student papers.

One teacher admitted that she tried to find and mark 100 percent of the mistakes "because parents like it." This technique, coupled with her strong belief that students needed lots of feedback on their ideas, led to papers that averaged eight responses per page and often resulted in a returned paper so full of marks and remarks that it seems likely a student would have difficulty figuring out what was worth attending to. Another teacher concentrated on two or three types of errors for each writing assignment, told the students when making the assignment which ones she would look for, and then tried to find 100 percent of these errors on each paper. This technique cut down on the time she spent marking papers, but she was not encouraged by any rapid improvement in correctness. A third teacher put a minus (–) sign in the margin beside each line that had an error in it in the belief that this was less punitive to students than pointing out the actual mistake. Because she worked with basic writers whose skills in this area were low, 90 percent of her responses on student papers were these minus signs. When papers were returned, a full class period was spent with students identifying and correcting their errors. Combine her marking emphasis with class time on error correction, and one can see the strong focus on correctness that this method produced: a silent message to these basic writers about the importance of avoiding error when one writes.

Symbols to ease the marking burden were used by all the teachers in my study: the standard "awks" and "frags," but idiosyncratic ones as well, such as one teacher's "T E" for a "target error" that had to be "terminated" by the end of the year. Only one of the teachers in my study told me he preferred to dismiss the problem as one that would take care of itself. "I mark the errors that bother me when I see them; it's not much of a problem," he said. The other teachers, however, seemed to support the statement quoted earlier: "I just can't reinforce this by doing nothing."

The problem writing teachers face when dealing with mechanical/grammatical error in student writing is a more complex one than simply deciding whether or not to ignore it. The visual signposts, the surface features and grammatical structures of English that readers expect, are certainly an important part of any written communication. Numerous surface errors *do* distract the reader, and we are all aware that society places great value on correctness as an indication of writing ability. Nevertheless, anyone who has read through a perfectly correct but perfectly empty student paper can verify the primary importance of *what* the student says regardless of how correctly it is stated. The dilemma, then, becomes one of balance and proportion in the writing program. Namely, *how does a teacher focus on content in student writing and still ensure that progress is also being made toward mastery of the mechanical and grammatical structures of written English?*

Recent research and theory in writing instruction suggests that this dilemma can be resolved by abandoning the traditional approach to error outlined above and working with other methods that are proving to be highly effective in helping students at all levels develop competence in the mechanical/grammatical aspects of writing. Before I discuss these new approaches to correctness, let me first present several key assumptions about the nature of the composing process and the way it is learned that provide the underlying rationale for the methods that follow.

Underlying Assumptions

Writing is a complex process, recursive rather than linear in nature, involving thinking, planning, discovering what to say, drafting, and redrafting. Writers who worry about mechanics while they are composing are not concentrating fully on what they have to say because it is difficult to do two things well at the same time, especially if neither task is yet completely under the writer's control. Therefore, any attention to correctness should be saved for *postwriting*—the final proofreading and polishing stages of a finished piece. Students should be told this, and teachers should not contradict this message by commenting on errors in early drafts, journals, or free writing unless they seriously interfere with meaning.

Learning to use the correct mechanical and grammatical forms of written language is a developmental process and as such is slow, unique to each child, and does not progress in an even uphill pattern. Weaver (1982) argues that "semantic and syntactic growth are normally accompanied by errors in language use" (p. 443). She demonstrates by tracing changing patterns in the kinds of sentence fragments students make from first through sixth grade. As the young writers in her study worked to express increasingly more complex ideas and to use more sophisticated sentence constructions, the kinds of fragments predominant in early grades disappeared, only to be replaced by others. First-graders, for example, produced numerous fragments that were explanatory clauses beginning with *because:*

I want a car. *because* I'm old enouf.

By sixth grade, types of fragments had blossomed to include a wide variety of subordinate clauses:

> Finally one day *when the machine spanked a kid, Billy.* Billy turned around and hit the machine.

> I would like to have a raffle. *So we can have some money for a special pro. in our room like roller-skating, skying* [skiing] *ice skating*

When students struggle to learn new skills such as using dialogue or writing a persuasive essay, they need time to master the unfamiliar aspects of mechanics and grammar that accompany them. To quote Weaver, "growth and error go hand in hand" (p. 443), which suggests that writing teachers must have a certain tolerance for error, accepting it as a normal part of writing growth.

The mechanical and grammatical skills of writing are learned when a writer needs to use them for real purposes to produce writing that communicates a message he or she wants someone else to receive. A piece of writing should not be seen as a test of the student's ability, or lack of it, to produce perfect prose, but rather as a chance for a developing writer to use all his or her present language capabilities to their fullest extent in producing a genuine written communication.

Responsibility for the correctness of any given piece of writing should fall mainly on the student, not the teacher. Students learn to become accurate and self-sufficient writers by searching for, finding, and correcting their own mistakes. They may fail to achieve perfection; they may miss many errors, in fact, but in the end they learn much more from identifying and correcting whatever errors they can find on their own papers and those of their peers than from the teacher's painstaking proofreading which may identify errors they don't understand or, worse yet, focus their attention on correctness instead of content. Copyediting is one of the skills a competent writer must learn, and it is never too early to start teaching independence in this area.

Students learn to write by writing, and they learn to control the mechanical and grammatical elements of written English by writing, revising, and proofreading their own work—with some help or direction from the teacher when necessary. They do not learn to write correctly by studying about writing or doing isolated workbook exercises unrelated to their own writing. In *The Art of Teaching Writing*, Calkins (1986) urges teachers to trust the "incidental learning" that takes place when students are actively and frequently engaged in writing (p. 199). They begin to read like writers and to view the world with a writer's eyes, not only for language and ideas but for the surface features of writing as well.

Methods

The following approach to correctness, culled from the work of such master-teachers as Donald Graves, Lucy Calkins, Ronald Cramer, Mina Shaughnessy, or experimented with in my own work with developing writers, views correctness within a larger framework that puts composing at the center of writing instruction. It also changes the teacher's role from drill sergeant/error hunter to coach/helper. If there is a common theme running through the methods below, it is that *revision is the key* to helping students master the mechanical and grammatical aspects of writing. When students view early drafts of their work as fluid, rather than fixed, they are free to concentrate on what they wish to say. Aspects of correctness can then be saved for final drafts with specific points of grammar and mechanics taught when necessary as students compose and revise their own writing. The techniques described below encourage students to work independently on correctness, show them how to become competent proofreaders, and at the same time suggest ways for a teacher to deal with the mechanical problems that appear on student papers. Although several of these methods were originally designed for elementary students, they are equally effective with secondary level and college students.

Let Students Write

The most important technique a teacher can use to guide students toward mechanically and grammatically correct writing is also the simplest: let them write. Let them write daily if possible and provide opportunities for them to experiment with all kinds of whole discourse from journals, letters, and personal essays to poems, short stories, and analytical prose. Mina Shaughnessy's (1977) work with adult basic writers at the City University of New York led her to observe that the single most important characteristic of these students was their lack of writing experience. She writes, "the basic writing student is . . . likely to have written 350 words a semester. It would not be unusual for him to have written nothing at all" (p. 14).

Let Students Read

A classroom environment rich with reading materials supports writing development, with frequent exposure to the language of written discourse and the patterns of Standard English. Students who grew up in households where "I seen" and "He has went" are acceptable forms of speech need to hear, see, and read standard forms of written English in the literature and nonfiction of the classroom. In the act of reading, even with the student's major emphasis on meaning-making, the mechanics of punctuation, spelling, capitalization, as well as standard forms of grammar and usage are visually present. Over time, these become absorbed as part of the student's linguistic knowledge. In a landmark study by Connors and Lunsford (1988) analyzing types and frequency of errors on college students' freshman composition papers, the researchers found such a preponderance of spelling errors they omitted spelling from their analysis. Combining spelling errors with other visual components of language, such as homophones, and comparing their analysis to similar studies done earlier in this century, they concluded that the error patterns in today's college freshmen "seem to suggest declining familiarity with the visual look of a written page" (p. 406). Our students are products of the media generation, not accustomed to spending sizable portions of their time reading. Consequently, one of the most important ways to help students develop their mechanical and grammatical writing skills is by immersing them in a rich and continuous classroom reading environment.

Provide Time for All Stages of the Writing Process

A third fundamental method for increasing correctness is showing students that writing consists of several overlapping steps: prewriting and planning, writing and revising, editing and proofreading. Or, as Kirby and Liner (1981) put it so aptly for students, "getting started, getting it down, getting it right, checking it out" (p. 8). Teaching effective strategies for each of these stages increases students' confidence as writers and allows them to concentrate their full attention on correctness at the stage of writing when it matters most.

Use Editing Workshops

A fourth basic method for working with correctness is the use of editing workshops—classroom time regularly set aside for final editing and polishing of papers that have already been revised for content. Delegating specific classroom time for this task is valuable in two ways: First, it gives students a definite message about both the importance of correctness and the appropriate time in the writing process to focus on it. Second, many strategies for effective proofreading and mastery of mechanical/grammatical skills can be incorporated into this workshop time while still keeping the classroom focus on the students' own writing. Four different activities teachers and students can engage in during an editing workshop are recommended throughout the literature on teaching the composing process.

MODELING   Many students, even at the college level, don't know how to proofread effectively. When directed to "check your paper for errors," they quickly scan over their work, perhaps adding a comma here or there or changing a spelling that suddenly looks odd. In *Children's Writing and Language Growth,* Cramer (1978) recommends modeling the editing process by obtaining permission from one student writer in the class to make a transparency of his or her paper for editing by the whole class on the overhead projector. Once the class has had a chance to read the paper projected on the screen, the teacher opens discussion by focusing on the content of the paper. "What do you like about this paper?" or "What has the writer done well?" are good questions to ask at this point. Then the teacher directs the discussion to proofreading by asking, "Can anyone find something that needs to be changed?"—a neutral question, suggesting error correction is a natural part of this stage in the writing process. As students identify and correct individual errors, the teacher corrects each on the transparency, giving a brief explanation of the reason for the correction, and also starts a list on the chalkboard of kinds of errors identified: spelling, capital letters, run-on sentences, etc. The teacher can point out errors the students don't identify and use this as an opportunity to discuss the error, or can stop when the class has corrected all the errors it can identify. The final step is for the students to apply this process to their own papers, using the list on the board as a guide for the kinds of errors to look for.

If this write/model/apply process is followed regularly, students receive numerous short lessons on grammar and mechanics plus the constant opportunity to apply these lessons to their own papers. The middle school teachers I work with in the Flint, Michigan, Community Schools have been using this modeling strategy with their classes with good success. Students get involved, arguing points of grammar with each other and voluntarily checking the dictionary. One teacher tells of the gradual inching up of student chairs to the overhead projector as they group-edit and the enthusiasm with which students approach their own writing after the modeling session.

INDIVIDUAL EDITING CONFERENCES   While students are actively involved in editing their own writing, the teacher can give individual help with proofreading by holding miniconferences. In *Writing: Teachers and Children at Work,* Graves (1983) describes brief conferences focusing on proofreading held with the writer when the paper is essentially completed and moving toward a final draft. The teacher quickly scans the paper, looking for recurrent errors, and tells the writer what kinds of proofreading activities are needed. This can be done in two- or three-minute conferences at the teacher's desk, or the teacher can move up and down the aisles, leaning over shoulders, and concentrating more attention on students whose writing would benefit from more help with mechanics. The dialogue might go something like this: "OK, John, looks like you're ready for a final proofreading and polishing. First I'd like you to circle all the words you think might be misspelled and look them up in the dictionary. Then work on complete sentences. There are several places in your paper where you've got two sentences strung together." The teacher might ask John to work with him in identifying the first few run-ons and correcting them before telling John to do the same throughout the rest of his paper and then let the teacher see it again. There could be a brief lesson on possessives for one student, another on *its, it's* for someone else. Never lingering for more than a few minutes with each writer, the teacher identifies an area for proofreading, illustrates what he or she means, and gets the writer started working independently. The eavesdroppers on either side of the aisles often learn as much as the student being worked with. "Can I help you with anything?" works well as an opening question from the teacher for it permits an immediate and accurate response to a student's need. Nancie Atwell (1987), in her classic text on teaching writing, *In the Middle,* describes longer conferences she holds with students periodically to teach the individual skills in mechanics and usage that each student needs. Atwell illustrates the kinds of skills she covers in individual editing conferences with a list of forty-eight "Sample Skills Taught in Editing Conferences" (pp. 110–111).

PEER PROOFREADING Another valuable way to work toward correctness during editing workshop time is to have students work together when proofreading. Students always say it is much easier to correct someone else's work than it is to identify errors in their own, and this technique depends on that perception. If writing is not seen as a *test* of an individual student's writing ability but as a process that is growing and developing, this method permits for learning by both writer and editor. Proofreading thus becomes a collaborative learning experience. When I do this with my own students, both basic writers and average freshmen, I usually put students in pairs after each has had a chance to proofread his or her own paper. The only rule I impose is that no corrections are to be made on the writer's paper without the knowledge and consent of the author. This means both writers must confer over any error on either paper and both must agree on the correction. I also ask that the editor initial all corrections he or she finds, which gives me some sense of the mechanical skills both the writer and the proofreader bring to the paper. If the two writers can't agree on an error, I am called over to make a decision, giving me a chance to teach a minilesson as I resolve the problem. Students enjoy being editors for each other, and I find that it takes a great deal of pressure off each writer to correct the work on his or her own. Peer proofreading can also be handled in groups of three or four students, who are instructed to pass their papers around the group, each student correcting any errors found. It helps if the groups are structured so that each one has a student good at spelling and mechanics.

MINILESSONS Brief ten-minute lessons on common mechanical problems can have immediate value when they are taught as part of a writing workshop. A short lecture at the beginning of a proofreading session can then be applied immediately to the students' own papers, reinforcing the new information through personal use rather than through a textbook exercise. Students can share problem sentences during these short sessions, ask specific questions from their own writing, and get help from the shared knowledge of the entire class. Teaching these skills and having students apply them while writing is in process produces much better results than teaching them from grammar/usage texts as isolated skills. By giving minilessons during writing workshop time throughout the school term or year, a teacher could easily review almost all the kinds of mechanical errors students make and never need to rely on a textbook or drill exercises to reinforce the learning. If several students in a class share the same mechanical/grammatical problem, grouping these students for a minilesson and then permitting them to work together to correct this error on their own papers can be highly effective. See Nancie Atwell's (1987) *In the Middle* for a fuller description of writing minilessons and a list of minilesson topics used in her own writing workshops with middle-school students.

Help Students Self-Edit

Several correction strategies are aimed at enhancing students' abilities to self-edit. Among the most useful are the following.

EDITING CHECKLISTS   These are lists of common errors that students can use as a guide when proofreading their own papers. Simple lists for young children can ask questions about spelling and capital letters, while older writers can be instructed to check their writing for a dozen or more surface features such as run-ons and fragments, subject-verb agreement, and possessives.

PROOFREADING STRATEGIES   Show students some methods to improve their own proofreading:

- run a blank sheet of paper slowly down the composition so you are forced to read one line at a time

- read one sentence at a time from the bottom up to take each sentence out of context and thus focus on errors, not meaning

- circle all suspected spelling errors before consulting a dictionary

- list three of your most frequent errors at the top of the paper, then read the paper three times, each time focusing on one of these errors

- read aloud to yourself or a friend, or read into a tape recorder and play it back

- have someone else—a classmate, parent, or the teacher—read the paper aloud to you, exactly as it appears on the page

AN EDITING CORNER   Something as simple as an editing corner heaped with handbooks, dictionaries, and a thesaurus can also help students become responsible for their own mechanical/grammatical correctness. The walls around the editing corner can be decorated with a chart on how to proofread, a list of spelling demons, rules of punctuation or capitalization, and examples of dialogue punctuated properly. One-page handouts with explanations and examples of common errors and ways to correct them can be filed in this corner along with displays of student writing taken through several drafts, including final proofreading. Students should be allowed free access to these materials as they write. They should be encouraged to use the corner to solve mechanical problems themselves.

Make Students Responsible for Developing and Monitoring Their Own Editing/Proofreading Skills

The ultimate goal of any approach to correctness is to have students become competent self-editors, recognizing and knowing how to correct any deviations from standard usage in their own writing. Keeping records of their own errors is one way of encouraging students to assume this responsibility. Some teachers just have students keep a sheet in their writing folder on which they record errors pointed out by the teacher or peers with the idea that they'll work to eliminate these errors in future papers. Madraso (1993) has students keep a three-column

"Proofreading Journal," with the first column for the error, the second column for the solution, and the third column for a strategy for spotting the error in the future. Andrasick (1993) uses a system for helping students recognize and learn how to correct their own individual error patterns. When reading student papers, she first responds to content, then goes back and indicates errors using a standard set of proofreading symbols. When students get their paper back, they transfer the list of errors for that paper to a 3 X 5 card, correct them on the paper with help from the teacher, peers, or a handbook, and then make a note on the card of the mechanical/grammatical error they will work on for the next paper. Each student has an ongoing card filed in the class "Goof Box" with this information listed for all their papers. After using this process for several papers, Andrasick asks students to review their "Goof Box" card and write a reflection, noting patterns of change—errors now eliminated and new ones that need attention. She also has them write about and share with each other the strategies they use to identify, learn about, and correct their own errors. With this system, students become consciously aware of their own editing skills, developing a sense of control over proofreading and error correction, and assuming responsibility for their own self-editing competence.

Abandon the Error Hunt

Another cluster of correctness strategies centers on marking techniques for the teacher, ones that differ significantly from the traditional "red-pencillitis" approach and are always preceded by classroom use of editing workshops and self-editing strategies.

BENIGN NEGLECT   Students involved for the first time in the process approach to writing, those newly engaged in journal-writing, prewriting exercises, multiple drafts, revision, and proofreading, can benefit from a period of teacher inattention to correctness when marking final drafts of papers. If students' previous writing instruction focused heavily on form and correctness, they need time to recenter their attention on what they have to say as writers and to learn the various composing strategies that will make writing more pleasurable for both the writer and the reader of his or her paper. If students are generating a great deal of writing and are frequently engaged in editing workshop strategies, the teacher can safely focus written comments on content. This benign neglect gives students a chance to internalize writing and proofreading skills and to demonstrate what they do know before the teacher begins to identify and work on areas of weakness.

SELECTIVITY   Rather than engage in intensive error correction when responding to student writing, teachers are encouraged by recent writing researchers and theorists to adopt a more moderate approach to error and to look for patterns in the errors an individual student makes. Research has never been able to show that circling all the errors—the error hunt approach to marking—makes a significant difference in writing quality; instead it discourages the student whose paper is full of mistakes and focuses students on errors instead of ideas. Students are more likely to grow as writers when the teacher's primary purpose in reading student papers is to respond to content. However, if attention to content and correctness are combined when marking papers, it is more helpful to select one or two *kinds* of errors the individual student is making than to point out every error in the paper. The teacher can identify a selected error, show an example or two on the student's paper, and either explain the correct form or direct the student to a handbook for further explanation.

ERROR ANALYSIS A third method for working with student error when responding to student writing, one that can be especially fruitful for the teacher, is to approach it from an analytic perspective. The composition teacher as error analyst looks for patterns in the errors of an individual student, tries to discover how the student arrived at the mistake by analyzing the error (i.e., is it lack of knowledge about a certain grammatical point? a mislearned rule? a careless error? overgeneralization of a particular rule? the influence of oral language?) and plans strategies accordingly. Kroll and Schafer (1978), Bartholomae (1980), and Shaughnessy (1977) have demonstrated the efficacy of error analysis in helping teachers better understand the source of student error as an aid to planning more effective ways of dealing with it.

Publish Student Writing

The final basic strategy recommended for working toward correctness is publishing. All writers, professionals as well as students, need a reason for laboring over a draft until it is perfect: The urge to see oneself in print can be a powerful drive toward revision and proofreading. Watch what happens when a class publication is handed out. Each writer is likely to flip immediately to his or her own work for a minute of personal pleasure before browsing through the rest of the book. Writing teachers need to take advantage of this human need to be heard, to leave a physical imprint on the world, by offering numerous opportunities for sharing and publishing: bulletin boards in the class and the hall, "paper of the week" on the door, individual books, dittoed class books, a classroom anthology of one piece from each writer that sits on public display in the library, writing as gifts for parents, pen pals, contests to enter, and a class newspaper.

Computers and Correctness

As the use of computers for writing has grown, so has the proliferation of studies examining the effects of computers on writers' processes and final products. Research results are mixed: While most researchers agree that students develop more positive attitudes toward writing and do more revision with computers, the effect on the quality of the papers themselves is contradictory. Numerous studies show computers have no effect on the overall quality of the papers; however, most of these studies were limited to a ten- or twelve-week period of study, perhaps too brief for computer use to impact writing improvement, especially since learning to use the computer often takes up instructional time at first. A 1992 study of eighth-graders who were already experienced computer users had more promising results. The researchers found that "papers written on computer were rated significantly higher" (p. 249) than handwritten papers in all four qualities assessed, including mechanics (Owston, Murphy, & Wideman, 1992). Concerned about the influence of spelling on the higher ratings assigned word-processed texts, the researchers assessed a random sample of papers from both categories, finding no difference in mean spelling errors between the computer-written papers and the handwritten ones, indicating that spelling did not bias the ratings. This study offers evidence that computers might provide yet another strategy for improving students' mechanical/grammatical skills.

At the present time, it makes sense to involve students in writing on computers as much as possible for ease of revision and the use of such writing aids as a spell checker, thesaurus, or grammar checker. Just remind students that the beautifully typed paper emerging from the printer still needs the same attention to mechanical and grammatical correctness that any piece of writing requires before it is ready for evaluation or publication.

Correctness in the Linguistically Diverse Classroom

Advocates for writing process instruction have been criticized for neglecting form and correctness in favor of fluency by those who don't fully understand the ways in which writing process instruction includes attention to all aspects of writing development. But criticism has also come from teachers of minority students. Delpit (1986, 1988) and Reyes (1992) have been critical of writing process instruction for speakers of nonmainstream dialects, such as blacks and ESL students, arguing that this method does not give these students explicit instruction in the standard literacy skills they need for access to higher education and the workplace. At first this position seems in direct conflict with the methods advocated throughout this article, and the danger is in misunderstanding their position as calling for a return to isolated instruction in grammar and mechanics. Yet both educators agree that skills must be taught within a context that encourages full development of linguistic skills and "critical and creative thinking" (Delpit, 1986, p. 384). It is my contention that, in the hands of a skilled teacher who fully understands ways to integrate skills instruction into a rich writing and reading workshop environment, writing process instruction would include whatever direct instruction was necessary for students to develop standard literacy skills. Minilessons in skills followed by direct application to students' own writing, extended minilessons that also include some practice exercises in the skill being taught (Weaver, 1996), individual conferences with the teacher to work at the specific skills each student needs, and an emphasis on preparing writing for publication, all give nonmainstream students the direct instruction necessary for developing standard English skills. Yet these strategies also provide a climate supportive of students' individual growth as thinkers and writers. Speakers of nonmainstream dialects and ESL students may indeed need more instruction in the mechanical and grammatical skills of Standard English than white middle-class students, but skills instruction for all students is best taught within the context of the writing process and in a classroom that stresses writing as a meaning-making and communicative activity.

Research Indications

As these methods for working toward correctness show, over the past two decades writing teachers and theorists have developed a body of techniques that can be termed a process-oriented approach to correctness, methods that help students master the mechanical/grammatical aspects of writing without making correctness the central focus of the composition program. Relatively few studies document the effectiveness of this approach. Mainly the literature on how to teach writing deals with the process as a whole and shows its effectiveness in improving the quality of student writing in all dimensions, including surface level correctness. However, two studies suggest specifically that working with correctness within the writing process is more effective than the traditional skills approach.

Calkins (1980), in "When Children Want to Punctuate: Basic Skills Belong in Context," reports on a 1980 study of teaching punctuation in the third grade. In one classroom the teacher taught language mechanics through daily drills and workbook exercises; her children rarely wrote. In another classroom the children wrote an hour a day three times a week with no formal instruction in punctuation. At the end of the year, the "writers" not only could define and explain many more marks of punctuation than the children who had been drilled in this (8.65 kinds as opposed to 3.85 kinds) but also were actively using these punctuation marks for real purposes in their own writing. Calkins notes that "When children need punctuation in order to be seen and heard, they become vacuum cleaners, sucking up odd bits from books, their classmates' papers, billboards, and magazines. They find punctuation everywhere, and make it their own" (p. 573).

·The second piece of research documenting the fact that developing writers *do* learn mechanical and grammatical skills through the process of writing is a 1984 study by DiStefano and Killion with fourth-, fifth-, and sixth-grade students. Students in the experimental group were taught by teachers trained in the process model of writing, while the control group students were exposed to a skills approach. Using pre- and postwriting samples in September and May, the researchers showed that students in the process model group did significantly better than those in the skills group in organization, spelling, usage, and sentence structure, with the latter three items ones that are usually associated with a skills approach. The students in the skills group did not do better than the process group on any of the three grade levels. The researchers conclude "that the writing process model takes into account skills such as spelling and usage as well as organization of ideas" (p. 207).

Despite the growth of the process approach to writing in the past ten years and its concomitant methodology for teaching mechanical/grammatical correctness within the context of writing, we do not have a body of recent research substantiating the efficacy of this approach. Teachers using these methods report student success along all dimensions of writing (for example, see Atwell, 1987, p. 259, on her students' performance on Maine's statewide writing assessment, and note the reports of other teachers in this volume). The need for research into this aspect of writing is crucial if we are to better understand how to help our students develop the full repertoire of writing skills they need for success in mainstream society. Research data will also help teachers promote these newer writing approaches with parents, administrators, and the public.

I suggest case studies of successful writing classrooms at all educational levels, with a particular focus on students' development of mechanical/grammatical skills, and longitudinal case studies of writing development in students from school districts that have adopted process approaches K–12. We must examine the interaction of teaching methodology, cognitive and linguistic development, and writing skill development as it occurs in rich reading/writing environments. In addition, we need comparative studies of mechanical/grammatical skill development in a variety of classroom contexts and with a variety of methodologies, attempting to better understand which approaches are most successful in helping students become more correct writers.

I also recommend that teachers continue to do informal research in their own classrooms, trying the correctness strategies described in this article, using the results to inform their own teaching practices, and sharing this information with fellow teachers. Formal and informal studies such as these would give educators the information needed to adopt strategies firmly grounded in research as well as in the best practice reported by successful writing teachers.

Conclusions

Writing instruction has long been dominated by an emphasis on correctness. Increasingly, however, as our knowledge of the writing process and the way it is learned grows, we are coming to understand that correctness develops naturally when students are continuously engaged in composing and revising activities that are meaningful to them. When young writers need a better understanding of mechanical and grammatical matters to ensure more effective communication of their ideas, they learn what they need to know to prepare final drafts for readers. The methods described above are designed to support this learning of the mechanical and grammatical elements of written language while still keeping writers focused on the content of their writing.

In compiling these techniques, I do not suggest that teachers either ignore mechanical and grammatical correctness in writing or replace grammar exercises and intensive marking with a heavy emphasis on editing workshops. Rather, I present these methods so that teachers will see them as evidence that skills *can* be learned in the context of writing and will, therefore, free students from the correctness focus in composition and permit them to find themselves as writers.

References

ANDRASICK, K. (1993). Independent repatterning: Developing self-editing competence. *English Journal, 82* (February): 28–31.

APPLEBEE, A. (1981). *Writing in the secondary school: English and the content areas.* Urbana, IL: National Council of Teachers of English.

ATWELL, N. (1987). *In the middle.* Portsmouth, NH: Boynton/Cook.

BARTHOLOMAE, D. (1980). The study of error. *College Composition and Communication, 31* (October): 253–269.

BRADDOCK, R., LLOYD-JONES, R., & SCHOER, L. (1963). *Research in written composition.* Urbana, IL: National Council of Teachers of English.

CALKINS, L. (1980). When children want to punctuate: Basic skills belong in context. *Language Arts, 57* (May): 567–573.

CALKINS, L. (1986). *The art of teaching writing.* Portsmouth, NH: Heinemann.

CONNORS, R., AND LUNSFORD, A. (1988). Frequency of formal errors in current college writing, or Ma and Pa Kettle do research. *College Composition and Communication, 39* (4): 395–409.

CRAMER, R. (1978). *Children's writing and language growth.* Columbus, OH: Charles E. Merrill.

DELPIT, L. (1986). Skills and other dilemmas of a progressive black educator. *Harvard Educational Review, 56* (4): 379–385.

DELPIT, L. (1988). The silenced dialogue: Power and pedagogy in educating other people's children. *Harvard Educational Review, 58* (3): 280–298.

DISTEFANO, P., & KILLION, J. (1984). Assessing writing skills through a process approach. *English Education, 16* (December): 203–207.

GRAVES, D. (1983). *Writing: Teachers and children at work.* Portsmouth, NH: Heinemann.

HARRIS, W. (1977). Teacher response to student writing: A study of the response patterns of high school English teachers to determine the basis for teacher judgment of student writing. *Research in the Teaching of English, 11* (Fall): 175–185.

HAYNES, E. (1978). Using research in preparing to teach writing. *English Journal, 67* (January): 82–88.

KIRBY, D., & LINER, T. (1981). *Inside out: Developmental strategies for teaching writing.* Portsmouth, NH: Boynton/Cook.

KROLL, B. & SCHAFER, J. (1978). Error-analysis and the teaching of composition. *College Composition and Communication, 29* (October): 242–248.

MADRASO, J. (1993). Proofreading: The skill we've neglected to teach. *English Journal, 82* (February): 32–41.

OWSTON, R., MURPHY, S., & WIDEMAN, H. (1992). The effects of word processing on students' writing quality and revision strategies. *Research in the Teaching of English, 26* (October): 249–276.

REYES, M. (1992). Challenging venerable assumptions. *Harvard Educational Review, 62* (Winter): 427–446.

ROSEN, L. (1983). *Responding to student writing: Case studies of six high school English teachers.* Ph.D. dissertation, Michigan State University.

ROSEN, L. (1987). Developing correctness in student writing: Alternatives to the error hunt. *English Journal, 76*, 62–69.

SEARLE, D., & DILLON, D. (1980). The message of marking: Teacher written response to student writing at intermediate grade levels. *Research in the Teaching of English, 14* (October): 233–242.

SHAUGHNESSY, M. (1977). *Errors and expectations.* New York: Oxford University Press.

WEAVER, C. (1982). Welcoming errors as signs of growth. *Language Arts, 59*, 438–444.

WEAVER, C. (1996). *Teaching grammar in context.* Portsmouth, NH: Boynton/Cook.

10   *Image Grammar*

HARRY NODEN

Introduction

Many writers through the ages have been influenced by art. Hemingway drew ideas from Cezanne's landscape paintings to create passages in his fiction. Ray Bradbury attributed his ability to write screenplays to his childhood love of comic book illustrations. Brian Jacques once explained that he "paints" his stories. In this chapter Harry Noden, an eighth-grade middle-school teacher and thirty-year veteran, describes his experiments encouraging students to approach writing as art by using grammatical structures as brush strokes.

Some days when my students come to class, we paint still lifes from models, both photographed and real. Some days we create action drawings based on video cuts from popular films. Some days we construct visual images from sound effects clues, and yet on other days we reflect on the image paintings of the great masters, masters whose work students scrutinize for homework. In many ways I teach a typical art class, but the supplies are far less expensive because we use notebook paper for canvas and words for paint. I teach eighth-grade English.

This approach to English as art developed from casual conversations with my old friend, art teacher Ken Gessford. In the early 1970s when Ken and I were both beginning our teaching careers in Ohio, we would often meet for coffee, lament over the poor showing of the Cleveland Browns, and talk shop—often discussing the similarities in our disciplines. We noted that the act of creation seemed to engage the writer and the artist in the same process, yet our respective disciplines encouraged very different styles of teaching. Art teachers traditionally taught by demonstrating and workshopping; English teachers taught by lecturing and testing. I couldn't help wondering how my classroom might change if I taught English like an art class.

One day, while in a whimsical mood I entered my classroom, paused to capture the attention of the class, and announced, "Today, we are going to paint pictures!" Cries of "Yeah!" rippled through my eighth-grade classroom. Those students who were struggling with the current grammar unit relished the opportunity to do anything but continue the agony of analyzing verbs, which to them was emotionally akin to the old "Wide World of Sports" portrayal of the agony of defeat.

Nadine asked, "Do you mean we are going to be able to paint? Like in color?"

"Yes," I replied, "especially in color."

"Can we paint airplanes?" asked Leroy. This held a special interest for Leroy. The pages in each of his class notebooks, where one might expect to find some course information or an occasional assignment, were instead filled with pencil sketches of airplanes, predominantly World War I biplanes flaming toward the ground.

"Sure. You can paint anything you like."

"What are we going to paint with," asked Anne, "markers?"

"No," I replied, "words."

Suddenly, the room grew silent. Then, a mix of quiet moans grew into a chorus of protests. This was not the anticipated answer my class had hoped to hear. They felt misled, that I was just setting them up for another grammar lesson, dressing the old standard grammar in an artist's smock. They were partly right. I wanted them to explore grammar. Our paint would be words and our brush strokes grammatical structures. However, as my students realized in the weeks that followed, this was something different, an approach to grammar unlike anything we had attempted before, an approach even the reluctant would come to enjoy.

Early Experiments in Image Grammar

My early experiments into what became *image grammar* began with exercises in a book entitled *Stop, Look, and Write* by Hart Day Leavitt and David A. Sohn (1964). The authors posed an interesting premise: provide students with images, teach them to observe carefully, and they will create more powerful sentences. Consequently, their book contained almost no instructional content, but rather a collection of fascinating photographs to inspire students to write. As the authors explained in the introduction, their approach was solely visual:

> The way you select words and organize them into whole compositions depends on the way you see human experience. If you literally do not see anything, you will of course have nothing to say. . . . Everything here aims at the expression of meaning in the most effective possible way, and this "meaning," this result of observation, must always include the PARTICULAR, the SPECIFIC, the DETAIL. (p. 9)

For two years I used this book as a primary writing source and discovered that the authors were right: writing from exciting images, students replaced worn clichés like "nice," "really great," "neat," "good," and even an occasional "gooder" with far more specific details, details of color, texture, sound, and smell. Their sentences became more sophisticated, more interesting, and their writing improved noticeably. Yet, their images still had an eighth-grade quality to them and fell short of what I considered possible. So, I continued to experiment and research.

Books by writers on writing, which rarely mentioned formal grammar, not only supported the notion of the writer as artist, but went further, giving detailed suggestions for building images. Robert Newton Peck (1980), for example, in his book *Secrets of Successful Fiction,* described "show and tell" as one of the major techniques for writing fiction:

> Readers want a picture—something to see, not just a paragraph to read. A picture made out of words. That's what makes a pro out of an amateur. An amateur writer tells a story. A pro shows the story, creates a picture to look at instead of just words to read. A good author writes with a camera, not with a pen.
>
> The amateur writes: "Bill was nervous."
>
> The pro writes: "Bill sat in a dentist's waiting room, peeling the skin at the edge of his thumb, until the raw red flesh began to show. Biting the torn cuticle, he ripped it away, and sucked at the warm sweetness of his own blood." (p.4)

Writers like Peck seemed to reaffirm the importance of painting images, of showing rather than telling. Consequently, I began to design lessons to raise the level of image consciousness among my students. For example, I would walk into a classroom, slam my books on a table, frown, and point my finger at a student, preferably one who occasionally tested the rules.

"You," I would shout. "You. Yes, you."

"Me?" the student would invariably reply.

I would scowl with a mean look of vengeance and extend my forefinger close to the student's face.

"Yes. I said you. How do you think I feel right now?"

"Huh?"

"You heard me. How do you think I feel right now?"

"Angry. But I didn't do it."

"Did I tell you I was angry?"

"No."

"Then how did you know? Show me some details."

This surprise introduction would lead to some laughter as students realized I was just teasing. Then the discussion would lead to show and tell, to the details the students processed, and from there to the concept of details in writing. Next, I conducted impromptu minidramas that students would perform, observe, and write about using concrete details that painted pictures rather than summarized feelings.

Another strategy that I borrowed from an article by Judithe Douglas Speidel (1977) attempted to increase the writing level of below-average students by having them describe reproductions of famous art works of the Renaissance and Baroque artists. Speidel collected hard data to demonstrate an "overall increase in the use of specific details and modifiers" (70). Almost eighteen years later I would participate in a workshop presented by Janice M. Gallagher in which she used a similar approach with gifted students.

In my replication of this approach, I used contemporary paintings that I downloaded from the Paris Web Museum (http://mistral.enst.fr/~pioch/louvre, February 1997). Although I didn't attempt to collect statistical data, I felt the exercise increased my students' awareness of details. Notice the intense attention to detail used by eighth-grader Chris Hloros in her description of a self-portrait by Picasso. Chris wrote this with no knowledge that Picasso had entitled the piece *Facing Death*.

> The feeling I think Picasso was trying to represent in this was that of sadness and depression. There are many clues. First off, the colors used in the painting are not bright. They are very dull and dreary, creating a mood of sadness and mystery. The blue gives you the feeling that this man is very unhappy with his life, and the green is a sickly color, making me think that this man is not in the best of health—maybe even in the last stages of his life about to die. The red in the eyes make them seem bloodshot. This may be from insomnia, possibly because of a horrific nightmare. His hair is also red, perhaps symbolizing blood or death on his mind. These colors truly add feeling to this painting.
>
> One thing that was very apparent to me was the shapes of teardrops used throughout the face. Picasso used a particularly large one that seemed to be in the center of the picture. This hints to unhappiness, possibly even a trauma that may have caused many tears to flow. Also, the nose is in the form of a teardrop, and also the eyes are almost teardrop shaped, creating a feeling of great sadness and depression.

I felt these excursions into artistic images improved students' use of grammatical structures, but hardly constituted a complete, or even partial, program for grammatical development. I looked for help in the current grammar texts, but this proved fruitless. At that time, in the early seventies, linguists were arguing the benefits of transformational and structural grammar, and traditionalists were calling for a "back to basics" movement. One camp referred to research studies like the one by Braddock, Lloyd-Jones, and Schoer (1963) that suggested there was little or no relationship between teaching grammar and improving writing. The other camp questioned the research and a few years later pointed to studies by Neuleib and Brosnahan (1987) and Kolln (1981) who argued that earlier research was flawed and that abandoning traditional grammar in its entirety was a little like putting a losing race horse out to pasture because the horse had an inept jockey who preferred riding backward.

As a teacher I felt frustrated. Neither camp offered proven classroom strategies to help kids write, and parents, aware of the linguistic-basics debate, looked to me for a definitive answer. So, I examined the advice of professional authors to learn how they acquired their artistic skills. Surprisingly, my journey uncovered some interesting relationships between art and writing. I learned that many writers have been profoundly influenced by images of art. To help him write descriptions of landscapes, Hemingway had studied Cezanne's paintings. Ray Bradbury had attributed his ability to write screenplays to his childhood fascination with comic books. Brian Jacques, advising aspiring writers on how to approach their craft, had proclaimed one word of advice: "paint." These discoveries suggested to me that imagery played a reciprocal role in the writing process, influencing how writers chose grammatical structures to create images and how images shaped the writers' choices of grammatical structures. Still, I could find no program for developing student writers as artists.

Encouraging kids to seek out images and show rather than tell further improved the writing of my students and added another dimension to the image techniques provided by Leavitt and Sohn (1964), but a critical question remained: What specific sentence techniques, what hidden brush strokes were authors like Steinbeck using that were unknown to amateurs?

The answer to these questions came from the work of Francis Christensen (1967). Christensen, an outspoken critic of traditional grammar, argued that scholars were absurd to expect grammar to carry over into writing when grammar instruction was not designed to help students write:

> It should surprise no one that no experiments, or so it has been reported, show any correlation between knowledge of grammar and ability to write. One should not expect a correlation where no relation has been established and made ground for instruction. (p. xiv)

In effect, Christensen was saying that the profession's approach to grammar was analogous to lecturing students on all the major swimming strokes and then testing their knowledge by requiring them to swim five laps in the pool. To solve this dilemma, Christensen analyzed the sentences and paragraphs of hundreds of well-known authors and pioneered a new rhetoric, a writing/grammar program designed to help students generate sentence structures like the pros. In his classic works *Notes Toward a New Rhetoric* (1967) and *The Christensen Rhetoric Program* (Christensen & Munson, 1968), he developed an extensive taxonomy of sentence structures, structures used by professional writers to build ideas and create images. His approach revolutionized the tools available to teachers to integrate writing and grammar.

A few years after reading Christensen's landmark study, I stumbled upon Virginia Tufte's *Grammar as Style* (1971), another extensive catalog of grammatical patterns used by professional authors. Tufte expanded the taxonomy of sentence structures identified by Christensen and provided additional tools for future studies in sentence combining and composing.

Selecting a Few Basic Brush Strokes

Of course, the problem I faced was how to adapt these sophisticated structures to my not-so-sophisticated eighth-grade students. I wanted to experiment with the techniques of Christensen—verb phrases, noun phrases, absolutes, appositives, participles, etc.—but many of my students were still struggling to compose a complete sentence.

To solve this problem, I decided to keep all activities and explanations at a level of artistic play, to make this approach as relaxing and enjoyable as recreational painting. Purposely avoiding extensive grammatical explications, oversimplifying definitions, and introducing structures as simple brush strokes, I began to teach students to create images with grammatical structures. Rather than attempting to define a participle as a hybrid adjective/noun and distinguish it from a gerund, I simply said "Try starting some sentences with 'ing' words. See if it gives your paragraph a feeling of more action. Many words that end with 'ing' are called participles. If you don't notice a difference, look at the passage from Hemingway's *The Old Man and the Sea* that I have bookmarked."

Using Christensen as a source, I began with four of the easiest structures at the simplest level: absolutes, participles, appositives, and adjectives out of order. I would demonstrate a grammar technique with a projected slide of a photograph from *National Geographic*, *Sports Illustrated*, or another image-rich magazine and then ask students to imitate my example, creating their own word painting with another slide. My eighth-graders composed pictures like these:

Absolutes

Mind racing, anxiety overtaking, the diver peered once more at the specimen.
Erin Stralka

I glanced at my clock, *digits glowing florescent blue in the inky darkness of my room*.
Jenn Coppolo

Jaws cracking, tongue curling, the kitten yawned tiredly, awaking from her nap.
Tara Tesmer

Appositives

The waterfall, *a tilted pitcher*, poured the fresh, pure spray into the creek.
Allie Archer

The volcano, *a ravenous god of fire*, spewed forth lava and ash across the mountain.
Ben Quagliata

The old Navajo woman, *a weak and withered lady*, stared blankly.
Jon Vadnal

The fish, *a slimy mass of flesh*, felt the alligator's giant teeth sink into its scales as it struggled to get away.
Lindsey Kannen

Participles

Melody froze, *dripping with sweat, hoping with all her might that they wouldn't hear the noise.*
Becky Swab

Flying through the air on the wings of a dream, the Olympic long jumper thrust the weight of his whole body forward.
Cathy Conry

The clown, *appearing bright and cheerful*, smiled and did his act with unusual certainty for someone who had just killed a man.
Christi Flick

The rhino, *caught in the tangled rope*, looked for freedom.
Erika Schreckengost

Adjectives Out of Order

The woman, *old and wrinkled*, smiled upon her newborn great-grandson with pride.
Stephanie Schwallie

The boxer, *twisted and tormented*, felt no compassion for his contender.
Chris Hloros

The cheetah, *tired and hungry*, stared at the gazelle, which would soon become his dinner.
Zach Vesoulis

Occasionally, to increase student awareness of punctuation, I would use an analogy recommended by Gary Hoffman (1986) in *Writeful*. Hoffman told his students to imagine that the comma controls a telescopic lens that zooms in on images. Using the basic sentence "The rhapis palm sat in a large, white container," he explained the concept this way:

> For instance, assume the branches of the palm are the detail of interest. Without any word of transition, only a twist of a zoom lens represented by a comma, the sentence can now read: "The rhapis palm sat in a large, white container, the branches stretching into the air." (p. 20)

The zoom analogy works nicely for punctuating absolutes, appositives, participles, and a variety of other grammatical brush strokes.

Once students had painted pictures in our in-class workshops, I noticed that the use of brush strokes began transferring to other writing. Eighth-grader Adam Porter, for example, created the following scene in a short horror story he wrote. Notice the blend of techniques, none of which were required as part of the assignment:

Then it crawled in. A spider, *a repulsive, hairy creature, no bigger than a tarantula,* crawled into the room. It crawled across the floor up onto his night stand and stopped, as if it was staring at him. He reached for a nearby copy of *Sports Illustrated,* rolled it up, and swatted the spider with all his might.

He looked over only to see a hideous mass of eyes and legs. He had killed it. Just then, another one crawled in, *following the same path as the first.* He killed that one too. Then another one came, and another and another. There were hundreds of them! *Hands trembling, sweat dripping from his face,* he flung the magazine left and right, *trying to kill the spiders,* but there were too many. He dropped the magazine.

Helpless now, his eyes darted around the room. he could no longer see the individual spiders. He could just see a thick, black blanket of movement. He started squirming as he felt their fang-like teeth sink into his pale flesh like millions of tiny needles piercing his body.

Similarly, using a photograph from *National Geographic*, Cary Cybulski employed a variety of techniques in her description of an old man hugging a cello:

The old man, *feeble and stiff,* tenderly embraced his beloved cello. A single tear slid down his wrinkled face. His arthritic hands shook as the bow quivered back and forth. He wore an out-of-style jacket, *an old fashioned plaid.* His shaggy eyebrows glistened with sweat, and his sideburns grew overgrown and wild. His cello, *a piece of art,* was old and had clearly been used. Decades of polishing made the wood shiny.

In a scratchy, weak voice, the old man cursed his hands for being so stiff and sore. He suddenly gasped as a spasm of pain swept through his arm. *Exhausted*, he gently lay his cello in the soft velvet case and lowered himself onto his bed.

As he lay there, memories of his childhood started to stir in his mind. He remembered coming home after school and practicing the cello for hours. He remembered playing solos in his high school orchestra, and then later in life playing with world known orchestras. *Smiling gently*, he brought his cello, *his life-long friend and partner*, close to him and fell asleep.

By the mid-1980s research had demonstrated positive gains in writing quality using sentence combining and composing. Research by Daiker, Kerek, and Morenberg (1986) at the University of Miami indicated that freshman composition students "who practiced sentence combining exercises for a semester wrote papers that were graded higher than those written by students who had not practiced sentence combining" (p. 4). Similar findings were published by Hillocks (1986) and Cooper (1973). These positive findings prompted the publication of two books that helped teachers develop programs for improving student sentence structure: *Sentence Composing: The Complete Course* by Killgallon (1987), aimed at high school students, and *The Writer's Options* by Daiker, Kerek, and Morenberg (1986), targeted more for college students.

While I used these works as major references for minilessons on combining and composing, I preferred to have students generate writing from images. I had read criticisms by Moffett (1968), Williams (1979), and Elbow (1985)—all of whom argued that combining sentences failed to engage students in the thinking process essential to writing. So, I was a little cautious about relying on text examples alone. From my own experience students seemed to progress to composing more rapidly with images, and they painted on a larger canvas, capturing longer sequences and more complex scenes.

Using Student Art to Improve Reading and Writing

Viewing sentence structure as art led in other artistic directions. I uncovered two books that described teachers integrating art, reading, and writing. In *Stretching Stories, Stretching Minds*, Phyllis Whitin (1996) describes how her seventh-grade students sketched their responses to text and then discussed their drawings to enhance their understanding of literature. Based on "sketch to stretch"—a teaching strategy first introduced by Harste, Short, and Burke (1988)—the book demonstrated, for me, the power of artistic images in meaning making.

In another fascinating work, *Envisioning Writing*, Janet Olsen (1992) described using student drawings to improve grammatical structures. Olsen suggested having students create "visual narratives," individual and sequential drawings that tell a story. Describing a pilot program she used with third- and sixth-graders, Olsen had students follow a four-step procedure. First, each student wrote a description, as in the paragraph below by one of her sixth-grade students:

The Big Guy

James weighs 240 pounds and use to be the champ. He beat Mohamad Ali for the crown. He's 38 know and he had drugs and pot. He's been in jail for 5 years and that ended his carrear. He's had a though time finding a job. His face is scared. He wares a ripped T shirt with knee pants. He's trying to make a come back in the boxing world. He's black. (54)

Then, the student created a drawing of the description. Next, the student discussed the details in the drawings with the teacher, collaboratively examining images in the paragraph and the drawing. After the discussion, each student rewrote his or her original paragraph using insights from the discussion to improve the written images. This is the student's revision of the previous paragraph:

The Big Guy

The lonely man stood in a ring holding tight to the ropes. His head was bald. His chest was hairy and sweaty. His legs looked like they were planted to the ground like Stumps. His muscles were relaxed in the dark ring. His mouth looked mean and tough the way it was formed. He was solid looking. His boxing gloves had blood stains on them. His still body structure glowed in the darkness. He braced himself against the ropes. His white pants had red stripes. the hair on his chin prickled out like thorns. (54)

I felt that Olsen demonstrated—much like the program of Leavitt and Sohn—that images, captured or created by students, can enhance writing.

Integrating Writing and Reading

Students seemed to enjoy approaching writing as art and many considered it play. So, I shouldn't have been surprised when not long after introducing image grammar to my kids, image techniques spontaneously entered our small group literary discussions. In answer to a question like, "Do you think this novel is a good one—why or why not?" students would respond, "I liked the way the author used absolutes and participles. It made you feel like you were right there." Comments like these transformed mediocre analysis into significant insights as students began transferring their perceptions of quality writing to an understanding of quality literature.

Prior to this, I felt student responses in small group discussions had been insightful when addressing feelings, associations, and observations about elements like character development and climax. However, observations on the craft of the author always seemed hollow and often went like this:

"I like the way Lois Duncan describes things," Heather would comment.

"In what way?" I would ask.

"It's just good."

"Oh. What in particular makes it good? Any specific words or phrases that stand out?" I would ask, prompting her.

"I don't know," Heather would say. "It just sounds really neat."

Sometimes I would beat the dead horse by probing further to have my students locate and read a passage, but after they read the selection, they often had no more to say than, "Yes, that's definitely neat, really neat." Christensen cut a trail through the jungle of syntax to the treasure of the writer's art, providing concrete explanations of why one piece of writing is exciting and another dull. In my eighth-grade classroom Christensen, taken at the simplest level, added a new dimension for our discussions of literature. With just a little understanding, students were able to evaluate a key ingredient in the writer's art—whether it was their own art or the art of professionals.

Exploring Film/Novel Images

After working with slide images and discussing images in literature, I decided to explore the visual world of films. I've long felt that best-selling novels adapt well into outstanding films in part because the images of the book provide a powerful visual guide for the director. The details of character, setting, and action scenes create an imaginary storyboard that simplifies photographic decisions. So, I decided to videotape excerpts from film versions of popular novels and match them with corresponding text from the book. In class, I would play the video cut and simultaneously project the author's writing on an overhead, so we could discuss how the words captured the images.

I wanted to take my students beyond still pictures. We had been painting slide images for some time, and now I wanted to move on to action images, images more indicative of writing about real life. The following are a few of the sample passages I matched with film images, often using an ellipsis to paste excerpts from the same scene and italics to emphasize the author's use of image grammar:

From Michael Crichton's *Andromeda Strain*:

Lieutenant Roger Shawn must have found the binoculars difficult. . . . His breath, *hissing out into the moonlit air*, would have fogged the lenses. He would be forced to pause and wipe them frequently, *using a stubby gloved finger*.

There is something sad, foolish, and human in the image of Shawn *leaning against a boulder, propping his arms on it, and holding the binoculars to his eyes*. Though cumbersome, the binoculars would at least feel comfortable and familiar in his hands. It would be one of the last familiar sensations before his death. (9)

From Peter Benchley's *Jaws*:

The only sounds were those he made breathing—*a deep, hollow noise as he breathed in, a soft thudding of bubbles as he exhaled*. . . . And then the black, fathomless eye, *seemingly riveted upon him*. The gills rippled—*bloodless wounds in the steely skin*. . . . He glanced downward, started to look away, then snapped his eyes down again. *Rising at him from the darkling blue—slowly, smoothly—was the shark*. (287)

I also used novels adapted from popular films to illustrate how professional writers captured the images of filmmakers:

From William Kotzwinkle's *E. T. the Extra-Terrestrial*:

Elliot looked up into enormous eyes, eyes like moon jellyfish with faint tentacles of power within them, *eyes charged with ancient and terrible knowledge, eyes that seemed to scan every atom of his body*. (33)

From *Raiders of the Lost Ark* by Campbell Black:

He stared at the bag, then at the idol in his hand, and then he was aware of a strange, distant noise, *a rumbling like that of a great machine set in motion, a sound of things waking from a long sleep, roaring and tearing and creaking through the spaces of the Temple*. (19)

Frequently, discussions of these passages would lead to observations about related techniques that were not my intended focus. The cut from *Andromeda Strain*, for example, spurred a conversation about how writers attempt to *hook* the reader in the beginning of a novel and eventually led to an examination of fictional lead paragraphs. The excerpt from *Jaws* led to a lesson on periodic sentences and periodic paragraphs, where an author holds the most important idea as a dramatic downbeat until the end of the sentence or paragraph.

Creating Art on Different Levels

From these spin-off discussions, I began to realize that image grammar embraces more than sentences. The construction of an artistic work requires image decisions at many levels—from brush strokes to design to the selection of the medium. Christensen (1967) had discussed this in a section of his book, *Notes Toward a New Rhetoric*. Daiker, Kerek, and Morenberg (1986) addressed this in *The Writer's Options* and Mina Shaughnessy (1977) alluded to this concept in *Errors and Expectations*. Shaughnessy explained, "The mature writer is recognized not so much by the quality of his individual sentences as by his ability to relate sentences in such a way as to create a flow of sentences, a pattern of thought that is produced, one suspects, according to the principles of yet another kind of grammar—the grammar, let us say, of passages" (226).

It seemed that in working with students, I needed to introduce image grammar on three levels: a grammar of brush strokes, a grammar of passages, and a grammar of genre. I could see that each level posed totally different constraints and freedoms for expression. An essay shapes paragraphs and sentences far differently than a short story. A nonfiction article demands certain types of paragraphs rarely found in a novel. Yet, each is an artistic medium.

This came home to me when I was teaching a drama unit to my eighth-graders and searching for some simple guidelines to help them write their own screenplays. On the recommendation of a friend, I sought out a book by Syd Field (1984) entitled *Screenplay: The Foundations of Screenwriting*. In the opening chapter, Field made a comment that confirmed my beliefs about levels: "If we were to take a screenplay and hang it on the wall like a painting and examine it," said Field, "it would look like this" (see Figure 10–1).

Throughout the book Field continued to explain how this diagram represented the conceptual scheme of most screenplays. I was intrigued, not so much by the specific wall hanging of a screenplay, but by the thought that each genre has its own wall hanging, its own shape influencing the writer/artist. Just a few months earlier, I had been teaching kids the shape of a nonfiction article, and at the beginning of the year we had experimented with graphic organizers, charting fictional plot lines.

I wouldn't ask a student to mold a sculpture and hand the student a set of watercolors, nor could I ask him or her to create an essay and hand the student tools for a short story. So if the art of image grammar is to be an effective tool for writing, it must extend beyond brush strokes to the layout of the canvas and beyond canvas to the selection of a medium.

A few days ago my friend Ken and I had coffee again. During the twenty-five years since we first started sharing ideas, the Cleveland Browns never did win a Super

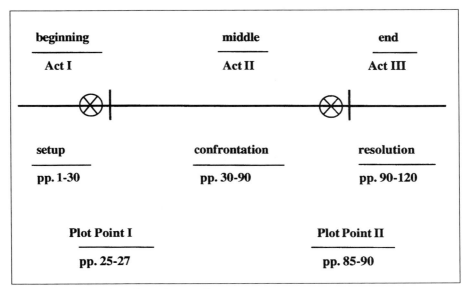

FIG. 10–1 *A painting of a script paradigm*

Bowl, but my approach to teaching grammar changed radically and became almost indistinguishable from Ken's approach to teaching art. This time we talked about workshopping, conferencing, portfolio assessment, and the artistic concepts of perception, production, and reflection. These days the harmony of visual art and image grammar seems natural, and I can foresee a time when the process of making meaning in art and writing will become a guide to making meaning in all disciplines.

References

BENCHLEY, P. (1974). *Jaws.* New York: Doubleday.

BLACK, C. (1981). *Raiders of the lost ark.* New York: Ballantine Books.

BRADDOCK, R., LLOYD-JONES, R., & SCHOER, L. (1963). *Research in written composition.* Champaign, IL: National Council of Teachers of English.

CHRISTENSEN, F. (1967). *Notes toward a new rhetoric.* New York: Harper and Row.

CHRISTENSEN, F. (1979). *The Christensen method.* New York: Harper and Row.

CHRISTENSEN, F., & MUNSON, M. (1968). *The Christensen program: The sentence and the paragraph.* New York: Harper and Row.

COOPER, C. (1973). An outline for writing sentence-combining problems. *English Journal, 62,* 96–102.

CRICHTON, M. (1969). *Andromeda strain.* New York: Knopf.

DAIKER, D., KEREK, A., & MORENBERG, M. (1986). *The writer's options.* New York: Harper and Row.

ELBOW, P. (1985). The challenge for sentence combining. In D. Daiker, A. Kerek, & M. Morenberg, *Sentence combining: A rhetorical perspective,* 232–245. Carbondale: Southern Illinois University Press.

FIELD, S. (1984). *Screenplay: The foundations of screenwriting.* New York: Dell.

HARSTE, J., SHORT, K., & BURKE, C. (1988). *Creating classrooms for authors.* Portsmouth, NH: Heinemann.

HILLOCKS, G., JR. (1986). *Research in written composition: New directions for teaching.* Urbana, IL: ERIC Clearing House on Reading and Communication Skills and the National Conference on Research in English.

HOFFMAN, G. (1986). *Writeful.* Huntington Beach, CA: Verve Press.

KILLGALLON, D. (1987). *Sentence composing: The complete course.* Portsmouth, NH: Boynton/Cook.

KOLLN, M. (1981). Closing the Books on Alchemy. *College Composition and Communication, 32* (2), 139–151.

KOTZWINKLE, W. (1982). *E. T. the extra-terrestrial.* New York: G. P. Putnam & Sons.

LEAVITT, H. & SOHN, D. (1964). *Stop, look, and write.* New York: Bantam Pathfinder Editions.

MOFFETT, J. (1968). *Teaching the universe of discourse.* Boston: Houghton Mifflin.

NEULEIB, J., & BROSNAHAN, I. (1987). Teaching grammar to writers. *Journal of Basic Writing, 6* (1), 28–35.

OLSEN, J. (1992). *Envisioning writing.* Portsmouth, NH: Heinemann.

PECK, R. (1980). *Secrets of successful fiction.* Cincinnati: Writer's Digest Books.

SHAUGHNESSY, M. (1977). *Errors and expectations.* New York: Oxford University Press.

SPEIDEL, J. (1977). Using art to teach writing. *Connecticut English Journal, 9* (1), 66–70.

TUFTE, V. (1971). *Grammar as style.* New York: Holt, Rinehart and Winston.

WHITIN, P. (1996). *Stretching stories, stretching minds.* Portsmouth, NH: Heinemann.

WILLIAMS, J. (1979). Defining complexity. *College English, 40,* 595–609.

11

Sentence Con
Notes on a New

DON KILLGALLON

Introduction

Killgallon begins by defining sentence composing and suggesting that teaching grammar is an ineffective way to improve students' writing, humorously describing how he learned this lesson through personal experience, and in effect inviting us to reflect upon our own experience. He describes how he stumbled upon the idea of having students imitate effective sentences from literature, leading Killgallon to develop activities for engaging in what he now calls "sentence composing." The heart of his article consists of samples of four kinds of activities: unscrambling, imitating, combining, and expanding, which are designed to promote students' use of more effective syntax, particularly the kinds of constructions used frequently by professional writers but seldom by students. Within the discussion of those activities for improved syntax, Killgallon explains how Francis Christensen's (1967) *Notes Toward a New Rhetoric* became the inspiration for his sentence composing techniques and textbooks.

Sentence composing is the regular use of four techniques designed to teach students to write sentences with structures resembling those of professional writers. A highly effective way to improve sentences by students of all abilities from middle school to college, it is easily learned by teachers and students. The four sentence composing techniques, described in detail later, all use sentences by professional writers with structural characteristics common among professionals, yet rare among students. With the techniques, students imitate those sentences through repeated practices and eventually use them in their own writing.

Little knowledge of grammar is needed. The activities of grammar—naming of sentence parts and parsing of sentences—dissect sentences:

> For all your rhetorician's rules teach nothing but to name his tools.
> Butler, *Hudibras*

Sentence composing doesn't name the tools, but instead, it uses them to build better sentences.

Now: The Research Story: An Idea Whose Time Was Long Overdue

After a two-year research project in which various textbooks on sentence improvement were piloted in Canadian schools, the Canadian Ministry of Education, the agency conducting the project, commented about the textbook series I wrote, *Sentence Composing*: "The best [textbook on sentence improvement] appears to be the Killgallon series" (Evans, 1987, p. 9).

Another comment from the research study highlights a significant offshoot of the sentence composing approach, namely a heightened awareness for students of literary style:

> Throughout the text, the author [Killgallon] emphasizes flexibility, comparison, judgment, and a variety of strategies closely related to effect. In some ways, the [Killgallon] series is an illustrated commentary on contemporary style—and a good one. (p. 8)

Although the result was revolutionary, the process was evolutionary. The seed for the sentence composing approach to writing improvement was planted in September of 1963, my first year as an English teacher, by a student whose last name I have forgotten but whose inadvertent contribution to the sentence composing approach I will forever acknowledge, a student named Barry.

Then: The Barry Story: An Epiphany from Parsing and Naming of Parts

Sitting at his desk with his upper torso hunched over, pencil in hand, Barry, one of the tenth-graders in my below-average English class, was about to take the ultimate test.

He was about to write what I hoped would be (after having received from me careful instruction in the parsing and naming of all its parts) the very best sentence he had written in his life. Ever.

In those first few weeks of that first year of my teaching career, I had discovered the severity of the writing problems of Barry and the others in his class. They couldn't write essays. I tried paragraphs. They couldn't write paragraphs. I decided to try sentences. I didn't have a clue as to how to actually teach writing: All I had done was tell them to write, and harp on the importance and joys of writing.

The harping wasn't helping.

Like so many in the profession, I expected them to write better without doing anything to help get them there. Francis Christensen (1967), that linguistic sage, told the hard truth: "In composition courses we do not really teach our captive charges to write better—we merely *expect* them to" (p. 129).

He was right. I had no idea how to teach somebody to write any more than I would know how to teach somebody to grow hair. But what could I, their teacher, do for Barry and his ilk, clueless, wordless, skilless? Grammar! Of course! Barry's class, before they could write, first needed a grammar tonic, a dose of vitamins A to V—adjective to verb! (Clearly, I hadn't heard about the research yet—you know, the conclusion that teaching grammar has little effect on students' writing. But Barry's story proves that it *did* have an effect. Not, however, the one intended.)

I taught Barry's class nouns, verbs, and the usual linguistic litany of things entombed in grammar textbooks since Gutenberg. We parsed. We named and underlined parts. We conjugated and cogitated. We even learned moral laws, including the heinousness of fragments and comma splices (mortal sins), and the horrors of split infinitives, unparallel series, danglers and squinters (venial sins). For a special treat, I interjected comic relief, something I thought would be amusing yet instructive, to illustrate how funny but foolish sentences became if writers slipped and sloppily committed a grammar gaffe. I wrote, "The little girl ate the food her mother gave her, and then she drank a beer," where the sin was an ambiguous pronoun. Hah.

The terminal activity of my grammar unit was to be the writing of one wonderful sentence: pristine, pertinent, pithy—and parsible. On that last day, in that final activity, everyone was going to write one memorable sentence. (Barry did not disappoint—at least in its memorability.)

The big day arrived. I gave Barry's class the entire fifty-minute period to plan, write, rewrite, polish, and perfect their single sentences.

And now came Barry's test, but also mine—a test of my effectiveness as a rookie English teacher, earnestly but ignorantly teaching the hodgepodge called *English*.

Barry's pencil was precariously poised to write that world-class sentence. When his pencil hit the paper line, my professional life was on the firing line.

As the class wrote, I observed Barry, the true test: He was unable to read beyond third-grade level, capable of no more than grunts during class discussions.

Now, however, he appeared to be giving his sentence his all. Deep in seeming concentration, he sat at his desk studying the blank lines on the paper before him, sometimes gazing at the ceiling as if to catch the muse in flight. Then, suddenly, his hand dashing out the words given to him by the ceiling muse, his pencil moving determinedly across the lines of the paper, eyes focusing on the words taking shape, Barry wrote his memorable sentence.

And here it is, the first time to see print. (I wouldn't have dared earlier.)

The elephant is a slow person. And there you have it. YIKES! On the hellish road of best intentions, I had obliterated Barry's already fragile thought process.

Over the following weekend, I graded their sentences. Although none equaled Barry's, many came close. I took stock and considered quitting teaching and enlisting in the Army, to spend my life in trenches of a different sort.

Barry had not failed. I had. I had quite clearly and wrongly assumed that, after all that naming of sentence parts and parsing of sentences, Barry would be cured of what Christensen called "syntactic anemia." I was wrong.

But wrong, too, was the research. Barry proved that teaching grammar *did*, after all, have an effect on his writing. Through it, he had contracted "verbal" schizophrenia.

I had to find a cure.

Having decided against joining the Army, I enlisted instead in a new campaign to right the wrongs I had inflicted upon my captive charges. I flushed out my mind. Unaided by grammar books, workbooks, or teacher's manuals, I took a fresh look at the process of writing, inspired by a wonderful little book I was currently reading: *Gift from the Sea* by Anne Morrow Lindbergh. At the beginning of a chapter, I was struck by one of her sentences. Here is what she wrote: *This is a snail shell, round, full, and glossy as a horse chestnut.*

That sentence, I thought, is what I had had in mind for Barry to write, a sentence rich in texture, structure, and thought. I picked up a pencil and wrote one like it, describing the first object my eyes landed on in my humble, rented furnished room—a cup of coffee. Here is what I wrote: *There is a cup of coffee, aromatic, rich, and refreshing as a hot shower.* Imitating Lindbergh's sentence took all of one minute.

Then I thought, what would happen if I asked Barry's class to imitate the same model, Lindbergh's sentence? The next day I did exactly that, but first I showed them my imitation of Lindbergh's sentence as an example. Then we, working together, wrote an imitation describing a book. And finally—the true test, which once again Barry was about to take—I asked each student to write an imitation. Here is what *Barry* wrote: *There is a flag, striped, colorful, and starry as a night sky.* Imitating Lindbergh's sentence took *Barry* all of one minute, and instantly killed the elephant who was a slow person!

At long last I had found a fertile field. And the seed planted there by Barry quickly took root, shot up, and grew into an approach to teaching writing I call "sentence composing."

Over the years my textbooks in sentence composing have been published for other Barrys. Thank you, Barry, for the epiphany, through which you changed a morphed elephant, grotesquely rendered, into a beautiful flag, described like a pro.

Barry succeeded because the task of imitating was for him, his classmates, and all of us as people, a natural learning method, activated at birth and used constantly throughout life. The marked success of sentence composing results from its use of a mimetic theory of language development. Mimetic theories to explain a child's development of speech are certain. A child learns to speak by imitating experienced speakers—usually parents and others who in the child's mind are speech experts. The modeling by parents of speech for their children activates the inborn speech potentiality. What they hear is what they say.

Sentence composing applies the same mimetic theory to a student's development of writing skill. A student can learn to write better sentences by frequently imitating experienced writers—professionals who in the student's mind are writing experts. The modeling process delivered through the sentence composing techniques (described soon) set the stage for students to learn how to write better sentences. What they read is what they write.

Repeated classroom exposure to sentences of professional writers—in effect the student's tutors—elicits attention to, understanding of, and, with practice, possession of those same structures. Because sentence composing activities saturate students with professional sentences, students learn to manipulate syntax to produce sentences that are structurally mature, coherent, organized, and stylistically varied—closely resembling those of professional writers.

The prerequisite saturation occurs through frequent practices using the four sentence composing techniques: *unscrambling, imitating, combining, expanding.*

Sentence Unscrambling

This is the process of listing the sentence parts of a professional sentence for the student to unscramble. Sentence unscrambling provides a close look at how professional writers structure their sentences. For example, here is a list of the sentence parts of a professionally written sentence:

- was immense

- its head rising high above them

- the tyrannosaurus rex

- out of sight

- the size of a two-story building

Students reassemble the sentence parts to produce coherent sentences, one of which may—although it is not essential—duplicate the author's original sentence, Unscrambling provides practice in moving sentence parts for variety in style.

Original: The tyrannosaurus rex was immense, the size of a two-story building, its head rising high above them, out of sight.
(Michael Crichton, *The Lost World*)

Subliminally, sentence unscrambling teaches the grammatical constructions—words, phrases, and clauses in all their variety—that make up the sentence parts in the scrambled list. More important, this sentence composing technique shows the *variable positions* in which those sentence parts may occur. Also, it helps slow or careless readers to discover interrelationships among ideas within an author's sentence because it demands close concentration on meaning.

Here's a variation on the unscrambling technique, a simple activity good for the middle school grades to provide beginning practice in the movability of sentence parts (Killgallon, 1997).

Sample Unscrambling Activity

Directions: The sentences below have movable parts that are <u>underlined</u>. Rearrange the parts to make new sentences.

Example
Original Sentence:
Tom was on his feet, <u>shouting</u>.
(Hal Borland, *When the Legends Die*)

Other Rearrangements:
<u>Shouting</u>, Tom was on his feet.
Tom, <u>shouting</u>, was on his feet.

---

1. Taran cried, <u>his teeth chattering violently.</u>
(Lloyd Alexander, *The Book of Three*)

2. The fog horn was blowing steadily, <u>once every fifteen seconds.</u>
(Ray Bradbury, *The Fog Horn*)

3. He sat on a rail fence, <u>watching the night come over Gettysburg.</u>
(Michael Shaara, *The Killer Angels*)

4. <u>Slowly</u>, <u>filled with dissatisfaction</u>, he had gone to his room and got into bed.
(Betsy Byars, *The Summer of the Swans*)

5. There are boys from broken homes, and boys who have been in difficulty with the law, <u>studying in the classrooms</u>, <u>working in the fields and in the workshops</u>.
(William E. Barrett, *The Lilies of the Field*)

6. Somewhere there, on that desolate plain, was lurking this fiendish man, hiding in a burrow like a wild beast, <u>his heart full of malignancy against the whole race which had cast him out</u>.
(Sir Arthur Conan Doyle, *The Hound of the Baskervilles*)

7. Alan made a business of checking his own reflection in the mirror, <u>giving Norris time to make a clean getaway</u>, while Keeton stood by the door, <u>watching him impatiently</u>.
(Stephen King, *Needful Things*)

8. <u>Standing in front of the room,</u> <u>her blond hair pulled back to emphasize the</u> <u>determination of her face,</u> <u>her body girdled to emphasize the determination</u> <u>of her spine,</u> <u>her eyes holding determinedly to anger,</u> Miss Lass was afraid. (Rosa Guy, *The Friends*)

9. She ate a great deal and afterward fell asleep herself, and Mary sat and stared at her and watched her fine bonnet slip on one side until she herself fell asleep once more in the corner of the carriage, <u>lulled by the splashing</u> <u>of the rain against the windows.</u> (Frances Hodgson Burnett, *The Secret Garden*)

10. The garden was <u>to the left of the barn and the pasture</u> hidden from the house by the smokehouse and a pecan grove and a row of little peach trees that <u>because of the drought</u> had dropped hard knotty fruit not even fit to make spiced pickle with. (Olive Ann Burns, *Cold Sassy Tree*)

Sentence Imitating

This is the use of sentences by professional writers as models for sentences written by students in which the structure of the model is retained, but the content is the students'.

The purpose of sentence imitating is to increase students' ability to vary sentence structure through a deliberate imitation of the structure of the model sentence. The ultimate goal of this sentence composing technique, equally true for all four sentence composing techniques, is independent mastery of the skill of sentence structure maturity. With regular and sufficient practice, that mastery will be demonstrated in the students' actual writing unaided by models. Like all of the sentence composing techniques, sentence imitating is an effective means for the attainment of that goal.

Model sentences for students to imitate are chosen for their possession of syntactic characteristics that are desirable but lacking in student writing. Here are a few typical models with imitations by tenth-grade students familiar with sentence imitating through frequent practices.

Models and Students' Imitations
1a. Model: The dark silence was there, and the heavy shapes sitting and the little blue light burning. (Ray Bradbury, *The Vintage Bradbury*)
1b. Student's Imitation: The dense fog was there, and the bloody bodies dying, and the torn white flag waving.

2a. Model: There was also a rhino who, from the tracks and the kicked-up mound of strawy dung, came there each night.
(Ernest Hemingway, *Green Hills of Africa*)

2b. Student's Imitation: There was also a turtle who, from the half-eaten tomato and the hole under the fence, had visited the garden that day.

3a. Model: His fingers smarting, the shamefaced Taran, the smallest and sassiest of the elves, hurried from the cottage and found Coll near the vegetable garden.
(Lloyd Alexander, *The Book of Three*)

3b. Student's Imitation: His body squirming, the blue iguana, the largest and most colorful of the iguana family, pulled himself out of the cage and found some food under a newspaper.

4a. Model: He heard every little sound of the gathering night, the sleepy complaint of settling birds, the love agony of cats, the strike and withdrawal of little waves on the beach, and the simple hiss of distance.
(John Steinbeck, *The Pearl*)

4b. Student's Imitation: He heard each little noise in the distance, the croak of the bullfrog, the rustling of the leaves in the trees, the clang of the wind chimes, and the whistle of the approaching train.

5a. Model: Near the spot upriver to which Mr. Tanimoto had transported the priests, there sat a large case of rice cakes which a rescue party had evidently brought for the wounded lying thereabouts but hadn't distributed.
(John Hersey, *Hiroshima*)

5b. Student's Imitation: At the place in the room where he had left his books, he found a stack of research articles, which had evidently been brought by several of the more academic students but had been returned by the teacher before they could be used.

Here's a high school activity that uses both unscrambling and imitating. Unscrambling strongly focuses students' attention on the structure of the sentence parts of the model, making imitation of those sentence parts easy (Killgallon, 1998b).

Sample Imitating Activity

Directions: Unscramble both lists of sentence parts to make two sentences that imitate the model. Then, imitate the model by writing your own sentence.

Model: The aftermath of the shooting was a three-ring circus, with the governor in one ring, with the prison in another, and with poor brain-blasted Percy Wetmore in the third.
(Stephen King, *The Green Mile*)

Scrambled Imitations

1a. and in the main office with busy administrators in high demand but low supply

b. in the guidance department with loads of schedule changes

c. was busy

d. in the cafeteria with huge lines

e. the opening day of school

2a. near the canal by the old barn

b. is a mile from the interstate

c. the nature trail

d. and near the old abandoned post office across from the church on Front Street

e. near the historic museum in the 19th-century village

Results:
Unscrambled Imitations of the Model Sentence

1. The opening day of school was busy, in the cafeteria with huge lines, in the guidance department with loads of schedule changes, and in the main office with busy administrators in high demand but low supply.

2. The nature trail is a mile from the interstate, near the canal by the old barn, near the historic museum in the 19th-century village, and near the old abandoned post office across from the church on Front Street.

Student Imitation of the Model Sentence

The tie-up on the highway was a mess, with traffic at a standstill, with police cars in the shoulders, and with a medical helicopter near the scene of the accident.

Sentence Combining

Here, students must impose a structure on a given amount of content presented as a list of sentences, by experimenting with possible combinations and then comparing their results with the original sentence. This kind of open-ended combining practice is especially good if students have previously done a lot of sentence composing activities that familiarized them with the kinds of constructions typical of professional writers. Here are three examples:

1. Sentences to Combine

a. He paused.

b. He was puffing noisily.

Original: He paused, puffing noisily.
(John Steinbeck, *The Red Pony*)

2. Sentences to Combine

a. His head was aching.

b. His throat was sore.

c. He forgot to light the cigarette.

Original: His head aching, his throat sore, he forgot to light the cigarette.
(Sinclair Lewis, *Cass Timberlane*)

3. Sentences to Combine

a. Bernard was waiting outside.

b. He was waiting on the landing.

c. He was wearing three things.

d. One was a sweater.

e. It was a turtleneck.

f. It was black.

g. Another was flannels.

h. They were dirty.

i. The third thing was slippers.

Original: Bernard, wearing a black turtleneck sweater, dirty flannels, and slippers, was waiting on the landing outside.
(Brian Moore, *The Lonely Passion of Judith Hearne*)

A more structured approach uses both combining and imitating to give students practice in the constructions typical of professional writers (the combining part) and to provide opportunities for using those same constructions (the imitating part). Here's a sample activity (Killgallon, 1997).

Sample Combining Activity

Directions: Combine the sets of sentences into one sentence by putting the underlined parts into the first sentence. Decide where the parts fit most smoothly into the first sentence. Add commas to punctuate the parts you insert into the first sentence. Finally, write an imitation of the sentence you produce, using your own content but the structure of that sentence.

Example

Set: The Horned King rode to the wicker baskets and thrust the fire into them. He did this <u>before Gwydion could speak again</u>. The Horned King was <u>bearing a torch</u>.

Combined: Before Gwydion could speak again, the Horned King, bearing a torch, rode to the wicker baskets and thrust the fire into them.
(Lloyd Alexander, *The Book of Three*)

Imitation: As the hitter darted toward first base, the pitcher, aiming with precision, threw the ball to the first base player and got the ball into the sweet spot.

---

1. Aunt Dorothy was waiting at the front door with her own small daughter. Aunt Dorothy was <u>tall and bony</u>. Her daughter was <u>Diane</u>.
    (Robert Lipsyte, *The Contender*)

2. There was a huge moulting stuffed moose head. It was <u>in the dining hall</u>. It was <u>over the stone fireplace that was never used</u>. The moose head was something <u>which looked somehow carnivorous</u>.
    (Margaret Atwood, *Wilderness Tips*)

3. Craig sat and waited for his father to tell him what he should do next. Craig was <u>calm now, at peace</u>. He sat and waited <u>just as he had done so many times as a child</u>.
    (Stephen King, "The Langoliers")

4. Perhaps an elderly gentleman lived there. He lived there <u>alone</u>. He was <u>someone who had known her grandfather</u>. He was <u>someone who had visited the Parrs in Cummington</u>.
    (Joyce Carol Oates, "The Doll" from *Haunted*)

5. The lawyer lay on an old Army cot. The cot was <u>in the closed anteroom</u>. It was one <u>he kept there for naps</u>. There was <u>a newspaper folded over his face as though he were a corpse being protected from flies</u>.
    (Frank Bonham, *Chief*)

Sentence Expanding

In this technique, an abridged version of a professional sentence is presented to students with places within it marked for expansion. In those places, students provide both the content and the structure in a way that will result in a smooth blend with the rest of the professional writer's sentence.

Abridged Version: / There stood / two squat old-fashioned decanters of cut glass / .

Original: In the centre of the table there stood, as sentries to a fruit-stand which upheld a pyramid of oranges and American apples, two squat old-fashioned decanters of cut glass, one containing port and the other dark sherry.
(James Joyce, "The Dead")

Sample Student Expansion

<u>When I entered the dining room</u>, there stood, <u>near the fresh loaf of bread</u>, two squat old-fashioned decanters of cut glass, <u>catching the sun's rays pouring into the room from the tear in the closed draperies</u>.

Notice that both the content and the structure of the underlined portions are original. In sentence expanding—unlike unscrambling, imitating, and combining—the student provides not just the content, not just the structure, but *both*. Success here strongly indicates that the student is well on the way to independent mastery of sentence variety.

All four sentence composing techniques, especially expanding, illustrate Francis Christensen's dictum that it is the "add-ons" that differentiate professional sentences from students' sentences. In other words, teaching students "add-ons"— namely, unbound words, phrases, dependent clauses—is the key to teaching the rhetoric of the sentence. As Christensen (1967) puts it, "The foundation, then, for a generative or productive rhetoric of the sentence is that composition is essentially a process of *addition*" (p. 130).

Also, I have found one of Christensen's most controversial assertions to be true through my work with students and teachers via sentence composing: "The mere form of the sentence generates ideas. It serves the needs of both the writer and the reader, the writer by compelling him to examine his thought, the reader by letting him into the writer's thought" (p. 131). All sentence composing techniques saturate students with new forms, namely various constructions used by professionals. Those constructions are the additions that professionals include frequently in their sentences. Once students acquire the same additions, the "forms" of those additions *actually promote the generation of ideas*. Christensen's theory, paraphrased, amounts to this: If you don't know how to say something, you can't say it. Imitating the additions of professional writers through the four sentence composing techniques provides *the how*, and also helps with *the what*.

As students become familiar with the kinds of additions common in professional sentences, they become adept at including them in expanding activities. Here's a sample activity (Killgallon, 1998a):

Sample Expanding Activity

Directions: Each sentence is a stripped-down version of a professionally written sentence. Expand the sentence to approximately the number of words in parentheses, which is the number in the original.

1. He can feel the eyes on him. (14 words)
   Original: <u>Standing in an aisle in a library</u>, He can feel the eyes on him.
   (Judith Guest, *Ordinary People*)

2. A pale silk scarf is tied around his neck. (29 words)

Original: <u>Above the open shirt</u>, a pale silk scarf is tied around his neck, <u>almost completely hiding from view the throat whose creases are the only sign of his age.</u>
(Philip Roth, *The Professor of Desire*)

3. The four animals continued to lead their lives. (30 words)
   Original: <u>After this climax</u>, the four animals continued to lead their lives, <u>so rudely broken in upon by civil war, in great joy and contentment, undisturbed by further risings or invasions</u>.
   (Kenneth Grahame, *The Wind in the Willows*)

4. He went into the kitchen. (31 words)
   Original: He went into the kitchen, <u>where the moonlight called his attention to a half bottle of champagne on the kitchen table, all that was left from the reception in the tent</u>.
   (Kurt Vonnegut, Jr., *Slaughterhouse-Five*)

The four sentences above clearly illustrate Christensen's theory about the importance of additions to professional sentences, accounting greatly for the expressive power in those sentences, which are typical of the way professionals write. The goal of sentence composing is to teach those additions by saturating students with professional models to imitate.

Sentence Composing: A New Rhetoric

In *Notes Toward a New Rhetoric* (1967) Francis Christensen said, "I want them [students] to become sentence acrobats, to dazzle by their syntactic dexterity. I'd rather have to deal with hyperemia than anemia" (p. 137). Sentence composing provides that acrobatic training. All four sentence composing techniques—unscrambling, imitating, combining, and expanding—use literature as a school for writing with a faculty of professional writers. The course that esteemed faculty brilliantly teaches—what Christensen called "syntactic dexterity"—is crucial to students' success as writers.

Christensen also advocated an integration of literature, writing, and grammar: "What I am proposing carries over of itself into the study of literature. It makes the student a better reader of literature. It helps him thread the syntactical mazes of much mature writing, and it gives him insight into that elusive thing we call style" (p. 137). Through sentence composing activities, students increase their understanding of, and consequent skill in, both literature and writing.

In the past, teachers neglected the sentence as a way to teach writing, using sentences instead as specimens for dissection, not as models for imitation. Only paragraphs, essays, and stories were used as models. After reading those longer models, students were told by their teachers, "Go, thou, and do likewise." Utterly unbreachable, the gap between the long professional model and the student's grasp of it was too wide, and so students were doomed to fail. The reach far exceeded the grasp.

With sentence composing, the gap sharply narrows because the model is graspable: It is *only one sentence long*. Students here, too, are told, "Go, thou, and do likewise." But this time, often amazingly, students ranging from our most challenged to our most challenging succeed. Here, with only a *single sentence* as the model, and with frequent imitation activities through the four sentence composing techniques, students are far more likely to succeed.

In the past, the sentence was used as an object of analysis, resulting in literary paralysis—the kind of activities I long ago inflicted on Barry and the other captive charges in my classroom. "The Barry Story" illustrates the stunted growth of those students from my misguided grammar unit. I had thought that dissection of sentences would lead to improved sentences, that *knowing* would result in *doing*. Nothing much happened.

Sentence composing reverses the order, on the assumption that *doing* results in *knowing*, that imitation leads to acquisition.

Much of the sentence composing approach owes a debt to the pioneering linguist Francis Christensen, the first to see the light, who wrote in *Notes Toward a New Rhetoric*, "If the new grammar is to be brought to bear on composition, it must be brought to bear on the rhetoric of the sentence. . . . With hundreds of handbooks and rhetorics to draw from I have never been able to work out a program for teaching the sentence as I find it in the work of contemporary writers" (p. 129).

Christensen's life's work inspired sentence composing, "a program for teaching the sentence as [it is found] in the work of contemporary writers." I am deeply grateful to him, my silent partner.

And deeply grateful to Barry, my silent mentor.

The foundation of the sentence composing approach is imitation. Everyone knows that a baby learns to talk partly by imitating the sentences of people who know how to talk. Every teacher of writing needs to know that a student can learn to write partly by imitating the sentences of good writers.

Imitation is sound pedagogy. With the sentence composing approach, students imitate the masters of the art of writing. Our job is to show them how. Otherwise—perish the possibility—in our very own classroom an unsuspecting elephant may be changed into, well, a slow person.

References

ALEXANDER, L. (1964). *The book of three.* New York: Henry Holt.
ATWOOD, M. (1992). *Wilderness tips.* New York: Bantam.
BARRETT, W. (1963). *The lilies of the field.* New York: Dramatists Play Service.
BONHAM, F. (1971). *Chief.* New York: Dell.

BORLAND, H. (1984). *When the legends die.* New York: Bantam.

BRADBURY, R. (1987). *The fog horn.* Mankato, MN: Creative Education.

BRADBURY, R. (1990). *The vintage Bradbury.* New York: Random House.

BURNETT, F. (1994). *The secret garden.* New York: Puffin Books.

BURNS, O. (1986). *Cold sassy tree.* New York: Dell.

BUTLER, S. (1993). *Hudibras.* Delmar, NY: Scholars' Facsimiles & Reprints.

BYARS, B. (1997). *The summer of the swans.* New York: Scholastic.

CHRISTENSEN, F. (1967). *Notes toward a new rhetoric.* Harper and Row.

CRICHTON, M. (1996). *The lost world.* New York: Ballantine.

DOYLE, A. (1995). *The hound of the Baskervilles.* New York: Puffin Books.

EVANS, P. (Ed.). (1987). *Beyond the 'ands' and 'buts': Sentence combining resources for integrated programs, grades 8–12, English and Anglais.* Toronto: Ontario Institute for Studies in Education (OISE) Press.

GRAHAME, K. (1990). *The wind in the willows.* New York: Dell.

GUEST, J. (1982). *Ordinary people.* New York: Viking Penguin.

GUY, R. (1996). *The friends.* New York: Henry Holt.

HEMINGWAY, E. (1996). *Green hills of Africa.* New York: Simon and Schuster.

HERSEY, J. (1989). *Hiroshima.* New York: Random House.

JOYCE, J. (1996). *The Dead.* New York: St. Martin's Press.

KILLGALLON, D. (1997). *Sentence composing for middle school.* Portsmouth, NH: Boynton/Cook.

KILLGALLON, D. (1998a). *Sentence composing for college.* Portsmouth, NH: Boynton/Cook.

KILLGALLON, D. (1998b). *Sentence composing for high school.* Portsmouth, NH: Boynton/Cook.

KING, S. (1992). *Needful things.* New York: NAL-Dutton.

KING, S. (1995). The langoliers. In *Four Past Midnight.* New York: NAL-Dutton.

KING, S. (1997). *The green mile: Complete stories.* New York: NAL-Dutton.

LEWIS, S. (1976). *Cass Timberlane.* Mattituck, NY: Amereon Ltd.

LINDBERGH, A. (1991). *Gift from the sea.* New York: Random House.

LIPSYTE, L. (1967). *The Contender.* New York: HarperCollins Children's Books.

MOORE, B. (1988). *The lonely passion of Judith Hearne.* New York: Little, Brown.

OATES, J. (1994). The Doll. *Haunted.* New York: NAL-Dutton.

ROTH, P. (1994). *The professor of desire.* New York: Random House.

SHAARA, M. (1996). *The killer angels.* New York: Ballantine.

STEINBECK, J. (1993). *The red pony.* New York: Viking Penguin.

STEINBECK, J. (1994). *The pearl.* New York: Viking Penguin.

VONNEGUT, K., Jr. (1985). *Slaughterhouse-five.* New York: Barron.

12 Breaking the Rules in Style

TOM ROMANO

> From this hour I ordain myself loos'd of limits and imaginary lines . . .
> —WALT WHITMAN

Introduction

Tom Romano describes how he has taught high school and college students how to communicate powerfully by breaking standard rules of writing. He introduces them to the stylistic options of "Grammar B," what rhetorician Winston Weathers calls "an alternate style." Romano focuses on the use of repetition, the sentence fragment, the labyrinthine sentence, orthographic variation, double voice, and the list.

Such stylistic rule breaking has a long tradition in the British and American literary heritage, dating back to the writing of William Blake and Laurence Sterne and including modern writers such as Joan Didion. Romano's contention is that purposeful rule breaking of standard English not only can lead to powerful communication, but also can help students evolve their voices, pay close attention to standard rules of writing style, and gain linguistic confidence and rhetorical flexibility.

Third-grader Justin is one of the best writers in class. He loves reading, revels in language, crafts stories that leave me in awe of his eight-year-old imagination and skill. In his latest piece of writing, one sentence reads, "I ate blugurt in the morning."

"What's blugurt?" I ask him.

"You know how you can put two words together to make one?" Justin asks, "like *can* and *not* make *can't*?"

"A contraction."

"Right. Well, blugurt is my combined word for blueberry yogurt."

★　★　★

Ninth-grader Dianna's paper about the Cleveland Browns' miserable losing streak has received 82 percent. Nine errors are marked; no teacher comments appear on the paper.

In one spot Dianna has written, "When asked about the Browns' record, quarterback Brian Sipe said, 'I don't know. There's just something wrong with the Browns.' Something wrong indeed!"

Something wrong indeed!—that nicely timed rhetorical phrase revealing Dianna's voice and ironic sensibility had been dutifully labeled "SF."

Patty, a high school junior, is reading *The Color Purple*, written primarily in protagonist Celie's African American dialect. One day I ask students to explain what they have learned about writing from the novels they are reading. Patty writes, "Alice Walker taught me that you can break the rules of writing I learned in tenth grade and write one of the best books ever."

During the time I wrote *Clearing the Way* (1987), I discovered a book in the Heinemann catalog that profoundly influenced my conception of what writing was, what it could be, and what I would teach. The book was *An Alternate Style: Options in Composition* by Winston Weathers (1980).

Certainly, the book is for composition scholars who seek greater knowledge of rhetorical theory. But the book is also for all who love linguistic innovation, stylistic experimentation, boundary-breaking written expression, and, above all, glorious human diversity. Weathers describes two ways of writing, two "grammars of style," as he calls them: Grammar A and Grammar B.

Grammar A you're familiar with: standard written English, traditional rules of style. It bows to the SAT English usage hoop that students must jump through. Grammar A is eminently acceptable and generally quite conservative. Fidelity to Grammar A has prompted many of us to say to students things like "Never begin a sentence with *and* or *but*" when we know that professional writers break that pseudo-rule whenever they must.

That's Grammar A, the grammar that we—among a phalanx of English/language arts teachers—move students to learn from kindergarten through graduate school. But according to Weathers, Grammar A is not alone. Also at large in the kingdom of writing is another grammar, an appealing rebel, illicit in most eyes, yet ubiquitous and purposeful. We English teachers should be forthright and honest and acknowledge this other way of writing, this other grammar of style: Grammar B, as Weathers calls it, "an alternate style."

Grammar B breaches the social amenities of Grammar A, taking liberties with Grammar A sentence structure, syntax, spelling, voice, and form. Grammar B breaks the rules of standard written English as a means of communicating powerfully. And it does this breaking, altering, and smashing with panache.

Don't be alarmed: Grammar B does not presage the decline of the West. Neither is it linguistic anarchy or grammatical promiscuity. Grammar B is nothing new. We've seen it in the writing of, among others:

Richard Brautigan

e. e. cummings

Emily Dickinson

Joan Didion

John Dos Passos

D. H. Lawrence

Gertrude Stein

Walt Whitman

Tom Wolfe

Virginia Woolf

Grammar B is no youngster, either. Weathers' earliest citation of alternate style usage in fiction is Laurence Sterne's 1760 publication of *The Life and Opinions of Tristram Shandy,* and in nonfiction, William Blake's prefatory remarks to each book of *Jerusalem* published in 1804. Writers have been using Grammar B for years, but especially since the mid-1960s when "new journalism" announced its presence through the work of Tom Wolfe and Truman Capote. Weathers writes:

> [Grammar B] is a mature and alternate (*not* experimental) style used by competent writers and offering students of writing a well-tested set of options that, added to the traditional grammar of style, will give them a much more flexible voice, a much greater communication capacity, a much greater opportunity to put into effective language all the things they have to say. (1980, p. 8)

Taking the persona of a student learning to write, Weathers asks that

> [I] . . . be exposed to, and informed about, the full range of compositional possibilities. . . . That . . . I be introduced to all the tools, right now, and not be asked to wait for years and years until I have mastered right-handed affairs before I learn anything about left-handed affairs. That, rather, I be introduced to all the grammars/vehicles/tools/compositional possibilities now so that even as I "learn to write" I will have before me as many resources as possible. I'm asking: that all the "ways" of writing be spread out before me and that my education be devoted to learning how to use them. (1980, p. 2)

I was excited by Weathers' inquiry into what many might consider this profane area of rhetoric. I developed a sense of urgency about my writing and teaching as I saw him treating with respect the unconventional stylistic maneuvers I'd admired over the years but never tried myself. Weathers approached his research in a scholarly, academic fashion. He catalogued the stylistic techniques of Grammar B, described them, and demonstrated how they might be used.

I found that Grammar B seeped into my own writing. Although no chapter in my first book, *Clearing the Way*, is about Grammar B, I was immersed in learning about it when I wrote Chapter 11, "Literary Warnings." You can see the influence of my study by the alternate style in which the chapter is written. My urgency about Weathers' research made me determined to bring Grammar B to my high-school students. But before I made such a bold move, I needed to talk about it.

I sought out Mark, my widely read friend and former student of eleven years earlier. I told him I'd never seen anything like Weathers' explanation of the alternate style, hearkened to the work of Tom Wolfe, e.e. cummings, and Ken Kesey that we'd admired and discussed over the years. "I'm hoping Grammar B will spur students to take chances," I told him. "I want them to astonish themselves. I want them to smash conventional rules of writing and cut loose."

Mark raised his eyebrows. "Looks like you're going to do what you've always done."

I blinked. He was right. For years I'd sought to free students from restrictions, to create an atmosphere that removed impediments to exploration and communication. But I'd never actively and single-mindedly pushed students to break conventional rules of writing as a way of writing effectively.

Even though I hadn't, however, over the years there had been memorable students with irrepressible voices who had surprised me with risk taking and originality. They were bellwethers. They knew intuitively that any rule of writing could be broken if the end result was writing that worked.

Style-Making Bellwethers

On a final essay exam in a high-school American Literature class, I asked students to write informative, well-supported essays in which they discussed five pieces of literature they had read over the semester:

1. the piece that revealed something startling or surprising about America's past

2. the piece you found most enjoyable

3. the piece most artfully put together

4. the piece that caused you to gain sympathy for a character you normally might not care about

5. the piece that most challenged your ideas or beliefs

Students could range freely over any of the poems, stories, essays, and books they had read during the semester. In fact, I listed the titles of everything we'd read to help jog their memories.

Here is a paragraph from David's essay:

Another book that shows just how much change has happened is *The Electric Kool-Aid Acid Test* (you're probably tired of hearing me talk about it). It was well written. I liked the way it looked on paper. How many books can you say that about? It looked good on paper. It had run on sentences in parts where the action seemed like it could go on forever and he just kept dragging the sentence out to keep you reading on, and on, and on. Then. All of a sudden. He would toss in a fragment sentence. He also had poems, songs, and the thoughts of the characters thrown into fully italicized paragraphs.
David Van Cleave
Junior, Edgewood High School

I hadn't taught the alternate style in that American Literature class, but David had read Tom Wolfe on his own. That was enough. David had learned about writing through reading. He was delightfully infected by Wolfe's exuberant voice, which demonstrated possibilities for supercharged prose.

In the same batch of papers was an essay from another junior, Becki. Ten months earlier, she had missed the first week of my writing class, each day sitting in the guidance office trying to talk a counselor into letting her drop the course. The counselor wouldn't comply with her request. So Becki and I spent the first weeks of school at loggerheads: she sullen and recalcitrant; I righteous and unyielding.

As the semester progressed and Becki grudgingly wrote, her strong voice piqued my interest. We softened our positions and gave each other a chance. Becki enjoyed writing; I enjoyed her feisty intellect and fearless yawp. Second semester she elected to take my American Literature class. Here is Becki's final essay exam, written in about thirty minutes—a double twisting, one-and-a-half off the high board, no second chance, no revision:

The reality. The pain. The loneliness.

All the endurance and loyalty involved with war is what I got from the novel *Johnny Got His Gun*. I never realized the true horror of war until this story. I cried when he did, laughed when he laughed, and felt the pain of being abandoned. Which is why "Richard Cory" ended his life. He wasn't happy with all his material things, no, not by far. He needed and so desperately yearned for love. And all he got was a lot of "oohs and ahs" by the peasants. He was at the end of his rope in the cold damp basement. His son witnessed his murder. Then, shortly, his own. His wife lay sobbing in her bed awaiting death, as did her daughter. Her daughter turns her face to the wall so as not to look death in the face when BANG. The cold hard iron doors shut. Shutting out the rest of the world His brother never wrote him. His parents were dead and he was in jail. Sitting, and thinking, thinking and sitting. I felt sorry for the poor guy. Growing up in the city can change a man for the worst. Unless you're Stony Decoco. Then you deal with life the best way you can. Day by day. Not getting too attached to anyone or anything for fear of change. Raising hell and earning money are two of the most important things to Stony. Who cares about love? Stony did. He loved Cheri

so much that every breath he took reminded him of her. Then she left him alone to face the world and being a survivor, he did.
Becki Strunk Thompson
Junior, Edgewood High School

It took me awhile to catch on to Becki's sophisticated discussion, which deftly blended one piece of literature into the next, one character into another. At one point—jumping the gun—I was saying to myself, Wait a minute, "at the end of his rope in the cold damp basement"? Richard Cory didn't hang himself. But I read on and was rewarded by Becki's subtle creation of language, literary interpretation, and compassion.

She expected me to have brains. Becki knew I had read all the literature she referred to. She had her audience pegged, but this was, after all, the final exam. So when it wasn't clear in her text which piece of literature she was writing about, Becki wrote the applicable title in the margin next to her discussion: Truman Capote's *In Cold Blood*, James Baldwin's "Sonny's Blues," and Richard Price's *Blood Brothers*—rhetorical elbows in the ribs in case I didn't get it.

So thoroughly delighted was I with Becki's linguistic performance that I telephoned her mother to extol Becki's stellar synthesis of literary knowledge, personal connection, and language use. When I called, Becki answered the telephone, rock music cranked up in the background.

"Mom's at work, Mr. Romano, I'm kicked back, listening to music and drinking a pop. School's out, man!"

"You deserve some laid back time," I said. "I called to tell your mom about your excellent essay."

"Yeah?" she said.

"Yeah, indeed," I said, "it made me sit right up and take notice."

Becki laughed. "I thought you'd like that."

For years my best writing students had been showing me that you *can* break rules of standard written English and write exceedingly well. With their example, my own delight in playful, innovative writing, and Winston Weathers' solid academic discussion of alternate style techniques, I was ready to bring Grammar B to my students. I've been doing it ever since, ten years now, with students junior high through graduate school.

Grammar B Stylistic Techniques

In the remainder of this chapter I'll demonstrate through the work of high school and college students some of the stylistic techniques Winston Weathers discusses in *An Alternate Style*, principally:

repetition

the sentence fragment

the labyrinthine sentence

orthographic variation

double voice

the list

Repetition

Grammar B certainly has no monopoly on the use of effective repetition. Repetition is a staple of effective writing regardless of the genre or style. Our lives thrive on repetition: our lungs expand and contract, expand and contract. The pulse at our wrists beats steadily on. In writing we love cadence and rhythm and rhyme. In Grammar B, however, repetition takes on even more importance. Grammar B, Weathers tells us, uses repetition "to achieve a kind of momentum in composition" (1980, p. 28). Here is a high-school junior playing around with repetition in a homework assignment:

> There were pans, there were pots, there were plates, there were glasses that had to be washed.
>   So I rubbed, scrubbed, polished, and rinsed the dishes clean.
>   I put them in the dish drainer to drip dry and they dripped in the sink.
>   Then I had to wipe the table, wipe the stove, wipe the sink.
>   I had to put the mound of dishes away in the cabinet under the counter.
> *Paula Perdue Cox*
> *Junior, Edgewood High School*

I love saying this piece aloud.
"cabinet under the counter"
". . . wipe the table, wipe the stove, wipe the sink."
Paula repeats sounds, words, and parallel patterns of phrases and sentences. And she knows intuitively that repetition is effective and then more effective when the repeated pattern is varied:

> There were pans,
> there were pots,
> there were plates,
> there were glasses that had to be washed.

The arrangement of the words makes me want to beat out their rhythm.

Writers in the alternate style also repeat ideas, even forms. They use everything from simple repetitions to repetends. The repetend is the unexpected repetition of a word, phrase, sentence, or passage. Remember "So it goes" in Kurt Vonnegut's *Slaughterhouse-Five*?

The Sentence Fragment

Elevating words or phrases to the level of sentence—albeit a fragmentary sentence in the eyes of Grammar A—"suggests a far greater awareness of separation and fragmentation" (Weathers, 1980, p. 19). A sentence fragment is a word or phrase torn from a continuous flow of discourse. It is no longer merely one word working with five, ten, twenty, or thirty others to create meaning within the confines of a traditionally defined sentence. The sentence fragment is isolated, emphasized, granted the integrity of beginning with a capital letter and ending with a period —usually.

Look at the lead to Chapter Seven of Richard Wright's *Black Boy*:

Summer. Bright hot days. Hunger still a vital part of my consciousness. Passing relatives in the hallways of the crowded home and not speaking. Eating in silence at a table where prayers are said. My mother recovering slowly, but now definitely crippled for life. Will I be able to enter school in September? Loneliness. Reading. Job hunting. Vague hopes of going north. But what would become of my mother if I left her in this queer house? And how would I fare in a strange city? Doubt. Fear. My friends are buying long-pants suits that cost seventeen to twenty dollars, a sum as huge to me as the Alps! This was my reality in 1924. (1937/1966, p. 178)

I've shared this passage with teachers and asked them to speculate about the effect of Wright's sentence fragments. Some teachers have said that the fragments emphasize the fragmented nature of his life at that point, the overwhelming nature of loneliness, fear, and doubt. Others have said that sentence fragments mirror thinking—the Vygotskian notion that inner verbal thought is composed of bursts of significant words that contain a shower of meaning for the thinker.

I asked students to experiment with sentence fragments in their writing. Chris wrote this:

I. Once. No. Many times.
Tried to ignore it.
But woke still. With my cat.
Walking. On my chest.
Licking. My face.
Chris Hardin
Senior, Edgewood High School

Chris' compact, radical use of sentence fragments startled me. Other students had used sentence fragments judiciously, mixing them with complete Grammar A sentences as Wright had done. Chris, I think, had been influenced by samples of writing from Gertrude Stein.

Why, I asked him, had he taken sentence fragments to such extremes?

"I wanted you to read every word," Chris said.

He achieved his purpose. I didn't skim the catwalk.

The Labyrinthine Sentence

At the opposite end of the sentence length continuum from the fragment is the labyrinthine sentence—not a lawless, poorly punctuated run-on sentence, but a finely crafted aggregation of words that weaves in and out, accruing information, riding rhythms of parallel sentence structure, tacking on phrases, clauses, and grammatical absolutes to form a sinuous sentence perfectly suited for some things we might describe or discuss.

Here is Tom Wolfe in *The Right Stuff* (1979), describing what it was like for test pilots in the 1950s to take jet planes beyond Mach one:

> To take off in an F-100 at dawn and cut in the afterburner and hurtle twenty-five thousand feet up into the sky so suddenly that you felt not like a bird but like a trajectory, yet with full control, full control of *five tons* of thrust, all of which flowed from your will and through your fingertips, with the huge engine right beneath you, so close that it was as if you were riding it bareback, until you leveled out and went supersonic, an event registered on earth by a tremendous cracking boom that shook windows, but up here only by the fact that you now felt utterly free of the earth—to describe it, even to wife, child, near ones and dear ones, seemed impossible. So the pilot kept it to himself, along with an even more indescribable . . . an even more sinfully inconfessable . . . feeling of superiority, appropriate to him and to his kind, lone bearers of the right stuff. (p. 30)

Weathers describes the labyrinthine maneuver as an "almost picaresque sentence" (1980, p. 18). Indeed, the sentence is a generative adventure, requiring the writer to provide more and more information to sustain it. The writer winds up her voice and lets spin. Here is a high-school senior describing what it's like in midwinter to catch a Toronto metropolitan bus to school:

> Waiting. For the bus. It takes a long time. In fact, it seems to take so long that your feet turn blue and your fingers become so numb that the book you were reading and were halfway through is now finished but the pages are stuck to your fingers so you have to pretend that you're still reading as you sway in and out of the bus shelter doorway hoping to catch a glimpse of the red rocket but instead your nose gets frostbitten and ice particles form in your hair, and as you return to safety your scarf blows away and you start coughing while out of the corner of your eye, you see the feeble lights on the bus approaching so you step up to the bus stop but the light turns yellow so the bus must stop and you feel the breath freezing in your throat and constricting your lungs, when all of a sudden the bus lurches forward and . . . *CHARTERED.*
> *Jennifer Alderson*
> *Senior, Woburn Collegiate High School, Toronto, Ontario*

Orthographic Variation

Weathers notes that one frequent characteristic of Grammar B is "a pressing against the walls of ordinary/orthodox vocabulary, a playing with words/word forms to achieve a special kind of lexical texture—a reading surface that is exciting and rebellious all at once" (1980, p. 30). That pressing against the walls is probably no more evident than it is in alternate stylists' use of orthographic variation.

And we teachers shudder.

Is there any surface feature of writing more glaring to the eye than spelling errors? If parents, administrators, and school board members have complained about any error in students' papers more than misspelled words, I don't know of it.

A parent's concern you will *not* hear:

"Ms. Dickson, I have a complaint about the writing my son is doing in your class."

"What's that?"

"His writing has no voice. It reads like the minutes from a meeting. I notice, too, that he doesn't use active verbs consistently. And there's an overall lack of concrete detail."

But you will hear plenty of carping about poor spelling, even though professional writers have been altering for years the way words look on the page. Here is John Dos Passos writing in *The Big Money* (1937/1961), describing the heinous rigors of assembly line production in Henry Ford's automobile plants:

> At Ford's production was improving all the time; less waste, more spotters, straw-bosses, stoolpigeons (fifteen minutes for lunch, three minutes to go to the toilet, the Taylorized speedup everywhere, reachunder, adjustwasher, screwdown bolt, shove in cotterpin, reachunder, screwdown bolt, reachunderadjustscrewdown-reachunderadjust until every ounce of life was sucked off into production and at night the workmen went home gray shaking husks). (pp. 56–57)

We want students to attain orthographic regularity in their writing, keeping in mind, of course, that standard English already permits some variation in orthography. On one high-school student's paper I had routinely circled the word *alright*, and told him the words he meant to spell were *all right*. He didn't see the point. I directed him to the dictionary. Later in the period, I came by his desk and asked what he had found.

He raised his eyes wearily. "They got yours; they got mine."

He showed me the citation. Sure enough, in that dictionary it was alright to spell *all right alright*.

Horrors, right? Slipshod standards. Riffraff corrupting our beloved English language. The same thing happened once when I circled *judgement* on a student's paper (a literate, capable student, I should add).

Good lessons for me from the populace. A poor speller myself, I'm all for simplifying English spelling whenever possible. During the copyediting of *Clearing the Way*, I argued for *dialog* instead of *dialogue*. And won. Then the copy editor upped the ante and suggested I use *monolog* instead of *monologue* and *catalog* instead of *catalogue*. I felt the sudden guilt and fear of conspiring in something unlawful. But I was giddy to go along with evolving the language.

Orthographic variations in Grammar B do not occur only when dictionaries grudgingly permit alternative spellings. Alternate stylists employ orthographic variation to meaningfully jolt readers. (E.g., The rule in one English Department was that three errors on a paper automatically equaled an *F*. Therefore, if a student's paper contained three spelling errors, the teacher assigned it an *F*—*automaniacally*.)

The proper word for orthographic variation, Weathers tells us, is not *misspelling*, but "calculated and controlled respelling" (1980, p. 30), which doesn't relieve teachers of their responsibility to continue to move students to orthographic regularity. I nervously imagine a scene in which a parent storms into a classroom, righteously waving her child's paper rife with spelling errors.

"How can you accept this writing?" demands the parent. "It's a spelling disaster!"

The teacher leans back in the chair, disdainfully waves a hand, and says, "Not to worry—those seeming errors are merely respellings."

It is, in fact, orthographic regularity that enables orthographic variation to be effective.

Observe the case of Erin, a young woman I met during the final semester of her senior year of high school. Erin was bright and polite. Her precisely clipped blond bangs corresponded to her meticulous daily attire. Her writing was cautiously restrained with no significant problems in grammar or usage. The only thing missing, for my taste, was a distinctive voice, a bond of meaning and style that would make her writing memorable.

At the time I met Erin, the high school featured a dynamic girls' basketball team. A number of the players were my students, so I went to a game. Erin, I found, was the point guard. In a basketball uniform she was daring, confident, and canny. She'd dribble the length of the court, pass the ball off to the corner, take it back at the top of the key, and launch an eighteen-foot jump shot. Erin played basketball with distinctive, undeniable voice.

Where, I wondered, was this young woman in my writing class? The labyrinthine sentence gave Erin a chance to blend her personas of outgoing, risk-taking athlete and reserved, obedient student. In the passage below, she used a labyrinthine sentence to cut loose on a roller coaster ride that rose with fond description, plunged to righteous indignation, and leveled off to a hard-won tranquillity. In addition to achieving full-voiced prose, Erin used orthographic variations and sentence fragments to highlight double meanings and communicate quiet commitment. Erin wrote about spring vacation in Florida, quite a contrast for students in the dreary, grimy-snowed winter of southwestern Ohio, where the biggest nearby body of water is the Ohio River.

> The waves are crashing down on white, sandy beaches as we take our morning walk, for the third day in a row, to celebrate the spring break and a get away from

city, schools, and familiar neighbors who seem to know all that happens whether at school, on a date, or inside our house, where no body should interfere, especially not those that are jealous because we get a Florida vacation while they sit at home, dreaming about the palm trees, the shining sand, glistening water and savage tans. The sights are many and varied and fill me with memories of things I might never see again. Return soon though. Eye will never forget these seven daze of onederful sites, clear beautiful sees, and a gorgeous state. Can't wait to come back. Will come back. Planning.

Erin Kash Allen
Senior, Edgewood High School

Erin's wrongfully right use of *eye, daze, onederful, sites,* and *sees* makes me stop and take note. Her multiple meanings emphasize the visual chasm between coastal Florida (with its beaches, palm trees, and expanse of blue sea) and southwestern Ohio in early spring (with its muddy hog farms, low rolling hills, and long stretches of brown-black earth waiting to be tilled and planted with corn and soybeans). Erin's orthographic variation puts me on my semantic toes, jolts me to attention.

So closely do I consider her surface text and meaning that by the time I get to *state,* I do not think *Florida* alone. Psychological state, I'm wondering? Emotional state? State of being? I don't know if Erin intended these meanings, but her playfulness alerts me to language. Seeming is not being. An intellect lurks behind the language play, an intellect that expects me to think.

Double Voice

Although we teachers press students to focus their writing, to straddle no fences, to argue either one side or the other in essays, Weathers notes that sometimes contrasting ideas are valid and opposing points of view equally interesting. Such complexity does not obfuscate or confuse meaning, but rather adds richness to it. Psychologist Jerome Bruner reminds us that often "depth is better achieved by looking from two points at once" (1986, p. 10).

Issues can be complex, and walking this earth are complicated people driven by motives both simple and multilayered. When we're fair, we know that each story has more than one side. Instead of discussing or rendering one point of view or idea, then its opposite, or minimizing one in favor of the other; a writer may employ double-voice, a stylistic maneuver that presents two sides simultaneously. Scott, for example, engages double-voice to indicate a hormonal dilemma and the probability of double dealing:

> Girl friend . . . Girl friend
> I love you.
> Only one for me
> Always and forever.
> Who's she?
> Always be together.

Is she new here?
Spend eternity together.
Do you know what her name is?
Scott Robinson
Senior, Edgewood High School

Writers may achieve double-voice many ways. One voice may appear in regular print, the other voice in italics or within parentheses. Voices may alternate sentence by sentence or paragraph by paragraph. Often double voices are set side by side in columns or paragraphs to emphasize the duality of two ideas or points of view. Such arrangement further suggests *synchronicity*—"all things present in the present moment" (Weathers, 1980, p. 35)—another characteristic of the alternate style, one which accounts for its plentiful use of present tense.

When my students experimented with the alternate style, I did the homework assignments right along with them. I needed to feel firsthand what purposeful, stylistic rule breaking was like. When we explored double-voice, I created my homework assignment the period before class met—just as many of the students did. As I watched my American Literature students take a test, I wrote what was on my mind:

The room is silent. Twenty-
five American Literature
students ponder, dig into
their minds, work hard to
formulate coherent thoughts
that will impress me with their
extensive knowledge of Henry
David Thoreau.

Oh, Jesus,
Thoreau—what a
conceited ass. He's
badgered me for two
weeks. I shoulda
read them essays!

Thoreau believed in the power
of the mind to plumb the depths
of thought and imagination, to
deal with intellectual subjects.

God, did Julie look
good last night!
Her hair, her eyes,
her wonderfully
luscious mouth, her

Radical political ideas, the
individual's relationship to
government. That's what Thoreau

dealt with in his seminal essay, "Civil Disobedience." And my astute essay question will lead students to confront crucial issues.

My stomach is rumbling like a distant thunderstorm. Pepsi for breakfast? Why did I do that!

Nothing can stop an individual who is determined, who advances confidently in the direction of his will, who leaves material possessions behind and seeks to know truth.

Time's awastin'. Better crank up the ol' B.S. machine.

The voice on the left is Teacher Tom. The voice on the right, I like to think, is George, the smart, likable, hulking wag, sitting in the last seat in the row by the windows. But soon after I wrote this, I realized that both voices were mine, the one on the right the sixteen-year-old Tom who still lives in me.

The List

Through a list a writer can quickly confront readers with abundant detail, enabling them to see an untainted, holistic picture. In list making, syntax and logical connections of language are not important. Simple, unexplained, occasionally poetic, the list usually appears in a column, one item per line, much like a grocery list. For practice the students and I did a quick-write and listed things we love. Here is the list I made:

students who speak the rude truth

Sharon's RX 7

gliding through water 900 meters into a swim

flesh

Mary Oliver

a book that makes me forget I'm reading

Wasatch Raspberry Wheat Beer

finding the precise word

Papa Bear's Pizza Oven in Canton, Ohio

GAP shirts

raw cherrystone clams

calamari

old photographs

Luciano Pavarotti

the 1930s

my daughter, upbeat

paperclips

my address stamp

newsy, full-voiced letters

Harry Crews

clear, honest intellects

connections that teach

Weathers explains that when making a list the writer simply provides "the data, the evidence, the facts, the objects" (1980, p. 20). The reader is left to bring meaning to them. The writer presents "a 'still life' of objects without indication of foreground or background, without any indication of relative importance, without any suggestion at all of cause-effect, this-before-that, rank, or the like" (1980, p. 20). Chad, who held Tom Wolfe in high regard and loved to write, play soccer, and deliver announcements over the PA system, dismissed the columnar list as "too much like a poem." In an alternate style piece about his visit to a college campus, Chad lists items that capture the feel of a young man's dormitory room:

> So after the coach leaves, I get a feel for what a college dorm room is like: Snipped-snaps of Jordan, Kareem, Bird, Tony Perez, a goldfish tank, paper, an Algebra III text, Diadora's crusted with dry mud, phone hung upside down on the wall, stereo singing softly with four speakers, a picture of a girl, Athens license plates tacked to the wall, Mousse and soap and toothpaste, and speedstick wedged tightly into a basket, draped with a towel like warm bread, a nerf basketball hoop jutting from the wall, a dead sock hanging on a makeshift clothesline, Tide.
> *Chad R. Pergram*
> *Senior, Edgewood High School*

Weathers writes about the objectivity of the list, about its nonjudgmental nature. It certainly can be that way. But the list can be calculated, too. The writer includes some items and excludes others. He orders the chosen items, too, maybe randomly, maybe not. In Chad's list I can't help but see both clutter and direction with "Tide" mentioned last to clean up the entire room.

Indeed, the list offers the writer opportunity to amass pointed detail in a particular context for devastating effect. Below is a poetic list rendered by a high school teacher as part of her research paper on Margaret Sanger, pioneering leader of the birth control movement in the United States:

1913 Methods for Birth Control

rue seed, castor beans
foam from a camel's mouth
pine bark and seaweed
stepping three times
over a grave

pomegranate peel
parsley and thyme
cedar oil
crocodile dung
churchyard luck

cabbage blossoms
root of spotted cowbane
holding the breath
great care and restraint

Dana Rickets
Teacher, Cottonwood High School
Salt Lake City, Utah

In the example below, Jennifer's list takes the form of a help-wanted advertisement for a cosmetic specialist in a fictional department store. Jennifer's absurd advertisement of the tacit qualities demanded of female cosmetic workers zings with social critique:

Help Wanted
Nymens Cosmetic Specialist

Attractive women ages 21–39
with prior cosmetic experience.
Must have excellent communication
skills. Single, nonmothers
preferred. Must be able to work

anytime Monday–Sunday including holidays. No wrinkles, age spots, facial scars, or bad teeth. Heavy foundation, panty hose, high heels and hairspray required. No sick pay or personal leave time. Overweight applicants and applicants with physical handicaps need not apply. No job security unless you maintain sales goals. Aggressive, self-motivated, persistent women only. Big busted blondes encouraged to apply. Actresses and anorexics preferred. Please contact Sherrie Airs at 231-2343 for an appearance interview.

Jennifer Pickering
Graduate student, Utah State University

Out of Weathers' definitions and my own examples of alternate-style maneuvers I'd found in literature, I created a packet that introduced students to Grammar B. We discussed Weathers' definitions, read aloud the examples, and sometimes puzzled over what was happening with the language (Gertrude Stein had us thinking hard). For homework assignments we wrote lists and double-voice pieces; we experimented with repetition, orthographic variation, and sentence form, both fragmentary and labyrinthine. Each day we shared writing, sometimes reading in a circle, sometimes putting our efforts on the chalkboard, opaque, or overhead. Our purpose was not to see who had done it right and who had done it wrong. Rather, by sharing the writing we saw the linguistic and personal variation that could exist in each Grammar B stylistic maneuver. That sharing became an instructive delight; the students' enthusiasm for rule breaking often turned those brief assignments into satisfying pieces of writing.

Some of the longer pieces students composed in the alternate style can be found in the appendix.

Can Students Get in Trouble for This?

After a workshop I conducted on Grammar B, a sixth-grade teacher told me he had shared the poetry of e.e. cummings with his students. They read the poems aloud and discussed the unconventional punctuation, spelling, and forms that cummings invented to communicate powerfully. The students delighted in the poet's rule breaking. Near the end of the discussion, however, one concerned soul in the back of the room raised a hand and asked, "Can e.e. get in trouble for this?"

It's a legitimate question. Will students get in trouble when they leave classrooms where Grammar B is permitted, even encouraged? One teacher accused me of teaching students to write "maverick essays." That sounded exciting, actually. But I knew what she referred to. In judging students' advanced placement exams, when anyone at an assessment table encounters an essay that breaks the standard or deviates from normal form, that essay is branded "maverick" and passed to the leader of the assessment table. My accuser believed this would mean curtains for the paper. Friends who have served as table leaders have told me, however, that if a Grammar B essay has a chance of scoring well with anyone at the table, it is likely to be with the leader, whose conception of effective writing often encompasses more than the traditional, thesis-driven, argumentative essay.

Never have angry or disenchanted former students contacted me to complain that I'd led them down a stylistically irresponsible path. Never that I know of has a student failed a future class because of our three-week foray into the alternate style. The worst that has happened involved one young woman who came back to visit the high school after her first semester at college. Cheryl told me that in her freshman composition class she had cast her first assignment in the alternate style. Her teacher found the essay interesting but didn't know what to do with it. He asked her to write in the conventional mode of essay writing for the remainder of the semester. She agreed to. I applaud the teacher's open-mindedness and straightforwardness. I applaud Cheryl's exuberant boldness and pragmatism. Four years later she became an English teacher.

Part of what we must teach students, of course, is sensitivity to audience, whether that audience be a teacher, an ailing grandparent, a newspaper's readership, a government bureaucrat, a grant-funding committee, or what have you.

I must admit, however, that socialization to the amenities of standard written English, both in surface features and in form, is not my major concern as a teacher of writing. In fact, I'd like to see more students using Grammar B writing techniques and purposefully breaking rules and pseudo-rules of standard style a lot more often in their writing. I'd prefer they do whatever necessary to generate original thinking and language than to slavishly heed the amenities of Grammar A.

As writing teachers, I don't think we have to fret much about socializing most students to the conventions of standard style. That socialization will occur *if students participate often in real literacy engagements*—writing frequently for their own purposes, reading frequently from the vast world of print. The bulk of what students read—particularly from textbook publishers—is written quite conventionally. Combine that reading experience with the patient teaching of editing skills within the context of their own writing, and most students will steadily move toward mastery of many standard conventions of composition.

In fact, purposeful rule breakers may be even more attentive to standard rules. The students most keenly aware of various school rules are not the student council representatives. It is the rule *breakers* who know the ins and outs of school rules.

What we teachers should worry about, however—what I am most concerned with—is our students' linguistic confidence. I want students to develop a willingness to be bold with language, to press forward with words. I want them to be versatile, daring, and practiced enough to readily interact with their writing, and to do so with imagination, logic, and originality.

For many students the alternate style was a liberation akin to the women's suffrage amendment. It was long overdue; it emboldened them; they were never the same after it. Cheryl, the student who confounded her freshman composition teacher with her Grammar B essay and later became an English teacher, echoed the sentiments of her classmates when she wrote,

> The alternate style adds freedom to do what we've always wanted to do but we always felt we'd get an F. This style enabled me to get what I really thought down on paper without worrying about structure. All of our class' pieces came out more truthful and, I think, interesting in the process.
> *Cheryl Eby*
> *Senior, Edgewood High School*

The students broke rules of writing and began ruling writing. In their alteration of standard style, they wrote with more purpose than ever before, paying closer attention to punctuation, word choice, and the forms they organically created. In paper after paper I saw evidence of intellect and intent, of students vitally aware of their role as writer, as maker and shaper of meaning through language.

"For the first time," wrote Teri, "I began thinking about the way my writing would look on the page."

Jon, a talented writer who had no trouble weaving flawlessly punctuated complex sentences, believed that purposefully using sentence fragments made him begin to think about the power of individual words. His voice expanded to include, as he put it, "terser sentences."

One student kept missaying the alternate style. Grinning and excited, he'd stride up to me before class. "Mr. Romano," he'd say, "are we working on our ultimate-style papers today?"

That made me nervous. For many students this paper *was* the ultimate style. Grammar B was freedom, license, escape from constraint. They saw Grammar B as a genre in itself, the ultimate genre. And what else could I have expected students to think? I'd driven them toward such thinking by doing an alternate style unit that required each of them to write an alternate style paper. I'd created a dichotomous monster. The students thought

There was straight writing over here, conservative, staid, safe, and sometimes boring.	But over here . . . over here was this "other" kind of writing—dangerous, rebellious, free of inhibitions.

I looked upon the alternate style differently. I saw Grammar B as a resource, offering writers further stylistic options—nontraditional ones, to be sure—but, as Weathers makes clear, no less legitimate and with ample precedent in our diverse literary heritage. In articles, in talks, in book reviews, in theses and dissertations as well as in fiction and poetry, we can often push the envelope, be a little more daring and adventurous in how we put words on paper. I wanted Grammar B techniques to become part of a versatile rhetorical repertoire that each of my students possessed, equally as useful, depending on content and audience, as conventional spelling, topic sentence–controlled paragraphs, thesis-driven essays, and argumentative idea development.

It seems to me that the most important aspect of Winston Weathers' Grammar B has little to do with orthographic variation, double-voice, or labyrinthine sentences. Of critical importance is the *spirit* of the alternate style, the implications it holds for nurturing all student writers, kindergarten through graduate school.

High-school or university students whose writing reflects their reading of Virginia Woolf and Allen Ginsberg often employ alternate styles of writing as they evolve original voices. Elementary school students whose writing repertoire includes invented spelling, drawings, speechmarks, and supplemental talk are also employing alternate styles—eminently appropriate ones—and they, too, are evolving original voices.

Iowa first-grade teacher Chris Rinner knows how his students readily create nontraditional techniques and forms: "They see writing as a way to make their point." And they make their points by using everything their new learning makes available. Weathers, in fact, maintains that Grammar B "is probably the fundamental and essential style, out of which a secondary Grammar A has been developed for specialized logic/clarity goals" (p. 51).

One of my high-school students pointed out that the alternate style "really helps writers understand their voices." I think he's right. My students—both in high school and college—pushed beyond boundaries of written expression, boundaries imposed both from without and within. They astonished themselves and learned about limits. Such self-understanding of the power and range of our voices is crucial to our maturation as writers. Voice is the vitality of a writer, both the root and point of growth. We write about personally important matters in many different genres and over a lifetime develop our voices.

We extend them, we adapt them, we learn with them. The alternate-style options explained by Winston Weathers let students participate in this development in new and exciting ways. Their visions became expansive, their language adventurous, their use of line and page inventive. Instead of wearing ruts in safe, beaten paths, my students broke new trails when their purposes demanded. They trusted both instinct and intellect, practicing possibilities, evolving their voices.

Appendix: Alternate Style Pieces

The Art of Learning Nothing
Biology—How to etherize tiny bugs so we can stare at their tails and wings and guess. Male or female? Which is more dominant? 25 percent chance of wrinkled winged female 25 percent wrinkled winged male 25 percent red-tipped female 25 percent red-tipped male . . . except red-tipped is a female trait so your whole experiment is now screwed up.

Reasons Why My Experiment Screwed Up
1. bugs etherized to death
2. bugs reproduced so much they changed color
3. bugs fried to death in incubator
4. bugs (male) were fags
5. stupid lab partners' fault—give them the F, not me
6. I don't have any idea
7. all of the above

What Was Avogadro's number again?
Kelvin's number?
Melvin's number?
H'm'ny MOLES . . . Molality. Molarity. Molecule. Molecular. Mole Method. What's the difference? I forget.

Charles' Law $\frac{V}{V_1} = \frac{T}{T_1}$

Boyles' Law $\frac{V}{V_1} = \frac{P_1}{P}$ put them in a pot and mix laws together and you get a

V that equals $V \cdot \frac{T_1}{T} \cdot \frac{P}{P_1}$ and Dalton's Law says the total pressure of a mixture of

gases is the sum of partial pressure and I'm totally drowning in the sum of equations.

Try something new.
200 + some pages of Indian history.
Wounded My Heart at Buried Knee
Wounded My Knee at Buried Heart
Buried My Knee at Wounded Heart
Then 284 pages of torturous philosophies for future scholars of the universe
"However this restriction may be opposed to natural right and to the usages of civilized nations, yet, if it be indispensable to that system under which the country . . ."

What was that?

Again.

Sigh.

"It is difficult to comprehend the proposition that the inhabitants of either quarter of the globe could have rightful original claims of dominion over the inhabitants of the other, or over the lands they occupied or that the discovery of either, by the other should give the discoverer rights in the country discovered . . ."

You said it. Great book you picked for us. Slam.

English can be fun. GRRammar!

We, us, them, they, their, there, they're, are, our, idea, idear, ideal.

Students scrunch over their desks scribbling and scratching their papers.

With pencil in hand and mouth, I nibble on the eraser and I sit . . .

  and sit . . .

       and sit . . .

Finally—

"Birds chirp at my bedroom window . . ."

No.

"Love, like a cancer—never a full recovery . . ."

Yuck. No.

"To be or not to be . . ."

That's not my question. No, that won't work either.

Nibble . . . Nibble . . .

              Chomp!

I spit the eraser from my tongue and stare at the dammed paper.

Let's try clots

CROTS!

crots, crots

SORRY

"autonomous unit characterized by the absence of any transitional device . . ."

huh?

D. H. Lawrence

my work	my crot
my crot	my life
my life	my crot
my crot	might rot

Karen Ballinger
Senior, Edgewood High School

Tucky House

It got its name when my brother was learning to talk. I spent half of my childhood there.

> Little red house on the hill
> overlooking a field of
> Bluegrass.
> Fresh scent of honeysuckle
> spread by the breeze.
> No T.V.
> No telephone.
> Only a wooden swing on the front porch.
> Large garden in the backyard:

> potatoespotatoespotatoespotatoespotatoes
> tomatoestomatoestomatoestomatoestomatoes
> lettucelettucelettucelettucelettuce
> onionsonionsonionsonionsonionsonionsonions
> Strawberries!

"Uncle Dale." A man of seventy-five years. He had white hair and whiskers to match. His crystal blue eyes sparkled beneath droopy eyelids. A grin continuously covered his face. The only outfit I can remember him wearing consisted of faded overalls, rugged work boots, and his old engineer's cap. Every time he saw me, he would tease and threaten to spank me. I knew he was only joking.

"Aunt Libby." Dale's wife. A tall, slender woman. Her silver-gray hair was swept into a bun, and a warm smile accompanied her piercing brown eyes. She always stopped by with a strawberry or peach cobbler for the "young-uns" (Yum, yum!).

When Kentucky is mentioned, many people think of hillbillies running around barefooted with a pig under one arm, trying to lead a stubborn old mule up a hill to the barn.

It's not like that.

Mornings. I roll over beneath the cozy blankets, yawn, and lie motionless. Sausage crackles in the skillet and the aroma fills the house. I open my eyes to be greeted by the sun's rays that gleam through my window.

Evenings. I sit on the back porch while Granny retells favorite stories of her childhood.

"When I was a youngster—about ten or twelve, there was this hillbilly singer—Red Foley, and his daughter was married to Pat Boone, well, when someone died, he stayed at our house in Corbin and wanted a chicken for the funeral, so my mother sent me out to get a chicken from the chicken coop, and the rooster got all roiled up, so later when this hillbilly guy was on the radio giving the names of people he wanted to thank, he didn't mention me, and I thought he should've 'cause of the trouble I went through gettin' his ol' chicken, well that just didn't do much for me . . ."

Horse and buggy . . .
milkman . . .
iceman . . .
walking to school . . .
Sunday drives . . .
sleigh ride down Cordon Hill . . .
camping in tents . . .
no cooler . . .
army cots . . .
courtin' at Cumberland Falls . . .
trip to Jelico . . .
bridge out . . .
Grandpa's coal mine . . .
not allowed in . . .
Carrol town . . .

                       Blink

                  Blink

             Blink

"Look, Granny.
the fireflies are out!"
Blink

              Stomp!
Blink

              Stomp!

                     Stomp! Blink
                        Clap!
                        "Gotcha!"

Relatives stop in unexpectedly. They are welcomed warmly and urged to stay for dinner and a good night's sleep. No matter how many people are crammed into the little house, the motto is: "The more the merrier!"

When I see a "Home Sweet Home" sign, I think of my Old Kentucky Home—'Tucky House.

Teri Baumgartner
Junior, Edgewood High School

References

BRUNER, J. (1986). *Actual minds, possible worlds*. Cambridge, MA: Harvard University Press.

DOS PASSOS, J. (1937/1961). *The big money*. New York: Washington Square Press.

ROMANO, T. (1987). *Clearing the way: Working with teenage writers*. Portsmouth, NH: Heinemann.

WEATHERS, W. (1980). *An alternate style: Options in composition*. Rochelle Park, NJ: Hayden Book.

WOLFE, T. (1979, 1980). *The right stuff*. New York: Bantam.

WRIGHT, R. (1937/1966). *Black boy*. New York: Harper & Row.

13

The Power of Dialect
Ebonics Personified

DENISE TROUTMAN

Introduction

Due to the "miseducation of the Negro" (Woodson, 1933, p. xx) and the vast majority of the U. S. populace, mythical notions about dialects, in general, and Ebonics, in particular, persist in spite of analyses showing the systematicity and logic of African American English. The mediaploitation surrounding the Oakland Unified School District's 1996 decision to recognize the legitimacy of Ebonics has intensified the existing myths. Sociolinguistic work appears vacuous, especially considering that the "Oakland Case" replicates significantly Judge Joiner's ruling in the "Ann Arbor Case." Clearly, negative evaluations of dialects in general and Ebonics in particular are still held by some key persons invested with teaching the children of Ebonics. I present the "low down" (key information) on Ebonics, as one example of a dialect with positive and powerful features. Too often television information programs about the Oakland Ebonics decision equated Ebonics with slang. I synopsize the distinctive features of Ebonics in an attempt to disambiguate slang and Ebonics.

Quiet as it's kept, a significant segment of Ebonics speakers of differing socio-economic statuses value their home language, even middle-class speakers. African American linguists, scholars, authors, poets, and pastors research, write about, and/or write in the discourse style of Ebonics, preserving and showing the value of the linguistic code.

Speakers outside of the African American speech community also show reverence for Ebonics, as language borrowings demonstrate. One television program is used as an example to demonstrate "covert prestige" held for Ebonics, as well as other borrowings.

Last, the implications of the present work are discussed as applicable to teaching contexts.

Among true language scholars, *all* varieties of a language are technically and appropriately called dialects. Traditionally, both linguists and lay persons view only the speech varieties of the powerless as "nonstandard dialects." In everyday interactions, "in one form or another, power informs all human relationships . . ." (Lakoff, 1990, p. 12).

Power, as an abstraction, is measurable along a continuum of physical features (Lakoff, 1990). Power, for example, can be measured by the act of decision making. Those persons making decisions about promotion and tenure in academia sit in positions of power. Decision making, then, has more strength, force, and impact than non-decision making. Power, as well, is measurable by the act of using language. When language and gender become key variables in a particular interaction, the linguistic variety used by men becomes the linguistic code of power. When language and socioeconomic status become the key variables, the dialect of wider communication becomes the linguistic code of power. Power, within this context then, is defined as having control over prized valuables within a society, such as monetary, educational, occupational, or material property, prestige (honor and respect usually due to property ownership), and "access to the creation and dissemination of knowledge" (Richardson, 1977, pp. 140, 189). In societies where one group dominates in social, political, and economic life, a disequilibrium will exist in the exertion of power, especially in interactions where age, race, gender, or socioeconomic status become marked linguistic variables. *Language is power.* The social dialect most often associated with those persons in power becomes the linguistic code of power.

The Power of Language

According to God's Word, language is powerful: "A man's [moral] self shall be filled with the fruit of his mouth; and with the consequence of his words he must be satisfied [whether good or evil]. Death and life are in the power of the tongue . . ." (Prov. 18: 20–21, *The Amplified Bible*). The power of language can be seen also in magical words. "Abracadabra" uttered over certain contents produces a changed outcome, by word alone. "Kazam," spoken by the right person, causes instantaneous transformations. Words have so much power that calling people "*out* of their names" (i.e., through racial epithets) oftentimes produces an irascible outcome.

Bosmajian (1973) effectively discusses the power of language in "Defining the 'American Indian': A Case Study in the Language of Suppression":

> The Nazis redefined the Jews as 'bacilli,' 'parasites,' 'disease,' and 'demon.' The language of white racism has for centuries attempted to 'keep the nigger in his place.' Our sexist language has allowed men to define who and what a woman is. . . . Through the use of the language of suppression the human animal can seemingly justify the unjustifiable, make palatable the unpalatable, and make decent the indecent. . . . Once one has been categorized through the language of suppression, one loses most of the power to determine one's future and most of

the control over one's identity and destiny. . . . There are degrees of control of one's destiny and degrees of suppression, but one element to be found in the various kinds of suppression is the use of language that attempts to justify the separation, enslavement, or eradication of the oppressed. Just as our thoughts can corrupt our language, so too can our language corrupt our thoughts, and in effect corrupt our behavior (pp. 89, 99).

Bosmajian's words are powerful and dense. As he explains, beginning with Columbus and other European invaders and extending into the present century, white Americans have used the power of language to redefine American Indians as savages, barbarians, and nonentities. As a direct result of redefinition, historically, white Americans felt justified in torturing, enslaving, and almost annihilating American Indians. In this instance, the thoughts of the white settlers affected their language and eventually corrupted their actions. A nation of approximately 4 to 8 million American Indians was almost annihilated through massive killings, disease, slavery, and war (Dinnerstein et al., p. 19). Bosmajian (1973) writes, "One of the first important acts of an oppressor is to redefine the oppressed victims he intends to jail or eradicate so that they will be looked upon as creatures warranting suppression and in some cases separation and annihilation" (p. 89). In Bosmajian's historic and linguistic explication, *words* are shown to be so powerful that they were used successfully in suppressing a whole nation.

The power of the word has long been established and acknowledged within the African American community. According to Smitherman (1977):

> the concept of Nommo, the magic power of the Word, was believed necessary to actualize life and give man mastery over things. 'All activities of men, and all the movements in nature, rest on the word, on the productive power of the word . . . The force, responsibility, and commitment of the word, and the awareness that the word alone alters the world. . . .' In traditional African culture, a newborn child is a mere thing until [its] father gives and speaks [its] name. No medicine, potion, or magic of any sort is considered effective without accompanying words. (p. 78)

Words hold so much power that a "war of mouths" (Smitherman, 1977, p. 79) is held before a war of arms, according to the African folk epic *Sundiata*.

> Even though [African Americans] have embraced English as their native tongue, still the African cultural set persists, that is, a predisposition to imbue the English word with the same sense of value and commitment . . . accorded to Nommo in African culture. Hence Afro-America's emphasis on orality and belief in the power of the rap which has produced a style and idiom totally unlike that of whites, while paradoxically employing White English words. (p. 79)

Language is power. Language is power*ful*. Those persons in powerful positions exert linguistic power. Such linguistically powerful persons are said to be educated, middle- and upper-class, holding high prestige and social status. Those persons who speak powerless varieties are characterized as little educated, working-class, with low prestige and social status. In short, they are considered untouchables, undesirables.

As sociolinguist Walt Wolfram (1986) explains, dialects that are more desirable can be identified according to the groups that are more desirable. Dialects labeled as "better" or "worse" are based on social stereotypes; thus, educated, urban, white, and middle-class are considered better than uneducated, rural, Black, and lower-class. African Americans are stereotypically viewed as poor, uneducated, gang members, or drug dealers. Ebonics, the speech variety spoken at least part of the time by 90 to 95 percent[1] of the African American population in the United States, as a result of undesirable traits associated with group members, is labeled as an undesirable, incorrect, powerless, nonstandard dialect of English spoken by a subculture.

The Problem to Be Investigated

In spite of all these linguistic technicalities, linguists and lay persons alike have not focused on two important areas: Not all Ebonics speakers are little educated, working-class, or of low social prestige and status. There is covert prestige held for this powerless speech variety.

Ebonics and the African American Speech Community

Due to inaccurate information society holds about dialects and languages, many African Americans hold high esteem for their linguistic heritage, regardless of their social status. This point becomes obvious when considering that Ebonics survives today, especially within many African American churches, fictional and nonfictional works, college classrooms, and among middle-class persons, though it is changing (as any language does). Below, I present the features of Ebonics occurring within the above specified contexts, yet will first briefly define the term Ebonics and list some of its most prominent features.

A Brief View of Ebonics

Despite some inaccurate media references equating the two linguistic codes, Ebonics and African American slang are not the same. Speakers of Ebonics may incorporate slang within their speech, yet slang is an effervescent, creative use of language that is age-graded, constrained primarily to morphology and syntax, and aims to keep outsiders out and insiders in, that is, to sustain a private code of communication. Young African Americans use slang items that I do not recognize or understand ("Oops, my bad"), although African Americans within my age group use slang items ("foxy mama") that I recognize and know based on the simultaneity of our rearing and the social, political, historical occurrences in the United States that impacted our lives. Regardless of age group, slang varies based on geographical location and is temporal.

Ebonics, in contrast, is here to stay—as long as its speakers survive. The term Ebonics derives from a fusing of the words "Ebony" and "phonics," first coined by a group of African American scholars in 1973 (Williams, 1975). Ebonics is also referred to as Negro nonstandard, Negroese, Black English (BE), Black Jargon, African-Negro Language, African American English (AAE), Pan African Communication Behaviors, the "language of soul," or "black talk" (Smitherman, 1977, p. 1; Blackshire-Belay, 1996, p. 15). Ebonics, regardless of the term used, is a linguistic system with distinct features in its phonology (sound system), syntax (sentence construction system), lexicon (vocabulary), and discourse structure (above the sentence level). Smitherman (1977) writes, "In a nutshell: Black Dialect is an Africanized form of English reflecting Black America's linguistic-cultural African heritage and the conditions of servitude, oppression, and life in America. Black Language is Euro-American speech with an Afro-American meaning, nuance, tone, and gesture" (p. 2). Further, Smitherman writes, Ebonics "is a language mixture, adapted to the conditions of slavery and discrimination, a combination of language and style interwoven with and inextricable from [African] American culture" (p. 3).

Some of the distinctive features of Ebonics follow. These linguistic features have their roots in West African languages, particularly those of the Niger-Congo region, and are not a result of haphazard or lazy articulation or lack of knowledge of a different linguistic system (i.e., the dialect of wider communication).

Phonology
Word-initial, voiced *th* is pronounced as *d*:
them —> dem, that —> dat

Word-final consonant clusters become simplified:
ho*ld* —> hole, pa*st*—> pass, de*sk* —> des, be*st* —> bes

Word-final, unvoiced *th* is pronounced as *f*:
Ruth —> roof, death —> deaf

(Smitherman, 1977, p. 7; Labov, 1972, pp. 15–20).

Syntax
Multiple negatives are permissible:
Don't nobody need nothing if they ain't gonna help.
Ain't nobody going nowhere wit no dirty clothes.

A highly marked aspectual system:

The coffee cold.	Right now, the coffee is cold.
The coffee be cold.	Usually, regularly
The coffee been cold.	Established in the remote past
The coffee been done got cold.	Stressed past, completed action

Absence of the verb *be* for static, fixed conditions or non-continuous activity:	We ready to go. They late.

LEXICON   The following words are part of the vocabulary shared by Ebonics speakers across the United States Regardless of geographic location, speech community members know the meanings of and use these terms, plus many more:

bad-mouthing: making negative points about a person or thing (e.g., "Who you bad-mouthing, now?")

born again: receiving new birth as a result of accepting Jesus Christ as Lord and Savior (e.g., "I thank the Lord that I been born again.")

CP Time: Colored People's time; a different system of time from European Americans', stemming from an Ashanti proverb cited in Berry and Blassingame (1977), "Ancient things remaining in the ear" (p. 516); an African system of time (e.g., "The meeting starts on CP Time.")

girl: a term of solidarity used between African American women (e.g., "Girl, you crazy.")

Uncle Tom: an African American male who is not loyal to the cause (the struggle of African Americans) and who seeks self-serving interests (e.g., "Many Blacks consider Clarence Thomas to be a true Uncle Tom.")

DISCOURSE   One major discourse pattern used by Ebonics speakers is signifying. Smitherman (1977) defines signifying as a game of insult used humorously to talk about a listener, who is within hearing range. The African American discourse rules specify that signifying does not take place behind a targeted listener's back, out of her listening range, though comments are made indirectly. The intent is for the targeted receiver of the signification actually to hear the comment; therefore, signifying behind a person's back does not accomplish the intended goal. This game is one of verbal wit, engaged in for fun or to make a point. When participants become serious, hurling true invectives, the game is over. Mitchell-Kernan (1972) provides some clear examples (323):

Context: One sister visits another sister's home. The latter sister feels, yet does not express before this exchange, that four children are enough and does not want another baby. She felt a bit upset when she became pregnant again and did not share with anyone that she was pregnant. At the time of this exchange, the pregnant sister had begun to show.
A: Girl, you sure do need to join the Metrecal for lunch bunch.
B: (noncommittally) Yea, I guess I am putting on a little weight.
A: Now look here, girl, we both standing here soaking wet and you still trying to tell me it ain't raining.

Context: In this exchange, Mitchell-Kernan engages in signifying with a young man in his early twenties. Two other young men of the same age are present also.
Young man: Mama, you sho is fine.
Mitchell-Kernan: That ain't no way to talk to your mother. (Laughter)
Young man: You married?
Mitchell-Kernan: Um hm.
Young man: Is your husband married? (Laughter) (p. 323)

Here, signifying occurs due to the indirection of the discourse. First of all, Mitchell-Kernan picks up on the young man's use of "mama," basing her comment on the premise that "if I am your mama, that is no way to talk to her" ("That ain't no way to talk to your mother.") The group enjoys Mitchell-Kernan's repartee (as the pause for laughter indicates) because it is clever and because she plays right along with the young man, showing her mental agility. The young man fires back with the point setting question, "You married?" After Mitchell-Kernan responds, the young man now scores the point with the question, "Is your husband married?" Here again, indirection occurs. The young man accepts Mitchell-Kernan's "um hm" reply that she is married. Yet he queries more importantly whether Mitchell-Kernan's husband accepts, believes, behaves as though he is married. (Touché!) The young man shows great skill in signifying with this witty response.

Ebonics: 'Live'

Most people hold the view that Ebonics exists only within the ranks of low socio-economic African Americans. Within the African American speech community, as is the case with other dialects in the United States, there is open recognition, acknowledgment, and pride in the home language.

Many African American linguists revere Ebonics, as becomes clear from their study of it, their scholarship and course offerings surrounding it, and their speaking the language. There is a rich body of work that focuses on describing and explaining the systematicity, uniqueness, and beauty in African American language. Smitherman's *Talkin and Testifyin* (1977) presents a historical, linguistic, and educational analysis of Ebonics in a very positive manner, with the distinctive feature of being written in both Ebonics and the dialect of wider communication. Baugh (1983), another African American linguist, also has recorded the regularity and systematicity of Ebonics. Rickford (1997), a Creolist, has chronicled the linguistic continuum of Ebonics from Africa to the Caribbean to the Sea Islands (off Georgia and South Carolina) and the United States mainland. Morgan (1989, 1991, forthcoming) and Troutman (1995, 1996a) have devoted research to describing the linguistic behavior of African American women, capturing their unique patterns in using language.

Many other middle-class African Americans show reverence for Ebonics through their works. Paul Laurence Dunbar, who followed in the footsteps of

Black poets Lucy Terry and Phillis Wheatley, was well known for his Negro-dialect poetry (Chapman, 1968) during the late eighteenth and early nineteenth century. Dunbar's poem "A Death Song" gives written permanency and historical chronology to features of Ebonics (Chapman, 1968, p. 356). Only one verse is cited here:

> Lay me down beneaf de willers in de grass,
> Whah de branch 'll go a-singin' as it pass.
>   An' w'en I's a-layin' low,
>   I kin hyeah it as it go
> Singin', "Sleep, my honey, tek yo' res' at las'."

Julianne Malveaux (1996), one of the few African American and female economists in the United States, writes positively in a newspaper column about the Oakland decision, calling the Oakland School Board members "visionaries of the future." John Oliver Killens (1971) captures the discourse style of Ebonics in the foreword to his book *The Cotillion*:

To Whom It May Concern
(and to all you all who ought to be)

I'm a writer, understand. And I just finished the novel that I'm forewording to you, dear readers. I used to write my novels as I lived them from Rio all the way to Zanzibar. In the oral tradition of my African ancestors.

  This book is kind of halfly autobiographical and halfly fiction, all based on facts as I have gathered them. I got my log together, baby, from the natural source, the horse's mouth and his hinder parts. Also from the lips of the sweetest girl on this terrible wonderful earth. Dig it, and like I went to one of them downtown white workshops for a couple of months and got all screwed up with angles of narration, points of view, objectivity, universality, composition, author-intrusion, sentence structure, syntax, first person, second person. I got so screwed up I couldn't unwind myself for days. I said, to hell with all that! I'm the first, second and third person my own damn self. And I will intrude, protrude, obtrude or exclude my point of view any time it suits my disposition. Dig that.

  . . . I decided to write my book in AfroAmericanese. Black rhythm, baby. Yeah, we got rhythm, brothers, sisters. Black idiom, Black nuances, Black style. (1–3)

In his decision to write in "AfroAmericanese," Killens demonstrates his love for the linguistic system.

  Pastor Sudduth, another example of a person within the middle-class who publicly acknowledges positive inheritance of an Africanized linguistic system, uses Ebonics features consciously from the pulpit. At different points, she encourages with "You go, girl." She rounds off pithy, salient points with "You hear me?" In one recent teaching, "The Significance of Behavior," Pastor Sudduth uses word play with the *be* in *behavior* and the acronym used by many scholars for Black English, BE:

In . . . [pastor's vernacular], BEhavior, our definition of BEhavior is the way that I BE to you or towards you, or against you. It's the way that I 'BE,' which is less than I AM. God is I AM because He's consistent. He never changes (Hebrews 13:8). But we are human BEings because we 'BE' one way to another and then 'BE' another way to the extent of becoming unpredictable. . . . The same way Jesus 'BE' at church is the same way He 'BE' at home or wherever. The way He 'BE' towards God the Father, He 'BE' the same way towards us and everyone else because He is not affected by the outside stimuli (external or internal) the way we are affected.

Pastor Sudduth and I have talked about Ebonics to the extent that we have even found biblical usages of BE (Black English), signifying that it must be legitimate if it is written in God's Word and that God ordained it from the beginning. Genesis 13:8 reads, "And Abram said unto Lot, Let there be no strife, I pray thee, between me and thee, and between my herdmen and thy herdmen; for we *be* brethren." "We be" is a regular grammatical construction in BE.

As an African American linguist who has studied, written about, and presented on Ebonics, I love the language. My love for it extends to the degree of passing it on to my children (who are acquiring proficiency in three linguistic systems), to the point of defending its existence, logicality, and rule-governedness in public lectures and professional writing, and especially to the degree of educating my family members of its origin, history, legacy, and value. My children are not cognizant of the Ebonics features that they use, yet I consciously spoke Ebonics around them. They heard their cousins using it, and as a result they learned to revere and speak Ebonics. By choice, I have just recently taught a graduate linguistics course entitled "The African American Speech Community," which focused primarily on scholarly work written on Ebonics and on encouraging graduate students to devote more attention to research in the area. My example, I believe, applies to a number of middle-class African Americans throughout the United States who have pride in their home language.

Ebonics and Covert Prestige

Although the stigma of Ebonics has been commonly acknowledged, its covert prestige is little recognized, especially in borrowings from Ebonics. Within sociolinguistics, covert prestige is associated with nonstandard varieties. Prestige is assigned to both standard and nonstandard varieties, yet with the latter type positive attitudes and attributes are "not usually overtly expressed and depart markedly from the mainstream societal values (of schools and other institutions) of which everyone is consciously aware" (Trudgill, 1983, p. 89). Ebonics speakers, clearly, attach overt and covert prestige to their linguistic variety due to their persistence in using Ebonics (thus, its survival); other speakers too attach covert prestige to Ebonics as evidenced in borrowings. Men, especially, are described as holding covert prestige for nonstandard varieties. In this section, I demonstrate the covert prestige of Ebonics and its powerful influence on a broader segment of United States society than typically identified.

BORROWING   In *Dictionary of Afro-American Slang*, Major (1970) writes that "a subculture always has a proportionately larger impact upon a dominant culture, rather than vice versa" (p. 11). The impact of African American culture upon the dominant, broader culture can be seen in:

young people's *sagging*, a popular style of wearing pants below the waistline

wearing braided hair or wearing beads in the hair

giving *high fives*, a stylized version of the common handshake currently used by sports players and all of the *cool generation*[2]

dancing the twist, the bump, the electric slide and especially those dances executed with hip-hop music

linguistic borrowings: "girlfriend" "You go girl" "I hear you"

the cover page of the *New York Times Book Review* (November 17, 1996), which was entitled "Yo Picasso!"

For the language borrowings, I provide a bit of contextualization. Many African American students, graduate and undergraduate, have informed me that they no longer use the newly created "girlfriend" due to its heavy usage by others outside the African American community. Television programs such as "Martin" introduced "girlfriend" usage to the broader community and sparked its borrowing. The African American students prefer a term relegated only to the African American community, thus dropping "girlfriend" and reverting back to "girl" usage primarily. "You go girl," an expression referring to a female who is admired because of some action, has crossed over into the dominant culture as evidenced in movies or television series that are not produced or written by African Americans. One of my jogging buddies, who is a European American female lawyer, readily acknowledges that she and her female associates use "You go, girl." "I hear you," used primarily as a back channeling device, similar to "uh-hunh" or "mhm" to show active listenership in conversations, means "I understand the point you are making" and may convey sympathy or empathy. Introduced within the African American community during the mid to late seventies, this statement moved quickly into broader usage. I remember the introduction of the expression among African Americans in my community and was flabbergasted when PBS news reporter Jim Lehrer used it on the nationally televised "MacNeil/Lehrer Report." "Yo," according to Smitherman's *Black Talk* (1994), can be used as a greeting, for example, "Yo, what up." Based on context, "yo" can also be used as an attention-getter "instead of saying 'Hey!' or 'Hey you!' [evolving] possibly from African American military men in the 1950s, who would answer 'Yo!' at roll call, whereas their European American counterparts would answer 'Yep!'" (Smitherman, 1994, p. 242). The *New York Times* reference (above) makes use of this latter interpretation of getting someone's attention.

Major (1994) refers specifically to the impact of African American culture on dominant culture via slang: "African American slang is not only a living language for Black speakers but for the whole country, as evidenced by its popularity decade after decade since the beginning of American history. The most recent example of this popularity is rap and hip-hop during the 1980s and the 1990s" (p. xxix). Again, slang is a subset of Ebonics; it does not make up the linguistic system in itself. Yet within this subsystem of Ebonics, the following are examples of borrowings:

homey, dude, homeboy, bad, chill, chill out, tripping, trip out, vibes, lighten up, bro, to the max, bogart, psych, flick, ride, threads, tube, weed, wheels, chick, fox/stone fox, turkey, grass, stoned, jam, out to lunch

Eble (1989) cites these slang items in *College Slang 101* yet does not credit them as stemming from the African American speech community. Through comparisons of collected items in African American–authored slang volumes (Andrews & Owens, 1973; Major, 1970, 1994), however, I have concluded that the listed slang items are of African-American origin (Troutman, 1996b).

In *Why Black People Tend to Shout: Cold Facts and Wry Views from a Black Man's World*, Ralph Wiley writes (1991) about language borrowing and covert prestige associated with Black language:

Speech? Why, it amazes some black people—specifically, me—to hear white people mumble snidely about the way black people are known to talk, with ever-widening dialectal form, then hear the same white people do their level best to talk the same talk about two years later. Mark Twain with Tom Sawyer and Huck Finn was aware of this predilection.... From ... right on to chill out to you got that right to you know it. You can watch a film where there isn't a black person in sight, just some young white people, and if you closed your eyes, you'd swear you were on the corner of 125th Street and Malcolm X Boulevard. High and low fives all over the place. (p. 39)

The Ebonics slang borrowing is synopsized by Flexner (cited in Major, 1994):

When we heard America talking, we heard Blacks talking.... The 'we' is Black and White.... The Blacks have influenced the American language in two major ways (1) by using many of their native (Black African) words and speech, and (2) by causing, doing, being, influencing things that have had all America talking, often using terms created or popularized by the Black presence and experience. (p. xxxiii)

Although she is not cognizant of it and although she has expressed opposition to Ebonics, Maya Angelou also shows covert prestige for the discourse style of Ebonics as seen in her poem "The Thirteens." The dozens is a discourse game engaged in by African Americans throughout the United States. In this game of wit and ingenuity, players engage in verbal warfare by talking about the opponent's mother typically, yet other relatives can be talked about as well. Today, this discourse form has come to be referred to as snapping. For example, one speaker can play the dozens or snap on another person by saying, "Your mother is so old, she owes *Jesus* food stamps" ("Snaps," 1997); or "Your mother is so old, she helped Moses edit down the *Eighteen commandments*" (Ibid.). (See the discussion of signifying, above.) Both comments produce laughter from listeners, even the recipient of the comments, given the appropriate context, because of the ingenious and spontaneous creation. Through the title of her poem, first of all, Angelou plays the signifying game. She does not play the dozens, as many African Americans boast of playing; she is so "bad," she plays the *thirteens*! Secondly, Angelou signifies on both Blacks and whites through the lines of the poem itself. In one verse (the Black thirteens), she condemns the recipient of her words, writing that she would call this recipient a dirty name if there were anything left to call him or her. In another verse (the white thirteens), Angelou writes that she would tell the recipient of these lines his or her real name if there were something worse to name her/him. Thus, through the title of the poem and the indirect hurling of insults within the poem, Angelou acknowledges familiarity with "the dozens" and demonstrates agility in playing the game. I would not want to be the recipient of the insults (the dozens-playing) in her poem! Through "The Thirteens," Angelou shows covert prestige for one prominent Ebonics discourse feature.

TOUGH GUYS Sociolinguistic research by Trudgill (1983) shows that men associate with (i.e., positively evaluate and favor) nonstandard forms. In self-evaluation tests conducted in Norwich (Britain), men reported using nonstandard speech forms more often than their actual speech (recorded in interviews) revealed. Unconsciously done, this male, nonstandard self-reporting suggests that men hold covert prestige for vernacular forms since they claim more frequent use of the less prestigious forms when in reality this is not the case. Trudgill's and others' research establishes that nonstandard varieties "have covert prestige not just for the working class but also for men" (Coates, 1986, p. 73). Such covert prestige can be seen for Ebonics.

Tough guys, be they college beaus or police officers, have to *talk the talk* in order to maintain an image of a *real* man. The linguistic variety chosen by *real* men tends to be nonstandard and in many instances tends to be Ebonics. On United States college campuses, graduates and undergraduates refer to their male counterparts as "dudes," "homies," or "homeboys." In order to greet another male, these students cooly inquire, "What's up" or "What's happening." The truly "copacetic" (i.e., calm) solicit "What up," using a slightly modified version that follows the grammatical structure of Ebonics (*be* absence for present tense, nonhabitual activity). The "Martin" television program regularly features this latter expression as disc jockey Martin rhetorically queries, "What up, Detroit?" Here, the popular television program may have been influential in the spread of a phrase already common within the African American speech community.

College male students, even younger males, in displaying coolness refer to other males as "man." My eleven-year-old African American son, in the appropriate setting, refers to his European American friends as "man" and they reciprocate. Male high-school teenagers and college students refer to each other as "man" also. Upon hearing this usage by non–African American males, I initially did a double take, pondering the borrowing.

For a very long time within the African American speech community, "man" has been appropriated in direct opposition to the historical and belittling use of "boy." To call male adults "boy" and to treat them that way was one further vehicle of emasculation commonly employed before and after the enactment of the Emancipation Proclamation. One dynamic of subordinate and superordinate relationships is that power can be exerted from below. In rejection of "boy" usage, African Americans exerted power from below by institution of the unwritten rule (circa post–Civil Rights movement) that African American males over the age of fifteen should not be called "boy," a rule which derived in direct opposition to historical oppression of African American males. This unwritten rule has become widespread throughout the United States, with a large segment of the populace being aware of and socialized in the application of the rule. The vociferous "I'm not a boy" has been uttered continually over the years by African American males as a mechanism for socialization of the broader culture to refrain from using "boy."

Today, still, the unwritten rule applies to persons outside the African American community (i.e., non-boy usage). Within the community, a different set of rules has been constructed (which is not fully elaborated here). For Ebonics speakers, the irreducible equivalent and substitute for "boy" became "man," to such a large degree that "man" even applied to young boys in the form of "little man." "Man" usage, then, stems from and continues within the African American speech community, typically applied African American male to African American male. The fact that "man" usage occurred within a non–African American male context was initially quizzical, yet hindsight brings clarity. Dominant group members have attached covert prestige to "man," thus co-opting its usage.

One further example demonstrating the covert prestige attached to Ebonics comes through the popular television program "New York Undercover," especially its two detectives. After viewing the series over a period of time and re-viewing several episodes, it became apparent to me that this popular program presented detectives so tough that they dress, walk, and talk tough.

Both detectives Williams and Torrez dress and behave very informally, very much in the style of the African American hip-hop culture. This informal dress, loose-fitting shirts and baggy jeans or pants along with tennis shoes, may seem to fit the detectives' undercover status, yet dressing in this way matches the tough guy stance. Torrez and Williams, that is, could not dress in the "down with the hood" manner, speak the "standard" dialect, and convincingly instill fear in drug dealers, murderers, and others in New York City. The "down" dress enables the tough guy status.

"Bopping," walking "in a certain rhythmic, graceful, cool way" (Smitherman, 1994, p. 68), also enables toughness, which both detectives engage in regularly. In order to indicate coolness and hipness, African American males of varying ages have bopped for years; walking otherwise sends too visible a signal of being a "lame," a person who is not with it (Smitherman, 1994). In one scene, Torrez enters the scene by bopping. In this same episode and regularly in the series, Williams bops. Both detectives rub their noses in the manner of African American males of the hip-hop culture, not because they itch, but to signify doubt or thought.

Besides clothing, body movements, and gestures, the mode and manner of talking further enables the detectives' "badness." In the United States, males cannot be "down," i.e., with it, hip, boss, slamming, jamming (Smitherman, 1994) in the hood and also appropriate power through the dialect of wider communication. It just ain't happening in New York City, tough city capital, especially with a hip (knowledgeable of the New York culture) African American and Puerto Rican detective. In this instance, Ebonics is used as the linguistic code of power. During two specific episodes of "New York Undercover," both detectives use "dis," "dat," "homey," "man," "ain't," "crib," "yo," and other African American expressions, such as "Ahm up on dat" and "You know what ahm sayin." Some examples are:

Williams: So homey how come you didn't tell 'er.
Torrez: Tell 'er *what*?
Williams: That Varrick is staying with your pops and you damn near consider him your uncle.
Torrez: (with an attitude) I told her what she needed to know. Now, I ain't got a problem with continuing on the case.
Williams: Ha-a-anh-h, Yo B, now you really think you gonna go after this guy you've known for your entire life like he's a stranger?
(Later scene)
Williams: I know that dis is your father but you saw the gun in his hand . . . It doesn't look good man.
Torrez: I don't care how it looks . . . dis is my father and ahm gonna find out.

In the second episode, Williams and an African American pastor use first syllable stress on certain words, which is characteristic of Ebonics speakers: *ad*dress, *po*lice. This same pastor uses loud-talking when the detectives arrest him. Loud-talking is another discourse pattern used by Ebonics speakers, whereby a speaker increases his speaking volume (though the volume may be still considered low), allowing others beyond an addressee to hear the exchange. It is precisely because of this loud talking (i.e., permitting others to be privy to a conversational exchange) that makes the act objectionable (Mitchell-Kernan, 1972). In the present instance, Pastor Harris loud-talks when Williams and Torrez are arresting him for questioning in connection with the burning of his church:

(The talk begins amicably between Pastor Harris, Torrez, and Williams, especially since Williams is a member of Pastor Harris's church.)
Pastor: Hope you got good news, J. C. [i.e., Williams].
Williams: Well, unfortunately not.

Torrez: Well, is there some place we can talk?

Pastor. *Right here*. I have no secrets from my congregation.

Torrez: Well, maybe you can tell us about that insurance policy you upgraded two months ago.

Pastor. (Walks over, closer to the congregation members) Oh, for crying out loud. I should have seen this coming.

Torrez: (Moves over, closer to Harris' new position) You know we can clear this up at the precinct.

Pastor. (Speaks loudly enough for congregation members to hear; loud-talking begins) Am I under arrest? (Congregation members begin to move in closer.)

Torrez: (Pause) Definitely not.

Pastor. (Angry, tight face) Am I a suspect? (Congregation members begin to encircle Torrez, Pastor, and Williams.)

Torrez: (Takes off sunglasses as opposition intensifies) Are we having a problem here?

Pastor. Are we having a problem? (Torrez glances over at Williams.)

Williams: I hope not.

Pastor. Then answer my question. Am I a suspect?

Williams: (Slowly) Until we can get this cleared up, Reverend (short pause), yes. (Pastor and congregation show expressions of disbelief.)

Pastor. (Loud-talking intensifies) Then take me in like a suspect. (Very aggressive, challenging stance) Arrest me, Detective Williams.

Torrez even loud-talks during the arrest scene, as a defense mechanism to get the church members to disperse after their pastor's arrest. He also uses an African American vocal quality in his delivery and hand gesture. The vocal quality and gesture add to the tough demeanor that Torrez needs to project, if he is to be given any credibility, respect, and authority in this situation:

Torrez: Alright people, there is *nothing* to *see* here, alright. Nothing to see here.

Torrez, later, uses the current African American pronunciation of "alright." When asked by his girlfriend about the performance of another detective, Torrez responds, "He did ahw-aight."

Both Pastor Harris and Williams signify during this episode. As the pastor is being arrested, he stops at the door of the detectives' car, saying, "It's alright. The *po*-lice are jus' doing their job." This comment is cutting since Pastor Harris means the opposite; the police are not doing their job because they have arrested the wrong person for the church burning. In an earlier scene, Williams engages in conversation with his ex-wife. While looking at a picture of their son, Williams comments, "He's got attitude to spare. Wonder where he got that from." Here Williams implies that their son got his aggressive, defiant disposition (Smitherman, 1994) from the mother.

Of course, in the episodes discussed and in the series as a whole, Williams and Torrez use the dialect of wider communication, also. This usage is expected because of the prime time slot in which the program is broadcast, the appropriateness of switching codes based on context, and the construction of believable characters. Yet, the fact that the writers and the producers of this series even permitted the features of Ebonics as demonstrated above is a message in itself. These persons give credence to the covert prestige of Ebonics, especially in exuding power.

Conclusion and Implications

Within the broader United States society and within sociolinguistics, socioliguists and lay persons have tended to overlook some very important dynamics concerning dialects of the less empowered, especially Ebonics. The two significant points made in this paper, again, are:

1. A large number of African Americans, particularly within the ranks of the middle class, hold allegiance, respect, and pride for their home language, whether it is called Ebonics, Black Language, or African American English. This point counters previous descriptions, reporting that Ebonics is spoken by "non-middle-class African Americans" (Fromkin & Rodman, 1993, p. 287; see also Trudgill, 1974, p. 59).

2. Although not openly acknowledged, covert prestige, and in turn power, is given to Ebonics, particularly by males. Through the use of specific vocabulary items, phrases, and nonverbal communication, tough guys co-opt Ebonics, even young male children.

"So What?" or "What Does It All Mean, John?"[3]

The two points given above have implications for the broader United States population and teachers. The information contained in this paper aims to dispel myths concerning Ebonics within the larger society. The name *Ebonics*, in itself, raises furious responses, even among some African Americans. Such fury emerges, in part, as a result of little knowledge and inaccurate information concerning Ebonics and has most recently emerged due to media misinformation about the Oakland Unified School District's decision on Ebonics. Even though sociolinguists have studied, described, and explained the Ebonics system since the 1960s and have published their findings, misinformation exuded forth from the media coverage of the Oakland decision. A gap obviously exists between the sociolinguistic literature and the information accessible to the general public. In fact, another "Black English Case" preceded the recent Oakland Ebonics case. Also called the "Ann Arbor decision," this initial "Black English Case" had little impact on the dispelling of myths and the dissemination of factual information. Recent television coverage (primarily), a large number of newspaper articles, radio broadcasts, and negative editorials and public opinion commentaries perpetuated myths. With accurate information in its hands, as presented here, the general public can develop informed positions.

For classroom purposes, I believe that teachers have to give greater "props" (respect) to Ebonics. Giving respect to students' home languages, in general, establishes a positive framework within which to help students grow and learn. Value for the home language transmutes to value for the student. The two entities are deeply integrated. According to general sociolinguistics, the home language is one that people typically value highly. It is the language of the closest family members and relatives, those whom we hold dearly. When others denigrate a speaker's home language, they are denigrating that person. Students, especially, can discern teachers that truly care, as displayed in teachers' reactions and treatment of the home language and the students themselves.

Through the information presented in the contents of this paper, I hope that teachers can recognize and acknowledge that Ebonics works according to a system, just as *all* language varieties do. Ebonics is a rule-governed language. In order to learn to speak it, individuals must learn the rules, again, as is true with other languages. Most important, I hope teachers can eradicate myths surrounding the language of African Americans. It is not haphazard, deficient, or the result of lazy articulation or any type of insufficiency. Before arriving on this continent, Africans already had a language system in place (in their brains). When humans over the age of thirteen learn a second language, the first language impacts the second one. Isn't this the case for first-language speakers of French, Spanish, German, and others when they learn a second language? In the United States, we have not applied the first-and-second language transfer to African Americans. Just as other African customs and practices survived the continental divide (such as art, music, medicine, folk tales, dance, religion, and food), the language patterns of Africans survived as well (Berry & Blassingame, 1977). African people were not "tabulae rasae" (blank slates) when they arrived in the Americas; thus, the linguistic system of Africa has placed its mark on Ebonics, even in its form and structure today.

Although controversy surrounded Ebonics and the "Oakland decision," making both the linguistic system and the Oakland School Board appear dubious, with a closer look we can identify the power and beauty of this socially constructed African American language.

Endnotes

1. Smitherman (1977) cites 80 to 90 percent as the number of African Americans speaking Ebonics "at least some of the time," while in her 1994 *Black Talk* she gives 90 percent as the statistic. Morgan (1994) asserts that statistics on the African American community have been inaccurately reported due to the number of middle-class African Americans not considered.

2. European American males in my daughter's third-grade class and my son's fifth-grade class signify their coolness by giving each other "fives" or "high fives" in the classroom or on the sports field.

3. I borrow this wording from the play *Day of Absence,* written by Douglas Turner Ward (1966). In the play, when all the African Americans disappear from a small town, one of the European American women asks her husband, "What does it all mean, John?"

References

ANDREWS, M., & OWENS, P. (1973). *Black language.* West Los Angeles, CA: Seymour-Smith Publishers.

BAUGH, J. (1983). *Black street speech.* Austin: University of Texas Press.

BERRY, M. & BLASSINGAME, J. (1977). Africa, slavery, and the roots of contemporary black culture. *Massachusetts Review 18* (3), 501–516.

BLACKSHIRE-BELAY, C. (1996). The location of Ebonics within the framework of the Africological paradigm. *Journal of Black Studies 27* (1), 5–23.

BOSMAJIAN, H. (1973). Defining the "American Indian": A case study in the language of suppression. *The Speech Teacher XXI* (2), 89–99.

CHAPMAN, A. (1968). *Black voices: An anthology of Afro-American literature.* New York: New American Library.

COATES, J. (1986). *Women, men and language.* New York: Longman Group.

DINNERSTEIN, L., NICHOLS, R., & REIMERS, R. (1990). *Natives and strangers.* New York: Oxford University Press.

EBLE, C. (1989). *College slang 101.* Georgetown, CT: Spectacle Lane Press.

FROMKIN, V. & RODMAN, R. (1993). *An introduction to language* (5th Ed.). New York: Harcourt Brace.

KILLENS, J. (1971). *The cotillion.* New York: Trident.

LABOV, W. (1972). *Language in the inner city.* Philadelphia: The University of Pennsylvania Press.

LAKOFF, L. (1990). *Talking power: The politics of language in our lives.* New York: Basic Books.

MAJOR, C. (1970). *Dictionary of Afro-American slang.* New York: International Publishers.

MAJOR, C. (1994). *Juba to jive: A dictionary of African American slang.* New York: Penguin Books.

MALVEAUX, J. (1996, December 31). Ebonics debate distorts needs of inner-city kids. *Detroit Free Press.*

MITCHELL-KERNAN, C. (1972). Signifying, loud-talking and marking. In T. Kochman (Ed.), *Rappin' and stylin' out.* Urbana: University of Illinois Press.

MORGAN, M. (1989). From down south to up south: The language behavior of three generations of black women residing in Chicago. Ph.D. dissertation, University of Pennsylvania.

MORGAN, M. (1991a). Language and communication style among African-American women. *UCLA Center for the Study of Women Newsletter* 7 (Spring).

MORGAN, M. (1991b). Indirectness and interpretation in African-American women's discourse. *Pragmatics 1* (4), 421–452.

MORGAN, M. (1994). The African-American speech community: Reality and sociolinguistics. In Morgan (Ed.), *The social construction of reality in creole situations*. Los Angeles: Center for African-American Studies.

MORGAN, M. (Forthcoming). Conversational signifying: Grammar and indirectness among African-American women. In E. Ochs, E. Schegloff & Thompson (Eds.), *Interaction and Grammar*. Cambridge, England: Cambridge University Press.

RICHARDSON, L. (1977). *The dynamics of sex and gender: A sociological perspective*. Chicago: Rand McNally.

RICKFORD, J. (1997). African-American language and culture: Roots and branches. Lecture presentation at Michigan State University, January 27.

SMITHERMAN, G. (1977). *Talkin and testifyin: The language of black America*. Detroit: Wayne State University Press.

SMITHERMAN, G. (1994). *Black talk: Words and phrases from the hood to the amen corner*. New York: Houghton Mifflin.

SNAPS (1997). Calendar.

SUDDUTH, E. (1997). The significance of behavior. Sermon, Doors of Healing Tabernacle Church, Lansing, MI.

TROUTMAN, D. (1995). The tongue and sword: Who is master? In G. Smitherman (Ed.), *African-American women speak out on Anita Hill–Clarence Thomas*. Detroit: Wayne State University Press.

TROUTMAN, D. (1996a). Culturally toned diminutives within the speech community of African-American women. *Journal of Commonwealth and Postcolonial Studies, 4* (1), 55–64.

TROUTMAN, D. (1996b). [Review of *College Slang 101*]. *Word 47* (2), 226–232.

TRUDGILL, P. (1974). *Sociolinguistics: An introduction*. New York: Penguin.

TRUDGILL, P. (1983). *Sociolinguistics: An introduction to language and society*. New York: Penguin.

WARD, D. (1966). *Day of absence*. New York: Dramatists Play Service.

WEAVER, C. (1997). Ebonics and the "parsley" problem. In C. Weaver (Ed.), *Lessons to share on teaching grammar in context*. Portsmouth, NH: Boynton/Cook.

WILEY, R. (1991). *Why black people tend to shout*. New York: Carol Publishing.

WILLIAMS, R. (Ed.). (1975). *Ebonics: The true language of black folks*. St. Louis: Institute of Black Studies.

WOLFRAM, W. (1986). *American tongues*. A videotape by A. Kolker & L. Alvarez. The Center for New American Media.

WOODSON, C. (1933). *The miseducation of the negro*. Washington, D.C.: Associated Publishers.

14 Ebonics and the "Parsley" Problem
Personal Reflections

CONSTANCE WEAVER

Introduction

Weaver first discusses the horrendous event that inspired Rita Dove's (1983) poem "Parsley," suggesting that this event is symptomatic of human beings' tendency to look down upon others, allegedly for language differences but more deeply for other reasons. She discusses the reciprocal relationship between attitudes toward others' language and attitudes toward the people themselves; clarifies the concepts of *language* and *dialect*; and gives examples of some regional dialect differences, demonstrating that dialects are patterned language (sub)systems.

Next Weaver explains the creation of the term "Ebonics" to delineate the linguistic and stylistic features of language that are used by African Americans—patterns that are often known collectively as "African American Vernacular English" (AAVE), a term currently popular among linguists. Weaver briefly discusses the African and pidgin/Creole heritage of AAVE/Ebonics, referring readers to Troutman's article in this volume for more details. The last half of the article focuses on the Oakland, California, Board of Education's resolution to value and draw upon Ebonics in educating African American students, especially in helping them master mainstream English, the "Language of Wider Communication." In the course of the discussion, Weaver briefly comments upon obvious sociopolitical issues. Returning to what she calls the "parsley" problem, she suggests that teachers have a responsibility to help decrease racism and ethnocentrism as well as to deal with language issues in the classroom.

When a colleague led me to read the poem "Parsley," by poet laureate Rita Dove, I was shocked at the horrendous event alluded to in the poem. In the first part, we experience the lives of Haitians working in the cane fields, the Blacks who lie down screaming. As uninformed readers, we do not yet understand the significance of their not being able to pronounce an *r*. But the General has found the word he wants: the Spanish word *perejil*. "Who says it, lives," we are told. But what about the others, those who cannot pronounce the word "correctly"? By the end of the poem, we realize that those who cannot pronounce the *r* in *perejil* will be killed. Rita Dove further explains in a footnote that "On October 2, 1957, Rafael Trujillo (1891–1961), dictator of the Dominican Republic, ordered 20,000 blacks killed because they could not pronounce the letter *r* in *perejil,* the Spanish word for parsley" (Dove, 1983).

What could have motivated such wholesale butchery? Surely it was not the mere inability to pronounce the *r.* The Haitians' pronunciation was used as an excuse for executing a people that Trujillo despised for other reasons. According to one biographer, Robert Crassweller (1966), it was nationalism, the history of strife with Haiti, and the fact that "the Dominican side of the border was becoming more Haitianized year by year" (p. 150) that motivated Trujillo's massacre—in addition, of course, to his personal ambition, which was insatiable. In Rita Dove's poem, though, there are hints that Trujillo may have despised the laborers, perhaps because they had not become assimilated Dominicans as his own mother had, or perhaps because he himself had worked among the cane laborers in his earlier years and he despised his own social origins (Crassweiler, 1966). Thus personal and political motivation might have coalesced for Trujillo, who in any case showed no concern or regret for the wholesale murders of the Haitian laborers.

The analogy is not perfect between Trujillo's execution of those who could not pronounce *perejil* "correctly" and the rest of us who may reject others supposedly because of their speech (though the analogy seems stronger in Rita Dove's poem than in Crassweller's biography).

Often we claim to be rejecting people because of their language usage, typically their dialect, but more basically we are rejecting the language because we see the people as different from us and, therefore, inferior to us (e.g. Gee, 1996). Thus those conversant in Received Pronunciation in Great Britain may look down upon Cockney, Northerners in the United States sometimes make fun of Appalachian and Southern speech, white Americans often reject the language patterns and slang reflective of Black origins, experience, and culture. On the other hand, the direction of denigration is not *merely* one way: that is, because we have learned—indeed, often been *taught* in school or at home—to reject or ridicule the language of some groups, our negative attitude toward their speech may increase or even initiate our rejection of the people themselves as "different," "other," even, somehow, "not as intelligent or good as I am." Language scholar Dennis Baron (n.d.) puts it succinctly: "Language both shapes and reflects reality" (the idea of language shaping reality generally being attributed to Edward Sapir [1921] and Benjamin Lee Whorf [1956]). Certainly, language shapes as well as reflects our *perception* of reality.

Over time, a vicious circle develops. Initially we—whoever *we* are—may have looked down upon certain peoples, but having learned to reject or ridicule their language as a means of denying them equality with us, we humans eventually reject the peoples partly *because of* their language difference. In this case, I use "language" to include "dialect"; the principle holds for both. As to the difference, the linguist Max Weinreich once wrote that a language is a dialect with an army and a navy. Dennis Baron explains this phenomenon nicely:

> We can say that two people use the same language if they can understand one another's speech. If they can't understand one another, they are speaking separate languages. But we define languages politically and culturally, as well as by degree of comprehension. Mandarin and Cantonese are not mutually intelligible, yet both are Chinese. They are held together on the mainland by an army and a navy and a common writing system, and they are held together internationally by a cultural definition of what it means to be Chinese. Serbian and Croatian are mutually intelligible, though they use different alphabets, but because of their armies they now live apart as separate languages. Noah Webster once argued that American and British English were separate languages. (Baron, n.d.; see also Baron, 1977; and Trudgill, 1983)

So linguistically, Ebonics may be considered a dialect of English, with discernable roots in West and especially Niger-Congo African languages, but *culturally,* Ebonics may be considered a language.

We teachers must, I think, try to help our students understand, appreciate, respect, and accept other cultures *and* their languages and dialects. Focusing on language/dialect and culture together is our best hope for lessening stereotypes about, and prejudices against, people we have traditionally regarded as different from us.

What Is a Dialect?

Linguistically, a dialect is a set of language patterns that differ noticeably from the patterns of other dialects within the same language (Wolfram, 1991). A key point is that dialects are not just slang and not merely "lazy" speech. Rather, they are a collection of linguistic patterns, involving not just vocabulary differences but also grammatical and/or phonological (sound) differences from other dialects. For example, Coke or Pepsi is "pop" here in the Midwest, but "soda" in the Northeast. However, the vocabulary differences aren't as noticeable as certain sound differences. People retaining the historical language patterns of the Northeast may say "bahn" for *barn* and "cah" for *car,* omitting the "r" from their pronunciation before a consonant or at the end of a word, particularly if it's followed by another word that begins with a consonant, as in *The cah should be in the garage.* However, these same speakers may add an "r" to nouns ending in an unstressed vowel: President John Kennedy's "idear," for instance.

In contrast, certain areas of the Midwest (such as southern Ohio and Indiana, where I come from) are distinguished by an added "r" in *wash* and *Washington,* which are commonly pronounced "warsh" and "Warshington." This difference seems to be confined to these two words, though, so it's hardly a "pattern." On the other hand, people from my original dialect area commonly pronounce a "short i" for a "short e" before a nasal sound, as in "pin" for *pen,* "mint" for *meant,* and "basemint" for *basement.* This is a pattern that South Midland speech (as linguists used to call it) have in common with so-called Southern speech. When I moved from the Ohio River valley to Michigan and began trying to teach the International Phonetic Alphabet to my college students, I discovered another patterned difference in the way we pronounced words like *father* and *awe,* which had two different *a* sounds for my students but were essentially the same for me. Also, I pronounced *war* as "wahr," while the native Michiganders pronounced it "wohr." These are patterned sound differences—phonological differences—between my original South Midland dialect and lower Northern dialect, as they used to be called.

As for grammatical differences, again I can illustrate from my own speech. When I first studied dialects in the late sixties and early seventies, I discovered that some of my patterns reflected Appalachian dialect—not surprising, I suppose, as I lived just across the Ohio River from Kentucky. These patterns involve mostly auxiliary verbs, and the one I still notice myself using occasionally is "used to could," rather than *used to be able to*—as in "I used to could do it." A similar pattern used in my household when I was growing up is "might could" rather than *might be able to*—as in "I might could do it."

So, What Is "Ebonics"?

No doubt you will have noticed that I've illustrated differing phonological and grammatical patterns in regional dialects specifically. Most people realize that there are educated people in other parts of the country who have some dialect patterns that differ from theirs (not to mention the much more noticeable pronunciation differences between American English, on the one hand, and both British and Australian English). However, people tend to regard the speech of the less educated or less affluent—the less powerful in society—as simply "wrong." They don't realize that these dialects too are patterned language systems, not aberrations from some linguistic norm. Neither do they realize that so-called standard dialects are not linguistically superior to other dialects of the same language; rather, standard dialects are labeled such as a means of "creating linguistic distance between a social elite and the vast majority of speakers by the attempt to impose a set of arbitrary rules" (Smith, 1997). Often, people's negative response to the less educated or less affluent's speech is accorded also to those dialects that reflect ethnic backgrounds other than European, such as the casual—and sometimes the formal—speech of many African Americans, to a greater or lesser degree. Thus in the United States, what's been called standard English is standard only in that it's the dialect of white supremacy (Sledd, 1969), or at least middle-class supremacy.

Sometimes this mainstream, prestige dialect is called "business English" or "the Language of Wider Communication" (CCCC, n.d.) to emphasize its acceptance in society at large, as opposed to acceptance only in certain regions or, more often, among certain social or ethnic groups primarily. However, linguists typically reject the term "standard English" because linguistically there is no *standard* from which all other dialects are derived. From one point of view, what's "standard" varies with context; that is, what's appropriate in a given context and situation might be considered "standard" for that context and situation, whether it be formal English or street talk. What's typically called "standard" English, though, is determined by who has the greatest power in society and government, not by the linguistic patterns themselves.

This broader discussion of "standard" and prestige dialects is important for understanding the currently popular concept of "Ebonics." The term "Ebonics" stems from a 1973 conference at which Black scholars in linguistics, education, and related disciplines rejected the work of white researchers who viewed Black language and culture as deficient (e.g., Bereiter & Engelmann, 1966). These Black scholars decided to coin their own term to define Black language from a Black perspective. Thus the term "Ebonics" was created, from the words "ebony" (black) and "phonics" (sounds). In creating the term, these scholars meant for the "sound" part to refer not just to the phonology of what had recently been called Black English, but to the total sound of speech that is uniquely Black in origin. As Robert Williams and Mary Brantley put it in their article in *Ebonics: The True Language of Black Folks* (1975),

> Ebonics, the essence of Black language, is to be viewed henceforth as creative Black expressions, both verbal and nonverbal, highly stylized in nature, rhythmic in sound, diversified in meaning and indigenous to Black people. These speech patterns have been developed by Blacks as a means of communication with one another. Ebonics is unique in both its stylistic and linguistic dimensions. (p. 133)

Williams and Brantley continue by mentioning some of the stylistic dimensions of Ebonics that were currently in vogue, such as rhyming, signifying, playing the dozens, jiving, capping, and rapping (see, for instance, Smitherman, 1986 and 1994; Kochman, 1972).

Nondominant dialects are maintained, of course, by cultural isolation, but also by cultural solidarity. As explained by Marcyliena Morgan in linguistic anthropology at UCLA,

> Like any languages and dialects, African American varieties of English, which range from that spoken by children and some adults with limited education to those spoken by adults with advanced degrees, are based on the cultural, social, historical, and political experiences shared by many people of African descent in the United States. This experience is one of family, community, and love as well as racism, poverty, and discrimination. (Feb. 1997)

Thus Ebonics was not merely a new term for what most linguists and sociolinguists (white) were then calling Black English—a term that has had other synonyms or near-synonyms, each an attempt to better define its origins and/or its users, among them African American English, Black English Vernacular, and most recently African American Vernacular English (AAVE). The phrase *African American* refers to the origin of the dialect in African American experience, while *vernacular* indicates that these linguistic patterns are typical of casual, "down home" speech. However, the term *vernacular* is not entirely satisfactory, since the language patterns in question are used among the educated and even in professional discourse by some African American scholars (Smitherman, 1972; Elgin, 1978). Discussions of Ebonics often focus on the linguistic aspects, as I shall do here. However, as Williams and Brantley (1975) explain, the term Ebonics was coined to make it clear that this speech was characterized by more than linguistic patterns. Indeed, it is characterized by the cultural experiences and language styles of African Americans from the days of slavery, and of Africans before they were brought to America as slaves.

Linguistically, the verb system of AAVE/Ebonics is perhaps the best indicator of its African origins. African American linguist John Rickford gives several examples (Dec. 1996) of the systematicity of its verb system, compared with the equivalents in mainstream or "standard" English:

1. AAVE: "She BIN had dat han'-made dress." (SE: She's had that hand-made dress for a long time, and still does.)

2. AAVE: "Befo' you know it, he BE DONE aced de tessts." (SE: Before you know it, he will have already aced the tests.)

3. AAVE: "Ah 'on know what homey BE doin." (SE: I don't know what my friend is usually doing.)

4. AAVE: "Can't nobody tink de way he do." (SE: Nobody can think the way he does.)

5. AAVE: "I ast Ruf could she bring it ovah to Tom crib." (SE: I asked Ruth if/whether she could bring it over to Tom's place.)

For more information on the features of this dialect, see Troutman, this volume (as well as several of the books and articles listed as resources at the end of this article).

People are typically aware that most African American teenagers can speak in Ebonics, and since teenagers use a lot of slang, Ebonics is often mistakenly assumed to be mostly a matter of slang and style. But as Rickford points out, few of the differences from the Language of Wider Communication that are found also in adult African American speech involve vocabulary or slang; most of the key differences are phonological or grammatical. And most confusing to those who do not speak the dialect are, of course, the grammatical patterns of AAVE/Ebonics.

Some linguists emphasize the parallels between today's AAVE/Ebonics patterns and the patterns found in West and especially the Niger-Congo African language systems. It is these scholars who are most inclined to consider AAVE/Ebonics a language, rather than a dialect of English (e.g., Denise Troutman; see her article in this volume). More often, however, linguists and sociolinguists have emphasized the historical development of this speech, which developed from a pidgin (a lingua franca used just for minimal communication between people who speak mutually unintelligible languages) to a Creole (the descendent of a pidgin, re-created by the children of the less powerful groups speaking the pidgin—e.g. Pinker, 1994), to a decreolized dialect of English that still has features in common with Gullah, an English Creole spoken on the sea islands off the coast of South Carolina and Georgia; with Creoles in the Caribbean; and with Hawaiian Creole, still known as Hawaiian "pidgin" (e.g. Rickford, 1996; Public Broadcasting Service, 1986; Burling, 1973; Dillard, 1972). Some features, especially the auxiliary verb features illustrated in sentences 1–3 above, could be attributed either to the African origins of today's AAVE/Ebonics or to its history as a trade (pidgin) language and subsequently as the language developed by the children of slaves in America (its Creole heritage).

Probably the majority of linguists and sociolinguists today consider AAVE/Ebonics to have roots in African languages *and* in the pidginization/creolization process, but nevertheless to be linguistically a dialect of English now, not a separate language. This explanation is given not only by White linguists (e.g., Burling, 1972) but by African American linguists as well (e.g., Baugh, 1983; Smitherman, 1986; Rickford [ongoing]). On the other hand, some of these same linguists are among those who speak of Ebonics as a *language* probably to express and bolster cultural solidarity among African Americans and/or to bolster the prestige of Ebonics in the society at large (Smitherman, 1997; Troutman, this volume; various sources in "The Real Ebonics Debate," 1997).

Ebonics in Oakland, California

Until 1996, the public had seldom encountered the term "Ebonics," since it was first coined in 1973 by Robert Williams, one of the Black scholars disturbed at white scholars' often narrow conception of the language indigenous to Blacks in the United States (Williams, 1975), and even more disturbed with their inclination to consider Black speech not merely different but deficient (one thinks, for example, of Bereiter and Engelmann, 1966). The term "Ebonics" resurfaced, though, in December of 1996, when the Oakland, California, Board of Education passed what has come to be known as the "Ebonics" resolution. After some revisions were made in response to criticisms (legitimate, I think), two key paragraphs of the resolution read as follows:

> NOW, THEREFORE, BE IT RESOLVED that the Board of Education officially recognizes the existence, and the cultural and historic bases of West and Niger-Congo African Language Systems, and these are the language patterns that many African American students bring to school; . . .
> BE IT FURTHER RESOLVED that the Superintendent in conjunction with her staff shall immediately devise and implement the best possible academic program for the combined purposes of facilitating the acquisition and mastery of

English language skills, while respecting and embracing the legitimacy and richness of the language patterns whether they are known as "Ebonics," "African Language Systems," "Pan African Communication Behaviors," or other description. . . . (Oakland Unified School District, 1997b)

To me it appears that the board was incorporating the original broad meaning of Ebonics that the creators of the term intended: namely, that the board (or at least whoever drafted the resolution) intended the term to refer to Ebonics in all its cultural and stylistic richness, not merely to its linguistic patterns.

Many of those who have studied the origins of AAVE/Ebonics emphasize the processes of pidginization and creolization in its history, as much as or more than the African language features carried over into AAVE/Ebonics (and even into general American speech, as far as vocabulary is concerned; see Troutman in this volume; Smitherman, 1986, 1994; and the PBS video *Black on White*, 1986). Indeed, the Oakland board of education was accused by the media and others of emphasizing the African origins of Ebonics and referring to it as a "language" (rather than a dialect) in order to obtain bilingual education funds for teaching these students to speak mainstream, "standard" English, a possible outcome that the board did not categorically deny. (For the board's response to criticisms, see Oakland Unified School District, 1997a.)

What informed linguistic scholars typically agree on, however, is restated in a resolution on the Oakland "Ebonics" issue from the Linguistic Society of America:

The variety [of English] known as "Ebonics," "African American Vernacular English" (AAVE), and "Vernacular Black English" and by other names is systematic and rule-governed like all natural speech varieties. In fact, all human linguistic systems—spoken, signed, and written—are fundamentally regular. The systematic and expressive nature of the grammar and pronunciation patterns of the African American vernacular has been established by numerous scientific studies over the past thirty years. Characterizations of Ebonics as "slang," "mutant," "lazy," "defective," "ungrammatical," or "broken English" are incorrect and demeaning. (Jan. 3, 1997)

Such enlightenment is part, I think, of what the Oakland, California school board was trying to accomplish in passing their resolution, complete with background information and a policy statement. As I read it, there are several aims explicit or implicit in this document.

In general, the document seems designed to bridge the worlds of those who mostly speak a dialect that reflects African American history, experiences, and culture and those whose dialect happens to reflect mainstream culture in the United States, at least socioeconomically speaking.

In particular, the Oakland "Ebonics" resolution seems designed first of all to affect the knowledge and cultural sensitivity of teachers, by

- encouraging teachers to become knowledgeable about Ebonics, both its history and its linguistic and stylistic patterns (incentives are to be offered)

- thereby encouraging teachers to accept Ebonics as a legitimate form of communication, worthy of respect and acceptance

- and thereby further increasing teachers' respect for and acceptance of the culture of the students they work with, and for the students themselves

Apparently Oakland's Board of Education did not intend for teachers to teach Ebonics, or to teach by using Ebonics in their own speech. However, they did intend for teachers to teach students about Ebonics, and to use the patterns of Ebonics as a starting point for understanding and appreciating mainstream English and its appropriate uses. Leanne Hinton (Feb. 1997), a professor in linguistics at the University of California–Berkeley, emphasized particularly the latter point after attending the board meeting where the Ebonics resolution was adopted: "This resolution is not about teaching [children to speak] Black English, but about the best way of teaching standard English. . . . By escaping the trap of thinking of non-standard Black English as a set of errors, and instead treating it as it really is, a different system, not a wrong one, standard English can be taught by helping children develop an awareness of the contrast between their two speech varieties, and learn to use one without losing their pride in the other."

Thus, it seems to me that the intent was to affect students and their learning in the following ways:

- to increase their self-esteem by increasing their appreciation of their African heritage

- to increase their willingness and motivation to learn mainstream English (because it is presented not as the "right" way to talk but as a potentially useful way to accomplish their own goals)

- to increase their respect for and rapport with their teacher (because the teacher has demonstrated understanding of and respect for their culture and for the students themselves)

- to improve their reading and writing skills and their academic achievement in general

In supporting the view that children's primary language/dialect should be valued, John Konopak of the University of Oklahoma points out that when standard English is considered the norm against which all other dialects should be measured, "the teacher has no responsibility to understand the student, only to inscribe upon her. Ebonics places a responsibility on the teacher/school/system" to listen to the children. Ebonics "acknowledges that the child—and by necessary extension, her community—not only has something important to say but also has the right to say it in ways that are meaningful to that community and that individual as part of a real, meaningful community" (1997).

It is important to note that most African American parents want to be sure that

African American children learn mainstream English in school (e.g. Delpit, 1986, 1988). They are convinced that so-called standard English is necessary to get ahead in mainstream society, even though fluency in the mainstream dialect(s) is no guarantee of success, or even of economic opportunity. Also, many African American students, especially teenagers and young adults, want to learn and use the dialect/language of the mainstream.

When parents and leaders in the African American community protest against linguists' or educators' concern for accepting and encouraging the maintenance of Ebonics, it is typically because they see the situation as an either/or phenomenon: either you teach Ebonics or you teach mainstream English. Thus if teachers are going to "teach Ebonics" (as parents may think of it) or encourage students to continue using Ebonics, they must be traitors to their race, if they're Black. If they're white, well then the teachers must be racist and must want to keep Blacks in their place—or so the reasoning goes. This was *not*, however, the intent of the linguists who first proposed using contrastive analysis to teach standard English to speakers of Black English (Fasold & Shuy, 1970), as it was then called, or to use beginning reading materials having Black English features to be contrasted with the same reading materials written in standard English (e.g. Baratz & Shuy, 1969; see also Rickford & Rickford, 1995). Nor is keeping Blacks in their place the intent of the Oakland, California, school board. On the contrary, they want to help African American youth become bi-dialectal and bi-cultural, so they can maintain their heritage but also have a chance to succeed economically and socially in mainstream America.

African American linguist John Rickford of Stanford University points out that in Norway, Sweden, Atlanta, Chicago, Oakland, and elsewhere, in programs that demonstrate the systematicity of the vernacular to students and contrast it with the standard variety, "kids learn to read and write more quickly and manage the transition to the standard more successfully than if schools attempt to ignore the vernacular or legislate its demise" (Jan. 23, 1997; Dec. 26, 1996).

In addition to what I think was the intent of the Oakland "Ebonics" resolution, I would also want, as a teacher, to deal with Ebonics (and by extension, other languages or dialects) in the context of studying the culture from which the dialect or language has arisen. For example, students of various ages could be introduced to slave songs, African American spirituals, as I was in music class during elementary school. But students should be introduced not only to the songs and the language patterns reflecting African Americans' linguistic heritage (e.g. Robinson, 1992), but to how slaves used the songs to communicate hidden messages with other slaves—messages like "It's time to head north to freedom," the coded message in songs like "Steal Away."

Furthermore, there are two more interrelated goals that I would specifically want to adopt. I'd want, on the one hand, to help prepare our youth to understand and operate in a world where racism and classism, monoculturalism and ethnocentrism still abound—think, for example, of the bombing of the federal building in Oklahoma City, the burning of Black churches, the rise of local militias, and the reemergence of the Ku Klux Klan and other white-supremacy groups. Certainly with the members of most such groups, we can see that linguistic prejudice not only stems from, but also promotes, the rejection of others. When people who so resolutely cling to racism and ethnocentrism have power in society, learning "mainstream" English is not going to help the less powerful very much, socioeconomically. Furthermore, governmental policy and recent legislation have had the effect (and probably the design) of further disenfranchising women and children and the poor in general, among whom are a disproportionate number of ethnic minorities.

Kevin Weston expresses it bluntly in an article in the *Los Angeles Times* (Jan. 5, 1997):

> We [African Americans] want an education for our people that exposes the true nature of this decadent American society. We want education that teaches our true history and our role in present day society. . . . Students [that is, African Americans in at least the Oakland, California school system] know they are receiving an inferior education that is preparing them for a shrinking welfare system or a booming penitentiary industry. But they feel powerless to change the way their education is administered.
>
> Ebonics opponents say black children must learn standard English to make them employable, to prepare them for a role in mainstream society. But as affirmative action is gutted and top-level discrimination revealed, where are the jobs that standard English is supposed to win us? Does corporate America have a new plan for us "black jellybeans" that we haven't been told about?

Clearly, Weston is right on target regarding the false promise of the alleged benefits of mastering mainstream, "standard" English. And yet, what do African American parents want for their children? Most seem to want their children to master mainstream English in school, in addition to having better schools, better instruction, and the respect of their teachers and peers. They know that while mainstream English is not a sufficient condition for economic success, it is often a necessary condition.

What, then, can we do as teachers? I would like to see more and more of us "problematizing" (e.g. Freire, 1985; Wink, 1997) the ways in which language and dialect are used as discriminators (e.g. Christiansen, 1994). Together, my students and I would ask questions like, Who benefits when we set up one dialect as "standard"? Who is hurt? How does linguistic prejudice reflect and promote stereotypes and prejudice against those of different races, cultures, and language/dialect communities? If we were to eliminate linguistic prejudice, would we humans find some other excuses for considering some group(s) superior and others inferior? What can we ourselves do to lessen such prejudices? How can we affect government policies so as to reopen the doors of opportunity to those oppressed by current policies?

In addition to addressing strictly language issues, then, I personally believe that we English language arts teachers have a moral obligation to engage students in discussion, reading, writing, and viewing experiences that will enable them to consider what I now think of as the "parsley" problem, thanks to Rita Dove's poem. That is, I think we need to investigate "man's inhumanity to man" (and woman's, too); to explore the roles we ourselves play in perpetuating this inhumanity; and to consider what actions we might want to take as moral and socially responsible human beings.

References

BARATZ, J., & SHUY, R. (Eds.). (1969). *Teaching black children to read.* Arlington, VA: Center for Applied Linguistics. (Available as a reprint from University Microfilms International in Ann Arbor, MI.)

BARON, D. (24 January 1997). Hooked on Ebonics. *The Chronicle of Higher Education,* B4–B5. <http://www.english.uiuc.edu/baron/essays/ebonics.htm>.

BARON, D. (n.d.). Oakland's Ebonics. *Linguist List, 8. 47.* <http://www.emich.edu /~linguist/issues/html/8–47.html#1> (1997, June 23).

BEREITER, C., & ENGELMANN, S. (1966). *Teaching disadvantaged children in the preschool.* Englewood Cliffs, NJ: Prentice-Hall.

BURLING, R. (1973). *English in black and white.* New York: Holt, Rinehart & Winston.

CHRISTIANSEN, L. (1994). Whose standard? Teaching standard English. In B. Bigelow, L. Christensen, S. Karp, B. Miner, & B. Peterson (Eds.), *Rethinking our classrooms: Teaching for equity and justice* (pp. 142–145). Milwaukee: Rethinking Schools.

CONFERENCE ON COLLEGE COMPOSITION AND COMMUNICATION (n.d.). *The national language policy* (leaflet). Urbana, IL: CCCC, National Council of Teachers of English.

CONFERENCE ON COLLEGE COMPOSITION AND COMMUNICATION (1974, Fall). *Students' right to their own language.* Urbana, IL: National Council of Teachers of English. (Drafted by M. Butler & the committee on the CCCC Language Statement.)

CRASSWELLER, R. (1966). *Trujillo: The life and times of a Caribbean dictator.* New York: Macmillan.

DELPIT, L. (1986). Skills and other dilemmas of a progressive black educator. *Harvard Educational Review, 56,* 379–385.

DELPIT, L. (1988). The silenced dialogue: Power and pedagogy in educating other people's children. *Harvard Educational Review, 58,* 280–281.

DILLARD, J. (1972). *Black English: Its history and usage in the United States.* New York: Random House.

DOVE, R. (1983). Parsley. From *Museum: Poems.* Pittsburgh: Carnegie Mellon University Press. Reprinted in N. Baym et al. (Eds.), *The Norton anthology of American literature* (4th Ed.), Vol. 2. New York: W. W. Norton Co.

ELGIN, S. (1978). Don't no revolutions hardly *ever* come by here. *College English, 39,* 784–789.

FASOLD, R., & SHUY, R. (Eds.). (1970). *Teaching standard English in the inner city.* Arlington, VA: Center for Applied Linguistics.

FREIRE, P. (1985). *The politics of education: Culture, power, and liberation*. South Hadley, MA: Bergin & Garvey.

GEE, J. (1996). *Socio linguistics and literacies: Ideology in discourse* (2nd Ed.). London: Taylor & Francis.

GRAHAM, L., & GRIFALCONI, A. (1971a). *David he no fear*. New York: Thomas Y. Crowell.

GRAHAM, L., & GRIFALCONI, A. (1993). *Every man heart lay down*. Honesdale, PA: Boyds Mills Press.

HINTON, L. (1997, February). (No title). In L. Monaghan (Comp.), Views of linguists and anthropologists on the Ebonics issue (Part 1). For the Society of Linguistic Anthropology. <http://www.leland.stanford.edu/~rickford/> (1997, June 23).

JONES, R. (1993). What's wrong with Black English. In P. Eschholz, A. Rosa & V. Clark (Eds.), *Language Awareness* (6th Ed.), (pp. 131–134). New York: St. Martin's.

KOCHMAN, T. (Ed.). (1972). *Rappin' and stylin' out: Communication in urban black America*. Urbana: University of Illinois Press.

KONOPAK, J. (1997). Ebonics. *Linguist List, 8*.150. <http://www.emich.edu/~linguist/issues/html/8–150.html#2> (1997, June 23).

LINGUISTIC SOCIETY OF AMERICA. (1997, January 3). Resolution on the Oakland "Ebonics" issue unanimously adopted at the annual meeting of the Linguistic Society of America. <http://www.sa.umich.edu/ling/jlawler/ebonics.lsa.html> (1997, June 23).

MORGAN, M. (1997, February). (No title). In L. Monaghan (Comp.), Views of linguists and anthropologists on the Ebonics issue (Part 1). For the Society of Linguistic Anthropology. <http://www.leland.stanford.edu/~rickford/> (1997, June 23).

OAKLAND UNIFIED SCHOOL DISTRICT. (1997a). Synopsis of the adopted policy on standard American English language development. <http://www.west.net:80/~joyland/Oakland.htm> (1997, June 23).

OAKLAND UNIFIED SCHOOL DISTRICT. (1997b). Amended resolution of the Board of Education adopting the report and recommendations of the African-American task force; a policy statement and [sic] directing the superintendent of schools to devise a program to improve the English language acquisition and application skills of African-American students. <http://linguist.emich.edu/topics/ebonics/ebonics-res2.html> (1997, June 23).

PINKER, S. (1994). *The language instinct*. New York: William Morrow.

PUBLIC BROADCASTING SERVICE (1986). *The story of English #5: Black on white*. PBS/FILMS Inc.

RETHINKING SCHOOLS. (1997). The real Ebonics debate: Power, language, and the education of African-American children. *Rethinking Schools, 12* (1).

RICKFORD, J. (1996a, December). Ebonics notes and discussion. <http://www.leland.stanford.edu/~rickford/ebonics/EbonicsExamples.html> (1997, June 23).

RICKFORD, J. (1996b, December 26). The Oakland Ebonics decision:

Commendable attack on the problem. *San Jose Mercury News.* <http://www. leland.stanford.edu/~rickford/ebonics/SJMN-OpEd.html> (1997, June 23).

RICKFORD, J. (1997, January 23). To the editors. *Newsweek Magazine.* <http://www. leland.stanford.edu/~rickford/ebonics/NewsweekLetter.html> (1997, June 23).

RICKFORD, J. (1997, February). (No title). In L. Monaghan (Comp.), Views of linguists and anthropologists on the Ebonics issue (Part 1). For the Society of Linguistic Anthropology. <http://www.leland.stanford.edu/~rickford/> (1997, June 23 Web search).

RICKFORD, J., & RICKFORD, A. (1995). Dialect readers revisited. *Linguistics and Education,* 7 (2), 107–128. <http://www.leland.stanford.edu/~rickford/ papers/DialectReaders.html> (1997, June 23).

ROBINSON, A. (1992). *The teachings drawn from African-American spirituals.* New York: Harcourt Brace Jovanovich.

SAPIR, E. (1921). *Language.* New York: Harcourt Brace and World.

SLEDD, J. (1969). Bi–dialectalism: The linguistics of white supremacy. *English Journal, 58* (December), 1307–1315.

SMITH, A. (1997, Feb. 1). Ebonics. *Linguist List, 8,* 150. <http://www.emich.edu/ ~linguist//issues/html/8–150.html#2> (1997, June 23).

SMITHERMAN, G. (1972). English teacher, why you be doing the thangs you don't do? *English Journal, 61,* 59–65.

SMITHERMAN, G. (1986). *Talkin and testifyin: The language of Black America* (2nd Ed.). Detroit: Wayne State University Press.

SMITHERMAN, G. (1994). *Black talk: Words and phrases from the hood to the amen corner.* Boston: Houghton Mifflin.

TRUDGILL, P. (1983). *Sociolinguistics: An introduction to language and society.* (2nd Ed.). New York: Penguin.

WESTON, K. (1997, Jan. 5). The state of ebonics and the relevance of a school's curriculum. *Los Angeles Times.* <http://jan.ucc.nau.edu/~jmw22/SF,LA,Chic. html/> (1997, June 23).

WHORF, B. (1956). *Language, thought, and reality: Selected writings.* Cambridge, MA: MIT Press.

WILLIAMS, R. (1975). *Ebonics: The true language of black folks.* St. Louis: Institute of Black Studies.

WILLIAMS, R., & BRANTLEY, M. (1975). Disentangling the confusion surrounding slang, nonstandard English, Black English, and Ebonics: Conclusion. In R. Williams (Ed.)., *Ebonics: The true language of Black folks.* St. Louis: Institute of Black Studies.

WINK, J. (1997). *Critical pedagogy: Notes from the real world.* New York: Addison-Wesley Longman.

WOLFRAM, W. (1991). *Dialects and American English.* Englewood Cliffs, NJ: Prentice Hall and Center for Applied Linguistics.

Other Resources: A Starter Bibliography

On AAVE and/or Ebonics, school success for speakers of AAVE/Ebonics, teaching mainstream/standard English, teaching AAVE/Ebonics speakers to read and write, cultural conflicts in learning mainstream/standard English and succeeding in school.

BAUGH, J. (1983). *Black street speech: Its history, structure and survival.* Austin: University of Texas Press.

BLOOME, D., & LEMKE, J. (Eds.). (1995). Special Issue: Africanized English and education. *Linguistics and Education, 7* (2).

CENTER FOR APPLIED LINGUISTICS (Ongoing). Center for Applied Linguistics Ebonics information page. <http://www.cal.org/ebonics/> (1997, June 23).

CHRISTIAN, D. (1994, December). ERIC Minibib, from *Vernacular dialects and standard American English in the classroom.* <http://ccat.sas.upenn.edu/~haroldfs/540/handouts/aave/aave.html> (1997, June 23).

DANDY, E. (1992). *Black communications: Breaking down the barriers.* Chicago: African American Images.

ERICKSON, F. (1987). Transformation and school success: The politics and culture of educational achievement. *Anthropology and Education Quarterly, 18,* 335–356.

FARR, M., & DANIELS, H. (1986). *Language diversity and writing instruction.* Urbana, IL: ERIC Institute for Urban and Minority Education and the National Council of Teachers of English.

FEIGENBAUM, I. (1970). The use of nonstandard English in teaching standard: Contrast and comparison. In R. Fasold & R. Shuy (Eds.), *Teaching standard English in the inner city* (87–104). Alexandria, VA: Center for Applied Linguistics.

FORDHAM, S. (1996). *Blacked out: Dilemmas of race, identity, and success at Capital High.* Chicago: University of Chicago Press.

LINGANTH (Ongoing). Home page. <http://www.beta-tech.com/linganth> (1997, June 23).

LINGUIST LIST (1997, May). Collection of resources on ebonics. <http://linguist.emich.edu/topics/ebonics> (1997, June 23).

MORGAN, M. (1994). Theories and politics in African-American English. *Annual Review of Anthropology, 23,* 325–345.

MUFWENE, S., RICKFORD, J., BAILEY, G., & BAUGH, J. (Eds.). (Forthcoming). *African American English.* London: Routledge.

OGBU, J. (1987, December). Variability in minority school performance: A problem in search of an explanation. *Anthropology and Education Quarterly, 18* (4), 312–334. (Ongoing). <http:www.dynateck.com/ebonics/organizations.html>. (1997, June 23).

RICKFORD, J. (Ongoing). Home page. <http://www.leland.stanford.edu/~rickford/> (1997, June 23).

RICKFORD, J. (1996). Regional and social variation. In S. McKay & N. Hornberger (Eds.), *Sociolinguistics for language teachers* (151–194). Cambridge: Cambridge University Press.

RICKFORD, J., & GREEN, L. (Forthcoming). *African-American vernacular English.* Cambridge: Cambridge University Press.

SCHIFFMAN, H. (n.d.). Partial bibliography: Use of vernacular languages, especially African-American vernacular English in education. <http://ccat.sas.upenn.edu/~haroldfs/540/handouts/aave/aave.html> (1997, June 23).

SCHIFFMAN, H. (n.d.). Annotated bibliography (no title). <http://jan.ucc.nau.edu/~jmw22/BiographicalSources.html> (1997, June 23).

SEYMOUR, D. (1971). Black children, black speech. *Commonweal Magazine,* November 19. In P. Eschholz, A. Rosa, & V. Clark (Eds.) (1997), *Language awareness* (7th Ed.). (151–159). New York: St. Martin's.

SHUY, R. (1970). Teacher training and urban language problems. In R. Fasold & R. Shuy (Eds.), *Teaching standard English in the inner city* (120–141). Arlington, VA: Center for Applied Linguistics.

SMITH, E. (1994). *The historical development of African-American language.* Los Angeles: Watts College Press.

SMITHERMAN, G. (Ed.). (1981). *Black English and the education of black children and youth.* Detroit: Center for Black Studies, Wayne State University Press.

SMITHERMAN, G. (1985). What go round come round: *King* in perspective. In C. Brooks (Ed.), *Tapping potential: English and language arts for the black learner* (41–62). Urbana, IL: National Council of Teachers of English.

SMITHERMAN, G. (1992). Black English, diverging or converging? The view from the National Assessment of Educational Progress. *Language Education, 6* (1), 47–61.

SPEARS, A. (1998). Black American English. In J. Cole, *Anthropology for the nineties* (96–113). New York: Free Press.

TAYLOR, H. (1991). *Standard English, Black English, and bidialectalism: A controversy.* New York: Peter Lang.

15

Meeting the Special Needs of the English as a Second Language (ESL) Students in Public Schools

MARY ANNE LOEWE

Introduction

In this chapter, Mary Anne Loewe discusses seven components of a whole language approach to English language instruction: immersion in language-rich environment; demonstrations of language use; high expectations of success; responsibility for learning placed on the students; frequent and varied language use; allowance for approximations of correct structures; and appropriate teacher response (Cambourne, 1988), in terms of how teachers can use them to help elementary-level nonnative English speakers achieve fluency and accuracy in English.

In the 1994–1995 school year, Michigan served more than 51,000 international students speaking over 100 different languages (Michigan Department of Education, 1995). Of course, Michigan is not alone; this is a nationwide phenomenon. Due to funding and staffing constraints, many of these students do not qualify for bilingual education, so the chances of mainstream teachers having sole responsibility for teaching them are very great. The twofold task that K–12 teachers normally take on, to teach both content and language, becomes more difficult when the students do not have English as a native language to support them in their learning. However, this formidable undertaking does not have to overwhelm the teacher. The content courses and the language development can support each other, with the content course serving as a context within which language acquisition is facilitated. Once the content is understood, the recycling, or repetition, of the vocabulary and syntax enables the students to acquire a more and more sophisticated command of their new language. They learn the material and how to talk/write about the material. This is the same goal that we, as educators, attempt to achieve with native English-speaking children.

A major concern of teachers and parents alike is the accuracy with which nonnative English speaking children come to use English. Teachers want to ensure that their students will succeed in their later studies and careers, and parents want everything for their children that America has to offer, including complete bilingual proficiency. Everyone agrees that the children should not only be literate in English, but also have a command of language that will enable them to participate in any career they may choose.

Increasingly, teachers are successfully utilizing whole language techniques in working with ESL students (Freeman & Freeman, 1992; Hsu, 1994; Jama, 1992; MacGowan-Gilhooly, 1991; Manning & Manning, 1989; Manning, Manning, & Long, 1994; Mills & Clyde, 1990; Nigohosian, 1992; Wilson, 1993). These techniques include immersing the children in a linguistically rich environment, demonstrating and modeling accurate English for the students, maintaining high expectations of success, giving the students responsibility for their learning, allowing many opportunities for the students to use the language, allowing the students to approximate accurate forms and structures, and responding appropriately to their attempts at English usage.

These techniques are key components of the whole language approach and form the basis of Brian Cambourne's 1988 model of literacy acquisition (see Figure 15–1). They are based on two assumptions about language learning which derive

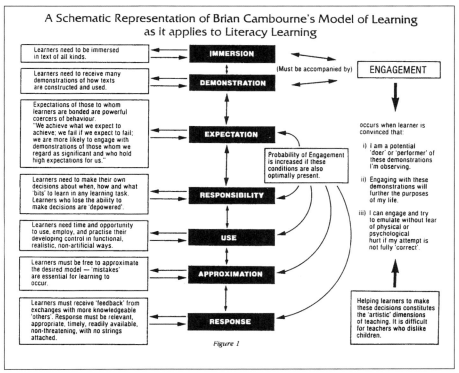

FIG. 15–1 *Brian Cambourne's Model of Learning/Teaching*
Source: Cambourne, B. (1988). The whole story: Natural learning and the acquisition of literacy in the classroom. Auckland, New Zealand: Ashton Scholastic, p.33.

from first language acquisition research. The first is that the oral and written forms of language are only superficially different and that the brain can learn to process oral and written forms of language in much the same way, provided that the conditions under which each is learned are also much the same. The second assumption is that, as stunning an intellectual feat as oral language acquisition is, it is achieved in an apparently effortless manner when the needed learning conditions are present (pp. 28–32).

Cambourne's model can serve as a model of learning for second language students, also, with a few accommodations.

The Student Should Be Immersed in Language

Being surrounded by language use is a necessary component in a child's acquiring his or her first language. As a child is learning to talk, the child is generally in the presence of an adult or other speaker of the language he or she is learning. We know the language the caregiver uses is somewhat simplified and the contexts under which the language is used are often ritualized and routinized. Bath time, story time, and meal time are prime examples of this. The child understands the language as it is used in a given context and is able to draw connections with other situations in which similar structures are used. Krashen (1985) calls this language *comprehensible input* and suggests that for language students, the most beneficial level of input for the student is just a little above the level of the child's language proficiency or at the i+1 level: Too low a level, and the child does not have anything to learn; at too high a level the language becomes noise.

There is little doubt that the ESL student in an American classroom is immersed in oral and written language, both of which serve as input if they are comprehensible and the student is engaged. Ensuring that the language is comprehensible for these students involves a few accommodations in how we present information.

Making Oral Language Comprehensible

1. Use the board or overhead projector to write down important words and point to these words as you speak. Using more than one modality (such as writing along with speaking) offers the student more than one path for processing the input. This is particularly useful for older students from alphabetic language backgrounds who may recognize words when written down that would ordinarily confuse them.

2. Use gestures. English as a second language teachers use gestures much more often than mainstream class teachers to help students understand what is said.

3. Use pictures or other visual aids.

4. Use routinized phrases. Phrases such as "Open your books to page N," used the same way every time they are uttered, allow the child to draw connections between that phrase and similar phrases used in books or said at different times. They serve as scaffolding in much the same way as caregiver talk does for the infant learning his/her first language, keeping the context stable so that the student can predict the usage (Ninio & Bruner, 1978).

5. Be careful to enunciate your words. Don't speak more loudly or slowly, but be more aware of the enunciation of content words. Speak with natural intonation and sentence structure, keeping in your speech function words, such as articles and prepositions. It is more confusing for an ESL student to be immersed in stilted, unnatural speech than in the more complex, natural speech the teacher usually uses.

6. Check for comprehension. Look at the student for confirmation of understanding. A simple nod from the student will let you know if you need to take other steps to be understood.

7. Have the students form buddies. Find someone who speaks the same language as the ESL student who can serve as a translator, or establish a buddy system with an American student who would be willing to explain class interactions. If students balk at being a constant buddy, there are variations on the buddy system that relieve the students from excessive responsibility for each other:
   A. The clock buddy—for each hour of the clock, students have different buddies. When that time comes, the students work on whatever task is at hand with that buddy.
   B. The two-minute (or one-minute) buddy—stop the class and have the students turn to their neighbors for two minutes and discuss a question that you pose from the material, or review with each other what was just learned (Levine, 1993).

Making Written Language Comprehensible

1. Read aloud to the students often from highly predictable books and picture books. (See Ammon & Sherman, 1996; Hamayan & Pfleger, 1987; Kinzer & Leu, 1992.) They are easily understood and keep the students engaged. Reading aloud also teaches narration skills, appropriate intonation, and grammar.

2. For older students, supply guided reading questions for all the reading assignments. This serves two purposes: It focuses the student on the part of the reading that is important and it helps the student learn organization markers such as those for sequence (first, second, third, then, before) and cause and effect (because, therefore). The knowledge of such markers is imperative for the students in their understanding of the passage and is a chronic problem for them.

3. Use graphic organizers. A graphic organizer is a visual display of the text.

Time lines and concept maps are examples of graphic organizers that students can create with each other, the teacher, or independently (Chamot & O'Malley, 1987).

4. Use a vocabulary card to illustrate the relationship between ideas in a text. Take a 3 x 5 card and divide it into four squares. On the top left square write the main idea or the main character from the reading; on the other squares write the supporting ideas or descriptions of the main character.

5. To the extent possible, contextualize the study. Revisit themes from the reading text throughout the day. Recycle the vocabulary, the grammar, and the organization of the reading in different units. The consistent theme serves as the scaffolding for the development of second language skills. The children encounter less new information, so they can focus their attention on other aspects of the language such as new grammar structures. Grammar structures can be directly taught as needed in mini-units, while discussing a text or helping students edit their papers. Atwell (1987); Calkins (1986); Chamot & O'Malley (1987); Clark (1992); Manning, Manning, & Long (1994); Short, Crandall, & Christian (1989); Levine (1993); Popp (1996); Routman (1991); Weaver (1994); and Weaver (1996) all offer suggestions on implementing theme explorations and/or contextualized grammar minilessons for many different grammar constructions.

Learners Need to Receive Demonstrations of How Texts Are Constructed and Used

Cambourne (1988) believes that without demonstrations, learning will not occur (p. 47). Make it a regular practice to demonstrate writing and reading to the students. Students whose native language is not English require more repetitions of demonstrations and more frequent demonstrations than native English speakers. An ESL student who is apparently proficient in conversational English may only understand 50 percent of the teacher talk in the classroom, so demonstrations become even more important. There are many areas in which demonstrations can help in the teaching of grammar:

1. Write paragraphs together with the students on an overhead projector.

2. Do sentence combining exercises with the students.

3. Edit a sample paper together.

4. Create a demonstration out of a read aloud by thinking aloud about the text as you read.

5. Use conferencing as an opportunity to repeat a demonstration for an individual student as the other students work.

Maintain High Expectations of the Student

Success is intrinsically motivating. Set high standards for the students, as close to the regular curriculum goals as possible, then help students achieve those standards. This entails understanding the students and the work they hand in. Students whose work is met with frustration, confusion, or even a raised eyebrow feel inadequate, different, and less likely to succeed. After all, if the teacher finds it a problem, it must really be a problem! This, in turn, increases the likelihood that the students will feel marginalized and pull out of the classroom community, or become mislabeled as difficult or cognitively deficient. Teachers need to demonstrate an understanding of and a respect for the students they teach. This can be done in a number of ways:

1. Research the cultures of the ESL students in your class. Look for cultural behaviors and values that might impact on the class processes. Some cultural values that may impact on a student's performance in English include the following:

    A. beliefs that the teacher should be the disseminator of information and that collaboration with peers is not profitable;

    B. beliefs that the student should not critically approach a text written by an adult;

    C. beliefs that boys and girls should not work together or be in the same class;

    D. beliefs that an individual student should never stand out from the crowd, even in a good way;

    E. beliefs that girls should never be in the position to instruct boys about anything; or

    F. beliefs that children should never address adults or look them directly in the eye.

Students and parents who come from these belief systems may feel they can adjust to the American classroom culture, but teachers may find that the students' performance suffers in these situations. Students stand to be mislabeled when the teacher is inadequately informed about the home culture. A good rule of thumb is to look to cultural differences first when students are performing in a way that is confusing. The more illogical or unexpected the behavior, the more likely it is that there is a cultural reason for it.

By the same token, demonstrate a respect for the students' cultural values by encouraging the student to talk and write about them. Kitagawa (1989) calls this "creating a mosaic in the context of cultural diversity. . . . Open dialogue and expressive writing are a meeting ground for all of us as members of the classroom community" (pp. 131–133). Content area study, such as science, may incorporate multicultural literature and approaches to teaching. Children from different ethnic backgrounds should be encouraged to make cultural connections as they learn about the contributions of different cultures to the subject matter (Offutt, 1996).

2. Know the language background of the students in your class. Students who come from oral cultures and some Eastern societies develop narratives and arguments differently from the British model which we teach in schools. Even a seemingly simple, risk-free event as show-and-tell can become problematic for students who develop narratives differently from Americans. For students who develop narratives episodically (that is, by telling all of the events that occurred around the main topic without directly addressing the topic), a read-aloud of a story developed linearly may not be understood. An older child may actually put a negative value on stories developed in an American style and resist writing in that way. See some of the following sources for information on the critical thinking patterns of various cultures: Barnhardt & Tonsmeire (1988); Freeman & Freeman (1989); Heath (1983); and Trueba, Guthrie, & Au (1981).

3. Show respect for the student's native language by allowing him or her to use it in class. Second-language acquisition studies now indicate that the first language can serve as a support for second language learning (Freeman & Freeman, 1992). Skills such as reading, acquired in the first language, we now understand can be transferred to the second. As children begin writing in English, they generally intersperse their native words into the text. This may be because the children understand the nuance of the foreign word better than an English equivalent, or it may serve as a placeholder that allows the student to continue writing without looking up the vocabulary word. Knowing the different reasons why a child may use a foreign word will enable the teacher to more accurately assess the writing skills of the student.

   Other ways the teacher can use the child's first language as a support for the second is to allow the child to compose in the first language and translate it with a buddy into English or to allow the child to teach aspects of his or her first language to the American students. Discussing the differences in their languages serves as a memory aid for students and will increase the accuracy with which the nonnative speaking students use English.

   Keep easy readers in the students' native languages available in the class. Reading in the native language helps the students retain their home language skills and also helps students in English by honing transferable reading skills (Wilson, 1993).

4. Resist assuming that immigrant children may take 5–7 years to catch up to the Americans in their academic language ability. Cummins (1981) and Collier (1989) differentiate between conversational language and cognitive academic

language, stating that while children may achieve total bilingual status in conversational English within a couple of years, they may never achieve bilingual status in their academic language for their entire school careers. This is because conversational English is highly contextualized, with the participants speaking of the "here and now," or of shared experiences, and it is cognitively less demanding than academic English. Academic English requires more linguistic elaboration because of the reduced context surrounding its use. There is real danger if teachers don't hold as high expectations as they should for the children, believing that bilingualism will take a very long time. The answer may be to add context to the study to help reduce the length of time required for acquisition. Perez (1996) illustrates the value of instructional conversations for syntax, vocabulary, pragmatics, and content acquisition. Students in her second-grade class took part in "conversations about concrete, contextualized learning experiences to form their own oral texts instead of being subjected merely to explicit lessons on 'how to talk'" (p. 174). They generated monthly lists of possible topics and from these lists the teachers would conduct an initial search for ideas and materials. The students then prioritized and voted on the list of topics to be discussed. During the conversation, the teacher would introduce the inquiry procedure (for example, an experimental procedure) and any vocabulary, without defining technical terms. The concrete experiences, limited use of native language, and the use of small group discussion served as scaffolding for the students' language development and promoted conversation (pp. 175–178). Other researchers discuss teaching language through a content course such as science, by teaching open-ended questions and writing strategies, using children's literature and ideas, and using E-mail technology to form science partners (Rubba, 1996; Offutt, 1996).

Give the Student Responsibility for His or Her Learning

Cambourne (1988) reasons that children learning their first language are responsible for determining which aspects of language with which to engage, although they "decide" quite unconsciously. He argues that we should expect the same of children in school. If children receive much comprehensible input and many demonstrations, they will choose the aspects of the language that are most important for them to learn to communicate in a given situation. Because these students come from cultures in which student responsibility means less teacher responsibility, they are sometimes more resistant than Americans to this practice. However, many of the activities we assign to Americans also work, with some encouragement, with ESL students.

1. Use portfolios to teach students how to self-assess their writing. Older students who are struggling to learn English are quite capable of identifying areas they need to improve in their writing.

2. Use jigsaw exercises. In jigsaw groupings, students join groups to study a segment of a particular text. When they become experts on this piece of text, they re-form into new groups that are comprised of representatives of each of the former groups. They are then responsible for teaching the other members of their new group about their segment of the text. Students must take notes on the content and ask questions in order to fully understand the text.

3. Give the students choices. Because ESL students may have limited communicative ability, the tendency is for the teacher or the other students to make the students' choices for them. It is much more profitable, although time consuming, for the participants to communicate the choices to the ESL student. The child learns both English and responsibility.

Students Must Be Allowed to Use the Language

Give frequent and meaningful opportunities for the students to use the language. Fundamentally, the purpose of learning a language is to provide a communication tool for the students. And, as with all other tools, it is best learned in a meaningful context. Students achieve facility and increasing accuracy in using a language when their attention is focused on conveying and receiving authentic messages—that is, messages that contain information of interest to the speaker and listener in a situation of importance to both (Rivers, 1987). The negotiation of meaning that occurs when students need to communicate for a purpose is essential to the acquisition of linguistic accuracy. Theme explorations offer students the opportunity to collaborate meaningfully on a project while honing their language skills. Popp (1996) offers this procedure for establishing a theme cycle:

1. Have the students vote on a list of themes to be explored.

2. When the list is completed, each student should take one home to parents. Enlist parents' help by asking if they have expertise, information, or materials to share about any of the topics. Resources may also be obtained from colleagues, the media specialist, and the local library.

3. Begin with the most popular theme. Ask children what they already know about the topic and what they would like to know. List their ideas in both categories on the board; then group the questions the children raise into research topics. Create an idea web.

4. Create research sessions. Each research session involves the following:
   a. a time to consult with other students and the teacher about individual problems;

b. an independent, paired, or group study period;

c. time to respond to what they are learning in writing and other means of expression such as drawing or making models;

d. time to share the day's discoveries in small groups or as a class; and

e. student self-evaluation of the day's work.

Consultation time: During this time students can share their frustrations with the research process. The teacher can conduct minilessons on the mechanics of research.

Study time: During this time students pursue their research in groups or individually.

Writing opportunities: Students may keep one journal to record what they have learned across the curriculum or they may keep separate journals for math, science, and social studies. Students may record part of what they have read and respond to it, or they may create a KWLCQ (What I know, What I want to know, What I learned, Connections with what I already know, and Questions I still have). In math, students may share their problem-solving strategies by responding to questions such as "I helped _____ with _____ problem. The difficulty seemed to be _____. My helping strategy was _____. In the end, he or she seemed _____ and I felt _____." In the early grades, students may write down math sentences they created through manipulatives. In social studies they can write about topics such as: people and places I wonder about, geography I notice, history that is happening, and current events that are happening.

Creative responses: Students may create maps or models, bulletin boards or posters, surveys or questionnaires, newspapers or letters to editors, alphabet books using alliterative sentences on the topic, or reenactments of historical events.

Share time: This gives the students time to share the excitement of their discoveries before the end of the day.

Student self-evaluation: Students rate themselves on a scale the class has developed and write reasons why they believe this is an accurate assessment of their performance that day (pp. 411–417).

A corollary to encouraging students to participate is that they should never be encouraged, even inadvertently, not to participate in the class, on the assumption that they can't use English well enough or will be embarrassed by their use of English. Students will be more likely to participate if the teacher does the following:

1. Continually invite the student to participate, creating a nonthreatening atmosphere. ESL students are usually shy and uncomfortable in an English environment. Special invitations will keep them from removing themselves from the classroom community.

2. Allow TIME for the student to participate. Nonnative speaking students take longer to process information; they take longer to move from one activity to another; they take longer to offer their opinions to the other students. Allow a longer wait time between asking a question and choosing a student to answer. This wait time makes educators a bit uncomfortable, but even a few seconds extension will allow the students to process the information and be prepared to participate in the class. Make it a practice to look for signs (such as forward moving body language, eye contact, or a smile) that the student has something to say, and then make time for him or her to say it.

3. Teach the ESL students polite ways of asserting themselves. During group discussions, ESL teachers encourage these students to give their opinions, assuming that shyness is the principle reason for the students' lack of participation. ESL students, however, have commented that even if they understand everything and want to participate in the discussion, the American students are just faster at "jumping into" a discussion. Even when ESL students understand perfectly well what is going on, chances are the American students will beat them "to the punch." At that point, the ESL students don't want to interrupt and so keep quiet. Teaching the students interrupting phrases to use to assert themselves into a conversation, and at the same time, preparing the American students to hear them, will allow more even participation in group activities.

4. Find creative ways of drawing out the ESL student and getting him or her to write in English. The February 1997 issue of *Teaching Pre K–8* describes how Paula Carter used clay to help her student feel better about writing in English. They would talk while the child worked with the clay, and the teacher would write down the spontaneous utterances the child said. This practice became a language experience for them, as everything written down became something the child could read back. After playing with the clay, the child wrote about the experience with the teacher's help. Providing concrete experiences for children, then asking them to write about them, is a very effective tool in literacy education.

Allow Students to Approximate Language Features

Nonnative English speaking students are attempting to learn a new language as they acquire new cognitive skills. Many of these skills, such as critical thinking skills, are not a part of their past cultural experiences. As Cummins (1981) indicates, as the cognitive difficulty of the task increases, the quality of the student's language, because of the explicitness required, may decrease. Here are two ways to help:
1. Giving the students places, such as journals, where they can write without fear of grades, and allowing them to make adequate use of the writing process

to revise their writing will ensure they will continue to use English even if unsure of its accuracy. Too much attention to accuracy of output will ensure that the child quits participating altogether. Dialogue journals, in which the teachers respond to the content of the student's writing, have been found to work very well in ESL classes (Clark, 1992; Hamayan & Pfleger, 1987; Manning & Manning, 1989). Gunkel (1991) describes the progress made by one Japanese student in the fourth grade who entered her class in September with very little knowledge of English. Her program incorporated the use of dialogue journals, read-alouds, and writing workshops. Figure 15–2 is a sample of Keisuke's growth in writing from September to February of that year. In that four-month span of time, there is a marked improvement in Keisuke's overall intelligibility. While it is not entirely grammatically accurate, there is little confusion in the February entry about what Keisuke wants to communicate. The sentence structure is markedly improved and Keisuke uses, not only declarative sentences, but questions and exclamations as well, with proper punctuation.

2. Celebrate the progress the international children make. By functioning in a second language classroom environment they are accomplishing a feat most of us have not had to attempt. Just by being there, they have already succeeded.

FIG. 15–2 *Keisuke's Dialogue Journals*

I. September
Dear Mrs. Gunkel,
thanks for letter.
Im work hard for book. and
read every night.
I liked japan house. put on
map Down and japan house
not in shoe on shoe off
to front Door.
I remember to school.
Playground is very wide and
not buy lunch.
Please teach america.
Sincerely,
Keisuke

II. February
Dear Mrs. Gunkel,
Did you finish my book
Covers remonade?
I think finished.
I have new story idea for animals.
Thinks use same time of
last one.
I went New York at Feb 16-19
I'm tired to walk.
I went soho, central park,
And going other!
Sincerely,
Keisuke

Source: Gunkel, J. (1991). Please teach America: Keisuke's journey into a language community. *Language Arts, 68*, pp. 303-304.

Give the Student an Appropriate and Timely Response

Keep the importance of grammatical accuracy in perspective. A good rule of thumb to follow is "fluency-clarity-accuracy" (MacGowan-Gilhooly, 1991). Focus first on helping students get all of their ideas down on paper, then help them with their argument, reasons, or logical development before addressing grammar. Then address the grammar as it applies to that particular piece. Let them say what they want to say, and help them learn the language to use for saying it. This is much preferable to dumbing down the curriculum in order to accommodate the child's language.

Don't attempt to address all the grammar issues at once, for each piece. Pick one or two that the student can work on by him or herself, or those that arise from the readings, and address only those. As the students progress, the teacher can choose more and more sophisticated constructions to address. Many of the grammar problems are shared by the American students: All students can benefit from minilessons on subject-verb agreement, appropriate use of tenses, and appropriate use of pronouns, for example.

Conclusion

Teaching ESL students in the regular elementary classroom can be a daunting task, but it does not have to be overwhelming. A whole language classroom, with its focus on individualized instruction and collaborative, contextualized learning, goes a long way in meeting the needs of these students.

References

AMMON, B., & SHERMAN, G. (1996). *Worth a thousand words: An annotated guide to picture books for older readers*. Englewood, CA: Libraries Unlimited.

ATWELL, N. (1987). *In the middle*. Portsmouth, NH: Boynton/Cook.

BARNHARDT, R., & TONSMEIRE, J. (1988). *Lessons taught, lessons learned: Teachers' reflections on schooling in rural Alaska*. Juneau: Staff Development Network.

BLAIR, D. (1990). *Science talk: Science in the ESL classroom*. Unpublished master's thesis. School for International Training, Brattleboro, VT.

CALKINS, L. (1986). *The art of teaching writing*. Portsmouth, NH: Heinemann.

CAMBOURNE, B. (1988). *The whole story: Natural learning and the acquisition of literacy in the classroom*. Auckland, New Zealand: Ashton Scholastic.

CARTER, P. (1997, February). Mother's words. *Teaching pre K–8, 27* (5), 51.

CHAMOT, A., & O'MALLEY, M. (1987). The cognitive academic language learning approach: A bridge to the mainstream. *TESOL Quarterly, 21* (2), 227–249.

CLARK, J. (1992). *Whole language literacy for at-risk learners.* Washington, DC: ERIC Clearinghouse.

COLLIER, V. (1989). How long? A synthesis of research on academic achievement in a second language. *TESOL Quarterly, 23* (3), 509–532.

CUMMINS, J. (1981). The role of primary language development in promoting educational success for language minority students. In *Schooling and language minority students: A theoretical framework* (pp. 3–49). Los Angeles: Evaluation, Dissemination, and Assessment Center, California State University.

DeCARLO, J. (1995). *Perspective in whole language.* Boston: Allyn and Bacon.

FERGUSON, P., & YOUNG, T. (1996). Literature talk: Dialogue improvisation and patterned conversations with second-language learners. *Language Arts, 73,* 597–600.

FREEMAN, Y., & FREEMAN, D. (1989). Bilingual learners: How our assumptions limit their world. *Holistic Education Review,* 33–39.

FREEMAN, Y., & FREEMAN, D. (1992). *Whole language for second language learners.* Portsmouth, NH: Heinemann.

GENESEE, F. (Ed.). (1994). *Educating second-language children: The whole child, the whole curriculum, the whole community.* New York: Cambridge University Press.

GORMLEY, K., & McDERMOTT, P. (Eds.). (1996). *Language and literacy spectrum. Vol. 6.*

GUNKEL, J. (1991). Please teach America: Keisuke's journey into a language community. *Language Arts, 68,* 303–310.

HAMAYAN, E., & PFLEGER, M. (1987). *Developing literacy in English as a second language: Guidelines for teachers of young children from nonliterate backgrounds.* Washington, DC: Center for Applied Linguistics.

HEATH, S. (1983). *Ways with words: Language, life, and work in communities and classrooms.* Cambridge: Cambridge University Press.

HSU, Y. (1994). *Whole language and ESL children.* Washington, DC: ERIC Clearinghouse on Language and Linguistics.

HUDELSON, S. (1989). *Write on: Children writing in ESL.* Washington, DC: ERIC Clearinghouse on Language and Linguistics.

KRASHEN, S. (1985). *The input hypothesis.* New York: Longman.

JAMA, V. (1992). *Integrating English as a second language instruction with the regular elementary- and middle-school curriculum: Can it work?* Paper presented at the Annual Meeting of the Teachers of English to Speakers of Other Languages, Vancouver, B.C., March 3–7.

KAMII, C., MANNING, M., & MANNING, G. (Eds.). (1991). *Early literacy: A constructivist foundation for whole language.* Washington, DC: National Education Association.

KINZER, C., & LEU, D. (Eds.). (1992). *Literacy research, theory, and practice: Views from many perspectives. Forty-first yearbook of the National Reading Conference.* Chicago: National Reading Conference.

KITAGAWA, M. (1989). Constructing a mosaic in the context of cultural diversity. In J. Jensen (Ed.), *Stories to grow on: Demonstrations of language learning in K–8 classrooms* (pp. 131–146). Portsmouth, NH: Heinemann.

LEVINE, L. (1993.). *Techniques for mainstream teachers of ESL students.* Washington, DC: TESOL.

MANN, V. (1997). A word is worth a thousand pictures: A writing project for the primary grades. *MinneTESOL Journal, Vol. 6,* 7–13.

MANNING, G., & MANNING, M. (Eds.). (1989). *Whole language: Beliefs and practices, K–8.* Washington, DC: National Education Association.

MANNING, M., MANNING, G., & LONG, R. (1994). *Theme immersion: Inquiry based curriculum in elementary and middle schools.* Portsmouth, NH: Heinemann.

MICHIGAN DEPARTMENT OF EDUCATION. (1995). *Michigan Department of Education Bilingual Students by District.* Lansing, MI.

MACGOWAN-GILHOOLY, A. (1991). Fluency first: Reversing the traditional ESL sequence. *Journal of Basic Writing, 10* (1), 73–87.

MIDDLEBROOKS, K. (1994). Whole language in today's ESL classroom. *English in Texas, 25* (4), 34–35.

MILLS, H., & CLYDE, J. (Eds.). (1990). *Portraits of whole language classrooms: Learning for all ages.* Portsmouth, NH: Heinemann.

NIGOHOSIAN, E. (1992). *Meeting the challenge of diversity: Applying whole language theory in the kindergarten with ESL Korean children.* ERIC Clearinghouse.

NINIO, A., & BRUNER, J. (1978). The achievements and antecedents of labeling. *Journal of Child Language, 5,* 1–15.

OFFUTT, E. (1996). *Teaching science in a multicultural world.* Parsippany, NJ: Modern Curriculum Press.

OYLER, C., & BARRY, A. (1996). Intertextual connections in read-alouds of information books. *Language Arts, 73,* 324–329.

PEREZ, B. (1996). Instructional conversations as opportunities for English language acquisition for culturally and linguistically diverse students. *Language Arts, 73,* 173–181.

POPP, M. (1996). *Teaching language and literature in elementary classrooms: A resource book for professional development.* Mahwah, NJ: Lawrence Erlbaum Associates.

RIGG, P., & ALLEN, V. (Eds.). (1989). *When they don't all speak English: Integrating the ESL student into the regular classroom.* Urbana, IL: National Council of Teachers of English.

RIVERS, W. (Ed.). (1987). *Interactive language teaching.* New York: Cambridge University Press.

ROBB, L. (1994). *Whole language, whole learners: Creating a literature-based classroom.* New York: William Morrow and Company.

ROUTMAN, R. (1991). *Invitations.* Toronto: Irwin Publishing.

RUBBA, P. (Ed.). (1996). *Proceedings of the annual international conference of the Association for the Education of Teachers in Science.* Pensacola, FL: Association for the Education of Teachers in Science.

RUPP, J. (1986). *Whole language in the elementary ESL classroom.* Paper presented at the annual meeting of the Teachers of English to Speakers of Other Languages, Anaheim, CA, March 3–8.

RUPP, J. (Ed.). (1994). *Elementary education newsletter.* The Official Publication of the ESOL in Elementary Education Interest Section. Vol. 15–16.

SHORT, D., CRANDALL, J., & CHRISTIAN, D. (1989). *How to integrate language and content instruction: A training manual.* Center for Language Education and Research, University of California Press.

TRAW, R. (1996). Large-scale assessment of skills in a whole language curriculum: Two districts' experiences. *Journal of Educational Research, 89* (6), 323–340.

TRUEBA, G., GUTHRIE, G., & AU, K. (1981). *Culture and the bilingual classroom: Studies in classroom ethnography.* Rowley: Newbury House.

WEAVER, C. (1994). *Reading process and practice: From socio-psycholinguistics to whole language.* Portsmouth, NH: Heinemann.

WEAVER, C. (1996). *Teaching grammar in context.* Portsmouth, NH: Boynton/Cook.

WILSON, K. (1993). *Whole language ESL: Reading, writing, and speaking.* Paper presented at the National Conference on Migrant and Seasonal Farmworkers, Denver, CO, May 9–13.

16 Implementing Whole Language in a University-Level ESL Curriculum

MARY ANNE LOEWE

Introduction

In the first section of this chapter, Mary Anne Loewe describes the whole language approach to language instruction and places it within the framework of current and past second language acquisition theory. She also offers guidelines for helping students achieve grammatical accuracy through awareness development and strategy training, contextualized instruction such as theme units, grammar instruction integrated into the other IEP program components of reading, writing, speaking, and listening, and the adoption of a student-centered syllabus.

The whole language approach to language instruction is actually a teaching philosophy that encompasses a number of different methodologies. Whole language teachers believe that students acquire language most successfully and easily when introduced to the language holistically; that is, when the big picture is experienced before any skill instruction is introduced, when class interaction involves authentic materials and meaningful language use, and when the instruction is student-centered. The whole language approach is clearly appropriate to meet the special needs of university ESL students. The necessity of whole-to-part instruction can be verified by considering the previous language learning experiences of international students in intensive English programs (IEPs). At Western Michigan University, international students enrolled in the IEP have studied grammar for an average of five years in their home countries; 20 percent have studied English for more than ten years. They still face six to nine months of additional instruction before they can assume university study. The use of authentic materials and meaningful communication is a motivational tool for the instructors. International students preparing for university study are particularly concerned with relevance; they are in the United States for a limited amount of time and are usually heavily monitored by family and sponsors. They rightfully challenge assignments that do not obviously relate to their goals of achieving fluent and accurate English usage. Last, because international students enter university-intensive English programs to achieve a variety of personal and professional goals and are in various stages of development, a student-centered curriculum allows the instructor to meet each of their needs by individualizing the instruction.

The term *whole language* carries with it different connotations for different groups. Because of its focus on process as well as product and its acceptance of the developmental stages of language acquisition as normal and largely idiosyncratic, in some circles whole language has undeservedly gained the reputation of being a philosophy under which language skills such as grammar and mechanics are ignored. In reality, the instruction of grammar and mechanics is dependent on the needs of the individual students. They receive direct instruction in the areas in which they require it but are allowed and encouraged to acquire language skills in much the same way as they did in their first language. The result is an improvement in writing fluency and critical thinking skills which far surpasses the accomplishments of students taught under previous teaching philosophies. The focus on communication strategy development as well as on the product teaches the students to monitor and correct themselves in order to continue to improve on their own.

Historically, whole language has been associated with literacy instruction at the elementary school level, but as second-language acquisition theory has developed over the past decade, particularly with regard to language learning processes and strategies and the role of interlanguage, we have become more aware of the similarities between children and adults as language learners (Crooks & Gass, 1993; Diller, 1978; Faigle, 1993; Feeley, Strickland, & Wepner, 1991; Flynn, 1986; Freeman & Freeman, 1992; Gaies, 1976; Gass & Madden, 1985; Gass & Selinker, 1992; Goodman, 1996; Kamii, Manning, & Manning, 1991; Kaspar & Blum-Kulka, 1993; Mitchell, 1982; Moll, 1990; Murray, 1980; Nehls, 1988; Selinker, 1991; Shank, 1986; Weaver, 1994). In this chapter I will place the whole language philosophy within the framework of past and current second language acquisition theory. In the second section, I will offer some guidelines for the implementation of a whole language philosophy in the university-level intensive English program.

Part I: Fitting Whole Language into Second-Language Acquisition Theory

The Empiricist School of Thought

Based on the structuralist view of linguistics that held that language study should be based on observable linguistic phenomena, the methods of language teaching under the empiricist school of thought replaced the old grammar-translation method of the early twentieth century. The principles that formed the foundations of the empiricist school included the beliefs that language is a set of habits;

language is speech, not writing; and teachers should teach the language, not teach about the language (Diller, 1978).

The Audio-Lingual Method of the 1950s and 1960s

The empiricist school was influenced strongly by the behaviorist model of learning, according to which children learn their first language through imitation and operant conditioning; the teaching methods included much pattern memorization and repetition, as in the audio-lingual method. The audio-lingual method was characterized by the focus on speaking and listening before reading and writing, memorization of dialogs created as *snapshots* of real language use, and imitation and repetition of language patterns. One technique in this method was the pattern practice drill of the following type:

Tape: Book. I have a book. Repeat after me.
Student: I have a book.
Tape: pencil
Student: I have a pencil.
Tape: I have a pencil.

Techniques such as this one were considered helpful for the students' development of automaticity in the language; through sheer repetition, students were thought to be able to form the speech habits for complete fluency. Because the freedom to make errors was so limited and error correction was so immediate, the students were thought not to learn *bad* linguistic habits. Pattern practice also helped students infer the rules of the language through learning the patterns. By learning the patterns, the students, by analogy, could create new utterances. Grammar rules were not directly taught, allowing instead for the students to *pick up* the rules intuitively as they had in their first language.

The Rationalist School of Thought

The attitude toward teaching language changed markedly with the publications of Noam Chomsky in the late fifties and sixties. His work in generative grammar formed the foundation of a linguistic theory that viewed linguistic structures as tied to meaning, a living language as one in which people can think, and the rules of the language as psychologically real. Chomsky introduced the notion that humans were predisposed to learn language, and changed the focus of language acquisition theory from an emphasis on the observable phenomenon to the interior processes. Children had the ability to figure out the rules of the language in spite of the "degenerate input" (ungrammatical and misspoken utterances) that surrounded them. The discussion turned to how this was accomplished. As Diller (1978) explained, "The learning of language is a problem-solving process; it is clearly not the mimicking of adult sentences" (p. 145). The comprehension approach to teaching (Winitz, 1981), which arose from this school of thought, had a significant impact on future teaching methods and techniques.

The Comprehension Approach

Comprehension was the key to the approach proposed by Winitz because all language that is ever learned was thought to be comprehended first. First-language acquisition theorists had noted that children acquiring their first language learned oral language before written and comprehended language before speaking. Children were considered to be speechless for the first year of life until they uttered their first words and did not utter those first words until they were ready. So, too, the language-learning student was free to converse whenever she or he felt ready, but was never required to because for adults, according to James Asher, "too early public utterance does interfere with language learning" (as quoted in Winitz, 1981, p. 46).

A second component of the comprehension approach was the new interpretation that the stages of acquisition were nonlinear. As Winitz stated, "Possibly the process that led to the acquisition of [a given phoneme] at six years [of age] began many years prior to this time. Six years may simply reflect the end point of a process which has been unfolding for some time. The evidence clearly supports the position that [that given phoneme] does not simply emerge at age six. In fact, it is produced, although, with less than a perfect record, many years prior to age six" (p. 3). This being true, the acquisition of specific grammar structures was also nonlinear and dependent on the knowledge of other grammatical structures. Figuring out the grammar of the language was a problem solving activity——one that children engage in naturally and unconsciously as they learn the fundamentals of their native language.

A number of teaching techniques arose out of the comprehension approach, one of which was Asher's total physical response. Using command forms only, the teacher instructed the students to perform certain tasks such as walking to the door, putting something on a table, or giving something to someone (Asher, 1969). As the students progressed, more and more sophisticated commands were given ("Take the paper from the student in the back of the room, roll it into a ball, and throw it away in the basket under the desk.") until the students felt comfortable enough to verbalize themselves ("Tell me what Juan just did.") and move into abstractions and tenses other than present. Students were not required to respond verbally until they felt comfortable doing so. The increasingly sophisticated, meaningful use of commands and the focus on comprehension first was thought to mimic the first language acquisition process, while giving a physical association to language served as a memory aid and a nonverbal means of response to a linguistic problem set (Diller, 1978, p. 149). No direct grammar instruction was conducted or thought necessary.

Krashen's *Natural Approach* (Krashen & Terrel, 1983) was another instance of the comprehension approach. The focus was on comprehension first, with the input that was optimal for comprehension established at the i +1 level, that is, just above the student's current competence level. Direct grammar instruction was again considered unnecessary, as the input was controlled in such as a way as to allow the students to infer and use the rules of the language.

In the eighties, new research by a number of child language theorists (see Gleason, 1993) confirmed that infants were not completely passive and silent until they uttered their first words and, in fact, made use of gestures and preverbal vocalizations to accomplish a variety of linguistic functions such as rejection, requests, and comments (p. 44). The discovery of children as active participants in a communicative network, even before speaking, took the importance off comprehension in favor of encouraging students to negotiate meaning with each other and work out communication while participating in meaningful activities or communicative tasks.

The Communicative Approaches

As Celce-Murcia (1991) describes the foundations of this approach, "communication is the goal of second or foreign language instruction . . . the syllabus of a language course should not be organized around grammar but around subject matter, tasks/projects, or semantic notions and/or pragmatic functions" (p. 461). Students are allowed to develop their linguistic competence by using the language in all four modalities of writing, reading, speaking, and listening without excessive attention to accuracy of output. The resulting in–class language use, or interlanguage, serves as comprehensible input for other language learners and offers the instructors insight into the language learning strategies and processes employed by students.

The Whole Language Philosophy

Clearly, the whole language philosophy is closely related to the communicative approach to language instruction. Its proponents believe that learning proceeds from whole to part, and that for optimal learning, the texts must be authentic, activities must be meaningful, and learning must be student-centered.

LEARNING PROCEEDS WHOLE TO PART   Child language acquisition studies have shown that children first learn language through routinized phrases and patterns (Gleason, 1993) and that children learn language more easily when they use the language in a context rather than complete isolated drill and kill exercises (Weaver, 1994). Cross-linguistic studies conducted by Slobin (1985) confirm that the universal aspects of child language acquisition are not so much in *what* the children are acquiring as in the *strategies* they use in the process. Phonological, syntactic, and semantic *overgeneralizations* are evidence that children form hypotheses about the rules of language and subsequently reformulate them based on the feedback they receive, progressively forming more and more highly sophisticated hypotheses. By the same token, there is evidence that second language learners acquire linguistic accuracy more easily by participating in communicative tasks (Dickens & Woods, 1988).

LEARNING OCCURS MOST SUCCESSFULLY WHEN INSTRUCTIONAL TEXTS ARE AUTHENTIC Texts that have been abridged and adapted are less rich and complex than those that have not been. They are shorter and the grammar structures are stilted and simplified. Authentic texts offer students access to more complex, real language structures, with more interesting characterizations and plots, than do controlled reading selections. The figurative use of language in literature, for example, requires students to respond on various levels. Lazar (1993) asserts that students become so involved in the plots and characters of an authentic story that a great deal of language may be absorbed in passing (p. 17).

LEARNING OCCURS AS THE RESULT OF MEANINGFUL INTERACTION Child language acquisition studies confirm that the child is a "social being, very responsive to caregivers, and draws caregivers into communicational interaction" from infancy (Gleason, 1993, p. 57). Both child and second language acquisition studies have shown that children learn language more easily when it is taught in a meaningful context rather than in isolation. The context serves as an aid to memory by helping students create mental linkages (Oxford, 1990), and also serves as comprehensible input through which the student can infer the rules of the language. There is evidence from second language research that basic skills such as grammar, vocabulary, and spelling are best learned from text-based or communicative tasks (Joe, 1995; Krashen, 1989; Krashen, 1993; Lightbown & Spada, 1993). The negotiation that occurs as a result of participating in meaningful interaction allows the student to proceed through the whole-to-part process, developing increasingly sophisticated hypotheses about the language. See any of the following resources for concrete suggestions for developing and using communicative tasks in the language classroom: Brown, 1994; Crook & Gass, 1993; Dickens & Woods, 1988; Johnson, 1982; Munby, 1981; Nunan, 1989; Rivers, 1987.

TEACHING SHOULD BE STUDENT-CENTERED Both first and second language acquisition researchers list stages of language acquisition. However, both bodies of researchers maintain that there are individual differences in the rate of development as well as the order of acquisition. The stages acquired are nonlinear; that is, structures may appear in one stage before a previous feature is mastered; children and adults skip stages, and all go through the stages at varying rates. Second language students in university IEPs arrive with varying levels of preparation. Even within a particular skill level at the university, the students have all completed different language curricula and for different lengths of time. They also have varying purposes for their attendance. During any given semester, the primary reason for attending is for preparation for university enrollment; however, many students (at Western Michigan University, approximately 10 percent) are interested in preparation for a business career or are tourists. A student-centered curriculum best meets all the varying needs of the students in the IEP.

Part II: Implementation of Whole Language in a Skill-Based Program

University-level intensive English programs generally maintain an isolated four-skill approach, four-level program: reading, writing, speaking, and listening, each offered at the elementary, intermediate, high-intermediate (or pre-advanced), and advanced levels. Upon arrival, students take a battery of standardized tests that place them into an appropriate level, then they progress through the levels either by semester-end standardized tests, teacher grades, or a combination of both. A number of university IEPs in the United States are abandoning this formula in favor of more contextualized study, by focusing on process, self-awareness, and strategy development; by offering content-based integrated skill classes; by combining grammar with other skill classes of speaking and listening, writing, and reading; and/or by making the syllabus more student-centered (Hafernik, Messerschmitt, & Vandrick, 1996). The next section suggests some ideas on implementing whole language in a university-level IEP that have proven successful in my classes.

Attention to Process, Product, Self-Awareness, Strategy Development, and Accuracy

Awareness Development

In developing their own awareness of the language learning process and the strategies they use, students will become more independent learners and more able to monitor themselves in their future use of English when their English instructor is not available. Clark and Ivanic (1991) cite the following advantages of raising awareness for the students' acquisition of writing.

1. It relieves anxieties.

2. It dispels misconceptions.

3. It puts important aspects of language skills on the agenda.

4. It provides a framework for students to reflect on their own experience.

5. It sets in motion a process of unlearning bad practices.

6. It provides a backdrop for all future activities.

7. It treats language as meaning in context.

8. It leads into talking about HOW.

9. It introduces terminology.

10. It helps students become more self-assured, responsible, and critical learners.

11. It is a catalyst for a student-driven syllabus.

12. It can serve as a useful research tool. (pp. 178–183)

Raising students' awareness of the learning process, their abilities, and their strategies assists the students and teacher alike. It helps the students reflect on and unlearn bad practices and misconceptions, and it introduces important language skills and vocabulary in context. For the teacher it can be an invaluable tool in planning an effective, student-centered syllabus.

It is often assumed that because the students in a university-level IEP are older and are literate in their own languages, discussing process awareness is therefore unnecessary. However, we know that the educational philosophy of many countries involves memorization and recall of grammar structures, and that class discussion, particularly in the Asian countries, is discouraged. In addition, students from other countries may indeed be literate in their languages, but their experience in the United States may be the first time they are required to use the more complex language of university study.

Process awareness development can take place with as simple an activity as a questionnaire asking the students what process they follow when they read or write in English, followed by a group discussion. For example:

1. How many drafts of a paper do you write?

2. What do you do when you sit down to write?

3. What does your workstation look like?

4. Do you let other people read your work?

5. When you are given a writing assignment, what do you do first?

6. When do you begin working on your writing assignments for school?

7. Are you a good writer?

8. What do you want to improve about your writing?

Otherwise, students may be asked to write a list of their problem areas in a separate page of their notebooks and rank them in order of importance. At the beginning of a writing unit, they may be asked to list one or more particular problem areas that they want to focus on; at the end, they could be asked to grade themselves on their success.

Strategy Training

As with process awareness development, strategy training enables the students to become independent learners and to continue to progress in situations when the teachers are not available. These strategies fall under the three main categories of memory, cognitive, and compensation strategies (Oxford, 1990). Figure 16–1 is a schematic of memory, cognitive, and compensation strategies as they relate to the direct language learning strategies that we teach our students. One strategy to aid in memory, for example, is for the students to create mental linkages. This can be accomplished by grouping ideas together, associating new words with previously learned words or into a larger context.

FIG. 16–1   *Diagram of Direct Language Learning Strategies*

I. Memory Strategies
    a. Place words into a context: associate them with something you already know.
    b. Associate new vocabulary with mental pictures or sounds.
    c. Review the material well.
    d. Act the idea out.

II. Cognitive Strategies
    a. Practice.
    b. Get the main idea quickly.
    c. Analyze or reason it out.
    d. Take notes, summarize, or highlight information.

III. Compensation Strategies
    a. Guess intelligently.
    b. Overcome limitations in speaking and listening (ask questions, use gestures).

Adapted from *Language Learning Strategies* by R. Oxford (1990), pp. 18, 19, 58.

Integrated Language Instruction

Thematic Units

Universities offer three kinds of content-based instruction: theme-based, or teaching all four skills of reading, writing, speaking, and listening, using thematically related material; sheltered courses, which separate second language learners from their native speaker counterparts in specially conducted content courses such as the one at the University of Ottawa; and the adjunct model, for which the students are actually enrolled in two courses: the university content course and a language course that is linked thematically such as the one at UCLA's Freshman Summer Program. All three types have been shown to be effective in assisting international students to adapt to university study and improve their academic language skills in each of the four modalities. Shih (1986) and Brinton et al. (1989) offer detailed discussions of the three kinds of content-based instruction offered for international students at the university level as well as samples of lesson plans for integrating language and content study.

In university IEPs, teaching through *theme units* in each class is one way of contextualizing the language study. Based on readings or audio or videotapes, the instructor creates a thematic unit that enables the student to acquire language using all four modalities and a variety of language functions. By contextualizing the instruction, the instructor "builds upon the students' previous learning experiences, allows a focus on use as well as usage, exposes the students to meaningful language use, takes into account the interests and needs of the students, and incorporates the eventual uses the learner will make of the language" (Brinton, Snow, & Wesche, 1989, p. viii). I have included a sample lesson on adventure travel in Appendix A. In this unit, the students read authentic materials, participated in class activities that were meaningful and relevant to their experiences, and worked cooperatively to complete a project. They read articles, brochures, maps, and library reference books. They wrote advertisements and business letters. They participated in group discussions, and gave and received directions. Their pronunciation as well as their oral and written accuracy were addressed.

Integration of Grammar Instruction into Other Program Components

As Nelson (1991) puts it, teach grammar within the context of writing. Nelson describes a five-year, fluency-first writing program at the postsecondary level. She suggests that changes in writing are preceded by changes in awareness and behavior first. When the students are freed from formulaic structures, organization patterns arise more naturally (p. 134); as the correctness anxiety that students feel is reduced, a real fluency and accuracy emerges. Speaking of Karin, an international student, Nelson writes ". . . As reliance on tacit knowledge grew, her drafts grew more nearly correct, at least where global or acquired features (like idioms, articles, prepositions, and the like) were concerned. Drawing on the textbook knowledge of grammar and mechanics that the memorized essay had displayed, Karin began correcting errors while reading aloud to the group" (p. 136).

A second program worth reviewing is that described by Adele MacGowan-Gilhooly (1991) at the City College the City University of New York. Reversing the traditional grammar-first sequence brought concrete evidence of its effectiveness in the form of higher scores on standardized reading and writing tests, as well as the qualitative evidence of improvement in the students' written work and reading abilities (p. 83).

The importance of increased self-esteem and risk taking should not be underestimated. In a whole language elementary school, first-grade children often are able to write one full page of understandable text. Second-graders draw concept maps, write first drafts, peer-edit, and rewrite. At the university level, elementary level ESL students write one full page or more of acceptable English texts. At the intermediate level, after five weeks, my students ask me, "How many pages do you want?" Not having been stifled by excessive attention to structure, the students become confident learners able to continue to progress on their own after they leave the ESL class.

Here are some suggestions for integrating grammar into the components of reading, writing, and speaking and listening in the university-level IEP.

TEACHING GRAMMAR IN READING CLASS   Immerse the students in authentic reading designed for American audiences, in and outside of the classroom. For lower-level ESL, children's books and books written for middle school or high school students offer somewhat simplified texts. For intermediate- to advanced-level students, magazines, novels, and the Internet provide authentic literature. Have the students keep reading logs consisting of summaries and opinions of readings. Begin each class with a discussion of the confusing grammar structure they have discovered in their readings.

Review the text for specific grammar structures. Discuss these structures and their effects on the writing, how they are used to show the relationship between ideas, or why the author made the decisions he or she did. This type of review introduces grammar as a discourse tool, illustrating the different grammar structures as they function in writing. The students may then be asked to assume the role of author and make similar decisions themselves in their writing.

Teach reading by means of the reading process: prereading, during reading, and postreading activities to help the students read for meaning and use appropriate reading strategies. Prereading activities help the students make connections between the reading topic and what they already know. Grammar is introduced without excessive direct teaching by having students conduct discussions which require the use of structures that are salient in the text or are suggested by it. (An example of this would be discussing "Is there life on other planets?" A negative response requires the use of contrary-to-fact conditional, for example, "If there were life on other planets, it would be different from our own.") Journal writing as a prereading exercise has a similar purpose. In Appendix B I have listed some more grammar activities that can arise from reading.

TEACHING GRAMMAR IN SPEAKING AND LISTENING CLASS   Immerse the students in oral language in and outside the classroom. Encourage students to monitor themselves by asking that they write down the grammar errors they hear themselves make every day. A variation is to have the students keep a log of interesting or confusing grammar structures they hear Americans say for discussion in class. Have them listen smart!

Have students tape-record their presentations and transcribe 5–6 sentences of their audio exactly. Then have them rewrite the sentences in correct English.

A variation of this is to have the students review a tape of their speaking in small groups, paying attention to specific grammar structures that they themselves have identified. Everyone in the group is responsible for helping identify the grammar problems.

TEACHING GRAMMAR IN WRITING CLASS   Teach writing by the writing process: prewriting, drafting, revising/editing, redrafting, publishing. Teaching the writing process puts grammar study in the revision/editing portion of the process and puts the attention on the entire composition process rather than only on accuracy. The process approach to writing allows the students to develop strategies for composing and editing so that they are able to continue to improve in their writing skills after they leave the ESL class. If they are going to the university or entering a profession that requires the use of English, the ESL class is only the beginning of their writing careers.

Negotiation of the Syllabus

The traditional syllabus design is "teacher-centered." Teachers develop the course goals, course content, and assessment tools. Turning the course around to one that is student-centered means involving the students in each aspect of the planning. Students assess their own problems and set their own goals; the course objectives arise from this information. Assessment is ongoing and is determined by the goals the students have set for themselves.

A student-centered curriculum is accomplished by asking the students their goals for the class. Weidauer (1994) and Nunan (1991) offer examples of goal assessment questionnaires to use to determine the course syllabus. Students are asked to rank their abilities in several language skills, mark the areas they are most interested in improving, then share this information with the teacher who can use it to review the goals of the class. Similarly, Angelo and Cross (1993) suggest a questionnaire on which students compare the instructor's stated goals for the course with their own goals. Again, they share their goals with each other and the instructor.

FIG. 16–2   *Goal Ranking and Matching Exercise*

What do you hope to get out of this course? Will it meet your needs and expectations? This exercise is designed to help you identify your learning goals and share them with the instructor. After you have completed it, you will learn what the instructor's goals are and see how well her teaching goals match your learning goals.

1.   Under the left-hand column, please list four or five learning goals you hope to achieve by taking this course.

2.   Then, using the right-hand column, indicate each goal's relative importance to you. Make the most important goal 1, the next most important 2, and so on.

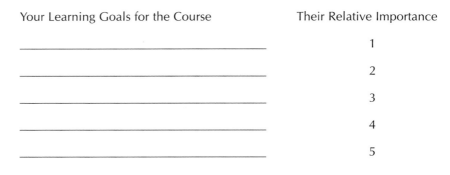

Your Learning Goals for the Course	Their Relative Importance
_____	1
_____	2
_____	3
_____	4
_____	5

Source: Angelo, T. & Cross, K. (1993). *Classroom assessment techniques: A handbook for college teachers (2nd ed.).* San Francisco: Jossey-Bass.

Taking the students' goals into account in syllabus planning helps assure that the students will see the relevance of the instruction and, subsequently, devote more energy to the tasks. It also makes the class more interesting, allowing each student to gain control over what he or she sees as important for his or her needs and experience level (Nunan, 1991, p. 22).

Conclusion

The role of grammar instruction has changed dramatically in this century with increased knowledge of the way children learn language. During the early twentieth century, language was taught mainly through the *grammar translation method.* As child language acquisition research progressed, direct grammar instruction nearly disappeared. Second-language learners were thought to be able to infer the rules of the language naturally, either by forming habits through sheer repetition of the structures (the *audio-lingual method*), or by receiving substantial amounts of comprehensible input (the *comprehension* and *natural approaches*). Now grammar instruction is experiencing renewed prestige on an as-needed basis. We know that children are active learners of their first language. They are responsive and interactive and negotiate with their environment from a very early age in order to figure out the rules of the language. In a parallel approach, second-language learners are immersed in communicative reading and writing events, developing strategies needed for becoming lifelong learners of languages. Skills such as grammar are acquired by the meaningful use of the language, through analysis and discussion of sentences in written texts and in their own speaking and writing, and in "teachable moments" of direct, individualized instruction.

Appendix A: Sample Theme Unit—Adventure Travel

Level: High Intermediate to Advanced

Skills: Reading: identification of main idea
determination of audience
vocabulary enrichment
map reading
scanning
using library sources

Writing: writing for different audiences
writing for different purposes (business and advertising)
composing/editing on computer

Speaking: fluency
vocabulary enrichment
pronunciation of numbers/names of cities and states
giving and receiving directions

Materials: "Been There, Done That," *Newsweek* magazine, July 19, 1993
Camping, rafting, or other travel brochures from AAA
USA road map
United States Chamber of Commerce Directory

Activities: Class discussion on the relationship between danger and excitement.

Small group discussion on *Newsweek* article: what kind of people enjoy which tourist destinations?

Small group work: location of tourist destinations named in the article on the map; discussion of location (including driving time) of these destinations in relation to each other, other states, Michigan, and the surrounding areas.

Students individually write a letter to the Chamber of Commerce of one tourist destination they would like to visit, asking for information about the site.

In small groups, students research a tourist area of their choice.

Students research the destination's location, things to do there, nearby places to visit, and available accommodations to create a travel brochure geared toward a particular audience. The brochure includes pictures and appropriate language and is formatted on computer.

Appendix B: The Reading Process and Grammar Instruction

Prereading Activities

1. predictions about the genre of the reading based on title, pictures, headings
2. journal writing followed by discussion in which students share their opinions about important questions suggested by the reading, using grammar constructions suggested by or contained in the reading
3. journal writing or group discussions that require the use of important grammar constructions in order to be accomplished

During-Reading Activities

1. "Jigsaw" activities: In small groups, students work collaboratively to study in depth one section of a text, then break into new groups in which each person shares information about his / her section of the text.
2. Critical analysis of summaries: The teacher gives students several different story summaries to determine which is most accurate.
3. Jumbled sentences reordering: Students reorder sentences that are out of sequence to create an accurate summary of the story.
4. Sentence combining: Students assemble sentences suggested by or taken from the text.
5. Grammar logs: Students write down their guess as to the meaning of a grammar item to confirm with each other, the teacher, or the grammar reference book.
6. Cloze exercises: Students practice in using strategies determining word meaning and grammar usage.

Postreading Activities

1. Students analyze different critical interpretations of the story.
2. Students write a review of the story.
3. Students analyze the components of a specific genre of writing and in small groups build a story from those components. They write the entire story together or begin the story together and finish it individually outside of class.
4. Students write an alternative ending to the story or its sequel using the narrator's point of view.
5. Students write diary entries or letters as one of the characters would have written them.
6. Students dramatize a scene from the text.

Appendix C: The Writing Process

Prewriting
1. Students freewrite for a short period of time on a topic.
2. Students read their freewrite to each other and receive feedback about what the others found most interesting, what they liked the most/least, and any suggestions of ideas to include.
3. Students then write a first draft of their paper, focusing on developing their ideas.

Editing
Edit first for organization and ideas; then for mechanics.

Peer Editing
1. Students read their papers aloud or distribute copies of them to small group. The instructor may provide a list of discourse and sentence level features for the students' use, or the students may review the papers based on their own stated writing goals.
2. The instructor puts sample papers on an overhead projector and conducts a group editing session.
3. The instructor pulls sample sentences with similar errors from students' papers for the students to discuss in small groups.
4. The instructor puts sample sentences on the board to use in sentence combining exercises.
5. For individual peer editing, the students complete a questionnaire to give to the author telling which parts of the writing were most interesting, which were most confusing, where more information would have been helpful, and where information could have been omitted.

Student-Teacher Conferencing
1. Read the student's draft and ask the student specific questions about his/her main idea. Ask for clarification of areas that are confusing.

Self-Editing
1. Give the students an editing guide giving strategies for editing, such as reading the text aloud, blocking out sentences, and reading the essay beginning with the last sentence first.
2. Encourage students to assess their learning by writing about or discussing certain changes they made in drafts, why they made those changes, and what they learned from the experience.

Source: Adapted from Lazar, G. (1993). *Literature and language teaching*. New York: Cambridge UP; and Weidauer, M. H. (1994). *Modern impressions: Writing in our times*. Boston: Heinle and Heinle.

References

ANGELO, T., & CROSS, K. (1993). *Classroom assessment techniques: A handbook for college teachers* (2nd Ed.). San Francisco: Jossey-Bass.

ASHER, J. (1969). The total physical response approach to second language learning. *Modern Language Journal, 53,* 3–18.

BLUM, J. (1984). *A guide to whole writing process.* Boston: Houghton Mifflin.

BRINTON, D., SNOW, M., & WESCHE, M. (1989). *Content-based second language instruction.* New York: Newbury House.

BROWN, B. (1994). Teaching adults ESL: A practitioner's guide. ERIC Document FL801118.

CELCE-MURCIA, M. (1991). Grammar and pedagogy in second language and foreign language teaching. *TESOL Quarterly, 25,* 3, 459–480.

CHOMSKY, N. (1965). *Aspects of the theory of syntax.* Cambridge: MIT Press.

CLARK, R., & IVANIC, R. (1991). *Consciousness-raising about the writing process.* New York: Longman.

COMEAU, R. (1987). Interactive oral language exercises. In W. Rivers (Ed.), *Interactive language teaching.* New York: Cambridge University Press.

CROOKS, G., & GASS, S. (Eds.). (1993). *Tasks and language learning: Integrating theory and practice.* Philadelphia: Multilingual Matters.

DICKENS, P., & WOODS, E. (1988). Some criteria for the development of communicative grammar tasks. *TESOL Quarterly, 22,* 4, 623–645.

DILLER, K. (1978). *The language teaching controversy.* Rowley, MA: Newbury House.

FAIGLE, L., CHERRY, R., JOLLIFFE, D., & SKINNER, A. (1993). *Assessing writers' knowledge and processes of composing.* Norwood, NJ: Ablex.

FEELEY, J., STRICKLAND, D., & WEPNER, S. (Eds.). (1991). *Process reading and writing: A literature-based approach.* New York: Teachers College Press.

FLYNN, S. (1986). Production vs. comprehension: Defining underlying competencies. *Studies in Second Language Acquisition, 8,* 2, 135–164.

FREEMAN, Y., & FREEMAN, D. (1992). *Whole language for second language learners.* Portsmouth, NH: Heinemann.

FRENCH, M. (1992). Grammar and meaning in a whole language framework. *Perspectives, 10,* 3, 19–24.

GAIES, S. (1976). Gradation in formal second language instruction as a factor in the development of interlanguage. Paper presented at the meeting of the Midwest Modern Language Association, November 4–7.

GASS, S., & MADDEN, C. (1985). *Input in second language acquisition.* Rowley, MA: Newbury House.

GASS, S., & SELINKER, L. (1992). *Language transfer in language learning.* Philadelphia: J. Benjamin.

GILLES, C., BIXBY, M., CROWLEY, P., CRENSHAW, S., HENRICHS, M., REYNOLDS, F., & PYLE, D. (Eds.). (1988). *Whole language for secondary students.* Katonah, NY: Richard C. Owen.

GLEASON, J. B. (Ed.). (1993). *The development of language.* (3rd Ed.). New York: Macmillan.

GOODMAN, K. (1996). *On reading.* Portsmouth, NH: Heinemann.

HAFERNIK, J., MESSERSCHMITT, D., & VANDRICK, S. (1996). What are IEPs really doing about content? Paper presented at the 27th Annual Conference of the Teachers of English to Speakers of Other Languages, Chicago, IL, March.

JAMES, C., & GARRETT, P. (Eds.). (1991). *Language awareness in the classroom.* New York: Longman.

JOE, A. (1995). Text-based tasks and incidental vocabulary learning. *Second Language Research, 11,* 2, 149–159.

JOHNSON, D., & JOHNSON, R. (1992). Having your cake and eating it too: Maximizing achievement and cognitive-social development and socialization through cooperative learning. Paper presented at the 90th Annual Convention of the American Psychological Association, Washington, DC, August.

KAMII, C., MANNING, M., & MANNING, G. (Eds.). (1991). *Early literacy: A constructivist foundation for whole language.* Washington, DC: National Education Association Professional Library.

KASPAR, G., & BLUM-KULKA, S. (1993). *Interlanguage pragmatics.* New York: Oxford University Press.

KRASHEN, S. (1989). We acquire vocabulary and spelling by reading: Additional evidence for the input hypothesis. *Modern Language Journal, 73,* 4, 440–464.

KRASHEN, S. (1993). *The power of reading: Insights from the research.* Englewood, CO: Libraries Unlimited.

KRASHEN, S., & TERREL, T. (1983). *The natural approach.* Hayward, CA: The Alemany Press.

LARSEN-FREEMAN, D. (1986). *Techniques and principles in language teaching.* New York: Oxford University Press.

LAZAR, G. (1993). *Literature and language teaching.* New York: Cambridge University Press.

LIGHTBOWN, P., & SPADA, N. (1993). *How languages are learned.* New York: Oxford University Press.

MACGOWAN-GILHOOLY, A. (1991). Fluency first: Reversing the traditional ESL sequence. *Journal of Basic Writing, 10,* 1, 73–87.

MITCHELL, D. (1982). *The process of reading: A cognitive analysis of fluent reading and learning to read.* New York: Wiley.

MOLL, L. (1990). *Vygotsky and education: Instructional implications and application of sociohistorical psychology.* New York: Cambridge University Press.

MUNBY, J. (1981). *Communicative syllabus design: A sociolinguistic model for defining the content of purpose-specific language programmes.* Cambridge: Cambridge University Press.

MURRAY, G. (Ed.). (1980). *Language awareness and reading.* Newark, DE: International Reading Association.

NEHLS, D. (1988). *Interlanguage studies.* Heidelberg, Germany: J. Groos.

NELSON, M. (1991). *At the point of need.* Portsmouth, NH: Heinemann.

NUNAN, D. (1989). *Designing tasks for the communicative classroom.* Cambridge: Cambridge University Press.

NUNAN, D. (1991). *Language teaching methodology: A textbook for teachers.* Englewood Cliffs, NJ: Prentice-Hall.

OXFORD, R. (1990). *Language learning strategies.* New York: Newbury House.

RIGG, P. (1991). Whole language in TESOL. *TESOL Quarterly, 25,* 3, 521–542.

RIVERS, W. (Ed.). (1987). *Interactive language teaching.* New York: Cambridge University Press.

SELINKER, L. (1991). *Rediscovering interlanguage.* London: Longman.

SHANK, C. (1986). Approaching the needs of adult illiterate ESL students. ERIC document ED316061.

SHIH, M. (1986). Content-based approaches to teaching academic writing. *TESOL Quarterly, 20,* 4, 617–648.

SHORT, D., CRANDALL, J., & CHRISTIAN, D. (1989). *How to integrate language and content instruction: A training manual.* Center for Language Education and Research, University of California Press.

SLOBIN, D. (Ed.). (1985). *The crosslinguistic study of language acquisition. Vol. 2: Theoretical issues.* Hillsdale, NJ: Lawrence Erlbaum.

WEAVER, C. (1994). *Reading process and practice: From socio-psycholinguistics to whole language.* Portsmouth, NH: Heinemann.

WIEDAUER, M. (1994). *Modern impressions: Writing in our times.* Boston: Heinle and Heinle.

WINITZ, H. (Ed.). (1981). *The comprehension approach to foreign language instruction.* Rowley, MA: Newbury House.

17 — Preparing Teachers to Teach About Language

DAVID FREEMAN AND YVONNE FREEMAN

Introduction

One of the goals the authors have worked toward has been to help teachers understand how to teach about language. A key reason why some teachers resist teaching about language is that their own understanding of grammar or linguistics is limited. The authors describe hands-on projects they use to help teachers "do linguistics" in the areas of phonology, morphology, and syntax. These projects lead to linguistics activities through which teachers can engage their own students. These activities help students understand the spelling system, how vocabulary develops, and what makes more complex writing. With increased knowledge of how language works, teachers can begin to make important curriculum decisions about what to teach and what not to teach in their grammar programs.

Teaching About Language

In many classrooms during language arts time, students learn language as they learn through language. In only a few classrooms is there also a focus on learning *about* language. Yet, Halliday (1975) reminds us that learning language, learning through language, and learning about language are all important. Students learn language, both oral and written, in classrooms where they read, write, and talk every day. They learn the content of math, science, social studies, and other subjects through language using their increasing language competence. But it is the rare classroom where students engage in meaningful and relevant study about language through inquiry projects that include linguistics. Why is this?

For one thing, teachers are very aware of the importance of helping students become competent readers and writers. They also know that they need to engage students in activities to develop the academic language needed to succeed in other content areas, like social studies or science. In addition, teachers recognize the importance of developing oral language, especially for students who speak other languages. These more pressing needs often push study about language to the back burner.

A second reason teachers don't often teach students about language in a meaningful way is that they don't regard this kind of study as significant. Their own experience helps shape this belief. They may have learned to identify parts of speech or to diagram a sentence during their elementary or high-school years, but that knowledge probably didn't serve a purpose for them in college or in their life outside school. Now they may see the need to teach grammar to prepare students for standardized tests or to highlight certain points of usage during the editing stage of writing, but they are often unsure of how to teach grammar in meaningful context (Weaver, 1996).

A third reason many teachers don't teach about language is that they really haven't been adequately prepared. While teachers may recognize gaps in other areas, and they may go back to universities for summer courses in math or reading, they don't generally flock to courses in language. Instead, the word "grammar" seems to strike fear into the hearts of even the most confident and competent teachers. "Linguistics" is equally frightening. The result is that teachers often avoid courses that would teach them more about language.

In many states with high populations of students who are designated as Limited English Proficient (LEP), recent teacher credentialing requirements include at least one course in grammar. Teachers taking the other required courses needed for working with English language learners, courses in second-language teaching methods and language acquisition, have seen the relevance of the new information not only for their second-language learners but also for their English-speaking students. The challenge for us as teacher educators is to help these teachers see how the new knowledge they are developing about language during their required grammar course can also benefit every student they teach.

In this chapter, we describe a course designed to introduce teachers to grammar in a way that they find relevant. This has been done in part by making connections between language structure and language acquisition. Our students, who range from elementary to adult-education teachers, have many second-language learners in their classes, and they are interested in learning about how students acquire a second language. An important general question, then, for our students is "What do students acquire when they acquire a second language?"

At the same time, we want teachers to begin to see grammar as a legitimate curricular area of study. We want them to involve their students in projects in which they explore different areas of language structure and use. The grammar course, then, must give all teachers, whether they have second language learners in their classes or not, the basic knowledge and skills they would need to lead students into these explorations.

In the sections that follow we describe this grammar course. It is divided into three sections: phonology, morphology, and syntax. For each area there is a related group inquiry project designed to explore a more specific topic such as the spelling system or teaching vocabulary. Because of the diversity in the teachers' backgrounds and interests, it has been important to build choice into the curriculum by having each student choose one of these areas to investigate in more detail. Often our teachers involve their own students in the investigation as they try out some aspect of language study in their classrooms. As we discuss the three group inquiry projects, we also describe related investigations individual teachers have carried out.

Phonology Project

The first area for investigation is phonology, the study of the sound system. Phonology connects easily with language acquisition since many studies of first-language acquisition focus on how babies acquire the sound system of their native language (Lindfors, 1987). Phonology is also of interest for second-language acquisition. Contrastive analysis studies have been carried out with various languages in order to predict which sounds in the language being learned will be most difficult to acquire for different kinds of second-language students (Lado, 1957). The study of phonology also provides important information for any teacher involved in debates over phonics or the teaching of spelling.

The phonology project is based on a study reported by Smith (1971). This study examined the sound-to-spelling correspondences from a sample of words taken from basal readers. The researchers found that the number of rules and exceptions needed to describe the correspondences was too great to be learned through direct teaching.

Our students replicate the process Smith described. Working in teams of three or four they start at some point in a book and select the first two hundred different words they find. They transcribe each word and then connect the phonemes with the spellings. For example, students would transcribe "apple," and then connect the sounds and spellings.

Making the sound-to-spelling matches is difficult and leads to good questions such as, "What do I do with a silent 'e'?" We point out that this problem is the same problem young writers encounter as they invent spellings. After transcribing all two hundred words and matching the sounds with the spellings, students make a list of possible spellings for each phoneme.

During class students develop a better understanding of the spelling system as we discuss D. W. Cummings (1988), who argues that spelling is systematic and that the system responds to three demands: sound, meaning, and etymology. Most words are spelled the way they sound. At the same time, we expect words that have the same root and convey similar meanings to be spelled the same way (*sign* and *signal* both have a *g*). Spellings also reflect word histories. A word like *avalanche* has a final silent *e* because English spelling retains its original French form.

Students are involved in different activities that help them understand that one spelling *pattern* can be pronounced in many ways and one spelling *sound* can be spelled in different ways. For example, students are asked to list words that demonstrate at least six different pronunciations of the pattern *ough*. Then they are asked to begin with a sound like /k/ and list all the possible spellings. Once they have written down the spellings, they investigate the contexts for each spelling. They find that /k/ is spelled *k* at the end of words where the *k* follows a consonant or a long vowel sound (*perk* or *peek*) and *ck* after a short vowel sound (*peck*). They also discover that exceptions like "trek" are borrowed words that reflect their history in the spelling.

Using this information and the data from their projects, they write their conclusions about teaching spelling. They often conclude that some spellings are so regular that students will simply acquire them. For example, the sound /b/ is usually spelled "b." A common exception is the "bb" spelling in words like "bubble," so they also consider some rules, like the doubling rule, that are worth teaching. In other cases, as with /k/, the students recognize the complexity involved. Some teachers have involved their students in the same exercise they have just completed. They ask students to brainstorm all the possible spellings of /k/ and then make generalizations about the different spellings. They use this approach for other minilessons in spelling as well.

In addition, our students review research on children's spelling development in English (Chomsky, 1970; Read, 1971; Wilde, 1992) and Spanish (Ferreiro & Teberosky, 1982). They bring in samples of children's writing for the class to analyze, and we discuss what kind of teaching might be appropriate for students at different developmental stages. For example, younger students would probably not benefit from the /k/ minilesson, but older students might. We also discuss differences between spelling development in English and Spanish since several of our students are bilingual teachers.

Wilde's book contains many ideas for spelling minilessons as part of writers workshop. We encourage teachers to read additional books that contain practical ideas on teaching spelling in the context of student writing. Books that teachers have found especially useful are Laminack and Wood's *Spelling in Use* (1996); Buchanan's *Spelling for Whole Language Classrooms* (1989); and Freeman and Freeman's *Teaching Reading and Writing in Spanish in the Bilingual Classroom* (1997). These books help teachers rethink their approach to teaching spelling. Each book emphasizes the importance of teaching spelling in the context of a comprehensive writing program.

We connect the phonology project with reading as well as with spelling. Students read K. Goodman's book *Phonics Phacts* (1993). This book helps them understand what phonics is and also helps them evaluate the proper role of phonics in a reading program. Although an understanding of phonology is not essential for an understanding of Goodman's book, it certainly helps. Students who have explored questions about the relationships between patterns of sounds and patterns of spellings as they carry out their projects develop a deeper understanding of the concepts Goodman presents.

Several teachers have used some of the ideas and activities from the graduate class to carry out individual investigations in the area of phonology with their students. Pam teaches second grade. Her students had memorized a poem that contained many "Ss," so Pam asked the students to go through the poem and decide what sound each "s" made. Then they made a graph where they listed the words grouped by sound /s/, /z/, or /š/ (when combined with "h"). Pam commented, "I was surprised at how interested my students were at finding out the different sounds the letter *s* made. As the day went on students found many other words in their reading that we added to our list." Through this simple procedure, Pam was able to help her students begin to develop an awareness of connections between sounds and spellings using an approach the students found interesting. At the same time, she began to pique their interest in one aspect of language study.

Mike, who teaches fourth grade, involved his students in a more complex investigation. He began by making a transparency of a poem his students were familiar with, Jack Prelutsky's "Nobody." The class read the poem together chorally. Then Mike asked them to work in small groups and look through the poem to find all the words with a "long e" sound. As Mike noted, "We did need to spend a few minutes at this point as some students did not know for sure the sounds of their vowels." Naturally, the students "knew" the sounds on one level: they could pronounce and recognize all the words. What Mike's students, like many other students, had trouble with was the more abstract task of identifying certain sounds as falling into a category called "long e." This knowledge about language is quite different from their working knowledge of language.

After several minutes, Mike asked a representative from each group to read their list of "long e" words. This led to good discussion, since some groups read words that had other sounds. Mike listed on the board all the words they found. Then he asked the groups to go back through the poem and list the spellings for each of these "long e" sounds. Mike demonstrated this procedure with the first couple of words on the list. Once more the groups went to work.

After they finished finding the spellings of all the words in the poem with "long e" sounds, groups reported back, and Mike recorded the results in chart form, writing the representative words under each spelling. He then asked his students if they could think of additional words that spelled the "long e" sound with other letters, and he added these to the chart. The students' final listing looked like the lists below:

ea	e	y	ee	ei	ie
eat	even	nobody	seems	receive	piece
reap	equal	friendly	green		
beat	me		teeth		
wheat					
neat					

When Mike asked his students what they had discovered from this investigation, they responded that they were surprised at all the spellings there were for this sound. They also pointed out that the letters that made the sound didn't always make it. For example, "y" made the "long e" sound in "nobody," but it made a different sound in "try." As a homework assignment, Mike asked his students to pick another long vowel sound, choose a page from the book they were reading, and find all the words with that sound. Working individually, students made a chart as Mike had with the sounds and spellings and brought their results back to class for discussion.

Mike had made his own list of "long i" words, and he showed students how he could use these words to create a poem. He wrote the first verse on the overhead:

> I saw a guy
> He had a pie
> He said he'd made it
> From a butterfly
> I wondered why?

Then students helped Mike to write additional verses using other words from the chart as well as words they thought of that had the "long i" sound. He invited them to use the words they had collected to make their own poems. Sarina wrote:

> In the night when
> My sister cries, I
> Hug her tight
> In my arms.
> But when I
> Cry, who's there
> for me?
> My sister.

These activities made Mike's students more aware of spelling patterns in English. At the same time, he engaged them in authentic reading and writing activities that helped them realize some of the techniques poets might use. Mike was able to take several of the ideas from the graduate class and adapt them for use with his fourth-graders. This is exactly the kind of result we had hoped for.

Morphology

The second project involves students in the study of morphology. Here the connection with second language acquisition is made clear as we study Krashen's theory (1982). This theory includes a natural order hypothesis that claims that people acquire different aspects of language—the sounds, the word structure, or the syntax—in a natural developmental order. Krashen based this hypothesis on studies of morpheme acquisition. For example, English learners acquire the plural "s" on words early, but the third person "s" (he walks) comes in much later. Until second language learners have had quite a bit of exposure to English, they will say things like, "He walk to school, teacher," despite direct instruction from teachers on the need for the third person singular present "s." Students understand Krashen's hypothesis better once they study English morphology.

An important related area for teachers of both second-language students and native speakers is the teaching of vocabulary. Two important questions are, "What do we know when we know a word?" and "How effective is it to teach vocabulary by teaching word parts?" In addition, as we study vocabulary we continue to think about spelling by looking at word histories, the process of assimilation many prefixes undergo, and the process of dropping "silent e" before adding a suffix.

The handout for the morphology project begins, "English teachers often try to find ways to help students increase their vocabulary. One way they do this is to teach students Latin and Greek roots, prefixes, and suffixes. The assumption is that students can use this information to determine word meanings. One question we might ask, though, is, 'What percentage of English words are formed this way?' An answer to that question might guide decisions about teaching vocabulary through teaching word parts."

One purpose of the morphology project, then, is to find out the percentage of words whose meanings can be determined by knowing the meanings of word parts. The project involves groups of students in analyzing the words from their phonology projects, this time looking at word types and structures. Groups first divide the two hundred words into content words (nouns, verbs, adjectives, and adverbs) and grammatical function words (prepositions, conjunctions, etc.). They subdivide the content words into three categories based on the kinds and number of morphemes: simple (one free morpheme—tree), compound (two free morphemes—workbook), and complex (a free morpheme and one or more bound morphemes—discover). Then students further divide the complex words by part of speech. Some teachers are not too confident about these parts of speech, and they have found Ruth Heller's series of illustrated children's books very helpful. For example, *Up, Up, and Away* is a book about adverbs. She has also written books about nouns, verbs, pronouns, prepositions, and adjectives (Heller, 1988, 1989a, 1989b, 1990, 1991, 1995, 1997). Teachers often buy these books to use in their own classrooms after we read them in the graduate class.

This reminder about parts of speech has enabled our students to capitalize on teachable moments. Sue teaches a multiage class with students in second through fourth grade. She found an opportunity to apply her study of parts of speech in her classroom. Sue explained the activity: "One morning we gathered at the carpet to brainstorm all of the words we could think of that had to do with the ocean." As students called out words, Sue wrote them on the overhead. She went on to explain what happened next: "I noticed immediately that all of the words they were calling out were nouns." Sue asked her students if the words had anything in common, and after some discussion the students decided the words named people, places, or things. One of the older children then recognized that these words are called nouns.

Next, Sue asked what else words did besides naming people, places, or things. The children talked about describing words and action words and some children remembered that these were called adjectives and verbs. Sue put up a large piece of butcher paper and divided it into three categories: nouns, verbs, and adjectives. Then she asked students to think up additional words for each category. This wasn't like a typical grammar lesson. It had emerged naturally from a class activity, and as Sue noted, "There was a lot of discussion and enthusiasm."

Sue extended this new interest in a subsequent minilesson on predicting syntactic cues. She gave students as a cloze exercise a story with key words missing. Under each blank, she wrote "noun," "adjective," or "verb." The children enjoyed this activity, and Sue used the opportunity to talk with them about the clues they could use to determine what part of speech would go in each blank. She encouraged them to use these syntactic cues to guess at words they didn't know as they read.

A final activity that again used students' new knowledge of parts of speech was the creation of a group poem. Sue had presented several "diamante" poems about sea animals to her students. These have the following diamond pattern:

The students noticed that each line had a different part of speech. They brainstormed additional vocabulary for each category and then wrote their own diamantes about different sea animals. Melissa chose to write about clams:

Melissa might have trouble finding a pearl in a clam, but her poem is indeed a gem.

Like Pam and Mike, Sue had made connections between the ideas from the graduate class and her own curriculum. She involved her students in a kind of language study that went well beyond traditional grammar lessons. Sue's students learned more about different parts of speech, and they used this new knowledge during reading strategy lessons and authentic writing activities.

The next step in the morphology project requires students to divide the complex words into two groups: those formed with inflectional suffixes like the past tense or the plural and those formed with derivational affixes. We discuss the idea that words with derivational affixes are formed by what linguists call word formation rules. For example, the suffix "er" can be added to verbs to create nouns like "farmer" or "teacher." Word formation rules such as this one are made up of three parts: a sound change, a category change, and a meaning change. In the case of the "er" rule, the sound change is simply the addition of the /ər/ sound. The category change is from verb to noun ("teach" to "teacher"). The meaning change may be expressed as "one who Xes" where X stands for the meaning of the root. That is, a "teacher" is one who teaches. Many new words enter a language or an individual's vocabulary through word formation rules like this one, although children or second-language learners may not even be aware of the process.

However, generally students find that only a small number of their original two hundred words were formed by word formation rules. About half the words in most samples are grammatical function words. Many others are simple words or complex words with inflectional endings like the plural "s." A further complication is that some complex words have Greek or Latin roots. For example, in a word like "product," "pro" seems to be a prefix and "duct" the root. There is an English word "duct," but the meaning of "product" can't be determined by using the knowledge of what "duct" means in English (in contrast with "aqueduct" where knowledge of English "duct" would help). We discuss how most English speakers learn the meaning of words like "product" directly, not by learning Greek or Latin roots and then putting the parts together to form the meaning of the whole word.

A further complication in using word parts to figure out word meanings is that prefixes often change to match the first sound in the root word. For example, a prefix like "in" assimilates in words like "illegal," "immature," or "irreverent." The study of assimilated prefixes not only helps students understand the difficulties of using roots, prefixes, and suffixes for determining word meanings but also helps them understand English spelling better. Many students find the study of assimilation interesting. It leads to questions about when spellings become fixed. Apparently, assimilation had already occurred in oral English before the spellings of words like "illegal" or "immature" were fixed by dictionary writers. On the other hand, more recent words like "input" don't reflect the actual pronunciation of the assimilated prefix in their spelling.

The morphology project also affords an opportunity for talking about spelling changes that occur when suffixes are added to words ending with a "silent e." We discuss the rule for dropping the "e," connecting it to the function the "e" served in the first place as well as the form of the suffix.

At the same time that students are investigating the efficiency of teaching vocabulary through teaching roots, prefixes, and suffixes, in class we look at the research that shows that students acquire vocabulary much faster through reading than through direct study of words or word parts (Freeman, 1991). Time spent teaching vocabulary is time taken away from reading. We also consider what it means to know a word. Students often think it just means knowing a synonym. However, the teachers soon come to realize that knowing a word also involves knowing its phonology (how to pronounce or recognize the sounds of the word), its morphology (its parts and what it can be combined with—is it "inproductive" or "unproductive"?), its syntax (what other words it requires—"put" takes an object and a location: I put the *car in the garage*) and its pragmatics (its level of formality).

Even though we want teachers to evaluate carefully the best way to help students develop their vocabulary, we also encourage them to involve students in language study for its own sake. Several of our students have decided to look at a particular affix. Rosalinda, for example, did her investigation into all the words with the suffix "ology." She found over one hundred such words. Rosalinda's final comment on her study was clever: "I have discovered that this study of the words that end in 'ology' could be called 'ologyology.'" Our students were aware of their classmates' explorations, and this led to productive collaboration. For example, another student brought in a book his fifth-graders liked. It's called *Grossology* (Branzei, 1995) and contains all sorts of "gross" things like mucus. In this way, Rosalinda's investigation could be linked to elementary curriculum.

Related to these investigations are explorations of word histories. We introduce etymology in class using a number of exercises from Tompkins and Yaden's excellent book, *Answering Students' Questions about Words* (1986). Students are always interested in how people's names become common nouns, so we give them a list of eponyms with obvious names like Elihu Frisbee and more difficult ones like J. G. Zinn, after whom the zinnia was named. We also consider how words such as "tangerine" or "spinach" reflect place names. Students are interested as well in the origins of animal names, and we ask them to look up the original meanings of a list from "aardvark" to "walrus." In addition, we ask students to figure out acronyms like "modem" or newly coined words like "bimoustrous" (computerese for a person who can use a mouse with either hand). We find that our students often use this new knowledge as they plan activities for their students. Rather than teach vocabulary directly, they involve their students in research about various aspects of English vocabulary including word histories.

Syntax

The third project focuses on syntax. The connection with language acquisition comes as we study some of the current research that focuses on the acquisition of syntax (Pienemann & Johnston, 1987) and on studies in Universal Grammar and second language acquisition (White, 1989). This leads to good discussions about the role of teaching in the process of second language acquisition (Larsen-Freeman &

Long, 1991). An additional topic of interest to all teachers is a consideration of what makes writing simpler or more complex.

As with the other projects, students work in groups of three or four. Each team chooses a passage of at least five sentences from a college textbook and a second passage from a children's book. They analyze each set of sentences. First, they decide whether a sentence is simple, compound, or complex by counting the number and types of clauses. Then they determine whether the sentence is in basic form or whether it has undergone a transformation like negative or passive. If the sentence is transformed, they rewrite it in underlying form. Then they diagram each of the sentences in the two sets. After analyzing the sentences, they write a conclusion in which they discuss which set is more complex and why they think it is more complex.

Teachers are often surprised as they work on the project at how much is left out of the surface structure of a sentence. For example, even in a seemingly simple sentence like "He wanted to win the race," a reader must recognize that "he" is the subject of both "wanted" and "win." Native speakers fill in these deleted items easily, but second-language students often have more difficulty. Our students also come to realize that more complex writing often contains a large number of these reduced clauses.

Another area that is seldom covered in traditional classes but comes up frequently when students try to analyze natural language is the use of two- or three-word verbs. For example, "look up" is a two-word verb in a sentence like "He will look up the answer." This use of "up" differs from its use as a preposition in a sentence like "He looked up the street." In the second sentence "up the street" is a prepositional phrase, but "up the answer" is not. Words like "up" combine with many verbs, so one assignment students have is to list at least one hundred verbs that take "up." We then discuss how the meaning of the verb plus "up" can't always be derived from the separate meanings of the two. When we "look up" a word in the dictionary, we don't look in a higher place. In class, we consider how difficult these two-word verbs are for second language learners. A further complication is that different languages use different combinations. A Spanish speaker, for example, might translate directly and say "He got married *with* her," instead of using the idiomatic English expression "He got married *to* her."

In the syntax project, students begin with complete sentences and try to figure out the parts that make them up. This process is like sentence combining in reverse. Once they have analyzed sentences, they understand better how they might work with students who write simple or compound sentences. They see that sentences might be combined by subordinating one clause to another. This approach better shows the relationships among the ideas. We discuss kinds of sentence combining exercises that have proved effective in helping students improve the quality of their writing. Good resources include books by D. Killgallon, *Sentence composing: The complete course* (1987), and W. Strong, *Sentence combining: A composing book* (1993).

In an introductory course like this, we can only begin to look at a complex area such as syntax. Even this introduction, though, is helpful to teachers. They come to realize that syntax is probably too complex to be taught directly through surface sentence patterns to second-language students. At the same time, they develop ways to analyze texts they ask students to read. Connie, for example, chose for her investigation to compare a story from a basal reader with one from a piece of children's literature. She found that in both stories the sentences she picked were all simple, but while the basal sentences were in basic form, three of the five sentences in the children's literature were transformed. For example, instead of having a prepositional phrase at the end (Toad and frog met each other in the garden) the sentence had been transformed to front the phrase (In the garden, toad and frog met each other). In this way Connie could apply the skills she had learned in the syntax project to evaluating the books in her classroom.

Conclusion

Most teachers do a good job of teaching language and teaching through language. However, teachers sometimes are hesitant to teach *about* language, often because they don't have enough background knowledge in grammar or because they haven't been exposed to ideas about ways to involve their students in linguistic investigations. After teachers have studied grammar more thoroughly by carrying out projects in the areas of phonology, morphology, and syntax, and particularly after investigating some area of language on their own, they are more apt to adopt a new approach and are better prepared to teach their students about language in new ways.

The changed attitudes toward grammar that teachers develop are often reflected in their course evaluations. One student, for example, wrote, "This course has made me take a look at what I taught to my students, and now I will go back and change some things that I will be doing with my students." This teacher doesn't have specific plans at this point, but the response suggests an openness to change.

A second teacher wrote a more detailed response:

By better understanding how the English language works, I can make better decisions on what [should] and in many cases what should *not* be taught. Knowing reasons why will give me a much better position when I'm trying to change some of the old, traditional ways (spelling lists and vocabulary lists to name two).

This teacher seems to have more definite ideas about areas of curriculum he wants to review, and since he knows more about "how the English language works," he feels more confident in undertaking this review. He can better explain the "reason why" if he takes a new approach to teaching spelling or vocabulary.

Even students who may not make major changes in their teaching sometimes begin to change their attitude toward grammar. As one quite honest student wrote,

"I found this class much more interesting than I anticipated. I expected to be totally bored."

No one course will change all students. Nevertheless, a worthy goal for any course is to build teachers' confidence and their knowledge base so they can examine their curriculum and make more informed decisions. With the public outcry for a return to basics, to teaching spelling and vocabulary in traditional ways and to teaching reading through a phonics approach, it becomes increasingly important for teachers to have this knowledge of grammar so they can most effectively teach language, teach through language, and teach about language.

References

BRANZEI, S. (1995). *Grossology*. Reading, MA: Planet Dexter.

BUCHANAN, E. (1989). *Spelling for whole language classrooms*. Winnipeg, Manitoba: Whole Language Consultants, Ltd.

CHOMSKY, C. (1970). Reading, writing, and phonology. *Harvard Education Review 40*, (2), 287–309.

CUMMINGS, D. (1988). *American English spelling*. Baltimore: Johns Hopkins University Press.

FERREIRO, E., & TEBEROSKY, A. (1982). *Literacy before schooling*. Translated by Goodman-Castro, K. Portsmouth, NH: Heinemann.

FREEMAN, D. (1991). Teaching vocabulary: What's in a word? In Goodman, K., Bird, L., & Goodman, Y., *The whole language catalog*, Santa Rosa, CA: American School Publishers.

FREEMAN, Y., & FREEMAN, D. (1997). *Teaching reading and writing in Spanish in the bilingual classroom*. Portsmouth, NH: Heinemann.

GOODMAN, K. (1993). *Phonics phacts*. Portsmouth, NH: Heinemann.

HALLIDAY, M. (1975). *Learning how to mean*. London: Edward Arnold.

HELLER, R. (1988). *Kites sail high: A book about verbs*. New York: Grosset and Dunlap.

HELLER, R. (1989a). *A cache of jewels and other collective nouns*. New York: Grosset and Dunlap.

HELLER, R. (1989b). *Many luscious lollipops: A book about adjectives*. New York: Grosset and Dunlap.

HELLER, R. (1990). *Merry-go-round: A book about nouns*. New York: Grosset and Dunlap.

HELLER, R. (1991). *Up, up and away: A book about adverbs*. New York: Grosset and Dunlap.

KILLGALLON, D. (1987). *Sentence composing: The complete course*. Portsmouth, NH: Boynton/Cook.

KRASHEN, S. (1982). *Principles and practice in second language acquisition*. New York: Pergamon Press.

LADO, R. (1957). *Linguistics across cultures*. Ann Arbor: University of Michigan Press.

LAMINACK, L., & WOOD, K. (1996). *Spelling in use: Looking closely at spelling in whole language classrooms.* Urbana, IL: National Council of Teachers of English.

LARSEN-FREEMAN, D., & LONG, M. (1991). *An introduction to second language acquisition research.* New York: Longman.

LINDFORS, J. (1987). *Children's language and learning.* (2nd Ed.). Englewood Cliffs, New Jersey: Prentice Hall.

PIENEMANN, M., & JOHNSTON, M. (1987). Factors influencing the development of language proficiency. In Nunan, D. (Ed.), *Applying second language acquisition research.* Adelaide: National Curriculum Research Centre.

READ, C. (1971). Pre-school children's knowledge of English phonology. *Harvard Education Review 41* (1), 1–34.

SMITH, F. (1971). *Understanding reading.* New York: Holt, Rinehart, and Winston.

STRONG, W. (1993). *Sentence combining: A composing book.* (3rd Ed.). New York: McGraw Hill.

TOMPKINS, G., & YADEN, D. (1986). *Answering students' questions about words.* Urbana, IL: National Council of Teachers of English.

WEAVER, C. (1996). *Teaching grammar in context.* Portsmouth, NH: Boynton/Cook.

WHITE, L. (1989). *Universal grammar and second language acquisition.* Philadelphia: John Benjamins.

WILDE, S. (1992). *You kan red this! Spelling and punctuation for whole language classrooms, K–6.* Portsmouth, NH: Heinemann.

Between Teachers and Computers
Does Text-Checking Software Really Improve Student Writing?

TIMOTHY BEALS

Introduction

For more than a decade teachers have encouraged students to use computer tools to help in the composing process—especially during the final stages. Today there are many software packages designed to suggest textual alternatives for greater clarity, consistency, and correctness.

This chapter examines one software package, Editor (Thiesmeyer & Thiesmeyer, 1990), which was created by the Modern Language Association especially for students and scholars. Beals then evaluates Editor's effectiveness in reducing the number and severity of distracting surface-level errors, using real writing samples of a student and a scholar. The chapter ends with suggestions and cautions for teachers who want to use text-checking software in the classroom.

In her chapter about assessment called "Responding to Student Writing," Nancy Sommers (1988) describes how she studied the commenting styles of thirty-five instructors and compared their comments with those generated by Writer's Workshop, a computer software package of twenty-three programs developed by Bell Laboratories "to help computers and writers work together to improve a text rapidly" (p. 171). Sommers reports that within a few minutes, the computer provided editorial comments on the student's text: identifying spelling and punctuation errors, isolating problems with wordy or misused phrases, and suggesting alternatives; offering a stylistic analysis of sentence types, sentence beginnings, and sentence lengths; and finally, giving the student essay a Kincaid readability score. The article concludes that there is a marked contrast between the teachers' comments and those of the computer, noting in particular how "arbitrary and idiosyncratic" most teachers' comments are. "Besides," Sommers concludes, "the calm, reasonable language of the computer provided quite a contrast to the hostility and mean-spiritedness of most of the teachers' comments" (p. 171).

If a computer can evaluate students' technique as well as most teachers—or better than most, as Sommers argues—then what is left for us teachers to do? More to the point, perhaps, can teachers and computers work together to improve student writing in the classroom and beyond? And what advantage, if any, do packages like Writer's Workshop and a host of similar programs have over traditional methods of reducing the incidence of distracting grammatical problems, encouraging stylistic effectiveness, and increasing overall writing quality? The answers may be found by examining what the architects of grammar and style checkers have designed their products to do and then determining how the programs really work in the classroom.

Methodology

For several years I have encouraged my first-year and advanced composition students to use the computer as an effective tool for planning, drafting, and revising. Besides the computer's obvious advantages over handwriting and typewriting for making quick, legible text changes, it has also had the useful, though rudimentary, ability to format text, check spelling, and determine word count in a reasonably simple, straightforward way. Today, however, most word processing software comes with an on-line thesaurus and grammar checker in addition to spelling and word counting utilities. And the sophistication of stand-alone grammar and style checkers has increased dramatically since their first appearance in the early 1980s.

My purpose in this article is to evaluate the theoretical and pedagogical assumptions of Editor—a program designed by the MLA especially for "writers, students, and instructors," and arguably the most sophisticated grammar and style checker available to students and scholars. Then I will evaluate both the program's general assumptions and specific suggestions against the best current theory regarding grammar instruction, and finally I will draw some conclusions about the use of text checkers in the composition classroom.

According to the program's creators, Elaine and John Thiesmeyer (1990), "Editor can be used both by teachers who wish to improve the writing styles of their students and by writers who wish to improve their own styles." Thus, to evaluate the assumptions behind the program I will examine the documentation that accompanies the program and then run two writing samples through the checker—one by a student and the other by a published writer. I have limited my writing samples to nonfiction pieces for both the student and published writer, since nonfiction writing is what college students are required to do most often, and because the nuances of creative writing—things like dialogue in fiction and drama or versification in poetry—tend to undermine the validity and effectiveness of the software.

Editor's Theoretical Assumptions: The Manual

We look first at the Editor manual to determine what the creators of the program intended to achieve. Elaine and John Thiesmeyer assert that the primary aim of Editor is to provide "a set of proofreading programs whose principal function is to look for clutter—that is, for usage problems and mechanical errors—in text ready for proofreading" (p. 7). While we will see next what the program does with "text ready for proofreading," already we notice that the program is not designed to check for stylistic, or even grammatical problems per se, but to detect those things that can be quantified (using the word *very* one too many times, for instance, or mistakenly repeating a word such as "the the").

Fair enough. Its creators point out correctly that "grammar and usage are not the same; thorough, accurate checking of grammar is not yet possible with computers. Editor makes no claim to be a full-fledged grammar checker, though it can find and report some grammatical problems in text" (p. 8). Instead, Editor is said to be an "electronic descendant" of Strunk and White's *Elements of Style*, with its emphasis on omitting unnecessary words, its delineation of selected rules of punctuation, and its chapter on "Words and Expressions Commonly Misused" (p. 7). Thus, Editor is not intended to be used to find erroneous instances of *to* when *too* was intended, but to find and point out such problems as redundancy, punctuation, and sexist language.[1] Seen for what it is, most scholars and students can recognize the usefulness—and limitations—of such a program for their own writing. The singular theoretical advantage of Editor, or presumably any other grammar and style checker, is its ability to address problems with surface structure; the primary limitation is its inability to improve the deep structure below the surface structure.

Drawing upon Noam Chomsky's transformational model of language, as well as subsequent generative semanticists and case grammarians, Constance Weaver (1979) and others have shown that sentences have both a surface structure and a deep structure. Weaver explains:

> On the one hand, a sentence obviously consists of a linear sequence of clauses, phrases, words, and sounds or letters; this may be termed surface structure. On the other hand, a sentence clearly has one or more meanings; this may be termed the deep structure. More technically, the deep structure consists of the underlying propositions and the relations among them. When we speak or write, we express propositions in language. When we listen or read, we determine propositions from language. (p. 7)

By this definition, grammar and style checkers like Editor are limited to identifying problems with the consistency or correctness of the surface structure, for computers cannot yet grapple with what a writer meant or intended to mean, or make inferences from surface structure to deep structure. And according to Noguchi (1991), Sedgwick (1989), and Bartholomae (1980), a student's ability to analyze and understand "correct" grammar and "proper" usage has little bearing on her ability to communicate clearly in writing. But here we must begin to see that while Editor is designed to aid writers by identifying structural problems, and while the correction of such errors can make a significant improvement in the piece's quality (Raforth & Rubin, 1984), it never claims to make writers more effective—just less offensive. The Thiesmeyers explain:

> Neither Editor nor any other computer program can help significantly with weaknesses in a text stemming from poor ideas. Ideas, coherence, logic, argumentative strategy—these are the bone and muscle of good writing. . . . Editor's business is writing's flesh—vocabulary, usage, mechanics, style. (p. 11)

How does it work? Let's investigate.

Editor's Pedagogical Assumptions: The Program

I tested the effectiveness of the program by using samples from one student and one published writer. The writing situation for both selections was essentially the same: they shared the same genre (book review), and had the same intended audience (generally sophisticated, educated readers).[2] Only the experience level was different: The student wrote her piece for my introductory English course called Freshman Rhetoric; the published writer wrote his piece for *The New Yorker* magazine.

Student Sample

The students in my first-year composition course were assigned a thousand-word essay to be written as if it were a review that might appear in *The New Yorker* "Books" department. They had read several reviews in the magazine during the semester but had not read the review by Stephen Greenblatt used later as a representative sample of published writing. Students were asked to review a book with which they were familiar, and they were encouraged to include a summary of the book as well as a discussion of its significance or relevance to their intended audience. Rachel's lead paragraph follows, exactly as it was submitted on October 14, 1993. It is shown here as it is represented in Editor's DRAFT mode, which includes all of the text with sentence numbers:

```
<1>P=/  J.R.R. Tolkien's award winning books The Hobbit and
the trilogy The Lord of the Rings (Ballentine; $19.80 four
volume set) are set in imaginary world of Middle-earth.
<2>Tolkien wonderfully creates a world, derived from our own,
yet complete in encyclopedic mythology. <3>Tolkien's work con-
sists of a myriad of creatures ranging from hobbits, elves,
dwarfs, orcs, to men, dragons, and wizards. <4>The hobbit,
```

```
Bilbo, is the main character in The Hobbit and, although he
remains a character in The Lord of the Rings trilogy, his
nephew Frodo picks up where his uncle left off and remains to
the end of the trilogy. <5>Although many characters weave in
and out of Tolkien's work, both hobbits remain the focal
points by which the magical ring must be found and preserved,
as in Bilbo's case, and destroyed, as in Frodo's case.
<6>Whereas The Hobbit offers an introductory view of Middle-
earth revealing wars, elves, dwarfs, kings, wizards, dragons,
and the magical ring, The Lord of the Rings displays the
increase of evil, ruin, wars, a brave hobbit, the destruction
of the magical ring, and the establishment of a long lost
kingship. <7>The reader is immersed into legends and lore as
Tolkien creates, page by page, the world of Middle-earth; a
Middle-earth that bears resemblance to our world yet is a sep-
arate entity in and of itself.
```

ANALYSIS   I selected this sample because it most nearly matched Greenblatt's review in length and style. (It is 228 words long and has 7 sentences for an average sentence length of 32.5 words.) While the text is basically sound, several mechanical and grammatical problems persist, both with the surface structure and with the deep structure. I will look first at what Editor concluded and then remark about the things the program did not recognize.

By using the USAGE component of the program, the program's main feature, Editor tagged four possible problems in the student's text:

1. It flagged "men" in the third sentence and labeled it a "Gender Specific Term."

2. The program highlighted the word "main" in sentence four, calling it a "Commonly Misused Term," suggesting instead either "principal," "chief," or "primary."

3. It flagged "and," in the fourth sentence and labeled it a "Probable Awkward Usage unless a later comma follows."

4. In the last sentence, it labeled "in and of" a "Probable Tautology."

Let's look at these objections one at a time. First, while the program thought it found an instance of "Gender Specific Term" with the use of "men" in the third sentence, it is probably the most accurate word in this case. Though women appear occasionally in Tolkien's fiction, male creatures—both man and beast—dominate the imaginary landscape. So here "men," rather than "people," or some other more general term, would be the most descriptive and logical word choice.

Second, Editor objected to the use of the word "main" in the construction "main character." Certainly one of its suggestions, "principal," could be successfully coupled with the word "character," while the other suggestions, "chief" and "primary," would be unusual. But by far the most common synonym for the protagonist of any story is "main character."

Third, the program determined that there could be a problem with the "and," construction in the fourth sentence "unless a later comma follows." Curiously it doesn't detect that another comma does follow. In fact, the problem occurs not because a comma follows the word, but because a comma does not precede it.

And fourth, the program identifies "in and of" as a "Probable Tautology," a description that would no doubt send this student scurrying to a dictionary. More to the point, perhaps, the phrase could easily be deleted, and it would probably strengthen the sentence to do so.

These are the only probable "errors" the program identified and brought to the reader's attention. But what of the matters it could have identified and an instructor may have marked?

In the first sentence alone, two unit modifiers—"award winning" and "four volume"—were not required by the program to be hyphened but could have been (although there is some disagreement among authorities about the use of hyphens in such instances). In the same sentence, the phrase "in imaginary world of Middle-earth" should include a definite article and read "in the imaginary world of Middle-earth."

Next, the "from . . . to" construction at the end of the third sentence should have an "and" in the transition and ought to be punctuated so that it reads, "from hobbits, elves, dwarfs, and orcs to men, dragons, and wizards." And in sentence four, the word "left" near the end of the sentence should be changed to "leaves" to maintain the present tense throughout. (The problem with the word "and" and the commas in this sentence was addressed above.)

The sixth sentence requires a comma after "Middle-earth," and the phrase "long lost," as a unit modifier, should be hyphenated. And in the final sentence, the semicolon following "Middle-earth" should be replaced with either a colon or a dash, since the clause that follows it is not independent.

These observations simply address the surface features of the paragraph, not the more important deep structure. But taken together, the program identified just four possible errors, only one of which could be taken seriously. Yet Editor missed at least nine other problems that could have been distracting to some readers, problems that should have been revised to eradicate surface errors and to address certain dilemmas at the level of the deep structure (see especially the vagueness at the end of the first and fourth sentences).

Professional Sample

For a published writer's prose sample, I turned to a recent issue of *The New Yorker*. In the October 11, 1993, issue, UC Berkeley professor and MLA author Stephen Greenblatt reviewed the book *Reading National Geographic* for the magazine. The lead paragraph of that article follows, again in the DRAFT mode generated by Editor:

```
<1>P=/ Years ago, driving in a rented rattletrap from Rissani to
Marrakech, across a wild and desolate stretch of the Atlas
```

Mountains, my wife and I sped past a shepherdess standing by the side of the road. <2>The woman was unveiled, young, and exceptionally beautiful. <3>She was wearing her wealth—dangling filigreed silver earrings, coin necklaces, elaborately worked bracelets—and as we passed she smiled and waved. <4>Her modest wave was an invitation, or so we chose to interpret it. <5>We jammed on the brakes, backed up, and rolled down the window. <6>My wife smiled, pointed to our camera, and asked in signs if we might take her picture. <7>Across the huge landscape, there was no one else in sight, no sound except the wind and the bleating of the lambs. <8>The shepherdess hesitated, evidently uneasy and uncertain. <9>I took some money from my pocket and held it out to her. <10>With some reluctance still, she reached out for it, then hunched into herself and allowed her picture to be taken. <11>When we got back to California and developed the film, we found the picture, all right, but it was rather different from what we remembered: we had a snapshot of a very thin, sombre, anxious woman entirely wrapped in mud-stained rags.

ANALYSIS   I selected this sample because it was written for a general audience by a well-known scholar. (It is 211 words long and has 11 sentences for an average sentence length of 19 words.)

Using the USAGE feature of the program again, Editor identified four possible problems in Greenblatt's text:

1. The program flagged the word "chose" in the fourth sentence, called it a "Commonly Misused Term," and suggested "choose" as an alternative.

2. It selected the word "rather" in sentence eleven and called it "Vague Diction if an adjective."

3. It selected the word "different" in sentence eleven, labeling it a "Commonly Misused Term" and suggesting either that it be replaced by "various" or "several" or be omitted.

4. The program labeled "very" a "Probable Empty Intensifier" in the last sentence.

First, the flagging of "chose" and the suggestion of "choose" is clearly wrong and could never work in this context.

Second, the word "rather" in sentence eleven, used here and everywhere as an adverb, is effective and clear enough when combined with the word "different."

Third, "different" could not be changed to either "various" or "several," and it certainly could not be dropped in this instance.

Fourth, while "very" could reasonably be construed as an "empty intensifier," it seems to add a deliberate force to the narrative, a force the author fully intended.

Interestingly, in this edited and published piece, Editor identified the same number of problems as were found in the student's lead paragraph. However, each of these probable "errors" easily could be defended from the point of view of both grammar and meaning. In fact, the only "problem" in Greenblatt's lead was the spelling of "sombre" in the final sentence, and spelling is a task Editor cannot perform.

Conclusions

These brief samples of both classroom and published writing reveal some real dilemmas facing teachers who want to integrate computers into the composition classroom. For instance, what do we do with Editor's suggestions when the "errors" are not really problems? Or, what do we do with the more numerous instances when Editor fails to identify legitimate problems with mechanics and usage? Perhaps most important, however, is there any way to link the correction of surface problems with the improvement of clarity or effectiveness at the deeper level of meaning and produce better writers? In short, should text-checking software like Editor be used in the classroom?

While every teacher will have to weigh the relative merits and drawbacks of such software as Editor in his or her own classroom, I can make three recommendations from my own experience: First is to investigate for yourself the claims and performance of any grammar or style checker. Ask around the department and see if you can get your hands on a copy of Editor or some of the dozens of other text-checking programs available. Read the manuals, compare the features, and test them out on your students' material and your own, but most important, go beyond what they claim to do and verify that they really fulfill what they promise. In addition to MLA's Editor, for instance, I also tested RightWriter (Macmillan), Correct Grammar (Houghton Mifflin), and Grammatik (Reference Software International), the three most commercially successful grammar and style checkers for IBM and Macintosh. In my own unscientific tests I found these programs to be more annoying than helpful, largely because they uncovered far more "errors" than there really were. Thus, be sure they perform and accomplish what you want to achieve in a way that is helpful and meaningful for you and your students.

Second, be honest with your students about your reasons for using a grammar checker. While the software can help eliminate some errors in text that is ready for proofreading, there is very little systematic or anecdotal evidence to suggest that grammar checkers actually help student writers produce more effective, error-free prose. The creators of Editor admit that it is not appropriate for use in the "early stages of composition." Rather, it is an "aid in proofreading, revising, and polishing completed drafts before they are submitted for evaluation or review" (p. 10). In other words, the grammar checker that works best works least. It is unrealistic to expect that computer software can locate problem areas or explain how to achieve greater effectiveness more proficiently or more carefully than a teacher.

Finally, recognize what the research has been saying about grammar for over fifty years: Teaching grammar in isolation, either in the classroom or on the screen, is not only unproductive but counterproductive (Hillocks & Smith, 1991). Using a grammar checker to do any more than identify certain features of a written piece's surface structure will surely meet with frustration—for you and your students. Although programs like Editor can "promote the habit and the skills of editing as a normal part of composition" (p. 12), by encouraging students to carefully examine their work on paper (the program does not allow on-screen changes), grammar checkers will never be able to assist our students directly until they can think and respond as we do. In one of their own most telling confessions, Elaine and John Thiesmeyer, both college instructors, write that "unlike a human editor or teacher, [Editor] does not acknowledge the good things you do—only the troublesome ones" (p. 8). We can do better.

Therefore, in spite of the alleged benefits of a program like Editor, and notwithstanding the legitimate criticism Nancy Sommers has directed at the way teachers have traditionally responded to student writing, tomorrow's classroom will probably not look that different from today's: a combination including measured use of text-checking software at the right time, and a generous amount of teacher interaction—both nurturing and critiquing—throughout the writing process.

Endnotes

1. Programs like this are especially nimble at catching sexist and inappropriately gender-based terms. Editor, for instance, is built with the assistance of works like the *MLA Handbook for Writers of Research Papers* (1995) by Joseph Gibaldi and Walter S. Achtert; *Language, Gender, and Professional Writing* (1989) by Francine Wattman Frank and Paula A. Treichler; and Rosalie Maggio's *Nonsexist Word Finder* (1987).

2. Maxine Hairston, in her book *Successful Writing* (1992), represents the "writing situation" as a communication square, the combination of *audience*, *purpose*, *persona*, and *message*. To this I add the dimension of *genre*, or the writing's characteristic form and function.

References

BARTHOLOMAE, D. (1980). The study of error. *College Composition and Communication, 31*, 253–269.

FRANK, F., & TREICHLER, P. (1989). *Language, gender, and professional writing: Theoretical approaches and guidelines for nonsexist usage.* New York: MLA.

GIBALDI, J., & ACHTERT, W. (1995). *MLA handbook for writers of research papers*. New York: MLA.

HAIRSTON, M. (1992). *Successful writing: A rhetoric for advanced composition*. New York: Norton.

HILLOCKS, G., & SMITH, M. (1991). Grammar and usage. In J. Flood, et al. (Eds.), *Handbook of research on teaching the English language arts* (591–604). New York: Macmillan.

MAGGIO, R. (1987). *The nonsexist word finder: A dictionary of gender-free usage*. Phoenix: Oryx.

NOGUCHI, R. (1991). *Grammar and the teaching of writing: Limits and possibilities*. Urbana, IL: National Council of Teachers of English.

RAFORTH, B., & RUBIN, D. (1984). The impact of content and mechanics on judgment of writing quality. *Written Communication, 1*, 446–458.

SEDGWICK, E. (1989). Alternatives to teaching formal, analytical grammar. *Journal of Developmental Education, 12*, 8–10, 12, 14, 20.

SOMMERS, N. (1988). Responding to student writing. In Tarvers, J. (Ed.), *Teaching writing: Theories and practice* (170–177). Glenview, IL: Scott, Foresman.

STRUNK, W., & WHITE, E. (1959). *The elements of style*. New York: Macmillan.

THIESMEYER, E., & THIESMEYER, J. (1990). *Editor: A system for checking usage, mechanics, vocabulary, and structure*. New York: MLA. Version 4.0 for MS-DOS and PC-DOS (IBM).

WEAVER, C. (1979). *Grammar for teachers: Perspectives and definitions*. Urbana, IL: National Council of Teachers of English.

CONTRIBUTORS

Timothy Beals is an adjunct professor of English at Cornerstone College in Grand Rapids, Michigan. He is also the managing editor of Discovery House Publishers and a student in composition theory and medieval studies at Western Michigan University.

Ellen Brinkley is an associate professor of English at Western Michigan University (Kalamazoo, Michigan). She works with preservice and practicing teachers of English language arts and directs the Third Coast Writing Project at WMU, a National Writing Project site. Her professional publications and achievements range from authoring a book on censorship, *Caught Off Guard: Teachers Rethinking Censorship and Controversy* (Allyn & Bacon, 1999), to chairing the group that designed Michigan's newly implemented statewide writing assessments. Ellen is one of the founders of a grassroots organization, Michigan for Public Education, a past president of the Michigan Council of Teachers of English, and a frequent presenter at such conferences as NCTE, IRA, and WLU. As a high-school teacher she helped establish an award-winning school-wide Writing Center and Writing Assistance Program.

Renee Callies currently teaches language arts to seventh graders at Gull Lake Middle School in Hickory Corners, Michigan. In her fourth year of teaching, she focuses on writing as a process, giving students time in class to practice and hone their skills. Hoping to make writing less of a chore and more of a delight, she continues to provide student choice, whenever possible, as a way to help reluctant writers get started. She recently finished a fellowship with the Third Coast Writing Project and is beginning work with the project on *Rural Voices, Country Schools*, part of Walter Annenberg's effort to improve the nation's public schools. Using writing project fellows from six sites across the United States, the network will document and celebrate the schools in rural communities. Renee has also presented her research on self-reflection as an enhancement to portfolio evaluation at the Michigan Council of Teachers of English.

Pat Cordeiro taught grades 1–6 for 18 years. Currently she is a professor at Rhode Island College and chair of the Department of Elementary Education.

Past president of the Whole Language Teachers Association, she is a member and chair of the Elementary Section Steering Committee of the National Council of Teachers of English. Her publications include: *Whole learning: Whole Language and Content in the Upper Elementary Grades;* an edited collection, *Endless Possibilities: Generating Curriculum in Social Studies and Literacy*; "Vygotsky in the classroom: An interactionist framework in mathematics," in *Interactionist Approaches to Language and Literacy*; "Messing up in science," in *Oops: What We Learn When Our Teaching Fails*; "Spontaneous and Scientific Concepts: Learning Punctuation in the First Grade," in *Whole Language Plus: Essays on Literacy in the United States and New Zealand*, among others. Pat's current research interests are in understanding the life and roles of children born into the "middle" place in the family and in systematically studying what "good" teachers do.

David Freeman directs the language development and TESOL programs and **Yvonne Freeman** directs the bilingual education program at Fresno Pacific University in Fresno, California. Both are interested in literacy education for bilingual learners. In addition to doing staff development with school districts across the country, they present regularly at international, national, and state conferences, including TESOL, NABE, CABE, NCTE, and IRA. In 1994–1995, they spent a year in Mérida, Venezuela, at the Universidad de Los Andes as Fulbright scholars. The Freemans have published articles jointly and separately on the topics of literacy, linguistics, bilingual education, and second language learning in professional journals and books. Their books *Whole Language for Second Language Learners* and *Between Worlds: Access to Second Language Acquisition* are published by Heinemann. *Between Worlds* received the Mildenberger Award from the Modern Language Association for outstanding research in the field of foreign and second language teaching. Their book *Teaching Reading and Writing in Spanish in the Bilingual Classroom* was published by Heinemann in early 1997.

As a secondary French and English teacher in Hawaii, **Jane Kiel** spent four years hoping "remedial" students could learn to enjoy their first language and helping gifted students learn a second. Now, as a day care provider and the mother of two young children, she has long been fascinated by language acquisition. In all the theory courses she took in college and graduate school, none provided as much insight into how children learn and acquire language as her years as a mother. Through watching young children struggle to learn about and gain some control over their environment, Kiel's philosophy of learning has taken a drastic turn. She now realizes that children learn an incredible amount on their own, without any drilling, flash cards, or unit tests. They learn because they have a need for the knowledge and, therefore, a desire to learn it. It is this innate quality of children that Kiel feels needs to be capitalized on when working with them as teachers. We must embrace the wealth of knowledge they already possess and help them to grow further. This is what she struggles to do as a mother and day care provider, and what she aspires to do as an educator.

Don Killgallon, who over his career taught secondary English to a boy named Barry and thousands of other students, currently teaches writing in colleges in Maryland. The approach he developed for writing improvement, called "sentence composing," has influenced the way teachers and students look at language, literature, and writing. Don is the author of *Sentence Composing* textbooks published by Boynton/Cook. His latest textbook series, published in 1997 and 1998 by Boynton/Cook, includes three volumes: *Sentence Composing for Middle School; Sentence Composing for High School;* and *Sentence Composing for College.* All of his textbooks focus on the sentence, in the past the most neglected unit of written composition, as the medium through which students can learn to write in ways resembling the writing of professionals. You can contact Don Killgallon through Boynton/Cook Publishers.

Mary Anne Loewe is an assistant professor in the Department of English at Western Michigan University, where she teaches classes on the reading and writing processes. Mary Anne has also served as coordinator of the International Teaching Assistant Training Program and as an instructor at the Career English Language Center for International Students at WMU, where she helped introduce a more holistic, integrated curriculum into a traditionally skill-based intensive English program. She has written articles and given workshops on contextualized grammar instruction and was the recipient of a Fulbright award to develop workshops for K–12 teachers of English as a foreign language in the Philippines.

Harry Noden, coauthor of *Whole Language in Middle and Secondary Classrooms*, with Rich Vacca, has taught full-time at Hudson Middle School for twenty-nine years and part-time at the University of Akron for seventeen years. In 1996, the Ohio Council of Teachers of English and Language Arts (OCTELA) selected Harry as the middle-school level Ohio Outstanding English Teacher of the Year. The same year, he received the NCTE Paul and Kate Farmer Award for the "Best Article of the Year" (middle-school category) published in *English Journal*. Harry has also served as coeditor and contributor, with Barb Moss, to the Professional Development Column in *Reading Teacher*. Several years ago, he created *Middlezine Magazine*, one of the first on-line magazines designed to showcase writing and art by middle-school students from around the world. Harry is currently teaching, writing electronic portfolios for Addison-Wesley, and working on a book entitled *Image Grammar*. He can be contacted at hnoden@uakron.edu.

Scott Peterson is a fourth-grade teacher in Mattawan, Michigan. With twenty-three years of teaching practice behind him, his hands are permanently stained with Magic Marker, and chalk dust runs in his veins. He believes that teachers must grow and change to meet the challenges of educating children for the twenty-first century, and he is constantly looking for new ideas and techniques to add to his repertoire. He is coauthor of the book *Theme Exploration: A Voyage of Discovery*.

Tom Romano teaches in the department of teacher education at Miami University. For seventeen years, he taught high-school students in southwestern Ohio before earning a Ph.D. in reading and writing instruction at the University of New Hampshire, where he teaches every other summer in the writing program. Tom's passions are spurring teachers to write, making a place for narrative thinking, and blurring the genres. He is the author of two Heinemann books, *Clearing the Way: Working with Teenage Writers* and *Writing with Passion: Life Stories, Multiple Genres.*

Formerly a high-school English teacher in the Philadelphia schools, **Lois Matz Rosen** is an associate professor of English at the University of Michigan–Flint, where she has directed the Writing Program since 1984 and teaches courses in writing, women and literature, and English education methods. Director of the Flint Area Writing Project from 1987 to 1994, she continues to give workshops on teaching writing and Writing Across the Curriculum for local schools and districts. Lois strongly believes in the power of writing to give students control over their lives and pleasure in their own creative processes. But she also knows that the freedom to think and plan and generate and create must be accompanied by attention to craft: the language, usage, and mechanical/grammatical skills that contribute to effective writing. She is presently chair of the Conference on English Education Commission on Teacher Education for Teachers of Urban, Rural, and Suburban Students of Color, a commission investigating ways to train English language arts teachers to be more effective in working with the racially, linguistically, and ethnically diverse populations of today's classrooms. Her coauthored reading methods text, *Multiple Voices, Multiple Texts*, is a psycholinguistic, whole language approach to secondary reading in the content areas.

Sue Rowe currently teaches language arts at Vicksburg Middle School in Vicksburg, Michigan. She has had experience with students of all ages at the secondary level, but opted to concentrate on seventh- and eighth-grade writing and literature classes early in her career. For the past ten years, she has worked with students of all ability levels, from special education to the talented and gifted. She is currently working on her master's degree in English at Western Michigan University and was a 1995 participant in the Third Coast Writing Project, one of the many National Writing Projects throughout the country.

Denise Troutman is associate professor of American Thought and Language and Linguistics at Michigan State University. She has taught writing courses to first-year students, especially students developing their writing skills, in addition to sociolinguistics, and introductory linguistics courses. Currently, Denise is working on descriptions of the linguistic behavior of African American women's language, which she has presented in special lectures and at conferences such as New Ways of Analyzing Variation in English (NWAVE, 1996) and Black Women in the Academy: Defending Our Name 1894–1994. Some articles published on this topic appear in *African-American Women Speak Out on Anita Hill–Clarence Thomas; Discourse:*

A Multidisciplinary Introduction; and *Journal of Commonwealth and Postcolonial Studies*, with a forthcoming article in *The Reader's Companion to U.S. Women's History*. Denise also presents papers dealing with the writing of Ebonics speakers at conferences such as the National Council of Teachers of English (NCTE) and Conference on College Composition and Communication (CCCC), with a publication appearing in *Writing in Multicultural Settings*. Denise states that "as a speaker of Ebonics, my teaching and writing focus on the value of this linguistic system, especially as a tool that facilitates written discourse and as a communication mechanism that captures humans' distinct language ability in a unique way."

Constance (Connie) Weaver is a professor of English at Western Michigan University, where she specializes in the teaching of language arts (reading, writing, and grammar). She is the author of various articles and the author or editor of several books. Those currently in print with Heinemann or Boynton/Cook are *Creating Support for Effective Literacy Education* (coauthored, 1996); *Teaching Grammar in Context* (1996); *Reading Process and Practice* (2d ed., 1994); *Success at Last! Helping Students with Attention Deficit (Hyperactivity) Disorders Achieve Their Potential* (edited, 1994); *Theme Exploration* (coauthored, 1993); *Understanding Whole Language* (1990). She has also published two previous books on grammar. Two edited volumes, *Reconsidering a Balanced Approach to Reading* and *Practicing What We Know: Informed Reading Instruction*, will soon be published by the National Council of Teachers of English.

Connie has also authored one videotape, *A Balanced Approach to Reading and Literacy,* and coauthored another, *Reading Strategies and Skills: Research into Practice.* From 1987 to 1990, she served as director of the Commission on Reading of the National Council of English. In 1996 she received the Charles C. Fries award from the Michigan Council of Teachers of English for distinguished leadership in the profession. Connie is also a cofounder of Michigan for Public Education, a nonprofit grassroots organization advocating equality and excellence in education.

Sarah Woltjer is currently teaching middle-school language arts. As a secondary education graduate of Calvin College in Grand Rapids, Michigan, she has enjoyed teaching at the middle-school level for the past three years.

INDEX

absolutes, writing about, 160
academic English, acquisition, 251
adjectives
    activities, 86–88
    descriptive writing without, 98
    minilesson on use of, 28–30
    out of order, writing about, 161
adverbials, punctuation of, 58–59
adverbs
    descriptive writing without, 98
    minilesson on use of, 28–30
African American English (AAE), 213,
        224, 232
African Americans
    Ebonics. *See* Ebonics
    power of word and, 211
    stereotyping of, 212
African American slang, 212–13, 219
African American Vernacular English
        (AAVE), 228, 233, 235
African Language Systems, 235
African-Negro Language, 213
Alderson, Jennifer, 192
Alexander, Lloyd, 174, 176, 178
Allen, Erin Kash, 195
alternate style. *See* Grammar B
Alternate Style, An: Options in Composition,
        185, 189
alternative hypotheses, 48–50, 51
American Indians, language used to sup-
        press, 211
Amplified Bible, The, 210
Anderson, H., 45
Anderson, R., 10
Andrasick, K., 148

Andromeda Strain, 165
Angelo, T., 271–72
Angelou, Maya, 219–20
"Ann Arbor (Michigan) case," 209, 224
Answering Students' Questions about Words,
        288
aphoristic/memorized hypothesis, 61
apostrophes. *See also* punctuation
    function, 56
    for possessive nouns, minilesson on
        use of, 33, 35–36
Applebee, A., 140
appositives, writing about, 160
Armstrong, M., 45
art
    relationship between writing and,
        158–59
    using student, to improve reading
        and writing, 163–64
    writing about, 157–58
"Art of Learning Nothing, The," 204
Art of Teaching Writing, The, 68, 133, 142
Asher, James, 263
Atwell, Nancie, 145
Atwood, Margaret, 179
audience, sensitivity to, 201
audio-lingual method for second-lan-
        guage acquisition, 262
awareness development in university ESL
        students, 266–67
"awkward," teacher's use of term, 111,
        113

babbling, 5
Baldwin, James, 189

editing (*continued*)

    skills, make students responsible for developing, 147–48

    teaching, 123–25, 130–32

editing checklists, using, 130–31, 147

editing conferences

    in action, sample conferences, 30–31, 127–30

    learning to use grammar with precision through, 120–35

    minilessons and, 124–26

    procedures, 125–26, 145

    teaching editing, 123–25, 130–32

    value of, 120, 132–35

editing corner, use of, 147

editing workshops, using, 144–46

Editor software

    examination of, 294–300

    impact of, on quality of writing, 300–301

Edlefson, Kathy, 133

Eeds, M., 10

Elbow, Peter, 110, 121

Electric Kool-Aid Acid Test, The, 188

elementary age children

    language acquisition in, 8–14

    punctuation, learning. *See* punctuation

Elements of Style, 295

Elley, W., 9, 13–14

empiricist school of second-language acquisition, 261–62

endline alternative hypothesis, 49, 50, 51

End of Education, The, 74

endpage alternative hypothesis, 48–49, 51

endstory alternative hypothesis, 49, 51

English as art, 155

English as Second Language (ESL) students

    appropriate and timely responses, giving, 256

    awareness development with university students, 266–67

    content-based instruction with university students, 268–69

    developing correctness with, 138, 150–51

    grammar instruction integrated into other university components, 269–71

    high expectations, maintaining, 249–51

    integrated language instruction with university students, 268–72

    language features, allow students to approximate, 254–55

    language, immersing student in, 246–48

    in Michigan, 244

    oral language comprehensible, making, 246–47

    responsibility for learning, giving student the, 251–52

    strategy training with university students, 267–68

    syllabus at university level, negotiation of, 271–72

    thematic units used with university ESL students, 268–69, 273

    university level curriculum, implementing whole language in a, 264–75

    use the language, frequent and meaningful opportunities to, 252–54

    whole language techniques used with, 245–46, 264–75

    writing and reading demonstrations for, 248–49

    written language comprehensible, making, 247–48

English Journal, 137, 138

environment, language acquisition and, 2, 4–5

Envisioning Writing, 163

ERIC (Educational Resources Information Center), 138

errors

    analyzing, 127–30, 149

    benign neglect of, 148

    correctness, developing. *See* correctness, developing

    dot-in-the-margin system, 127, 131

the error hunt, 139–41, 148–49
    abandoning, 148–49
    frustration of teachers over, 139
    pattern of, 48–52, 143
    postwriting attention to, 141–42
    selectivity and, 148–49
    students' response to making, 44,
       101, 133
    symbols, use of, 140
    treatment of students', 32–33, 36,
       110–17, 118, 125–29, 133–34,
       139–41
Errors and Expectations, 166
E. T. the Extra-Terrestrial, 165
expanding, sentence, 179–81
expanding a term in a relation, 7
extended minilessons, examples of,
    26–33, 35–36

Facing Death, 158
Faigley, L., 62
feelings activity, 92–93
Ferreiro, E., 47–48, 61
fiction, techniques for writing, 157
Field, Syd, 166
films, writing about, 164–66
five parts of the sentence, 50
"fluency-clarity-accuracy," 256
Fog Horn, The, 174
Form-Correction Response, 139
fragments, 51
Freeman, David, 279
Freeman, Yvonne, 279
Friends, The, 175
functional structure, concept of, 49
Furness, E., 61

Gallagher, Janice M., 158
Gardner, J., 60
George, Jean Craighead, 88
Gessford, Ken, 155, 166
Giacobbe, Mary Ellen, 45, 74, 75
Gift from the Sea, 172
Gill, T., 76
Ginsberg, Allen, 203
Gleason, J. B., 265

God's Gift of Language Series, 18
"Going by the Rules: Conventions of
    Written English," 138
Goodman, K., 282
"Goof Box," use of, 148
Grahame, Kenneth, 181
grammar. *See also* punctuation
    aspects of grammar to teach, select-
      ing, 21–24, 123–25
    breaking the rules, teaching writing
      by. *See* rule-breaking, stylistic
    correctness, developing. *See* correct-
      ness, developing
    course for teachers. *See* teaching
      about language, preparing
      teachers for
    effective instruction, 74–77, 123–25
    formal instruction, effectiveness of,
      71–74, 75, 95, 98, 159
    historical overview of instruction,
      18–19
    image. *See* image grammar
    research on teaching of, 19–21,
      151–52
    syntax development and grammar
      instruction, 12–14
    teaching grammar in the context of
      writing. *See* teaching grammar
      in the context of writing
    texts, references for, 33–35
    use of grammar-checking computers.
      See computers
    whole language programs, grammar
      instruction in, 261
Grammar A, 185
"Grammar and Beyond," 138
Grammar as Style, 159
Grammar B
    defined, 185–86
    double voice, 190, 195–97
    labyrinthine sentence, 190, 192
    list-making, 190, 197–200
    orthographic variation, 190, 193–94
    possible negative ramifications for
      students, 200–203
    repetition, 189, 190

Kerek, A., 162, 166
Kesey, Ken, 187
Kiel, Jane, 1
Killens, John Oliver, 216
Killer Angels, The, 174
Killgallon, Don, 162, 169, 289
Killion, J., 151
King, Stephen, 174, 176, 179
Kirby, D., 144
Kitagawa, M., 249
Koch, Kenneth, 80
Kolln, Martha, 20
Konopack, John, 236
Kotzwinkle, William, 165
Krashen, S., 14, 246, 263, 284–85
Kress, G., 45, 62

labyrinthine sentence, 190, 192
Lakoff, 210
Lamb, H., 13
"Langoliers, The," 179
language
    acquisition. *See* language acquisition;
        second-language acquisition
    defined, 230
    nonstandard, societies' treatment of,
        210, 212, 229–31
    power of, 210–12
    preparing teachers to teach about.
        See teaching about language,
        preparing teachers for
    and reality, 229–30
language acquisition, 1–15
    babbling, 5
    cognitive capacity, 1–3, 246
    early language acquisition, 2–3, 5–8,
        264
    in elementary years and beyond,
        8–14
    environment, 2, 4–5, 246
    factors that enable, 1–5, 245–46
    innate need/desire to communicate,
        2, 3–4
    mimetic theory of language devel-
        opment, 172–73
    physical development, 1, 3

second-language acquisition. *See* sec-
    ond-language acquisition
single-word utterances, 5–6
spelling, 11–12
stages, 5–8
syntax development, 6–8, 12–14
vocabulary acquisition in elementary
    school, 9–11
word combining, 6–8
"language of soul," 213
"Language of Wider Communication,
    the," 231
Larsen, S., 11
Lawrence, D. H., 186
Leavitt, Hart Day, 156
Lehrer, Jim, 218
"less is more," 18
Lewis, Sinclair, 178
lexicon, Ebonics, 214
Life and Opinions of Tristram Shandy, The,
    186
Lilies of the Field, The, 174
Limited English Proficient (LEP), 280
Lindbergh, Anne Morrow, 172
Lindfors, J., 2, 6
Liner, T., 144
Linguistic Society of America, 235
Lipsyte, Robert, 179
list-making, 190, 197–200
Loewe, Mary Anne, 244, 260
Lonely Passion of Judith Hearne, The, 178
Los Angeles Times, 238
Lunsford, A., 26, 143

MacGowan-Gilhooly, Adele, 269
MacNeil/Lehrer Report, 218
Madraso, J., 147
Major, C., 219
Malveaux, Julianne, 216
Mangubhai, F., 13–14
Martin, 218, 220
Mason, G., 12
McDaniel, H., 12
McNutt, G., 11
McQuade, Finlay, 19–20
Mead, Beth, 127

periods. *See also* punctuation
    alternative hypotheses for placement, 48–50
    correct usage, microlesson for teaching, 128–29
    early learning of, 40–48
    learning by older writers, 51–52
    placement as process, 55
    sequence of learning, 48–51
    teaching about, 60–62, 128–29
personal involvement of students, importance of, 68
Peterson, Scott, 67
Phonics Phacts, 282
phonology, of Ebonics, 213, 233
phonology project, 281–84
phrase, teaching concept of, 21
phrase structure alternative hypothesis, 49
physical development, language acquisition and, 1, 3
Picasso, 158
Pickering, Jennifer, 200
pidgin, 234, 235
poetry
    adjective activities, 86–87
    color poem activity, 82, 84
    comparison poems activity, 80–82
    diamante poems, 286
    encouraging risk taking through, 117–19
    fall poem activity, 96–99
"Polishing, Proofreading, Publishing," 138
Popp, M., 252
portfolios with ESL students, use of, 251–52
Postman, Neil, 74
power
    defined, 210
    of language, 210–12
Power Writing program, 100, 102
predicate/subject activity, 78–80, 81
Prelutsky, Jack, 283
preschoolers, language acquisition, 2–3, 5–8
prewriting experiences, 28, 30, 96
Price, Richard, 189

professional writers material, use of, 173–81
Professor of Desire, The, 181
pronouns referents, unclear, 101
"Proofreading Journal," 148
publishing student writing, 149
punctuation. *See also* grammar
    characteristics of today's, 57–59
    defined, 39, 55–56
    early learning, 40–48
    editing process and learning, 52–54, 62, 125
    function of, 55–57
    importance of, 39, 40
    learning by older writers, 51–52
    as negotiable, 45, 57–59
    prior experience and, 55
    as process, 54–55
    sequence of learning, 48–51
    teaching about, 23, 60–63
    theory of, toward a, 59–60

Quirk, R., 49

Raiders of the Lost Ark, 165
rationalist school of second-language acquisition, 262–63
reading
    demonstrating to ESL students, 248–49
    integrating writing and, 164
    letting students read, 143–44
    phonology project connected to, 282–84
    spelling acquisition and, 12, 282–84
    syntax development and, 13–14
    university ESL instruction, teaching grammar in reading class, 270, 274
    vocabulary acquisition and, 9–11, 288
reality, language and, 229–30
"Reasons Why My Experiment Screwed Up," 204
Red Pony, The, 177

The editor and publisher wish to thank those who have generously given permission to reprint borrowed material:

"Teaching Grammar in the Context of Writing" by Constance Weaver originally appeared as "Teaching Grammar in Context" in *English Journal* (vol. 85, Nov. 1996). Reprinted by permission of the National Council of Teachers of English.

Figures 2–1, 2–2, and 2–6 originally appeared in *Teaching Grammar in Context* by Constance Weaver (Boynton/Cook, A subsidiary of Reed Elsevier Inc., Portsmouth, NH, 1996).

"Developing Correctness in Student Writing: Alternatives to the Error Hunt" by Lois Matz Rosen was published in an earlier version in *English Journal* (vol. 76, no. 3, March 1987). Reprinted by permission of the National Council of Teachers of English.

Portions of "Sentence Composing: Notes on a New Rhetoric" by Don Killgallon originally appeared in *Sentence Composing for Middle School* (1997), *Sentence Composing for High School* (1998), and *Sentence Composing for College* (1998) by Don Killgallon (Boynton/Cook, A subsidiary of Reed Elsevier Inc., Portsmouth, NH).

Portions of "Breaking the Rules in Style" by Tom Romano originally appeared in *To Compose: Teaching Writing in High School and College, Second Edition,* edited by Thomas Newkirk (Heinemann, A division of Reed Elsevier Inc., Portsmouth, NH, 1990); in *English Journal* (vol. 77, no. 8, December 1988) published by the National Council of Teachers of English; and in *Writing with Passion: Life Stories, Multiple Genres* by Tom Romano (Boynton/Cook, A subsidiary of Reed Elsevier Inc., Portsmouth, NH, 1995).

Figure 15–1 from *The Whole Story: Natural Learning and the Acquisition of Literacy in the Classroom* by Brian Cambourne. Copyright © 1988. Published by Ashton Scholastic, Auckland, New Zealand. Reprinted by permission of the Publisher.

Figure 15–2 from "Please Teach America: Keisuke's Journey into a Language Community" by Jean M. Gunkel. From *Language Arts* (68, 1991). Copyright 1991 by the National Council of Teachers of English. Reprinted with permission.

Figure 16–1 adapted from *Language Learning Strategies* by R. Oxford. Copyright © 1990. Published by Newbury House. Reprinted by permission of Heinle & Heinle.

Figure 16–2 adapted from *Classroom Assessment Techniques: A Handbook for College Teachers, Second Edition,* by Thomas A. Angelo and Patricia K. Cross. Copyright 1993 Jossey-Bass Inc., Publishers. Reprinted by permission.